Media, Sex, Violence, and Drugs in the Global Village

Media, Sex, Violence, and Drugs in the Global Village

Edited by
Yahya R. Kamalipour
and Kuldip R. Rampal

ROWMAN & LITTLEFIELD PUBLISHERS, INC.
Lanham • Boulder • New York • Oxford

ROWMAN & LITTLEFIELD PUBLISHERS, INC.

Published in the United States of America
by Rowman & Littlefield Publishers, Inc.
4720 Boston Way, Lanham, Maryland 20706
www.rowmanlittlefield.com

12 Hid's Copse Road
Cumnor Hill, Oxford OX2 9JJ, England

British Library Cataloguing in Publication Information Available

Library of Congress Cataloging-in-Publication Data

Media, sex, violence, and drugs in the global village / [editors] Yahya R. Kamalipour
and Kuldip R. Rampal.
   p.   cm.
   Includes bibliographical references and index.
   ISBN 0-7425-0060-8 (alk. paper)—ISBN 0-7425-0061-6 (pbk. : alk. paper)
   1. Mass media—Social aspects.   2. Mass media and culture.   3. Sex in mass
media.   4. Violence in mass media.   5. Drugs and mass media.   6. Developing
countries—Civilization—Western influences.   7. East and West.   I. Kamalipour,
Yahya R.   II. Rampal, Kuldip R., 1946–
HM 1206 +
302.23—dc21   2001019882

Printed in the United States of America

For
Mah, Daria, Shirin, and Niki
and
SR

Contents

Figures

Tables

Acknowledgments

In completing this project, we have benefited from the kind support and co-operation of many people throughout the world. Foremost, we would like to offer our deepest gratitude to the contributing authors of this book because without their genuine interest, hard work, and support, this project could not have materialized. Also, we would like to thank the authors' colleges, universities, and organizations for providing them with financial, research, administrative, and secretarial support during the course of this project.

Furthermore, we are indebted to the following individuals, at our respective universities, for their valuable support and encouragement throughout this project. At Purdue University Calumet, we are grateful to Sandra Singer, vice chancellor for academic affairs; Dan Dunn, acting dean of the School of Liberal Arts and Social Sciences; Saul Lerner, former acting dean of the School of Liberal Arts and Social Sciences; and Susan Van Til, secretary, Department of Communication and Creative Arts. At Central Missouri State University, we want to acknowledge the support of Robert Schwartz, dean of the College of Arts and Sciences; Terry Rodenberg, director of the Office of International Programs; and Bruce Swain, chair of the Department of Communication.

We are very grateful to Brenda Hadenfeldt, Jennifer Knerr, the production and marketing departments, and everyone else at Rowman & Littlefield Publishers, who contributed to this book through its many stages.

Of course, we are indebted to our respective families and friends for their unconditional love, emotional support, and understanding throughout this project. A special note of thanks goes to Sarita Rampal for her thoughtful comments on the dynamics of media globalization, which were very helpful in the conceptualization of this project.

Introduction

Yahya R. Kamalipour and Kuldip R. Rampal

Long before Marshall McLuhan proclaimed the impending emergence of the "global village" that would result from the development of modern communication technologies, controversial American author Herbert Schiller was warning about the social implications of America's cultural influence on the youth in developing countries through Hollywood movies and television programming. Writing in *Mass Communication and American Empire* in 1969, Schiller quoted Wilson P. Dizard, a former director of the United States Information Agency, as saying that "American TV products, for better or worse, are setting the tone for television programming throughout the world. . . . The United States now leads all other countries combined twice over as a program exporter" (Schiller 1969). Schiller had argued that the implications of the cultural influences brought about by American programming in the developing world were far-reaching. "Everywhere local culture is facing submersion from the mass-produced outpourings of commercial broadcasting in the United States," he said, adding, "To foster consumerism in the poor world [through American entertainment programming] sets the stage for frustration on a massive scale" (Schiller 1969).

At the dawn of the twenty-first century, the dominance of America's cultural products globally remains unparalleled. The *Washington Post* reported on October 25, 1998, that international sales of American popular culture products totaled $60.2 billion in 1996. The article quoted sociologist Todd Gitlin, who called American popular culture "the latest in a long succession of bidders for global unification. It succeeds the Latin imposed by the

1

Roman Empire and the Catholic Church, and Marxist Leninism imposed by Communist government" (Farhi and Rosenfeld 1998).

Expanding democratization around the world following the demise of the Soviet Union and the accompanying economic liberalization in many countries in the 1990s have further strengthened the appeal of Western democratic market societies and their cultural values. Exposure to these values has been greatly enhanced by the information revolution, with its global satellite television and that truly revolutionary medium, the Internet. In mid-February 2000, there were 200 million subscribers to the Internet worldwide, including 100 million in the United States. By 2005, one billion people—a sixth of the world's population—are expected to be online. The global village is increasingly becoming a reality also because of the worldwide operations of Western media conglomerates, such as those of Rupert Murdoch and TIME-Warner communications, which make sure that the viewer in Colombo or Taipei is no less informed about the latest antics of *The Bold and the Beautiful* than the viewer in New York or London.

The editors of this book, having traveled to many countries on at least five continents, have seen firsthand the reality of the pervasiveness of American culture through movies and television programming. American television is practically everywhere, and young people are tuning in at a viewing scale unparalleled in the ratings levels of indigenous programming. When the Singapore Broadcasting Corporation, for example, canceled MTV for contractual reasons in 1994, young Singaporeans spoke out in frustration and rejected an alternative local music video program as "unexciting." MTV has not only been a vehicle for the globalization of American music but has attracted a young audience throughout the world, including countries such as Saudi Arabia, Iran, Kenya, and Chile.

And in India, as a result of the government's "open skies" policy since the introduction of economic liberalization in 1991, Murdoch's Hong Kong–based STAR-TV has become readily available through hundreds of cable television operations all over urban India. Practically overnight, millions of Indian television viewers, long used to the government-run TV stations' staid educational programming and dramas based on often tiresome Indian mythology, found themselves tuning in to the likes of *Baywatch, Dallas,* and *Dynasty.* In a land where kissing has never been allowed in Indian movies or television programming, TV viewers could now experience the sex, violence, and drug culture long decried even in the West. Even in countries where satellite receiving dishes are illegal (e.g., Iran and Saudi Arabia), millions of people install and disguise such equipment so that they can view Western and non-Western satellite television channels, including STAR-TV, Zee-TV, MTV, CNN, SKY-TV, and Fashion TV.

Hundreds of articles have been written around the world to analyze the phenomenon of media globalization. The refrain "Western cultural imperialism," heard from the developing world since the 1960s, has become louder in this age of global television and the information revolution. As the reader will note from the research studies and essays in this book, there are many concerns about the implications of Western global television, and the domestic productions inspired by it, in the areas of sex, violence, and drugs. Occasionally, the concerns are expressed in a highly dramatic manner. For example, an Associated Press news story from India on December 26, 1994, said that residents of a high-rise apartment building in Bombay, frustrated with increasing promiscuity among their teenage children exposed to Western and local commercial television, dumped their television sets in tandem out their windows. The state government in Maharashtra, whose capital is Bombay, asked its culture minister to police sexually suggestive lyrics in movies and music video programs.

Authoritarian and totalitarian states, on the other hand, simply ban such programming, censor it heavily, or take other extreme measures. For example, while this introduction was being written, a story from the *Hindustan Times* (April 5, 2000) reported that in Karachi, Pakistan, a progovernment Pakistani extremist group, modeled on the Taliban of neighboring Afghanistan, launched a campaign against "un-Islamic" practices in Pakistan, where satellite television is very popular, by rounding up and burning "satanic" television sets. Hundreds of people gathered near a mosque to watch the show staged by activists of the Tehrik-e-Insdad Munkirat, or movement for prevention of evil practices, as they destroyed TV sets. "These gadgets are satanic devices which corrupt people and society," said one of the leaders of the group.

Are such public and government reactions to media globalization warranted? Is there any research-based evidence showing that the portrayal of sex, violence, and drug use in popular programming and movies has harmful effects on children or any other age group? If politicians and scholars from the developing world were to put aside the baggage of "Western cultural imperialism" for a moment, another relevant question would remain: Are there any positive effects of media globalization? What of the "empathy" factor established by the sociologist Daniel Lerner back in his 1958 landmark work, *The Passing of Traditional Society*, in which he argued that wider exposure to mass media enables consumers to relate to higher order needs, motivating them to realize those needs. The authors in this book address these and related issues. This anthology, with contributions from fifteen media scholars from around the world, covers both the theory of media effects and case studies of individual countries grappling with the social implications of Western media imports, and similar local productions, in the areas of sex, violence, and drugs.

The reader will note that several authors in this anthology also address the significance of the political variable in assessing the social implications of media globalization. For example, does India's democratic political system, which by nature points to an open skies and liberal media policy, exacerbate the negative effects of the often permissive offerings of Western television and movies? At the same time, for example, does Egypt's essentially authoritarian political system and the resulting protective media policy lessen the negative influences of the globalized Western media?

This book should be of particular interest to students, teachers, and researchers in a variety of disciplines, including mass communication, international communication, intercultural communication, international relations, cultural studies, and journalism.

REFERENCES

Farhi, Paul, and Megan Rosenfeld. 1998. American pop penetrates worldwide. *Washington Post*, 25 October.

Hindustan Times. 2000. Campaign against un-Islamic practices. 5 April. www.hindustantimes.com.

Lerner, D. 1958. *The passing of traditional society: Modernizing the Middle East*. New York: Free Press.

Schiller, H. 1969. *Mass communication and American empire*. Boston: Beacon.

1

The Paradox of Media Effects

Thomas J. Roach

Do mass media tell us what to think? The latter half of the nineteenth century began with newspaper editor Horace Greeley sending the population west and closed with publisher William Randolph Hearst promoting war with Spain. In the first half of the twentieth century, reluctant Americans were rallied to fight in World War I, Orson Wells dramatized the H. G. Wells novel *War of the Worlds*, creating a nationwide panic, and the Nazi party gained control of the government in Germany, all with the help of new methods of mass communication. Do mass media still hold these powers, or is the public less naive? This chapter considers the debate over media effects in a broad historical perspective and rethinks some of the popular assumptions of the twentieth century.

THE MEANINGS OF MASS AND MEDIA

The most misunderstood issue concerning mass media is their relationship to mass democracy. Mass media often are accused of encumbering democracy, but mass democracy without mass media is inconceivable. The Greek prototype for modern democratic states was born in cities where participation was limited to relatively small numbers of citizens. Early modern democracies had similar constraints. At the time of the American Revolution, the thirteen colonies were much closer to the Greek model than to the mass democracy model into which they evolved. The significant seat of power was the state, not the federal government. Oratory and small partisan printing presses provided all the communication opportunities that seemed to be required. Over two hundred years later, the population of metropolitan Chicago is approximately the size of the population of the thirteen colonies at the time of the ratification of the U.S. Constitution. A mass democracy by the end of the nineteenth century, the United States required mass communication, and mass communication required mass media.

Perhaps no event in U.S. history is as significant as the expansion of the voting population; almost 250 million people now are governed by institutions designed to govern 6 million or 7 million. The capacity of the individual to participate in or even to monitor the affairs of state is diminished greatly. Because *mass communication* means sending one message to many receivers, this process, by definition, does not allow interaction over a broad range of issues. Perhaps mass media do not make mass democracy possible as much as they make the appearance of mass democracy possible. But given that *mass democracy* is a contradiction in terms, a somewhat participative state bureaucracy with the illusion of classical democratic principles may be the best configuration possible. The complaint that mass media are inhibiting democratic institutions may reflect a desire on the part of the critic to have mass media simply portray a different fiction.

While the word *mass* too often may be overlooked, the word *media* too often is overworked. Literally, *media* signifies a technology and an industry of presses, wires, tubes, and broadcast signals. Other technologies have revolutionized lifestyles, yet there is no similar interest in indoor plumbing, air conditioning, or even automobiles. Clearly, mass media are significant because they facilitate mass communication, and mass communication is part of the process by which mass societies work out their identities and their goals. However, while the technology of mass media may make mass communication possible, its role in producing what are called media effects is incidental. If people could broadcast their thoughts to a mass audience using telepathy, all of the effects concerned would still exist. Most of the time when we say *media effects,* we mean *mass communication effects.*

RHETORICAL TRADITION AND MASS COMMUNICATION

Before the development of the printing press, rhetoric was recognized as the only means of exercising power through communication. Rhetoric is the art of communicating to produce an effect. Throughout history, rhetoricians served as either teachers of public speaking or public spokespersons. In terms of traditional rhetorical theory, the most significant difference between contemporary and classical communication is audience size. In classical rhetoric, formulas for producing effects dealt mainly with message quality because the size of the audience was fixed by the limitations of the human voice. Mass communication, by eliminating the proximity requirement, made audience size a variable. For the last one hundred years, the formula for influence has been message quality plus audience size equals influence.

What was called oratory is now channeled through print, radio, and television advertising, print and electronic journalism, and various mass audience communication processes, such as the radio talk show and e-mail. Historically, someone seeking help from a professional communicator looked to rhetoricians and lawyers for assistance. The advent of mass societies and mass media has caused professional communicators to become experts in message preparation and mass communication technology. The professional rhetorician is now a public relations practitioner.

The problem of explaining effects of mass communication is exacerbated when too much attention is paid to the historical novelty of dissemination processes and too little attention is paid to ancient processes of public address and deliberation. Like Oedipus, twentieth-century media critics often have studied details without considering context. The abundance of literature on mass media has much more to say about the agency of change than it does about what is being changed. Thus an erroneous argument is made by omission: that media effects override the process by which humans exchange, accept, and reject ideas.

However, there is little evidence that one hundred years of mass media have changed the human side of the communication equation. The invention and investigation of arguments are as essential to discourse as they were in classical times, and arguments still depend on logical, emotional, and ethical proofs. In the final analysis, the advent of the mass society and the development of mass media have had much more impact on public speaking than they have on public speeches.

News that rhetorical inquiry survived the century of mass media has not escaped scholars of classical rhetoric. Lloyd Bitzer hot-wires traditional rhetorical theory into the matrix of mediated mass democracy in his seminal essay "Political Rhetoric." Bitzer explains how rhetoric, now acting through mass media, is still at work engaging motives, principles, thoughts, arguments, and sentiments for the purpose of forming attitudes and assisting judgment in civic affairs. According to Bitzer, if propaganda is effective, it is not because of technology; rather it is the result of blind faith and a lack of critical thinking (1998, p. 4).

Bitzer also accounts for messages that are not mediated electronically. Political rhetoric takes place at campaign rallies, in deliberations in capital offices, in "robust persuasive speeches," and in "quiet, informative discourses meant to assist decision-making" (p. 13). He points out that all of these messages are political because they conduct the public's business. Either they

take place within deliberative bodies or they rally support for issues in order
to influence deliberative bodies.

THE EFFECTS DEBATE IN THE
RHETORICAL TRADITION

Perhaps nothing unmasks the primacy of rhetoric over mass communication
technology more clearly than the fact that classical Greeks engaged in the
effects debate over two thousand years before the advent of mass media. In
his fourth century b.c. dialogue, the *Gorgias,* Plato denounces unethical rhetorical practice for its undesirable effect on public discourse. Substitute the
words *media effects* for the word *rhetoric* and *public relations practitioner* for
rhetorician and *orator,* and this dialogue becomes strikingly familiar.

Plato states his case through a fictional rendering of Socrates, who had
already been martyred by state execution for the crime of corrupting youth.
Socrates states that when the city holds a meeting to elect state physicians or
shipwrights, to decide to build a wall or a harbor, or to choose generals or
dispatch troops, the rhetorician should refrain from giving advice. Only the
craftsmen, master builders, or generals should speak. A fictional Gorgias,
based on the fifth-century teacher of rhetoric known for his florid speaking
style, reminds Socrates that the building of the docks, walls, and harbors of
Athens was done on the advice of Themistocles and Pericles, two orators.
Socrates asks what power orators possess that gives them so much influence.
Gorgias explains that rhetoric embraces all the arts. He believes that in any
contest between a rhetorician and a craftsman, the rhetorician would win the
election. No craftsman can speak on any subject as persuasively as a rhetorician. According to Gorgias: "The rhetorician is capable of speaking against
everyone else and on any subject you please in such a way that he can win
over vast multitudes to anything, in a word, that he may desire" (Plato 1988,
p. 15).

Rhetoric is the means by which a culture articulates its identity and establishes its goals. For classical Greece and for most nations in the twenty-first
century, the rhetorical give-and-take over choices, issues, and sentiments is
the heartbeat of culture. At its core, the debate about media effects is necessarily preoccupied with what may lie coiled about this most vital social
organ. Whether it be the serpentine wires of mass media or the beguiling
rhetorical practice of demagoguery, the threat is essentially the same. The
technology and the methods of communication both call for attention if they
threaten to interfere with the articulation of cultural identity and goals. But
angst over mass communication effects originates in the historical debate
over the uses and misuses of rhetoric.

THE CENTURY OF MASS
COMMUNICATION

The twentieth century was marked as much by irony as by progress. It was anointed with wave after wave of promising technological innovation and defiled by World War I, the Bolshevik Revolution, European fascism, World War II, nuclear warfare, China's Cultural Revolution, and global spasms of ethnic cleansing—events so apocalyptic they have given the Napoleonic Wars and the American Civil War of the previous century a romantic cast. The Century of Progress was a period of radical cultural change realized through weapons technology, facilitated by communication technology, and paid for with the lives of 20 million Russians, 6 million Jews, and the populations of two Japanese cities.

Early media critics attempted to explain the role of mass media in bringing about these apocalyptic events, but the first investigations into media effects were actually trial-and-error experiments on an unsuspecting public. A committee of public relations practitioners, expert in using the new electronic media, prepared the United States to enter World War I. The same strategies and tactics were used in different languages with different flags to legitimize the pathological regimes of Joseph Stalin, Adolph Hitler, and Mao Zedong. More recently, when Iraq invaded Kuwait, the Kuwaiti royal family hired an international public relations firm based in the U.S., which successfully promoted the idea of an international rescue mission. In the twentieth century, mass media meant mass power. Some wanted to understand it; some wanted to have it.

THE CRITIQUE OF MEDIA EFFECTS ON
THE PUBLIC SPHERE

The primary location of mass communication effects studies has been the arena in which citizens publicly engage one another in debate over civic issues—the public sphere. All forms of self-government, be they ancient or modern, occur in some variation of a public sphere in which public debate can influence state authority. As the reference to Plato's *Gorgias* points out, there are similarities between concerns over rhetorical practice in the public sphere of Athens and concerns over media effects in the modern public sphere, but it is also useful to consider the differences.

When the real Socrates delivered his "apology," it was intended only for the citizens of Athens. His actual words faded and were lost before his physical presence succumbed to the hemlock he drank. We speculate that he might have hoped the memory of his argument would affect the behavior of his audience and perhaps even affect the quality of debate in the public sphere.

However, while Socrates had a great deal of control over the effect generated by his argument, he was helpless when it came to disseminating his message. The fact that this is one of the most widely read speeches in Western history has everything to do with message quality and, at least as far as Socrates was concerned, nothing to do with message dissemination.

If Socrates, a human agent of communication, is compared with a technological agent of communication (e.g., Gutenberg's printing press), the juxtaposition of the words *media* and *effects* becomes a crude analogy. Gutenberg's invention had no awareness of audience, nor could it anticipate that it would one day be used to produce Adolph Hitler's *Mein Kampf* or Chairman Mao's Little Red Book. Mass media have had a profound impact on the modern public sphere, but there is no cybernetic will. Herein lies the essential paradox: mass media produce an effect, but they have no intent. Given the etymological context of the word *effect*, its attachment to the word *media* is a personification that obfuscates the essential role of human agents and rhetorical strategies.

The investigation into effects in communication begins with the Sophists in classical Greece. For the Sophists, communication was the art of persuasion, in other words, the art of producing an effect. Later, rhetorical theorists like Aristotle also identified rhetoric with effect, although not as directly. For Aristotle, rhetoric was the art of discerning the best available means of persuasion, and persuasion was part of a process by which people discerned the truth. This definition persisted through modernity.

In 1925 Herbert A. Wichelns in "The Literary Criticism of Oratory" renewed the vows between rhetoric and effect. He linked rhetorical criticism with the study of how effect is produced: rhetorical criticism "regards a speech as a communication to a specific audience, and holds its business to be the analysis and appreciation of the orator's method of imparting his ideas to his hearers" (1980, p. 67). This is called neo-Aristotelian criticism because it uses the classical canons as models for the study of public speaking. Neo-Aristotelianism was the dominant mode of rhetorical criticism until the 1960s, and it was the first contextual frame used to explain media effects.

It was inevitable that the question of media effects would be framed by neo-Aristotelianism. There was a critical tradition of studying effect in speeches, and a parallel line of investigation developed for examining effects produced by mass media. However, the relationship between public speakers and media is only analogous. While both may produce effects, the former is generated by a human agent to achieve a goal, and the latter are the incidental outcome of communication technology interacting with culture. More accurately, the most salient examples of propaganda at midcentury were rhetorical strategies amplified by mass media.

The strongest, most persistent case for pure media effects concerns propaganda. The term *propaganda* has been in circulation at least since 1622, when

Pope Gregory XV appointed the College of Propaganda, a committee of cardinals to oversee foreign missions. This early usage of the term referred to the dissemination of information about the faith. However, propaganda took on pejorative connotations after it was used to describe ways in which communication technology helped rally support for the Nazi party in Germany and spread confusion and disunity among its enemies. Given this new context, the term *propaganda* linked media effects to a human agent and contextualized media effects in a way that was parallel to effects in the neo-Aristotelian rhetorical tradition, thus making media effects easier to comprehend.

The name most associated with propaganda is Joseph Goebbels. He was charged with communicating and justifying Adolf Hitler's policies. Goebbels helped construct the Hitler myth in the 1920s and was instrumental in negotiating Hitler's rise to power. Hitler rewarded Goebbels by naming him minister of popular culture and propaganda (it is interesting that at this early date the Nazis recognized a link between communication technology and culture). Goebbels had authority over the German press as well as radio, film, and theater. His main tool for reaching large audiences was radio. He also eliminated opportunities for public dissent and made it compulsory to listen to Hitler's speeches. He did some of his most infamous work during the invasion of France:

> To spread alarm and despondency among the French, his broadcasters reported rumors that the Reynaud government was fleeing from Paris, urged all French patriots to withdraw their savings before the Nazis confiscated the banks, gave advice about how to avoid a non-existent cholera epidemic, spread rumors of peace talks and then claimed that the British had torpedoed them. Goebbels's radio programs also quoted the forged diary of a British soldier describing his sexual exploits with French wives, advised the hoarding of food, and described imaginary Nazi atrocities in ways likely to encourage flight and clog French roads. (Craig 1996, p. 10)

Goebbels's horrific success wielding the power of mass media justified even the most paranoid fears of media effects.

However, it was not mass media but Goebbels the human agent capitalizing on what now can be seen as a historical anomaly that achieved these results. Yes, he took advantage of emerging communication technology, but he was also dealing with a naive public. Others would try, but no one since has achieved such profound results. Recent events have shown that similar tactics within the Soviet Union were less successful, and no government or corporation in Western Europe or the United States has matched Goebbels's absolute control over the channels of mass communication. In retrospect, early twentieth-century propaganda was the exception, not the rule. It married unethical rhetorical strategies to new methods of mass communication and deceived an unsuspecting public. Scholars who recognized these complex circumstances shifted away from the neo-Aristotelian model of media effects and propaganda.

After studying the post–World War II environment in the United States, Elihu Katz and Paul Lazarsfeld (1955) suggested a more sophisticated model of media effects. In their pioneering research, they looked at political issues, buying habits, and film choices in Decatur, Illinois. They concluded that, while mass media frequently introduced new information, personal influence was more dominant than media influence. Mass media was seen primarily as a powerful disseminator of messages. Their "two-step-flow" theory shifted the critical focus to more indirect media effects like agenda setting. The old neo-Aristotelian propaganda theories came to be known pejoratively as the naive model or the hypodermic needle model. The terms illustrated what researchers believed was a naive notion that mass media injected opinions into an undiscerning public. For the most part, serious academic research has continued to reject hypodermic needle theories.

Popular preoccupation with the naive model was resuscitated by Vice President Spiro Agnew in three speeches delivered in 1969 and 1970. While a close reading of Agnew's arguments reveals his objective was most likely to control mass media, not to make it more democratic, he nevertheless sparked new fears of propaganda-like media power. Agnew, speaking for the administration of President Richard Nixon, offered a catalog of media effects relating mainly to broadcast news. His initial concern was that journalists had voiced reactions to a Nixon speech on Vietnam without giving the public enough time to consider the message on their own. This argument has less in common with criticism than it does with actual propaganda.

Notably, Agnew identifies his topic as "the television news medium" and not news commentators or producers (Agnew 1989, p. 66) and claims that "no medium has a more profound influence over public opinion" (p. 66). Agnew attacks the mediators and the closed system in which he believes their opinions are formed, but as he frames the issues, the overriding, largely unspoken influence on public opinion is the medium of television itself. He does not consider that journalists might not be influential and that if they are influential, it might be because they are better informed than the average citizen or that, in part, journalists are the public. Journalists are relevant to Agnew mainly because of their unlimited access to what he believes are powerful hypnotic airwaves. He claims that Nixon worked hard on his speech, and the public might have liked it more had not television commentators interpreted it for them. In the future, he thinks television commentators should observe a moratorium of at least twenty-four hours before critiquing presidential speeches.

Here is the paradox that characterizes this speech and much of the discourse that it generated: Agnew panders to a deliberative public sphere, but the normative rhetoric outlined by his rules could only restrict public debate. As in Nazi Germany, he would have arguments presented without being tested through deliberation. In his version of the public sphere, mass media would not invigorate public discourse; they would fossilize it. This is media criticism as rhetorical strategy.

In the end, Nixon and Agnew only provided further evidence to support Katz and Lazarsfeld's argument that the American public is not as gullible as was once believed. Because of their prominent public roles, Nixon and Agnew were able to command the attention of the mass media and gain access to the public sphere. They carried out what might have seemed like devastating attacks on newspaper reporters and broadcasters, but there was no public outcry for journalistic abstinence. By 1974, the United States had withdrawn from Vietnam, and Nixon and Agnew were driven prematurely from office.

Agnew's argument has been extended by other political figures, most notably by Gary Hart (in 1987) and by George Bush (in 1988) for the purpose of deflecting unflattering news coverage of their political campaigns. Academic research for the most part has continued to explore the indirect effects of mass media.

CULTURAL EFFECTS OF MASS MEDIA

By the 1980s the cultural effect of mass media was becoming more disturbing than any negative impact they might have on public deliberation. From a cultural perspective, mass media are significant not only because they disseminate arguments, but also because they demonstrate behavior. Additionally, the very existence of mass media changes the way we communicate and therefore the way we live. The former concern is manifest in the argument that sexual promiscuity or violent behavior may be learned from movies or song lyrics. The latter concern generates the argument that the education process is impaired by mass media generated expectations of entertainment and nonlinear communication.

Every social institution in the world copes with cultural media effects. Religious and political leaders and parents struggle to contextualize information, behaviors, and paradigms of thought that were previously inaccessible for youth. The impact of cultural media effects on these groups is particularly devastating because they hold the responsibility of maintaining cultural norms. A focus of culture-building efforts is educating youth. It is an almost universal practice to protect the young from exposure to things like violence and sexual stimulation until they have acquired habits of reason and judgment that will allow them to make safe, culturally acceptable choices. However, if a home has a computer, a television, or even a radio, parental control over social initiation is problematic.

Moreover, it is now apparent that no political or cultural mechanism has demonstrated potential for neutralizing or modifying social changes facilitated by mass media. Censorship is unacceptable because it compromises the principles of publicity and uninhibited public debate, principles that give rise to and sustain self-government. Government censorship runs the distinct risk of allowing minor threats to freedom like Agnew and Nixon to become major threats to freedom like Goebbels and Hitler. And even if censorship were desirable, how could it be realized in a communication environment that has added Web pages, satellite dishes, and twelve-page-per-minute computer printers to established media such as broadcast radio and television, phone lines, and film?

WHO IS NAIVE?

President Woodrow Wilson is typical of twentieth-century political leaders in that he was less concerned with inhibiting the influence of mass communication and mass media than with exploring and expanding it. He put the nation's most accomplished public relations professionals on a committee headed by George Creel and charged them with generating public support for U.S. entry into World War I. The activities of the Creel committee were the acknowledged textbook for Nazi propagandists in Europe. After shilling for two world wars, mass media lost much of their ability to inject opinions into an unsuspecting public. Opinion research following World War II began to show that mass media had a greater influence on the agenda of public discussion than they did on the outcome of public discussion. Thus the view from the twenty-first century seems to show that that state manipulation of mass media was countered by the emergence of a media-skeptical public.

More recently, concerns developed over media effects on culture. Radio and the record industry were subjects of attacks claiming that jazz and later rock music were bad influences. Eventually similar public arguments attacked television and film for portrayals of people engaging in sexual activities, using illegal drugs, and committing acts of violence. Another category of negative influence addressed the simplistic, often inaccurate stereotyping of gender, race, or cultural identity. Both hypotheses—that mass media injects opinions in a mass audience and that people will mimic behavior they experience through mass media—are incorporated in the argument of cultural imperialism. It may be too early to tell, but it is possible that just as the public learned to distrust mass-mediated political messages, it also will learn to distrust mass-mediated cultural messages.

Regrettably, more is known about mass media and those who abused it than is known about the abused masses. One theme that runs through both the propaganda and the cultural impact theories of media effects is that the public is passive and undiscerning. To propaganda critics, this means people will believe what they are told, and to the cultural influence critics, it means they will imitate behavior they observe.

Did the century end as it began? Is the individual still a helpless Victor Frankenstein victimized by a mass media that he created but no longer controls? One solution is to make everyone who views political messages and cultural products through the mass media as informed and discerning as media critics. Essentially, this is what rhetorical theorists always have mandated. Democracy requires leaders and citizens with skills in rhetorical inquiry. Citizens who can be manipulated by media propaganda also can be manipulated by rhetorical demagoguery. Those participating in the effects debate for two thousand years before the advent of mass media generally agreed that the determining factor in assessing propaganda influence is the weakness of the receiver, not the strengths of the channel or the sender. Theirs is a simple solution that skirts the need for censorship. One might imagine that if Quintillion, Cicero, and Aristotle were alive today they might argue that if there will be a form of self-government, then the citizen must be a discerning critic of public debate. And if there will be a democracy in the twenty-first century, then it will be a mass democracy, and the citizen must be a discerning critic of mass communication as well.

REFERENCES

Agnew, Spiro. 1989. Speeches on the media. In Tom Goldstein, ed., *Killing the messenger: One hundred years of media criticism,* 66–85. New York: Columbia University.

Bitzer, Lloyd F. 1998. Political rhetoric. In Thomas B. Farrell, ed., *Landmark essays on contemporary rhetoric,* pp. 1–22. Mahwah, N.J.: Hermagoras.

Craig, Gordon A. 1996. The devil in the details. *New York Review of Books,* September 19, pp. 8–12.

Katz, Elihu, and Paul F. Lazarsfeld. 1955. *Personal influence: The part played by people in the flow of mass communication.* New York: Free Press.

Plato. 1988. *Gorgias.* New York: Macmillan.

Wichelns, Herbert A. 1980. The literary criticism of oratory. In Bernard L. Brock and Robert L. Scott, eds., *Methods of rhetorical criticism: A twentieth-century perspective,* pp. 40–73. 2d ed. Detroit: Wayne State University.

2

Social Implications of Media Globalization

Nancy Snow

Today's commercial media are truly global, influenced by deregulation of media ownership, privatization of television, and new communications technologies that have created media giants owned by transnational corporations (TNCs). Gone are the days when media were defined by national boundaries and national values, although U.S.-based broadcasting networks still hold onto their outdated monikers: National Broadcasting Company (NBC) or the American Broadcasting Company (ABC). As Christopher Dixon of Paine Webber states, "What you are seeing is the creation of a global oligopoly. It happened to the oil and automotive industries earlier this century; now it is happening to the entertainment industry" (Duncan 1998, p. 4). The six key transnational corporations that make up the global media system are AOL Time Warner, Disney, Bertelsmann, Viacom, News Corporation, and the latest entry, Vivendi Universal, which merged with media company Seagram in 2000 to form Europe's answer to AOL Time Warner.

HOLLYWOOD AND THE GLOBAL MEDIA

These companies in turn own almost all the major Hollywood studios and the cable channels and television networks that air the movies.

The social implications of the Hollywood media portend the direction in which the global media are heading. George Gerbner, a pioneer in systematically examining television programming content and dean emeritus of the Annenberg School of Communication at the University of Pennsylvania, has collected data over thirty years that show how Hollywood marketing has influenced social reality. The Cultural Indicators Project relates recurring features in the television world to media policy and viewers' conceptions of reality. The results of this long-term research are revealing: there exists a lack of diversity (or whitewashing) in the media, with virtually every racial and ethnic class disproportionately absent. Further, television emphasizes stories of conflict, violence, and the projection of white male prime-of-life power. Not surprisingly, viewers who see members of their own group underrepresented but overvictimized (which means all minorities on television) develop a greater sense of apprehension, mistrust, and alienation, what Gerbner calls the "mean world syndrome" (Gerbner 1996, p. 31). Gerbner's prescription for change, which I share, is that we must increase public participation in cultural decision making; otherwise the new digital communications technology of today, driven by privatization and a global thirst for profit, will remain unaccountable to truly democratic requirements for diversity representation in employment, programming, and ownership.

THE DIVERSITY DIVIDE IN THE
GLOBAL MEDIA

The media globalization age in which the world lives is quintessentially American—technologically superior, commercially driven, and suspicious of central (i.e., governmental) authority. This is the age of the World Wide Web, direct broadcast satellites, twenty-four-hour cable news channels, global e-mail, and digital telephony. It is an age brought to you by "your" sponsor: America Online, AT&T, Microsoft, Sprint, CNN, Disney, and a handful of other American-based global corporations, some of which were obscure or practically nonexistent a decade ago. As Robert W. McChesney notes (1999), "the hallmark of the global media system is its relentless, ubiquitous commercialism" (p. 108).

Despite this, many Americans believe that the global media age has dramatically altered their lives, and mostly for the better, according to a July 3, 1999, national survey of Americans by the Pew Research Center for the People and the Press. Americans embrace the new communication technologies (e-mail, cellular phones, and the Internet) but enthusiasm for these new communication technologies differs dramatically along generational and racial lines. Three-quarters of Americans under age fifty say the Internet is a change for the better, compared with barely half (51 percent) of those aged sixty-five and older. Parents of minority children are the least convinced of the benefits of television: 66 percent of them say that television was a change for the better compared to 78 percent of others. A growing media divide characterizes the new generational and diversity gap. The paradigmatic shift to the latest digital technology holds out the promise of greater diversity of sources and perspectives than ever before. But it also presents a danger to democracy, as voices that lack access to the new technologies lose ground in the ferocious battles for market shares and profiteering among the digital dominants.

A half century ago, most Americans got their news and information about the culture from a local newspaper, a few television channels, and perhaps a few neighbors. The promise of the global media age includes a healthy skepticism of the old media and government sources as a multiplicity of channels, both traditional and alternative, proliferates on the Internet. Populations in less developed countries that mostly grew up on a single voice controlled by the government are finding new sources that challenge the orthodoxy. Those who seek to exercise central control of information are frustrated by the global media age, while those who value freedom and democracy have cause to celebrate its arrival. Unlike state monopolies, global media systems are not tools of tyrants or dictators.

Yet optimism for technological integration brings along its accompaniment—fragmentation. Global corporations that own the media are lobbying for minimal governmental interference in their business, including regulation and taxation. Democratic governments, traditionally protectors of the public good, are becoming handmaidens to electronic commerce on the World Wide Web, supporting commercial transactions, protecting intellectual property, and facilitating e-commerce.

The majority of the world's population will not be able to compete in a media age defined by economic globalization in which efficiencies of scale produce rapid winners and losers. The illiterate and disenfranchised in all countries will be unable to participate, much less compete. Absent new methods (and movements) of distributing wealth more equitably, chaos will ensue.

The last decade of the twentieth century built a foundation for global media determinism. For the wired generation, there is no point of return to a simpler, gadget-free time. This is why the first decade of the twenty-first century is so critical in the movement for democratic communication and public determination of our cultural environment.

BUILDING A CULTURAL ENVIRONMENT MOVEMENT AROUND GLOBAL MEDIA

The global media age is part of the cultural environment—the public space of our times—that is already dominated by a few private global media and telecommunications conglomerates driven by the marketing imperative. The two largest global media firms with household names, AOL Time Warner and Disney, have seen their non-U.S. revenues increase from around 10 percent in 1990 to 35 percent in 1996, with the expectation that the figure will top 50 percent early in the twenty-first century. That global media dominance spells trouble for global grassroots citizens who wish to use these media outlets (or build their own!) for activism, advocacy, and movement politics. Public attention must be paid and action taken to counter the rush to total media monopoly. The purpose of this chapter is to confront the global media age in the name of true democracy and to work to restore the airwaves to the people, their rightful owners.

Over five years ago, the private media broadcast industry won its greatest victory in the history of American politics over the public airwaves. Not surprisingly, the American public was the last to know. This is because this victory came in the form of a giveaway, a something-for-nothing, or something-for-too-little, proposition. This giveaway is the purest form of corporate subsidy that results from special interest money dominating the American political process. At the stroke of a pen in the halls of the U.S. Congress, the Telecommunications Act of 1996 was passed, which handed over the new digital spectrum, worth up to $70 billion in the federal Treasury, to the broadcasters. The Federal Communications Commission (FCC), the U.S. government agency that oversees and monitors the public airwaves, was prohibited from auctioning off the airwaves, thanks to the high-powered arm-twisting of the National Association of Broadcasters (NAB). These free digital licenses will allow American broadcasters to air digital programs in the next few years. Broadcasters paid nothing to the public for the right to air programming over the public airwaves, and an opportunity was lost to set aside public-interest programming in the digital spectrum.

The American public may have been in the dark in 1996, but the emerging controversy surrounding the digital giveaway is becoming an opportunity in 2000 for a number of citizen groups to play a significant role in challenging the public interest mandates of the broadcasters. They include People for Better TV (www.bettertv.org), a national coalition that includes the American Academy of Pediatrics, the Civil Rights Forum on Communications Policy, Communication Workers of America, Consumer Federation of America, Cultural Environment Movement, Fairness and Accuracy in Reporting, Globalvision, League of United Latin American Citizens, Media Education Foundation, NAACP, National Council of Churches, National Organization for Women, Rocky Mountain Media Watch, all of which are composed of individual citizens who seek debate over and analysis of media democracy concerns. These include requiring broadcasters to devote meaningful coverage to public affairs, monitoring broadcaster responsibility toward children and youth, and supporting measures that promote racial, ethnic, and gender diversity in media programming and employment. The National Association for the Advancement of Colored People (www-.naacp.org) announced on July 12, 1999, that it would open a Hollywood bureau to monitor diversity in television and the global Hollywood film industry. Kweisi Mfume, president and CEO, said the step was taken in response to a virtual whitewash in American television programming for the fall 1999 prime time television lineup. Although African Americans compose 13 percent of the general U.S. population, this number is not having an appropriate presence either in front of the camera or behind the scenes. For Latinos and Native Americans, the opportunities are even fewer. Lack of opportunities creates feelings of marginalization as 62 percent of African Americans and 63 percent of Latinos feel that television entertainment shows do not represent them accurately. Mfume's message is designed to "send a strong, clear signal that the frontier of television must reflect the multi-ethnic landscape of today's American society." The NAACP campaign is an effort to restore national television to a showcase for its best writers, directors, performers, and artists, without regard to digital diversity divides.

Two reports in 1998 reached a similar conclusion: the United States has a digital divide along ethnic lines. *Closing the Digital Divide: Enhancing Hispanic Participation in the Information Age,* by the Tomas Rivera Policy Institute (TRPI), and *Falling through the Net II: New Data on the Digital Divide,* by the Commerce Department's National Telecommunications and Information Administration (NTIA), concluded that two American minority groups, African Americans and Latinos, were lagging far behind whites in their levels of telephone usage, personal computer ownership, and online access.

What these reports show is that the ability to communicate is a basic human right that is denied to some according to their ability to gain access to technology. Without basic telecommunications services, groups are not able to fully participate in the global economy, participate meaningfully in political discourse, or even socially interact with the global village. A third report by the Benton Foundation, *Losing Ground Bit by Bit: Low-Income Communities in the Information Age,* recommends that American government and society commit to universal access and keep pace with changing technology. Universal access is defined as access to a personal computer with a World Wide Web browser, a personal Internet e-mail address, and the capacity to make one's own information available via the Web.

Making the global media age safe for democracy is a daunting challenge, as many analysts point to the declining quality and diversity in programming. Dan Werner, president of MacNeil-Lehrer Productions, is concerned that the lessons of the past few years in television news, after saturation coverage of Princess Diana and Monica Lewinsky, is that more news outlets do not lead to better coverage, just endless repetition. For example, the following is a list of the number of minutes of network news coverage of the deaths of various celebrities during the first five weekdays following their death: Princess Diana (1997), 197 minutes; Princess Grace (1982), 24 minutes; John Lennon (1980): 59 minutes; Elvis Presley (1977): 31 minutes.

William F. Baker, coauthor of *Down the Tube: An Inside Account of the Failure of American Television* (1998), bemoans the attention to lurid details and wild speculation that the media adhere to these days: "More and more, we see news coverage linked to the entertainment sensation of the moment. The 'true facts' behind the movie-of-the-week is now often the lead story on the evening news. This is not merely an attempt to grab hold of the eyeballs of viewers in an over-saturated marketplace. In many cases, it is also a direct result of the media mergers that have put the purveyors of entertainment and supposedly objective information under the same roof and urged them to cross-pollinate in the interest of boosting profits" (p. 686).

The profit payoff for America's leadership in global media technology and content is evident. Newspapers have added technology and Internet sections, magazines like *Wired* for the online entrepreneur are common, but the social change outcomes are only now being realized. Like many contemporary scholars, I recognize the contradictory trends of integration and fragmentation that characterize information and communication. The global information revolution, with its focus on borderless speed and efficiency, is occurring as the finite ecosystem called earth experiences its own growing pains: The U.S. Bureau of the Census predicts that the global population will increase by 50 percent in the next 50 years from today's 6 billion to more than 9 billion. By 2050, the population of today's Global North (relatively rich, industrialized nations) will represent only 12 percent of the world's population. A shrinking percentage of the world's population will continue to accumulate a greater percentage of the world's wealth, a trend that is likely to accelerate destabilization in international relations.

Regrettably, we live in an age when governments are witnessing their budgets decrease as the influence of the multinational corporations that operate digital media technology expands proportionately. These corporations hold no allegiance to any particular country. They can decide where jobs will be, and by choosing the countries in which they will locate or do business, they decide what laws they will obey. They have the flexibility to employ child labor, to pay very low wages, and to select locations that are willing to exchange environmental damage for jobs. Their public policy emphasizes continued downsizing of government budgets, particularly in the regulatory sector, and a declining tax base from which to protect the public domain. The reality of the global media age is that citizens can allow their civilization to accommodate itself, willy-nilly, to the market dictates of information technology, or they can attempt to advocate policies that will influence it for the public good.

RECLAIMING A DEMOCRATIC CULTURE
IN THE GLOBAL COMMERCIAL AGE

As an academic and a social activist, I aim in this chapter to address how the global media can encourage an active global civil society that will reassert the public domain as a place in which democratic culture, and not just commercial culture, flourishes. Democratic culture is indeed under threat in the digital commercial age. As Mark Lloyd, executive director of the Civil Rights Forum on Communications Policy, remarks, "There is no question that the merger of computers and satellite and other communications technology has created a breathtaking global business. But communications is not merely a business. It is a means of binding the nation together. It is a public good. This notion, of communications as a public good, is as old and enduring as the postal system established under Benjamin Franklin. As the founders realized, a strong communications system and public access to information is good for commerce but it is essential to democracy" (1998, p. 1).

Democracy falters in a global media age because the selling of goods and not the telling of stories now drives our means of communication. It is clear that the global media system serves mostly advertisers and shareholders. For the world's wired generation, most of what we know, or think we know, we have never personally experienced. We live in a world erected by the stories we hear and see and tell, mostly from television. The traditional public service role of the public airways has been marginalized.

Television broadcasting is the most concentrated, homogenized, and globalized medium. The top hundred advertisers pay for two-thirds of all network television. Four networks, allied to giant transnational corporations—our private "Ministry of Culture"—control the bulk of production and distribution, and they shape the cultural mainstream. Other interests and minority views, as well as the potential to challenge dominant perspectives, lose ground with every merger. What are some consequences of this cultural monopoly? Even though there are many channels, what counts is what is on them. Multiplicity of channels does not guarantee diversity of content.

VIOLENCE AND THE GLOBAL MEDIA

Humankind may have had more bloodthirsty eras, but none was as filled with images of violence as the present. We are awash in a tide of violent representations such as the world has never seen. Images of expertly choreographed brutality drench our homes. There is no escape from the mass-produced mayhem pervading the life space of ever larger areas of the world. Broadcasters are licensed to serve "the public interest, convenience, and necessity." They are also paid to deliver a receptive audience to their business sponsors. Few industries are as public relations conscious as television. What compels broadcasters to endure public humiliation, risk the threat of repressive legislation, and invite charges of undermining health, security, and the social order? The answer is not popularity. The usual rationalization—that television violence "gives the audience what it wants"—is disingenuous. As the trade knows well, violence is not highly rated. But there is no free market or box office for television programs through which audiences can express their wants. The usual question is, Does media violence incite real-life violence? But the question itself is a symptom of the problem rather than a diagnostic tool. It obscures and, despite its alarming implications and intent, trivializes the issues involved. Television violence must be understood as a complex scenario and as an indicator of social relationships. It has both utility and consequences other than those usually considered in media and public discussion. And forces other than free expression and audience demand drive it.

Violence in drama and news demonstrates power. It portrays victims as well as victimizers. It intimidates more than it incites. It paralyzes more than it incites. It defines majority might and minority risk. It shows one's place in the "pecking order" that runs society. Media violence is but the tip of the iceberg of a massive underlying connection to media's role as universal storyteller and an industry dependent on global markets. These relationships have not yet been recognized and integrated into any theory or regulatory practice. Television, for instance, has been seen as one medium among many rather than as the mainstream of the cultural environment in which most children grow up and learn. Traditional regulatory and public-interest conceptions are based on the obsolete assumption that the number of media outlets determines freedom and diversity of content. Today, however, a handful of global conglomerates can own many outlets in all media, deny entry to new and alternative perspectives, and homogenize content. The common carrier concept of access and protection applicable to a public utility such as the telephone also falls short when the issue is not so much the number of channels and individual access to them but the centralized mass production of stories to grow on.

Violence in the media is an integral part of a system of global marketing. It dominates an increasing share of the world's screens despite its relative lack of popularity in any country. Its consequences go far beyond inciting aggression. The system inhibits the portrayal of diverse dramatic approaches to conflict, depresses independent television production, deprives viewers of more popular choices, victimizes some and emboldens others, heightens general intimidation, and invites repressive postures by politicians that exploit the widespread insecurities that it itself generates.

The First Amendment to the U.S. Constitution forbade the only censors its authors knew—government—from interfering with the freedom of their press. The First Amendment does not protect the people from corporate censorship. The Founding Fathers had no experience with corporations at that time because it wasn't until the late nineteenth century that corporations were established. Since then, large conglomerates, virtual private governments, have imposed their formulas of overkill on media they own. Therefore, raising the issue of overkill directs attention to the controls that in fact abridge creative freedom, dominate markets, and constrain democratic cultural policy.

In the United States, we claim to honor free speech as one of our most treasured constitutional protections, but we continue to leave free speech unprotected in the unregulated market. The federal government has the power to correct this, but only if the people have the political will to see that it is corrected. The First Amendment was written to protect the free speech of individual citizens foremost, not the rights of private industry. The free speech rights of viewers are harmed if the government continues to leave diversity of expression to the prerogative of television broadcasters.

Behind the problem of media violence is the critical issue of who makes cultural policy on whose behalf in the electronic age. The debate about violence creates an opportunity to move the larger cultural policy issue to center stage, where it has been in other democracies for some time. The convergence of communication technologies concentrates control over the most widely shared messages and images. Despite all the technocratic fantasies about hundreds of channels and antiviolence posturing by the mass media, it is rare to encounter discussion of the basic issue of who makes cultural policy. In the absence of such discussion, cultural policy is made on private and limited grounds by an invisible corporate directorate whose members are unknown, unelected, and accountable only to their clients.

We need to ask the kinds of questions that can place the discussion of television violence as a cultural policy issue in a useful perspective. For example, What creative sources and resources will provide what mix of content moving on the "electronic superhighway" into every home? Who will tell the stories and for what underlying purpose? How can we assure survival of alternative perspectives, regardless of profitability and selling power?

Those who are benefiting the most from the global media age are the producers and consumers who have the most money. Choices are rampant for those with the largest incomes, while the poor and those who reside in less populated rural areas stand to lose out the most. Deregulation in the media has so far produced a mere handful of corporations and mega media mergers that are forging their own exclusive arrangements and a dominant control of the global market. Finally, the advertising and marketing needs of the giant media corporations, not consumer choice, are determining programming content.

The 1999 *UN Human Development Report* states that "the collapse of space, time and borders may be creating a global village, but not everyone can be a citizen. The global, professional elite faces low borders, but billions of others find borders as high as ever" (1999, p. 31). Some of the highest borders are in the telecommunications sector. There are more computers in the United States than in the rest of the world combined. The same personal computer that costs a month's wage for the average American takes eight years' income for the average Bangladeshi citizen. Thailand has more cellular phones and Bulgaria has more Internet users than all of Africa combined, except for South Africa (p. 62).

According to the report, the road to communications wealth for countries—in the areas of production, patents, and technology—is increasingly dominated by a few countries and companies (1999, p. 68). This means that uneven and unequal development is likely to continue as long as the marketplace and the search for profits determine social and political outcomes.

THE NEXT STEP: A CITIZEN RESPONSE

This chapter has highlighted the hype and gory tendencies of global media and their social and cultural implications. Here are some activities that you can do to help build a global cultural environment movement that resists cultural homogenization and works to diminish the hypercommercial aspects of global media in favor of democratic and diversity alternatives:

- Oppose global media domination and work to abolish existing concentration of ownership and censorship (both of and by media), public or private. This involves extending rights, facilities, and influence to interests and perspectives other than the most powerful and profitable. It means including in cultural decision making the less affluent, more vulnerable groups who, in fact, make up the majority of the population. These include the marginalized, neglected, abused, exploited, physically or mentally disabled, young and old, women, minorities, poor people, recent immigrants—all those most in need of a decent role and a voice in a freer cultural environment.
- Seek out and cooperate with cultural liberation forces of other countries working for the integrity and independence of their own decision making and against cultural domination and invasion. Learn from countries that have already opened their media to the democratic process. Help local movements, including those in the most dependent and vulnerable

countries of Latin America, Asia, and Africa (and also in Eastern Europe and the former Soviet republics), to invest in their own cultural development; oppose aggressive foreign ownership and coercive trade policies that make such development more difficult.

- Support journalists, artists, writers, actors, directors, and other creative workers struggling for more freedom from having to present life as a commodity designed for a market of consumers. Work with guilds, caucuses, labor, and other groups for diversity in employment and in media content. Support media and cultural organizations addressing significant but neglected needs, sensibilities, and interests.

- Promote media literacy, media awareness, critical viewing and reading, and other media education efforts as a fresh approach to the liberal arts and an essential educational objective on every level. Collect, publicize, and disseminate information, research, and evaluation about relevant programs, services, curricula, and teaching materials. Help organize educational and parents' groups demanding preservice and in-service teacher training in media analysis, already required in the schools of Australia, Canada, and Great Britain.

- Place cultural policy issues on the social-political agenda. Support and, if necessary, organize local and national media councils, study groups, citizen groups, minority and professional groups, and other forums of public discussion, policy development, representation, and action. Do not wait for a blueprint but create and experiment with other ways of community and citizen participation in local, national, and international media policy making. Share experiences, lessons, and recommendations and move toward a realistic democratic agenda.

Fewer sources fill more outlets more of the time with ever more standardized fare designed for global markets. Global marketing streamlines production, homogenizes content, sweeps alternative perspectives from the mainstream, and moves cultural policy beyond democratic or even national reach. There is no historical precedent, constitutional provision, or legislative blueprint to confront the challenge of the new consolidated controls that really count—global conglomerate controls over the design, production, promotion, and distribution of media content and the iniquitous portrayals and power relationships embedded in it. We must build our own controls now and make the democratic right to communicate a central tenet of the global human rights agenda.

REFERENCES

Baker, W. F. 1998. The lost promise of television: Eyeballs for sale. *Vital speeches of the day* 69, no. 22: 684–689.

Baker, W. F., and G. Dessart. 1998. *Down the tube: An inside account of the failure of American television.* New York: Basic.

Duncan, E. 1998. Wheel of fortune? Technology and entertainment survey. *Economist,* November 21, p. 4.

Gerbner, G. 1996. The hidden side of television violence. In G. Gerbner, H. Mowlana, and H. I. Schiller, eds., *Invisible crises.* Boulder: Westview.

Lloyd, M. 1998. "The airwaves belong to the people: The role of the storyteller in communications policy." Remarks before the National Alliance for Media Arts and Culture Conference, Pittsburgh, Pa., October 22.

McChesney, R. W. 1999. The media system goes global. In *Rich media, poor democracy.* Urbana: University of Illinois Press.

———. 1994. "Rethinking U.S. broadcasting history." In *Telecommunications, mass media, and democracy.* New York: Oxford University Press.

Media Channel (www.mediachannel.org/ownership). Provides media ownership figures.

National Association for the Advancement of Colored People. 1999. "NAACP blasts TV networks' fall season whitewash: NAACP Hollywood bureau to monitor diversity in TV and film industry." NAACP press release, July 12.

New Internationalist. April 2001. Special issue on global media.

Pew Research Center for the People and the Press. 1999. *Public perspectives on the American century: Technology triumphs, morality falters.* Washington, D.C.

United Nations Development Program. 1999. *Human development report.* New York: Oxford University Press.

3

A Global Perspective on Internet Sexual Content: Nations' Values as Predictors of Internet Web Sex Pages

James A. Danowski and Junho H. Choi

Cybersex—pornographic content and related sexual activities on the Internet and World Wide Web—has been approached from a variety of perspectives. Although many writers make reference to the global nature of the technology, there have been no studies that systematically investigate global Internet sex in an empirical manner. Studies of sexual Internet content have yet to systematically analyze nations as units of analysis.

Some observers take a commercial vantage point and suggest that pornography on the Net is a valuable stimulant to the growth of the Internet, claiming that pornographic material has historically provided the economic engine to initially drive development of each new medium (Tierney 1994). Rosoff (1999) states that sex on the Net is the quietest big business in the world, attracting tens of millions of users. "Respectable" Web businesses rely on it for advertising dollars. He observes that online pornography was the first consistently successful e-commerce product and played a major part in the Internet's explosive growth. Moreover, he argues that adult sites gave us technological advances in advertising, user tracking, and e-commerce that have now spread throughout the Web. Rosoff quotes Lee Noga of content provider ZMaster as saying, "If there's something successful and new happening on the Internet, there's probably somebody with an adult background heading it."

Tedesco (1998) claims that sex sites on the Internet are a significant source of e-commerce revenue. He cites a report from Forrester Research that a handful of generic pornography sites is generating between $150 million and $200 million a year, with a secondary tier generating an additional $50 million, and commercial opportunity remaining across the adult spectrum.

Others see Internet sex as part of a powerful twenty-first-century sexual revolution. Maxwell (1997) foresees a long-term trend of increased sexual openness, gay marriage and legal prostitution, sex on the Internet, virtual sex, and devices for heightened stimulation. Currently, a number of articles in professional journals of sex therapists and educators see the Internet as a valuable resource for sex education. Targets include the general public in different countries (Gotlib and Fagan 1997; Lunin, Krizanskaya, Melikhova, Light, and Brandt-Sorheim 1997; Barak and Safir 1997), undergraduate coeducational students (Rosen and Petty 1995), undergraduate feminists (McCormick 1997), and even adolescents (Roffmann, Shannon, and Dwyer 1997).

Sex therapists have largely taken a positive view of Internet sex. Newman (1997) focuses on how a person with an unwilling partner can fulfill paraphilic desires (considered sexual perversions) on the Internet or can find evidence to convince their partner that the desired paraphilic behavior is "normal." Leiblum (1997) categorizes clinical issues stemming from involvement with "netsex" into three overlapping categories: (1) those involving gay, straight, or transgendered individuals, (2) those involving couples, and (3) those involving individuals with paraphilias. Kim and Bailey (1997) detail cases in which the Internet was used by paraphiles to disperse and obtain material, as well as to interact with others for paraphilic fulfillment. The authors discuss the roles of sex educators, therapists, and researchers in working with Internet-gratified paraphiles who find gratification through the Internet.

Nevertheless, other viewpoints are less supportive of Internet-related sexual behaviors. Schnarch (1997) argues that global computer networks are not advantageous for the development of intimate relationships, communication skills, and contact without anxiety or exposure. He argues that consumers readily embrace the supportive rationalizations some of his therapist colleagues offer for Internet sexual relationships because it is what they want to hear. He states that technologies which make it easy for self-presentation and limited self-confrontation are likely to promote dependence on other-validated intimacy. They do not stimulate self-validated intimacy in poorly differentiated people.

Some authors (Durkin 1997; Davis, Mcshane, and Williams 1995) approach the subject from the point of view of criminal behavior, its punishment and control. They stress how pedophiles (child molesters) use the Internet to traffic in child pornography, engage in sexual communication with children, locate children to molest, and communicate with other pedophiles. On the other hand, some researchers suggest ways to gather data from children over the Internet for sex research purposes (Binik, Mah, and Kiesler 1999).

Media studies scholars have treated the Internet and related computer-mediated communication technologies as a virtual space in which marginal groups can structure their identities, including sexual ones (Jones 1997; Sproull and Faraj 1997). Gay men (Shaw 1997) and lesbians (McCormick and Leonard 1996), as well as women seeking cybersex (Blair 1998), have been studied, with the standard critical studies assumption that sexuality is socially constructed. Rival, Slater, and Miller (1998) present a counterargument. Having investigated Internet sexuality, as well as sexual behaviors in traditional societies, they posit that the utopian definition of sexuality as sexual desire is too divorced from more basic archetypal love, domesticity and reproduction. They argue that debates about the possibilities of human sexuality and associated political intervention will make no significant progress until people stop repeating that "sexuality is socially constructed."

Although a diversity of perspectives undergirds current scholarship on the Internet and sexuality, there is no systematic research at the societal level on how values are related to Internet sex. Accordingly, the goal of this chapter is to focus on the societal values that predict development of Internet sex Web pages by studying thirty-nine societies from around the world using the World Values data from the early 1990s (Inglehart 1997). In addition to providing values data for our research, the work of Inglehart (1997) and colleagues provides a conceptual basis for our hypotheses linking societal values with Internet-based pornography. The theoretical formulation gives a route to understanding what kinds of societal values are associated with such content and why.

THEORETICAL FRAMEWORK

Materialist and Postmaterialist Value Systems

Inglehart (1997) focuses attention on what he calls "postmaterialist" values, akin to postmodernism. In contrast are the "materialist" values that dominate in newly industrialized or industrializing societies, and "traditionalist" values that he argues precede industrialization. In materialist societies there is considerable insecurity about economic resources. The result is a value system that differs from the one in advanced industrial societies which no longer have widespread uncertainty about the more basic physical needs of living. Table 3.1 shows the basic value differences between materialist and postmaterialist societies.

During the last two decades people have witnessed major political and economic changes around the globe, such as the collapse of the Soviet Union, democratization in Asia and Latin America, and a reshaping global economy, among others. Abramson and Inglehart (1995) argue that political and economic changes are associated with changing value priorities in a society. In their perspective, value changes reshape the nature of political cleavages (Abramson and Inglehart 1995, p. 1). They also see the spread of postmaterialist values as important in the growth of democratization (p. 3). The materialist/postmaterialist profile also varies according to the degree of economic development (p. 117), a thesis for which they found empirical support in the 1990–1991 *World Values Survey* (p. 127). On the average, countries having high levels (not growth rate) of economic development, as indicated by a high per capita GNP, have high levels of postmaterialism. Given their perspective that values are cognitive mobilizers of political, economic, and cultural changes, the conceptual dimension of materialist/postmaterialist values appears useful in understanding the trends of transforming global cultures.

It should be noted that just as within a society there is likely to be a mix of materialist and postmaterialist values, as evidenced in data from the World Values Surveys, there is also variance across nations. Recognizing this variation, some observers may argue that across nations, value systems represented by these two poles are moving in parallel, instead of materialist values

Table 3.1. Security and Insecurity: Two Contrasting Value Systems

	Materialist Societies	Postmaterialist Societies
1. Politics	Need for strong leaders Order Xenophobia/fundamentalism	Deemphasis on political authority Self-expression, participation Exotic/new are stimulating
2. Economics	Priority to economic growth Achievement motivation Individual vs. state ownership	Quality of life is top priority Subjective well-being Diminishing authority of both private and state ownership
3. Sexual/family norms	Maximize reproduction, but only in two-parent heterosexual family	Individual sexual gratification Individual self-expression
4. Religion	Emphasis on higher power Absolute rules Emphasis on predictability	Diminishing religious authority Flexible rules, situational ethics Emphasis on meaning and purpose of life

evolving into postmaterialist values. Such a perspective may appear valid based on a cross-sectional snapshot of national value differences; but when change since the early 1980s is analyzed empirically, the validity of a parallel worlds assumption is challenged.

Values and Sexual Media Content

Considering the sexual components of different value systems, coupled with an assumption that production of media content has some relationship to cultural values, one would expect that sexual values are associated with the amount of available media content about sexuality. We expect that societies which are more postmaterial develop a greater number of Internet Web pages with sexual content. This is because Inglehart's postmaterialism includes a focus on freedom of expression, exotic and new stimulation, individual sexual gratification, less importance placed on two-parent families and children, diminished religious authority, and situational ethics. His treatment offers reasons that explain these associations. These are not reviewed here.

The relationship between postmaterialist values and sexual content on the Web is important to investigate not only as an academic theory-building exercise but because of important policy issues that have arisen. As expansion of sexual freedom and expression appears to be a global trend, there has been an associated move toward a global framework for Internet regulation of pornography on the Net. An example is the INCORE (Internet Content Rating for Europe) initiative, which seeks to foster a global standard for rating Web content on such dimensions as pornographic and racist content (www.incore.org/what/what.htm).

Nevertheless, in this chapter we will see if the amount of pornographic sexual content in nations can be predicted based on the nature of their dominant values. If this is the case, then the theoretical explanations that have been offered for societal value changes can also explain the growth of pornographic content on the Web. This potentiality expands the possible payoff from predicting in what kinds of societal value systems pornographic content is more evident.

Questions of Causality

In terms of causal direction of development, Inglehart (1997) stresses that there is no one-way linear causation of postmaterialist values in the transition from an industrial, materialist society. Rather, he argues that the values are mutually causal. This reasoning leads to the hypothesis, although not testable in the current research, that the increased availability of sex content on Internet Web pages stimulates development of postmaterialist values in societies that are currently material or traditional.

Inglehart sees the changes toward more postmaterialist values as cohort-based. Individuals in their late teens and early adult formative years are thought most likely to develop postmaterialist values, while the older generations retain the values they developed in their youth. As a result, he sees intergenerational variation in postmaterialist values, with the whole society shifting more in that direction due to generational replacement.

Given this perspective, we would expect Internet Web sex pages to develop more in societies in which youth have more access to the Internet. In societies that have younger populations we would expect faster distribution of postmaterialist values across society, as younger cohorts are larger in size and come to dominate older cohorts more quickly. Given the generational time frame for change, we expect to observe more variation in postmaterialist values also associated with Web sex pages. This is because societies that have had sufficient generational replacement to have a dominant profile of post-materialism still have members whose values are otherwise. Thus postmateri-alist societies are also societies with more diversity in these values.

Part of postmaterialism is more emphasis on flexible rules. This, coupled with the diminishing importance of two-parent heterosexual families with children, is likely to be associated with fewer restrictions on sexual Internet content. The focus on freedom for individual sexual gratification will out-weigh concern for the harm to youth that pornographic material may cause. Moreover, there is likely to be more pedophilic sexual material.

PRIOR EVIDENCE OF AND ACADEMIC LITERATURE ABOUT SEXUAL CONTENT ON THE INTERNET

One of the top words consistently entered into various search engines on the Internet has been "sex." (the top 100 list of search terms is available at www.searchterms.com). A search on April 17, 1999, using this word in Alta Vista resulted in 12.6 million hits of all types. Infoseek returned 11.2 million hits, and Hotbot returned 2.8 million Web pages. The search engine Deja-news, which searches the content of newsgroups, returned 96,491 hits. A content analysis of newsgroup sex stories (Harmon and Boeringer 1997) identified the following overlapping categories and percentages: nonconsent, 41 percent; female/female homosexuality, 36 percent; bondage, 24 percent; discipline, 23 percent; intentionally inflicted pain, 22 percent; pedophilic sex with adults, 19 percent; torture, 12 percent; group sex, 8 percent; mind control sex, 5 percent; and incest 5 percent. Other Internet sexual content is diverse. Alta Vista's engine suggested related search subtopics associated with the single term "sex," including sex stories, animal sex, anal sex, free sex, oral sex, sex with animals, gay sex, group sex, sex passwords, sex games, sex chat, sex pictures, interracial sex, and child sex.

Focusing more on the interactive communication processes associated with sexual themes, Danet (1998) sees Internet-based synchronous chat and gender games as particularly suited to sexual play, textual masquerade, the performance of gender, textual cross-dressing, and gender neutrality. Noonan (1998) reviews the major segments of the Internet in which sexual content resides and conjectures about their psychological significance. Argyle and Shields (1996) argue that the Internet allows users to envision other users' bodies and engage in forms of public sex over the computer wires, elaborating sensual fantasies and sexual dialogues in "hotchats" and "cybersex." Lamb (1998) studied personas of individuals in online chat rooms that were supposedly for youth. The researcher reports that less than 10 percent of the visitors appeared to be genuine youth. Two-thirds were judged to be adults masquerading as children to engage in cybersex. These behaviors mainly involve masturbation while reading the sexual activities of others or casting mutual fantasies. In addition, pornographers were reported to be 25 percent of those online in the youth groups studied.

Hypotheses

Deriving from the basic nature of postmaterialist value constellations articulated by Inglehart and associates, the study reported in this chapter posed five hypotheses and tested them.

Hypothesis 1: The less important are children in societies, the greater the prevalence of sexual pages on the Web from those societies. Incidents of sexual exploitation of children on the Internet are widely publicized, as are concerns about children having access to what is considered adult content. The life cycle of news story topics is such, however, that no enduring attention has been paid to children's interests by central actors in the Internet community, or in wider circles within the advanced industrial societies in which the Internet has flourished.

Given the increased attention to adults' subjective gratification in postmaterialist societies, except for children's apparently expanding role as objects of sexual desire among adults, children may become less important overall in such societies. As this occurs, we expect greater numbers of Web sex pages originating in these nations.

Hypothesis 2: The less that traditional values for raising children are thought important in societies, the greater the prevalence of sexual pages on the Web from those societies. Inglehart's (1997) theorizing suggests that traditional values societies focus on raising children to be obedient and religious. Materialist societies, occupied with economic growth, place more attention on raising children to have determination and thrift, and to accumulate money and things. Postmaterialist societies focus more on teaching children independence, responsibility, imagination, and tolerance for diverse kinds of people. Accordingly, the less traditional the values of child rearing, the greater the number of Web sex pages originating from a society.

Hypothesis 3: The greater the value placed on nontraditional moral values in societies, the greater the prevalence of sexual pages on the Web from those societies. Traditional morality sees good and evil as clear-cut and distinct, transcending particular situations, enduring in definition, and rooted in a timeless divine authority. Proponents of a postmodern morality, on the contrary, see good and evil as a fundamentally humanistic construction. Postmodernism rejects the possibility of objective, natural law bases for right and wrong. It places the locus of moral judgment fully within the subjective domain of individuals or within the consensus of a social group.

In postmaterialism some moral judgments are left to individuals' subjective perceptions and justifications. At the same time, some moral judgments are placed in the hands of the majority or the dominant coalition, which, although perhaps not representative of the majority, is politically dominant and fosters secular legislation of situational morality. In both of these micro and macro subjective views of morality, what is thought right or wrong changes over time, depending on the social actors' evaluation of perceived personal or group gains or losses in situations. As the situational ethical envelope expands, when questions of morality arise, even the most fundamental words used within the culture to describe experience can be subject to attempted situation-specific renegotiation. An example was President Clinton's infamous rhetorical move as he testified in his impeachment trial, during which he sought to engender new meanings for the word "is."

Accordingly, in societies embracing situational and/or relativistic morality to a greater degree, societal members are more likely to see justification for what were traditionally considered immoral sexual behaviors. There is likely to be greater perceived justification for two such behaviors measured in the World Values surveys: homosexuality and prostitution. There is also likely to be greater perceived justification for divorce because it would be seen as more often situationally and subjectively necessary. Respect for parents can also be expected to be diminished because their exercise of parental authority would be seen less as automatically justified and more open to question by children and others based on situational factors.

This reasoning supports the hypothesis that societies with more nontraditional moral values have more sex Web pages originating from them. Production and distribution of sexual content are more situationally evaluated with respect to morality. This expands the pool of such content as ethical flexibility and latitude regarding its acceptable production and use increases.

Hypothesis 4: The less the importance of religious values in societies, the greater the prevalence of sexual Web pages from those societies. Organized traditional religion, according to Weber (1958), has decreasing authority and respect in the period of modern societal values preceding the postmodern. There is a distancing of religion from the public sphere. A secular, rational-legal system becomes the primary authority structure in those societies. Inglehart (1997) argues and shows some evidence for the notion that societies which abandoned religious authority first—the societies that were primarily Protestant—more quickly developed a materialist society that evolved sooner into a postmodernist society. The postmodern emphasis on subjectivism, situational ethics, nontraditional moral values, as well as its focus on New Age beliefs that organized religion excessively constrains human spirituality, leads to the hypothesis that as the importance of religious values in societies declines, the number of sexual Web pages originating from those societies increases. Institutional religion has explicit norms that define as improper the production and use of pornographic content and other sexual content not designed to exclusively support procreation within religiously approved marriage.

Nevertheless, even within the most postmaterialist societies, one may expect to find religious content on the Web, given the capability for religious groups to create Web content that fits their values and social programs. A feature of more postmaterialist societies is higher valuation of freedom of expression. Some postmaterialist societies have vocal religious minorities, which in some ways may reflect these groups' attempts to oppose the dominant postmaterialist values in their societies. Regardless, it is expected that societies with more postmaterialist values have more sexual Web pages.

Hypothesis 5: The greater the postmaterial values in societies, the greater the prevalence of sexual Web pages from those societies. A consideration of the empirical data from the 1990s surveys shows clearly that Inglehart's postmaterialism scale is closely associated with a number of other social values, some of which have already been discussed. Nevertheless, it is useful to examine the scale itself in developing the reasoning for this hypothesis: (1) seeing that people have more to say about how things are done at their jobs and in their communities, (2) giving people more say in important government decisions, (3) protecting freedom of speech, (4) progressing toward a less impersonal and more humane society, and (5) progressing toward a society in which ideas count more than money.

The first two elements of the index tap the concept of personal freedom and control over individual environments. This emphasis on individual autonomy supports individuals having the freedom to pursue the sexual gratification of their choice. The third element, about freedom of speech, is also consistent with individuals having freedom to produce and consume sexual messages. Many pornography purveyors in societies that value freedom of speech point to this as justification for their distribution of such content.

The fifth element of the index emphasizes the importance of ideas. If sexual ideas are considered important, this value for ideas would be consistent with a value on sexual fantasizing. These reasons provide justification for the hypothesis that the greater the postmaterialist values in societies, the greater the origination of sexual Web pages from them.

DATA AND PROCEDURES USED
TO TEST HYPOTHESES

Nations Studied

As described in the codebook for the data included in Inglehart (1997), a large group of research organizations coordinated their activities to conduct a forty-three-nation world values survey of representative samples carried out in 1990–1993. This enables comparisons across societies representing almost 70 percent of the world's population. They cover a wide range, from societies with per capita incomes as low as $300 per year, to those with per capita incomes as high as $30,000 per year. The societies range from established democracies with market economies, to ex-socialist states and authoritarian states.

Operational Definitions

We took the data from the 1990–1993 surveys of forty-three nations (World Values Study Group 1994) and, aggregating data by nation, computed the mean and standard deviation values for the variables used in this study. The new data set had an *n* of 43, representing one case for each nation. To obtain our data on Internet development by nation, we used the counts of Internet hosts found for the biannual January 1999 robot search of hosts by domain name that Net Wizards conducts (www.isc.org/ds/WWW-9901/report.html). A host is a server on the Internet, and some analysts project that the number of actual computers using the Internet averages approximately ten times the number of hosts.

In terms of the kind of Internet sex we would study here, we decided to focus on Web pages rather than newsgroups (Harmon and Boeringer 1997) or chatting. There is textual sexual content on newsgroups, but it is several orders of magnitude less in volume than sex Web pages. Sexual chatting on a one-to-one level, such as through ICQ software, cannot be studied without participant observation techniques. We did not wish to become sexually involved with subjects, nor did we believe that the campus committee for protection of human subjects would approve such research even had we wanted to conduct it. Likewise, we did not wish to engage in-group chatrooms such as Lamb (1998) did to study their sexual discussions. The kind of Internet sex content that is more prevalent and tractable to the national level is Web page sexual content, so we restricted our research to that arena.

For the sex Web page data capture we used the only search engine we could identify that would allow us to search for hits within particular domain names while at the same time searching for words in titles. This was Alta Vista. We used the same domain names for countries as for the data on number of hosts. As we searched within domains, we searched for the word "sex" in the title of the Web pages. For comparison purposes, we also did domain searches without specifying where in the Web page the word "sex" should appear. Alta Vista returned a value for the count of such pages. To test for the reliability of the search results, we ran the search at different times on four different days—April 11, 1999; April 27, 1999; April 30, 1999; and May 1, 1999—and correlated the results. The correlation coefficients of the log-transformed counts with sex in titles ranged between .96 and .97. This is evidence of high reliability in the normalized search output. So we averaged the log-transformed values at the four points in time to create the basic index of sex in the titles of Web pages for societies. The correlation for the log of the variable that indexed "sex" anywhere in the Web page correlated .97 with the log of the counts examining only titles. (Log transformation is standard practice for transforming skewed distributions to render them more normal.) Our original reasoning, therefore, for looking only at titles, which was that foreign language pages would use English in titles to attract more browser hits and so we would get a more international picture from the title only search, turned out to make only a minor difference.

To assess the reliability of the hosts variable in measuring Internet development, we also did a search on number of Web pages having the domain name of each nation using Alta Vista. The two measures were highly correlated at .89 for the raw values, and .91 for the log of the raw values. The Alta Vista results of searching for the total number of Web pages per domain name, done on April 29 and May 1, gave exactly the same results. Given the goal of this research to measure societal differences in Web sex pages, we thought it most appropriate to produce a proportion of Web sex pages so as to control for the total number of pages. This ratio was computed by dividing the averaged log of the number of sex Web hits by the log of the total number of Web pages per domain. This produced a relative index of Web sex per domain name.

As table 3.2 in the results section shows, there is wide variation in number of hosts, Web pages, and sex pages across the nations. Postmaterialism was operationalized with a twelve-item scale that we described earlier (see Abramson and Inglehart 1995 for details). Inglehart's (1997) states that gay and lesbian support is the strongest component of postmaterialist value changes. There are two items measuring homosexuality values: (1) "On this list are

Table 3.2. Hosts and Sex Hits by Countries

Country	HOSTS	HOSTLN	DOMWEB	LNDOMWEB	SEXAVE	LNSEXAVE	HOST+WEB	SEXRATIO
USA	7,236,406	15.79	18,354,115	16.73	491.25	7.21	32.52	.22
Japan	1,687,534	14.34	6,174,902	15.64	379.00	7.07	29.97	.24
Britain	1,423,804	14.17	6,817,370	15.73	2,027,00	8.68	29.90	.29
Germany	1,316,893	14.09	4,523,658	15.32	4,557.50	9.32	29.42	.32
Canada	1,119,172	13.93	3,140,772	14.96	893.50	7.70	28.89	.27
Nether.	564,129	13.24	1,309,581	14.09	1,176.75	8.06	27.33	.30
Finland	546,244	13.21	445,940	13.01	202.00	6.21	26.22	.24
France	488,043	13.10	1,149,423	13.95	92.50	5.60	27.05	.21
Sweden	431,809	12.98	1,596,055	14.28	1,188.00	8.04	27.26	.29
Italy	338,822	12.73	1,377,952	14.14	210.00	6.17	26.87	.23
Norway	318,631	12.67	472,864	13.07	265.25	6.47	25.74	.25
Denmark	279,790	12.54	760,822	13.54	301.50	6.75	26.08	.26
Spain	264,245	12.48	1,074,622	13.89	147.50	5.83	26.37	.22
Switzer.	224,350	12.32	1,213,974	14.01	828.25	7.54	26.33	.29
Brazil	215,086	12.28	1,332,950	14.10	418.00	6.89	26.38	.26
S. Korea	186,414	12.14	537,757	13.20	63.50	4.98	25.33	.20
Belgium	165,873	12.02	485,546	13.09	107.50	5.56	25.11	.22
Russia	147,352	11.90	1,371,910	14.13	461.75	7.36	26.03	.28
S. Africa	144,445	11.88	394,939	12.89	284.25	6.54	24.77	.26
Austria	143,153	11.87	519,067	13.16	245.50	6.51	25.03	.26
Mexico	112,620	11.63	410,124	12.92	43.50	4.64	24.56	.19
Poland	108,588	11.60	324,138	12.69	798.25	7.32	24.28	.30
Hungary	83,530	11.33	197,240	12.19	59.75	4.85	23.53	.21
Czech.	73,770	11.21	459,584	13.04	245.50	6.66	24.25	.27
Argentn.	66,454	11.10	373,166	12.83	46.25	4.89	23.93	.20
Ireland	54,872	10.91	267,818	12.50	37.00	4.63	23.41	.20
Portugal	49,731	10.81	193,497	12.17	3.75	2.67	22.99	.12
Turkey	32,496	10.39	232,920	12.36	8.00	3.05	22.75	.13
Chile	30,103	10.31	99,642	11.51	1.00	1.37	21.82	.06
Estonia	21,969	10.00	71,183	11.17	24.50	4.37	21.17	.21
Iceland	21,894	9.99	107,081	11.58	19.25	4.20	21.58	.19
Slovenia	17,836	9.79	71,640	11.18	8.00	3.02	20.97	.14
China	17,255	9.76	301,031	12.61	5.25	3.03	22.37	.14
Romania	16,659	9.72	57,408	10.96	15.00	2.95	20.68	.14
India	13,253	9.49	22,074	10.00	.75	1.27	19.49	.07
Latvia	10,345	9.24	47,050	10.76	19.50	3.74	20.00	.19
Lithuan.	10,147	9.22	82,060	11.32	9.25	3.33	20.54	.16
Bulgaria	7,425	8.91	23,674	10.07	4.00	2.32	18.98	.12
Belarus	718	6.58	35,859	10.49	.50	1.36	17.06	.08
Nigeria	410	6.02	386	5.96	.00	.00	11.97	.00

Note: HOSTS = number of hosts, HOSTLN = natural log of hosts, DOMWEB = total Web pages for domain, LNDOMWEB = natural log of total Web pages, SEXAVE = average number of sex Web pages over four points in time, LNSEXAVE = natural log of average number of sex Web pages, HOST+WEB = natural log of number of hosts plus natural log of number of Web pages, SEXRATIO = natural log of sex Web pages divided by HOSTWEB.

various groups of people. Could you please sort out any that you would not like to have as neighbors." (One of the groups was "homosexuals.") The values were dummy-coded as 1 = mentioned and 2 = not mentioned; (2) "Please tell me for each of the following statements whether you think it can always be justified, never be justified, or something in between. The respondent was handed a card with a ten-point scale anchored with "never" at one end and "always" at the other. Homosexuality was one of the items presented in this manner.

Values toward another form of individual sexual gratification were measured using the same procedure asking about "prostitution." Likewise individuals were asked about "divorce." Justification of each is consistent with a more strongly postmaterialist orientation. Another question asked how many times the person had been married. One item asked whether individuals should have complete sexual freedom.

Values toward children and their upbringing in traditional two-parent heterosexual families were operationalized with several types of items. One asked respondents to rate how important having children was to a successful marriage. Other children-related items included questions asking how many children if any the respondent had had, how many were living at home, and what the ideal number of children is. Respondents were also given a list of qualities and were asked to rate the importance of the following for child rearing: (A) good manners, (B) independence, (C) hard work, (D) feeling of responsibility, (E) imagination, (F) tolerance and respect for other people, (G) thrift, saving money and things, (H) determination, perseverance, (I) religious faith, (J) unselfishness, and (K) obedience.

Interviewees were also asked whether a home with both a father and a mother is necessary for a child to grow up happily, whether a woman has to have children in order to be fulfilled, whether a working mother can establish just as warm and secure a relationship with her children as a mother who does not work, whether a preschool child is likely to suffer if his or her mother works, whether what most women really want is a home and children, whether being a housewife is just as fulfilling as working for pay, whether having a job is the best way for a woman to be an independent person, and whether both the husband and wife should contribute to household income.

Parental respect values were measured by asking respondents to agree with one of these two statements: (A) Regardless of what the qualities and faults of one's parents are, one must always love and respect them or (B) One does not have the duty to respect and love parents who have not earned it by their behavior and attitudes.

Religious values were measured in several ways. One item asked respondents to state whether they believed there was a clear right and wrong or whether it depended on the situation. Another set of items asked about particular religious beliefs, while another asked whether the Church was adequately addressing a list of issues.

Findings

Table 3.2 shows the values indices based on the number of hosts, Web pages, and sex page variables by country.

In the results to follow, signs of correlations should be ignored because of differences in coding direction of scales across variables, but the wordings reflect the proper directionality of the associations. The +var designation means that the variance on the value item within societies was correlated with a higher ratio of sex pages. The -var designation means that decreased variance within societies was correlated with a higher ratio of sex pages. No hypotheses about variance were formed, but these results are included because of their potential value for future research.

Hypothesis 1: The less important are children in societies, the greater the prevalence of sexual pages on the Web from those societies.

+var .67 (p < .001) Children not important to successful marriage
−var −.43 (p < .005) Fewer children living at home
−var −.30 (p < .03) Have had fewer children

The hypothesis is supported.

Hypothesis 2: The less that traditional values for raising children are thought important in societies, the greater the prevalence of sexual pages on the Web from those societies.

.52 (p < .0005) Teaching children hard work not important
.38 (p < .08) Teaching children obedience not important
.34 (p < .03) Teaching children religious faith not important
+var .31 (p < .03) Teaching children good manners not important

The hypothesis is supported.

Hypothesis 3: The greater the value placed on nontraditional moral values in societies, the greater the prevalence of sexual pages on the Web from those societies.

+var .59 (p < .0001) Homosexuality justifiable
+var .51 (p < .0005) Prostitution justifiable
+var .47 (p < .002) Suicide justifiable
.47 (p < .001) Divorce justifiable
+var .51 (p < .0005) No duty to respect parents unless earned it
.25 (Ns) People should be allowed complete sexual freedom

Given that five of six indicators show support, the hypothesis is supported.

Hypothesis 4: The less the importance of religious values in societies, the greater the prevalence of sexual Web pages from those societies.

.51 (p < .001) Less agreement life meaningful only if believe in God
.51 (p < .001) Less agreement suffering meaningful only if believe in God
.47 (p < .003) Less agree death has meaning only if believe in God
.53 (p < .001) Church does not give adequate answers to social problems
.52 (p < .001) Church does not give adequate answers to moral problems
.52 (p < .001) Church does not give adequate answers to problems of family
.37 (p < .02) Church does not give adequate answers to spiritual problems
.39 (p < .07) Think less about the meaning and purpose of life
.34 (p < .02) Good and evil depend on the situation

The hypothesis is supported.

Hypothesis 5: The greater the postmaterial values in societies, the greater the prevalence of sexual Web pages from those societies.

.49 (p < .001) Postmaterialist values (4 items)
+ var .46 (p < .002) Postmaterialist values (12 items)

The hypothesis is supported.

Discussion and Interpretation of Findings

We found support for each of the hypotheses. Countries that have more sexual Web content place less importance on children, have less traditional child-rearing values, have more nontraditional moral values, place less importance on religion, and are more postmaterialist. Because these values are associated with postmaterialism in Inglehart's conceptualization, that theory sees extensibility through our findings. The theory provides a framework to explain the availability of pornographic message content. Also, the theory leads to the expectation of increasing amounts of such sexual content on the World Wide Web as more societies change from primarily materialist to postmaterialist.

The trajectory of societal value change evidenced empirically in the successive waves of the World Values survey data since the early 1980s appears so far to be non-monotonic. In other words, the direction of change has not reversed. Given the theoretical importance of economic security in fostering a shift from materialist to postmaterialist values, one would expect that the direction of change would alter only if there were widespread and enduring reductions in global economic health.

Limitations

This study examined Web pages containing the word "sex" in the Internet domains of each nation studied in the World Values Survey. A domain name is an addressing construct used for identifying and locating computers on the Internet. The procedure we used ignored the .com domain, yet that domain contains millions of sex content Web pages. To get an estimate of the international distribution of Web sex pages in the .com domain, on May 12, 13, and 24, 1999, we conducted two analyses in which we used a periodic sampling of .com sex Web pages from three search engines, Hotbot, Alta Vista, and Excite. We looked up the registration information for the .com address in the Whois (www.whois.net) database through Network Solutions (www.-networksolutions.com), which is a provider of domain name registration services. Whois is a searchable database maintained by Network Solutions that contains information about networks, networking organizations, domain names, and the contacts associated with them for the com, org, net, edu, and ISO 3166 country code top-level domains, as well as the protocol, or set of rules, that describes the application used to access the database. Other organizations have implemented the Whois protocol and maintain separate and distinct Whois databases for their respective domains.

The Hotbot sample contained 100 hits, the AltaVista sample 141, and the Excite sample 100 hits. The three samples yielded similar results. The Hotbot sample had 79 percent of the Web sex pages from the United States, while the Alta Vista sample had 65 percent and the Excite sample had 78 percent, for an average of 74 percent. Table 3.3 shows the other distribution of pages in the samples across other countries. The fact that approximately 74 percent of the .com Web sex pages are of USA origin indicates that the U.S. totals are heavily underestimated. Nevertheless, the fact that we log the number of hits variable greatly reduces the variance as it normalizes, so that the net result of doing an expanded .com investigation would have little effect on the correlations and findings reported in this study.

Another consideration is that some of the Web pages we captured with our search were not pornographic. We used a key word "sex" for our research. This captured Web pages of pornographic materials but also of other sex information, such as demographic, medical, homosexual, HIV/AIDS, sex education, and gender issues. We believe, however, that using the general key word "sex" is appropriate to our research scheme. Our primary research questions are the relationships between social values and sex-related materials on the Web, not particular kinds of sexual content. Nevertheless, our qualitative observations indicate that the social values on sex appear associ-

Table 3.3.   Dot Com Samples and Countries of Origin

Country	Hotbot	Alta Vista	Excite
USA	79	91	78
Canada	4	13	2
United Kingdom	7	7	5
Bahamas	0	9	2
Austria	2	2	5
Netherlands	0	4	2
Australia	3	1	0
Sweden	1	2	0
Russia	1	2	0
Denmark	1	1	0
Panama	0	0	2
West Indies	0	2	0
Germany	0	1	1
Norway	0	1	1
Singapore	1	0	0
Croatia	1	0	1
United Arab Emirates	0	1	0
France	0	1	0
Italy	0	1	0
Switzerland	0	1	0
Costa Rica	0	0	1
Cayman Islands	0	1	0
Total	100	141	100

Note: (1) Hotbot had 2,784,970 hits with a search keyword, sex in the .com domain. It produced 1,000 results (Web pages), but some of them belong to the same site. All of them were porn sites because the search engine organizes the results with high relevancy, which orders Web pages with other frequent query keywords such as porn, hard-core, XXX, and so on. A systematic sampling was conducted resulting in a sample size of 100.

(2) Alta Vista: we used the commands *domain:com* + *title:sex* and returned 278,294 pages. Because the engine shows only the first twenty pages of hits (400 hits), we conducted a systematic sampling on two different days, using random selection of hits on a page, to arrive at a sample size of 141 hits.

(3) Excite has an advanced Web search feature that allowed us to search for the word "sex" only in .com sites. It was not possible to restrict the keyword to titles. The engine returned 473,460 hits. We used a systematic sample of every third hit until we reached a total of 100.

ated with the amount of pornographic materials and other sex-related discourses in cyberspace. Perhaps because traditional media have restricted both to a greater degree, the Internet has become a public space in which expression on sex-related issues is voiced to a greater degree. For most countries, the preponderance of Web pages on sex are pornographic in nature. To provide evidence, we generated aggregate data from the Alta Vista search engine in which we used Boolean expressions to eliminate pornography-related pages. The results show that only 17 percent of sex pages do not contain the pornographically related words listed in table 3.4.

Another limitation is that we did not do a more systematic content analy-

Table 3.4.   Search Results of Nonporn Web Pages with "Sex" Keyword (Alta Vista Advanced Search Mode)

Boolean Expression	Hits
sex	7,157,728 (all languages)
sex AND NOT porn	3,856,786 (all languages)
sex AND NOT nude AND NOT nudity	3,192,547 (all languages)
sex AND NOT xxx	3,067,282 (all languages)
sex AND NOT adult	2,503,712 (all languages)
sex AND NOT porn AND NOT xxx AND NOT nude AND NOT nudity AND NOT adult AND NOT adults	1,621,599 (all languages)
sex AND NOT porn AND NOT xxx AND NOT nude AND NOT nudity AND NOT adult AND NOT adults AND NOT fuck AND NOT slut AND NOT cock	1,526,587 (all languages)
sex AND NOT porn AND NOT xxx AND NOT nude AND NOT nudity AND NOT adult AND NOT adults AND NOT fuck AND NOT slut AND NOT cock	1,230,611 (English)

Note: Performed at 10:30 A.M. CST, May 13, 1999.

sis of Web sex pages. We did not feel this was central to the research goals of this chapter, given observations some have made that there is similarity of pornography across various media such as print, video, and the Web. We were also struck by the observation in the Harmon and Boeringer (1997) study: "The PI of this study found it necessary to seek professional debriefing through the counseling services offered at the university after conducting this analysis. Caution and careful preparation is advised in expanding and replicating this research" (online source, not paginated). The authors of this chapter do not use pornography and did not wish to expose ourselves to it for this research. One undergraduate researcher, however, claimed to have conducted a detailed content analysis of online pornographic materials (Rimm 1995). His research was featured as a cover story in *Time* magazine and he testified before a congressional committee, but his research was widely attacked in the scholarly community (http://ecommerce.vanderbilt.edu/cyberporn.debate.html) for misrepresentation of aspects of his design and interpretations.

Searching using the English word "sex" in titles of Web pages revealed prevalence within pages in other languages, but the word was not translated into the various national languages for the searching. This is because virtually all sexual Web pages from various countries use the English word "sex" to increase the visibility of their Web pages for search engines. This and other related English words are put into the Meta Names for the Web page. The search engines read these Meta Names, but they are not visible to the typical user.

Furthermore, because subscription to the pay-per-view sex Web sites is conducted by normal methods of e-commerce, such as use of international credit cards, this further contributes to the use of the English form of the word "sex." Moreover, the characteristics of network users, found in studies to be more highly educated and higher in socioeconomic status (College Board 1999) are likely to be knowledgeable of the English language regardless of country of residence.

The study reported in this chapter shows the predictors of later sexual Web page development with a lag of six to nine years. Inglehart (1997) found in a study of value change in twenty-three societies from the early 1980s to the early 1990s that the average percentage change across the nations over the ten-year period is 15.7. Thus the current study is likely to underestimate the relationships between values and development of sex Web pages. Given the slow change in values, the lag in our study between the values data and the Web sex data suggests that we have a virtual cross-sectional design. Nevertheless, the interpretation of a lagged design showing time order between values and later sex pages may also be warranted.

Questions of mutual causality arise. Does greater prevalence of sex Web pages accelerate value change in societies? Answers to this question must await a repeat of the World Values study in the early 2000s.

Conclusion

This chapter has focused on nations' values and the proportion of their Web pages that have sexual content. We found support with data from thirty-nine nations for the hypotheses that countries have more sexual Web content that: place less importance on children, have less traditional child-rearing values, have more nontraditional moral values, place less importance on religion, and are more postmaterialist. Pornographic Web content penetrates the globe with over 12 million head page addresses. Based on the current findings, it is reasonable to hypothesize for future research that as the Internet grows worldwide, the prevalence of this content will increase. This theory suggests that this will accelerate societal value changes in the postmaterialist directions we have observed.

REFERENCES

Abramson, P., and R. Inglehart. 1995. *Value change in global perspective*. Ann Arbor: University of Michigan Press.

Argyle, K., and R. Shields. 1996. Is there a body in the net? In R. Shields, ed., *Cultures of Internet: Virtual spaces, real histories, living bodies*, pp. 58–69. London: Sage.

Barak, A., and M. Safir. 1997. Sex and the Internet: An Israeli perspective. *Journal of sex education and therapy* 22: 67–73.

Binik, Y., K. Mah, and S. Kiesler. 1999. Ethical issues in conducting sex research on the Internet. *Journal of sex research* 36: 82–90.

Blair, C. 1998. Netsex: Empowerment through discourse. In B. Ebo, ed., *Cyberghetto or cybertopia? Race, class, and gender on the Internet*, pp. 205–217. Westport, Conn.: Praeger.

College Board. 1999. Technology increases gap in education. Available at www.collegeboard.org/policy/html/paadmit.html.

Danet, B. 1998. Text as mask: Gender, play, and performance on the Internet. In S. Jones, ed., *Cybersociety 2.0: Revisiting computer-mediated communication and community. New media cultures*, pp. 129–158. Thousand Oaks, Calif.: Sage.

Davis L., M. Mcshane, and F. Williams. 1995. Controlling computer access to pornography: Special conditions for sex offenders. *Federal Probation* 59: 43ff.

Durkin, K. 1997. Misuse of the Internet by pedophiles: Implications for law enforcement and probation practice. *Federal probation* 61: 14–18.

Gotlib, D., and P. Fagan. 1997. Mean streets of cyberspace: Sex education resources on the Internet's World Wide Web. *Journal of sex education and therapy* 22: 79–83.

Harmon, D., and S. Boeringer. 1997. A content analysis of Internet-accessible written pornographic depictions. *Electronic Journal of Sociology* 3. Available at www.sociology.org/content/vol003.001/boeringer.html.

Inglehart, R. 1997. *Modernization and postmodernization*. Princeton: Princeton University Press.

Jones, S. 1997. *Virtual culture: Identity and communication in cybersociety*. London: Sage.

Kim, P., and J. Bailey. 1997. Side streets on the information superhighway: Paraphilias and sexual variations on the Internet. *Journal of sex education and therapy* 22: 35–43.

Lamb, M. 1998. Cybersex: Research notes on the characteristics of the visitors to online chat rooms. *Deviant behavior* 19: 121–135.

Leiblum, S. 1997. Sex and the net: Clinical implications. *Journal of sex education and therapy* 22: 21–27.

Lunin, I., J. Krizanskaya, L. Melikhova, L. Light, and P. Brandt-Sorheim. 1997. Use of the Internet for sex education in Russia. *Journal of sex education and therapy* 22: 74–78.

Maxwell, K. 1997. Sex in the future: Virtuous and virtual? *Futurist* 31: 29–31.

McCormick, N. 1997. Celebrating diversity: Feminist sexuality education in the undergraduate classroom. *Journal of psychology and human sexuality* 9: 37–69.

McCormick, N., and J. Leonard. 1996. Gender and sexuality in the cyberspace frontier. *Women and therapy* 19: 109–119.

Net Wizards. Available at www.nw.com.

Newman, B. 1997. The use of online services to encourage exploration of ego-dystonic sexual interests. *Journal of sex education and therapy* 22: 45–48.

Noonan, R. 1998. The psychology of sex: A mirror from the Internet. In J. Gackenbach, ed., *Psychology and the Internet: Intrapersonal, interpersonal, and transpersonal implications*, pp. 143–168. San Diego: Academic.

Nordenstreng, K. 1984. *Mass media declaration of UNESCO*. Norwood, N.J.: Ablex.

Nordenstreng, K., and T. Varis. 1974. *Television traffic—A one-way street? A survey and analysis of the international flow of television programme material.* Paris: UN-ESCO.

Rimm, M. 1995. Marketing pornography on the information superhighway: A survey of 917,410 images, descriptions, short stories, and animations downloaded 8.5 million times by consumers in over 2,000 cities in forty countries, provinces, and territories. *Georgetown Law Review* 83: 1849–1934. Available at http://trfn.clpgh.org/guest/mrstudy.html.

Rival, L., D. Slater, and D. Miller. 1998. Sex and sociality: Comparative ethnographies of sexual objectification. *Theory, culture, and society* 15: 295–321.

Roffmann, D., D. Shannon, and C. Dwyer. 1997. Adolescents, sexual health, and the Internet: Possibilities, prospects, and challenges for educators. *Journal of sex education and therapy* 22: 49–55.

Rosen, E., and L. Petty. 1995. The Internet and sexuality education: Tapping into the wild side. *Behavior research methods, instruments, and computers* 27: 281–284.

Rosoff, M. 1999. Sex on the Web: An inside look at the Web porn industry. Available at www.cnet.com/Digdispatch/dispatch342.html.

Schnarch, D. 1997. Sex, intimacy, and the Internet. *Journal of sex education and therapy* 22: 15–20.

Shaw, D. 1997. Gay men and computer communication: A discourse of sex and identity in cyberspace. In S. Jones, ed., *Virtual culture: Identity and communication in cybersociety,* pp. 133–145. London: Sage.

Sproull, L., and S. Faraj. 1997. Atheism, sex, and databases: The Net as a social technology. In S. Kiesler, ed., *Culture of the Internet,* pp. 35–51. Mahwah, N.J.: Erlbaum.

Tedesco, R. 1998. Porn sites making hay: Online adult business is generating $200 million-plus in revenue a year. *Broadcasting and cable* 128: 64.

Tierney, J. 1994. Porn: The low-slung engine of progress. *New York Times,* January 9, p. B1.

Weber, M. [1904–1905] 1958. *The Protestant ethic and the spirit of capitalism.* New York: Scribner's.

World Values Study Group. 1994. *World Values Survey, 1981–1984 and 1990–1993.* Computer file. ICPSR version. Ann Arbor: Institute for Social Research producer; Ann Arbor: Inter-university Consortium for Political and Social Research.

4

North America's Cult of Sex and Violence

Rose Dyson

Media response was immediate following the Columbine High School massacre in Colorado on April 20, 1999, in which fifteen people were killed and almost as many injured. As in the previous year, following similar shootings in Jonesboro, Arkansas, pundits argued over who was at fault. American radio talk show host Rush Limbaugh warned his listeners against "useless" demands for gun control or anything so rash as solutions from the government in Washington. Others called for widespread objection to popular culture in which movies, language, and music glorify violence.

Amid hand-wringing officials and grieving parents, few concrete plans surfaced for the prevention of similar occurrences. With massive coverage bordering on voyeurism, the focus, instead, was on prayer for the victims and their families, more compassion for those who are "different," emphasis on the "complexity" of the causes, and either praise or criticism for emergency response teams. Media savvy teenagers gave their own interpretation of events, providing clues and insights into the dimensions of the problem. On the whole, widespread denial of warning signs, both local and global, was the predominant theme. In Canada, a similar shooting occurred one week later that left one teenager dead and another seriously injured at a high school in the small Alberta town of Taber. Media attention shifted briefly to analysis of the coverage and the role it played in spawning what was widely regarded as a copycat crime.

Since then, as reported in the *Los Angeles Times*, July 21 1999, petitions signed by prominent Americans have called on Hollywood to adopt a new code of conduct and demonstrate commitment in addressing this epidemic of violence. In response, major advertisers such as Proctor and Gamble, General Motors, IBM, and Sears have pledged to pay for the development of more "family-friendly" shows. The U.S.-based Parents Television Council, led by media personality Steve Allan, is featuring full-page advertisements in major dailies advocating direct appeal to TV sponsors. Meanwhile, in Canada, despite mounting protests in California over jobs and productions being lost to "Hollywood North," which offers the cheaper dollar and subsidies, most people have yet to wake up to the fact that their own tax dollars are now paying for the local economic boom in the cultural industry, much of which is fueled by themes of sex and violence (Advertisers 1999, p. C4; Saunders 1999, p. C1).

The issues of harmful fallout from such content have now been with us for several decades. But as experts continue to conduct endless studies and argue about how these should be addressed, the problem escalates. Pendulum swings between public outcry and relative indifference are not new. These cycles usually begin with a demand for curbs followed by government-initiated inquiries, which in turn spawn promises from industry for self-regulation. Some evidence of greater responsibility surfaces—such as cancellations of Marilyn Manson shock rock concerts immediately following the shootings in Colorado—until the furore dies down and it is back to business as usual.

This chapter provides a critical analysis of these patterns in North America with particular emphasis on experiences in Canada in the past two decades. Specific ways in which dominant media interests tend to diffuse and undermine community protest are discussed in an effort to provide better understanding of how these pitfalls might be addressed by public educators.

STUDYING THE PROBLEM

By 1977, the issue of television violence, which had predominated in the early part of the decade, was beginning to recede. In broadcasting circles, competition for ratings became the major focus with the attention of critics drawn to a new development: the steady, calculated infusion of sexually suggestive themes, references, and language in television programming. Observations on the part of both researchers and commentators within the mainstream media indicated a gradual departure from existing standards of decorum in network codes, with themes of illegitimacy, abortion, incest, homosexuality, rape, and extramarital affairs becoming increasingly evident.

These were accompanied by endless controversy over harmful effects (Withey and Abeles 1980, p. 130).

In 1970, the U.S. *Report of the Commission on Obscenity and Pornography* gave pornography a clean bill of health. It was followed by the U.S. Surgeon General's Report on television violence in 1978 with proponents emphasizing that what was true for violence in television programming would also hold true for sexually explicit material, and that a more systematic approach to the total context in which these materials were used, and their use encouraged, had to be taken into account (Bogart 1980; Withey and Abeles 1980). Subsequent studies have included the U.S. *Final Report of the Attorney General's Commission on Pornography* released in 1986, also known as the Meese Commission Report.

Edward Donnerstein, an American psychologist and a major researcher on the subject of violence and sexual explicitness in the media, was one of its key witnesses. He reported that "individuals exposed to certain types of materials respond with blunted sensitivity to violence against women, calloused attitudes about rape, and sexual arousal to rape depictions and laboratory simulations of aggression against women" (Donnerstein, Linz, and Penrod 1987, p. 5). In a book that followed the Meese Commission, his stated aim was to go beyond its findings, but in fact little new discussion was offered apart from a criticism of the Meese Commission recommendations, particularly the call for an expansion of existing obscenity statutes and stricter enforcement of these laws. Donnerstein and his colleagues argued, instead, for "educational programs to mitigate the effects of sexual violence in the media" (p. 174). This has since become an observable pattern in reported findings on pornography.

In a paper presented at the annual meeting of the Scientific Society for the Study of Sex in San Diego, California, in 1992, feminist scholar Gloria Cowan spoke on three issues: the lack of attention paid to degrading and dehumanizing pornography and the imprecise selection of materials in research studies, the distortion of findings by researchers, and the inconsistencies in statements made by some pornography researchers. Sometimes the long-term harmful effects of X-rated material without violence are recognized. At other times, they are not. As Cowan pointed out, one shortcoming in the work done on pornography in general is that, too often, researchers are overly committed to their own version of what they perceive to be the appropriate focus and tend to concentrate too heavily on discrediting the findings of other researchers. Another reason for inconsistencies is a political or ideological distaste for recommendations that have wide-ranging legal solutions.

In studies released through the LaMarsh Centre on Violence and Conflict Resolution at York University in Toronto in 1989 on attitudes and behavior regarding pornography, sexual coercion, and violence among adolescents and young adults, psychologist James Check found that young people aged twelve to seventeen years tend to be the primary consumers of pornography and rely on it as a form of sex education. Also, 37 percent had expressed an interest in watching sexually violent scenes such as rape, torture, and bondage whereas adults tended to express very little interest in such scenes (Check and LaCrosse 1989). Since then, of course, an entire generation of adolescents has grown up with sustained patterns of addiction to violent pornography, which accounts in part for the steady increase in demand for and consumption of the genre. This, in turn, is fueled by producers and distributors offering an increasing array of bizarre themes. In his 1997–1998 *Annual Report* for the Ontario Film Review Board, Chairman Robert Warren said, "The main characteristics of the past fiscal year were larger volumes of submitted product, especially of the adult sex genre, and increasingly difficult classification decisions as film makers try to extend the boundaries of what is acceptable to the community" (Warren 1998, p. 2).

THE FRASER COMMITTEE REPORT

In Canada, a major study on issues involving sex and violence commissioned by the federal government known as the Fraser Committee Report was released in 1985. In the end, because it was fraught with ambiguities and claims of inconclusive evidence, the government itself ultimately rejected it. The committee deliberately ignored findings released at the second Symposium on Pornography and Media Violence held in North America at the University of Toronto on February 5, 1984, despite the fact that the event was specifically timed to coincide with its scheduled hearings in Toronto, and that committee members were present and later provided with transcripts (Fraser 1985, p. 101; Epstein 1984).

Participants at the conference included over thirty prominent American and Canadian researchers, writers, community activists, educators, health care workers, members of the media, and municipal politicians. Among them were Donnerstein, Zillmann, Bryant, Malamuth, Check, Singer, Huesmann, Eron, Radecki, and U.S. Surgeon General C. Everett Koop. Koop emphasized that violence throughout North America had reached epidemic proportions and that media violence, pornographic and otherwise, was a major causal factor. More action was demanded and a follow-up study to the Fraser Report was done by the Ministry of Justice (Dyson 1995). A series of bills to amend the Criminal Code on definitions of pornography were then introduced in the House of Commons at one time or another, all to no avail, until May 1993, when a new child pornography bill was introduced and subsequently implemented.

INDUSTRY-ORCHESTRATED PUBLIC
RELATIONS

The reasons for the delay of almost ten years for this particular initiative are various. One of them was the result of well-funded and well-orchestrated propaganda campaigns from pornographic media interests opposed to any interference with their corporate activity. An example manifested itself in the form of a "leaked" memo from Argyle Communications, Inc., at the time the Toronto affiliate of Gray and Company, a large Washington, D.C., based public relations agency. In Canada, the Metro Toronto Residents Action Committee on Violence Toward Women and Children (METRAC) distributed it. The memo included an outline of a campaign being launched for the purpose of discrediting the U.S. Meese Commission Report. One of the agency's strategies read as follows:

A way must be found to discredit the organizations and individuals that have begun to disrupt the legitimate business activities of publishers. . . . This can be accomplished by creation of a broad coalition of individuals and organizations opposed to the Commission's findings and recommendations . . . these new groups would include academics, civil libertarians, religious leaders, civic and community leaders, politicians, columnists, commentators and entertainers. It might be called "Americans for the right to read" or "The First Amendment Coalition." (Johnson 1986, p. 4)

Evidence of these strategies being implemented included a series of public meetings held throughout Toronto, mainly in public libraries, but without panel representation in defense of the bill. Soon there was a visible shift in the balance of coverage on the issue of pornography that had hitherto appeared in mainstream newspapers. In my own analysis of ninety-three articles that appeared in the *Toronto Star* over a period of fifteen months from the time the bill was first introduced into the House of Commons on May 4, 1988, until it was declared virtually defeated on July 14, 1989, and eventually died, only six could be described as reflecting the position of the Justice Department, where the bill had first been drafted (Dyson 1995).

A protest was registered with the Ontario Press Council on January 11, 1988, accusing the *Toronto Star* of inaccurate, misleading, and biased reporting by feminist and legal scholar Reva Landau. But it proved to be useless. The newspaper's response was that the bill was a complex one that had been interpreted in "different ways by different people" but that their columns reflected the views of a major segment of the cultural community (Dyson 1995). It was not clear if they were referring to the artistic community, the movie distributors who have always contributed so much to the newspaper's advertising revenue, or both.

Landau's experience, which resonates with similar complaints filed with the Ontario Press Council by C-CAVE members since, serves to demonstrate how biased in favor of the press these councils can be (Dyson 1999). They underscore the continuing need for impartial media councils and an ombudsman acting solely in the public interest, as recommended by at least one major Canadian inquiry into the subject of media violence in the past (LaMarsh Commission Report 1977). Only now is the need for vigilance at the international level becoming increasingly urgent.

CANADIAN INITIATIVES
IN THE EARLY 1990S

In 1993, the Canadian government's Standing Committee on Culture and Communications made two recommendations. First, that the federal minister of justice take the necessary measures to develop criminal legislation to control slasher and snuff films in conformity with the Canadian Charter of Rights and Freedoms. Second, that this be done in collaboration with the minister of finance, who should revise the customs tariff as required to ensure that it complements the necessary amendments to the Criminal Code. One result was that in July 1993 a child pornography bill was passed that makes the production, distribution, and possession of child pornography a criminal offence in Canada, punishable by up to five years in prison for simple possession of the illicit material. Under this legislation, any film, magazine, or video that shows explicit sexual activity involving people under eighteen or adults pretending to be under eighteen is considered child pornography.

Opposition to the legislation, which appeared in the media immediately after its adoption, was reminiscent of that expressed to previous bills on pornography. Amid calls to have it revoked, the usual objections surfaced. The law was passed with "undue haste," was badly flawed because it is too broad, allowing for too much "misadventure" on the part of police forces and border guards, that the burden of proof rests with the accused, that merit can only be assessed after the fact and that "artists" whose defense is unsuccessful risk going to jail (Harris 1993, p. C1).

The first artist to be charged under the new legislation was Eli Langer, who had five oil paintings and thirty-five pencil drawings depicting sex with children seized from the Mercer Union art gallery in Toronto on December 15, 1993. In his well-funded defense, amply supported by prominent members of the arts community and media industry in Canada acting as expert witnesses, Langer argued that he did not use models, that his work was the product of his imagination, and that it involved a serious "exploration of the phenomenon of sexual intimacy between adults and children" (Exhibit busted, 1993, p. 11).

On April 20, 1995, the Ontario Court ruled that the paintings and drawings seized by police should be returned to Langer because the seizures violated his constitutional right to free speech on the basis of demonstrated artistic merit. The presiding judge also ruled that the legislation was valid and that the protection of children takes precedence over the right to free speech (Downey 1995, p. A6). In October 1995, Langer's appeal to the Supreme Court was also denied (Top court refuses, 1995, p. A4).

By 1999, however, the legislation was again in jeopardy following a decision from Justice Duncan Shaw of the B.C. Supreme Court when he dismissed two charges of possession of child pornography against John Robin Sharpe of Vancouver on the basis that possession of child pornography "is not a reasonable limit on freedom of expression guaranteed by the Charter of Rights and Freedoms" (Matas 1999). This time, the federal government intervened in order to protect its legislation. The B.C. Court of Appeal has since upheld the lower court decision and the matter is now before the Supreme Court of Canada.

Despite persistent attempts to have the legislation dismantled, the authorities have seized numerous caches of child pornography. One of the first examples occurred in October 1993, when five people were arrested in what was described as the largest seizure of child pornography in Canadian history (Wilkes 1993, p. A11). Only now, police argue that the B.C. court decisions have seriously impeded their ability to lay charges.

LIMITATIONS TO NEW LEGISLATION

In the spring of 1993 both Blais and federal MP Otto Jelinek supported a proposal to broaden the legal definition of obscenity to include undue exploitation of crime, horror or cruelty, and violence that is degrading and dehumanizing, even if it contains no sexual element, this component was not included in the bill that became law in July 1993. Consequently, other manifestations of the problem continue to proliferate. In 1992, one of these surfaced in the form of serial killer board games marketed by Diamond Distributors, a U.S. company with branch offices in Burnaby, British Columbia, and Edmonton, Alberta. Described by B.C. reporter James Risdon, these games were packaged in their own plastic body bags, complete with illustrations, a bag of twenty-five babies, four serial killer figures, crime and outcome cards, and instructions (Risdon 1992, p. 1). The games also inspired a similar genre of violent entertainment called "True Crime Trading Cards," produced by Eclipse Books in California. According to one newspaper account, they outlined the killer's criminal history with a photo that carried a watercolor likeness of either the killer or the victim (Killer cards 1993, p. B6). In many instances, the killer's history included an addiction to pornography.

In 1994, the Canadian government's Standing Committee on Justice and Legal Affairs drafted amendments to the Criminal Code on these crime cards and board games that would have legalized their commercial use and sale to anyone over the age of eighteen years. C-CAVE and victims groups represented by parents whose children had been murdered by serial killers argued against them on the basis that such amendments would normalize this kind of entertainment by putting the government's stamp of approval on its legal sale to anyone at all (Dyson 1995).

Other limitations to the Criminal Code on pornography and media violence have surfaced in Ontario government debates on the subject of interactive video games (Mackie 1993, p. A3). Public protests over this new genre of violent entertainment revolved around CD-ROM discs first marketed by Sega entitled Night Trap. The game featured actual images of women rather than cartoon-like characters. On *CBC Midday Television*, July 15, 1993, the company vice president, Jeff McCarthy, described the trend toward more realistic video games portraying more sex and violence as the generation of children reared on video games got older. Opposition critics argued that voluntary controls by the industry were not sufficient while the Ontario attorney general, Marion Boyd, countered that drafting legislation to control video games was extremely difficult and would require federal–provincial cooperation to overcome jurisdictional limits. In the end she resorted to the same timid solution as California Attorney General Dan Lungren. Both called on video game manufacturers and retailers to "voluntarily" remove from the market games that contained graphic, gratuitous violence. Once again, history was repeating itself as officials carefully emphasized that they were not proposing "censorship or mandatory government action" but appealing instead to industry leaders for both corporate and personal responsibility (Lungren 1993). Meanwhile, a review of Night Trap in the *Wall Street Journal* described the game as having the sound and feel of a B-grade slasher film, providing a glimpse of where video games may be headed in the future (Mackie 1993, p. A3).

In public statements made on behalf of Sega, Jeff McCarthy pointed out that the company was doing its "best to inform consumers and parents . . . and would soon introduce a ratings sticker on each game sold (Dawson and Harvey 1993, p. 16). The stickers, it was reported, like movie ratings, would advise parents in three categories: GA for general audience, MA-13 for mature audiences, and MA-17 for adults only. Few observers have ever believed that ratings and warning labels are very helpful for a variety of reasons, among them the well-grounded evidence that anyone who engages in this form of entertainment is at risk and that once a product is on the market, children of all ages invariably end up with access to it. By the end of the year, in response to public protests, it was announced that Night Trap would no longer be distributed in Canada, although there was subsequent evidence of the game being distributed in certain parts of the country. Minor variations continue to be released into the market with no serious objections from anyone (Dyson 1995).

VALUES AND TECHNOLOGY
CONVERGING

The urgency and seriousness of problems posed by new interactive technology was stressed by University of Florida–based social scientist, educator and toy designer, Eugene Provenzo in 1993 when he attended a conference in Toronto on electronic child abuse organized by the now defunct Institute for the Prevention of Child Abuse. He warned parents about the potent impact and increased dangers of ever more graphic depictions and diversified forms of violence on the market as the technologies converge.

There are, of course, numerous examples of how violent pornography as entertainment and violence in real life are converging, with boundaries between the two becoming increasingly blurred. One example involves the life and crimes of Canadian serial killer Paul Bernardo and his wife, Karla Homolka, who was his accomplice. In 1994, I participated in a televised forum at the Stephen Leacock High School in the greater Toronto area not far from where Bernardo grew up. Because he also lived in the greater Toronto area, the social impact of the crimes with which he was charged and subsequently convicted—which included not only murder but videotaped accounts of how he tortured his victims—was strongly left throughout the region. Paris Black, who hosted the event, focused attention on the fact that Bernardo, when he was first put in jail, received thousands of letters from young female fans. This is, of course, not an isolated example of serial killers attracting adoring female fans, but all of them must surely be regarded as a manifestation of what U.S. Surgeon General C. Everett Koop meant when he said a decade earlier at the University of Toronto that violence in the media has become one of the most serious mental health problems facing North America.

Throughout the summer of 1993, intense public interest, both inside and outside of Canada was focused on the charges faced by twenty-three-year-old Karla Homolka in St. Catharines, Ontario, who was sentenced to twelve years in prison for manslaughter in the death of teenagers Leslie Mahaffy and Kristin French. A press ban was imposed on publication of the evidence because Paul Bernardo, her estranged husband at that time, still faced two charges of first-degree murder in connection with the deaths. The presiding judge closed the courtroom to the general public and prohibited the media from publishing or broadcasting any details about the circumstances of the deaths. Judge Kovacs stated that Bernardo's right to a fair trial on the murder charges had to take precedence over freedom of expression. His decision precipitated an avalanche of media attention and debate, offering the public an unprecedented opportunity to observe the expression of *institutionalized* violence in the media when the overriding consideration is profit.

Although the need to protect the families and communities traumatized by the murders was not stipulated as a factor for imposition of the ban, it was soon apparent that the ban would have that side effect. When Debbie Mahaffy was interviewed for *Maclean's* magazine, her comments underscored the potential for justification of the ban on humanitarian grounds alone. She said, "My emotion coming out of court was one of despair. It was like my daughter had just died again. . . . It aches to be constantly reminded" (Brady 1993, p. 17).

The day after the Homolka trial was concluded, representatives for the *Globe and Mail*, the *Toronto Sun*, and the CBC announced that they had planned an appeal. John Cruickshank, then managing editor of the *Globe and Mail*, explained that "the overall issue the court will be asked to decide is whether the 'enormous public interest' in the proceedings can be reconciled with the valid interest of ensuring a fair trial for Ms. Homolka's estranged husband, Paul Bernardo, on two charges of first-degree murder" (Claridge 1993, p. A4). For Cruickshank, the need for the victim's families to be spared unnecessary additional pain and suffering was a nonissue. Similarly, the prurient and voyeuristic implications involved in the enormous public interest, evident in the lines that formed outside the courtrooms whenever the court was in session, were ignored.

A number of lawyers commented on the validity of the ban, among them Nancy Toran-Harbin, a Toronto-based victims rights activist. She argued that the impact of communications technology on the public court is increasingly in danger of transforming it into a "tabloid court." Said Toran-Harbin:

> During the past ten years, there has been a burgeoning recognition within the justice system of a pressing need to address the short and long term impact of violent crime upon victims of violence. It is now accepted that damage is not confined to the primary victim, but rather extends to a group of secondary victims comprised of the victim's family and intimate circle. In addition, it is now being recognized that a larger constellation of individuals can, to a significant degree, be detrimentally affected, namely, the peers, friends and acquaintances of the victims and their families. (1993, pp. 111–112)

Prior to the commencement of the Homolka trial, through newspaper accounts, the public had already been made aware of the many horrifying aspects relating to the case. Consequently it was difficult to rationally conclude that somehow justice would be better served through publication of additional minute details about, for example, the last words uttered by two terrorized children. Indeed, if we accept the premise that it is desirable for the justice system to treat victims of crime with at least as much regard and humanity as the accused, the need to explore methods that aim toward such attainment is long overdue.

Reported instances in which publicity surrounding the graphic details of brutal murders have served as blueprints for further crimes have become routine. A serial killer who is able to successfully conceal evidence, even temporarily, poses a significant ongoing threat to public safety, and, in response, the justice system is required to interpret and determine a balance in the face of competing values and needs. Clearly, distinctions need to be drawn between public voyeurism and the public right to information, with more emphasis placed on determining what it is the public really needs to know. As Toronto criminal lawyer Edward Greenspan pointed out, "The public's essential right to know doesn't mean they have the right to know everything . . . immediately. Consider," he said, "the example of a victim in a sexual assault case. We protect their identity, for good reason" (Cheney 1993, p. D1).

Imposition of the ban fueled press speculation on how it might be enforced. Legal options available to Attorney General Marion Boyd to lay criminal charges against both cable television outlets and stations that distributed shows violating the ban were countered by industry spokesmen with the familiar argument that the company viewed itself only as "the carrier of information, irrespective of its content" (Tyler 1993a, p. A10).

Cross-border complications prompted Bob Rae, then premier of the Province of Ontario, to accuse the U.S. media of showing disrespect for Ontario's judicial system by publishing details of the Karla Homolka trial that the Canadian media were banned from reporting (Cheney 1993). By that time, however, most coverage in Toronto was focused on the ban's impact on basic rights to freedom of the press. In the *Toronto Star* Osgoode Hall law professor Alan Young commented on the "foolishness" of the court decision while lauding Canadian laws in general. He explained that Canadian judges have been able to shield courtroom testimony in a way that American judges can not because of differences in the power relationship between their media and justice system (Tyler 1993b, p. A4).

In Toronto, Brian Greenspan, past president of the Criminal Lawyers Association, pointed out that the press ban on the Homolka trial was by no means the first one to be imposed in Canada. What was new, he said, was the reaction of the media. He also commented on fundamental differences between the American and Canadian judicial systems, such as the methods by which witnesses are questioned, which tend to precipitate the requirement of a ban in Canadian court cases more often. He also urged the Canadian public not to allow themselves to be held hostage by the American media.

Nelson Thall, president of the Marshall McLuhan Centre on Global Communications in Toronto, observed that although the court had acted in good faith to protect Paul Bernardo's right to a fair trial, it had, through its ignorance of the ground rules of the new media environment, taken actions that had resulted in the opposite effect. Judge Kovacs, he said, had made an error in not excluding all electronic media and allowing only the press to cover the case (Thall 1993, p. A18).

Sheila Kieran, a former journalist and director of the Ontario government, appointed the LaMarsh Commission, which reported on violence in the communications industry in Canada in 1977. She warned everyone not to be taken in by the continent-wide display of "self-righteous indignation" from the media industries. "They insist their job is to ensure that you live in a free and open society, protected against dictators who can't wait to subvert justice and strangle your access to information. Hardly. The first job of your newspaper or television station is to make money" (Kieran 1993, p. A27). She also pointed to the growing chasm between Canadians, their politicians, media editors, and owners:

> It is insulting to suggest people are too passive to defy a court order. That order, in fact, seems to many people a difficult but reasonable compromise between an open society and the need to ensure a fair trial. Perhaps that is why the streets are not filled with hordes demanding to know, *this very minute*, every appalling detail of how two lively young women were murdered. The media seem oblivious to the fact that, for each of the people who rushed across the border to wallow in the horrific details in U.S. newspapers, thousands were apparently content to live in a country where the presumption of innocence and the right to a fair trial are considered something more than mere obstacles to test the press's cunning and perseverance. (Kieran 1993, p. A27)

In the aftermath of the high school shootings in Littleton, Colorado, and Taber, Alberta, and the extensive coverage that followed in both countries, these deliberations now seem distant and rather quaint.

LOCAL AUTHORITIES IGNORE
CORPORATE GREED

There have been other examples of the media industry's cynical disregard for the public interest stemming from the murders of the Mahaffy and French girls. One month after conclusion of the Bernardo trial, Bret Easton Ellis, author of the hideously sadistic novel *American Psycho,* a book identified as a blueprint for Bernardo's behavior and crimes by the Crown Attorney's office during the trial, appeared in Toronto as part of Harbourfront's International Festival of Authors. Harbourfront is primarily funded by the Canadian taxpayer, which means that the same public traumatized by the trial and mourning for the children Bernardo murdered was, in effect, paying to provide a forum and publicity for one of his favorite authors. This happened despite objections from across the country to distribution of the book in Canada when it was first published, preceded by considerable controversy in the United States. The book had also been ruled inadmissible by the judge during pretrial arguments in the Bernardo trial, on the basis that the contents were so vile and vicious that if read in whole or in part by the jury the book would have a significant prejudicial effect (Cairns and Burnside 1995, p. 3). Nevertheless, Ellis was showered with publicity while in Toronto, from the *Toronto Star* and the *Globe and Mail* and from public broadcaster TV Ontario when host Steve Paikin interviewed him during a main stage reading, followed by book autographing (Dyson 1999).

Public officials ignored objections from C-CAVE and other community organizations that, in the aftermath of the Bernardo trial, we were not only funding violent material known to have a harmful effect, but promoting and sanctioning it, and giving its author a voice even after it has been clearly identified as the favored reading material of a "multiple child rapist/murderer." In 1999, despite renewed protests from C-CAVE, city officials approved a permit for Lions Gate Entertainment, based in Vancouver, to proceed with the film production of *American Psycho,* based on a script adapted from the book by Canadian director and producer Mary Harron (Slotek 1999). The major justification for proceeding, both on the part of Harron and two women interviewed with me on *CBC TV News* and *Canada AM,* April 8, 1999, was that the book is a fine satire, depicting the styles and trends of the 1980s. Both York University–based feminists, they stated that they had found the book extremely funny, including the scenes in which women's heads were being lopped off or their bodies connected to jumper cables from the back of automobiles. This is clearly an ominous trend in mainstream definitions of humor. The two killers in the Colorado school massacre in April 1999 were reported to have interspersed their shootings with howls of laughter. Countless researchers have commented on how the absence of fear and indignation from these kind of depictions and their replacement with humor is in itself a grave demonstration of values distortion and desensitization (Dyson 1999).

There have been other examples of poor judgment on the part of Toronto municipal officials from the standpoint of the public interest. Also in 1995, from February 2 to April 8, Harbourfront Art Gallery, the Power Plant, hosted an exhibition entitled *The American Trip* in which it purported to offer "the latest on artists in the forefront of expression of outlaw activity."

Print material accompanying the exhibition explained that the purpose was to "highlight disillusionment with the American Dream" and to "challenge the boundaries of censorship." Displays involved the theme of "teenage lust" experienced by outlaw artists drifting in and out of jail. Accompanying photographs focused on drugs, sex, violence, and rock 'n' roll with references to preadolescent children. Another portion of the exhibition celebrated images of sex and death with themes of kids killing parents along with the world of bike gangs with their dress codes and symbols. There was an exploration of the "psychopath and con man transformed from outlaw to celebrity with serial killers used as examples. All of this was mounted in an exhibition at public expense to "test the boundaries of censorship."

INTERNATIONAL RESPONSES

Throughout the world, community activists, government officials, and legal experts, concerned with the proliferation of hate on the Internet, are taking note of modest gains being made on the issue of child pornography. This was evident at two international symposiums on the subject held in Toronto, one in September 1997 and the other in March 1999. In a 1998 report based on an international comparative review of policy approaches conducted by Heather DeSantis for the Department of Canadian Heritage, it was noted that in many jurisdictions existing laws concerning hate and illegal materials are being applied to the Internet. So far, Germany is the only country to have successfully introduced entirely new telecommunications legislation to deal with the Internet, but there is growing support among other countries as well for multilateral initiatives despite the contentiousness of issues surrounding freedom of speech. Also, Internet service providers are developing codes of conduct in response to the worldwide impetus for self-regulation.

These are all laudable and necessary initiatives, but the urgency for more effective strategies intensifies as a siege mentality mushrooms in our schools and cities. Distortions to the democratic process itself, brought on by globalization, trade liberalization, and, as George Gerbner frequently points out, increasing reliance on sex and violence as cheap industrial ingredients because they sell well in a global economy and translate easily into any language, must be challenged. As every aspect of the current economy becomes reordered by currency speculators and advocates of "free" trade, the crisis for the survival of democracy itself deepens. The Cultural Environment Movement (CEM), founded by Gerbner in 1996 to meet this crucial challenge of our time and now supported by over 250 independent organizations in every state in the United States and over sixty other countries, must be accelerated. Ways in which *institutionalized* violence is maintained and protected by public relations expertise have been persuasively argued by Joyce Nelson, Noam Chomsky, Robert McChesney, and Nancy Snow among others (Dyson 1999). Meanwhile, the potential for eruption of real-life violence from frustration and anger about the possibility of changing America's cult of sex and violence at all, deepens. Road rage, air rage, and other manifestations of what George Gerbner calls "the mean world syndromes" are already upon us. Apathy is another by-product from diminishing faith in public institutions, evident in low voter turnout during elections all over North America.

Other developments, particularly in the United States, include the growing interest in class action lawsuits such as the one launched in 1999 in Louisiana against Oliver Stone and others responsible for the production and distribution of the film *Natural Born Killers*. It set the stage for another lawsuit, the US$130 million action in the state of Kentucky against selected media outlets precipitated by a school shooting in 1997 (Edwards 1999). In Canada, victims' legal advocates collaborated with American counterparts, and in Toronto C-CAVE cohosted a panel discussion at the University of Toronto on November 30, 1999, featuring Scott Newark, special counsel to the Ontario Office for Victims of Crime; Miami lawyer Jack Thompson, acting for the families in the Kentucky lawsuit, and David Grossman, a psychologist and retired U.S. lieutenant colonel who is widely regarded as one of the world's foremost experts in the field of human aggression and the roots of violence. The purpose was to examine the possibility of adapting the American lawsuit strategy to the Canadian experience.

Since World War II American civil action lawsuits have resulted in sweeping consumer protection legislation. Canadian observers regard this as evidence that criminal and statutory proceedings as a force in law are being overshadowed. Although the tendency in Canada has been to rely more on the regulatory model, Canadian civil rights lawyers are predicting that American initiatives on media issues will have a significant impact on Canadian civil courts and potential damages awarded. In these cases public opinion is swayed, not by moral or legal imperatives, but on the matter of compensation for damage caused. For community activists and educators this is good news. There is already evidence that insurance rates for movies dealing with violence have risen dramatically in the months following the massacre in Littleton, Colorado (Quill 1999, p. 17). Although a more litigious society is an acrimonious and less desirable alternative to more peaceful forms of conflict resolution, these law suits may, nevertheless, provide some badly needed impetus for better public education on civil liberties issues and the distinctions that need to be made between individual freedom of expression and corporate freedom of enterprise.

66   Rose Dyson

REFERENCES

Advertisers planning to pay writers for "family" shows. 1999. *Globe and Mail*, August 13, p. C4.

Attorney General's Commission on Pornography. 1986. *Final report of the Attorney General's Commission on Pornography.* Washington, D.C.: Government Printing Office.

Bogart, L. 1980. After the surgeon general's report: Another look backward. In S. Withey and R. Abeles, eds., *Television and social behavior: Beyond violence and children,* pp. 103–134. Hillsdale, N.J.: Erlbaum.

Brady, D. 1993. A mother's grief. *Maclean's,* July 19, p. 17.

Cairns, A., and S. Burnside. 1995. Bernardo trial: Life imitates "art." *Toronto Sun,* September 1, p. 3.

Check, J., and V. LaCrosse. 1989. Attitudes and behaviour regarding pornography, sexual coercion, and violence in Metropolitan Toronto high schools. Report no. 34. In *The LaMarsh research programme reports on violence and conflict resolution.* Toronto: York University.

Cheney, P. 1993. Do we really need to know? *Toronto Star,* July 3, p. D1.

Claridge, T. 1993. Media outlets plan appeal of publication ban: Globe, Sun, CBC to argue judge made legal errors. *Globe and Mail,* July 7, p. A4.

Commission on Obscenity and Pornography. 1970. *Report of the commission on obscenity and pornography.* Washington, D.C.: U.S. Government Printing Office.

Cowan, G. 1992. "Degrading/dehumanizing pornography: The costs of denial." Paper presented at the annual meeting of the Scientific Society for the Study of Sex, San Diego, Calif.

Dawson, A., and I. Harvey. 1993. Video "game" under attack. *Toronto Sun,* July 14, p. 16.

Donnerstein, E., D. Linz, and S. Penrod. 1987. *The question of pornography: Research findings and policy implications.* New York: Collier.

Downey, D. 1995. Art works ruled no risk to young. *Globe and Mail,* April 21, p. A6.

Dyson, R. A. 1995. "Doctoral thesis: The treatment of media violence in Canada since publication of the LaMarsh Commission Report in 1977." OISEUT, National Library, Ottawa.

———. 1999. *Mind abuse: Media violence in an information age.* Montreal: Black Rose.

Edwards, S. 1999. Eerily familiar death spree puts Hollywood on trial. *National Post,* April 22, A13.

Epstein, D. 1984. *Symposium on pornography and media violence.* Toronto: C-CAVE/OISE. Video recording.

Exhibit busted. 1993. *Now,* December 23–29, p. 11.

Fraser, P. 1985. *Pornography and prostitution in Canada: Report of the Special Committee on Pornography and Prostitution.* Vols. 1–2. Ottawa: Ministry of Supply and Services.

Gerbner, G. 1991. The second American revolution. *Adbusters,* Fall-Winter, pp. 8–10.

Harris, C. 1993. Organizations fear child-porn bill threatens artists. *Globe and Mail*, June 30, p. C1.

Johnson, S. 1986. June 5. Pro-pornography "leaked" memorandum. In METRAC, *Pornography and free trade: A time for action* (Toronto: METRAC Publishers), appendix A, pp. 1–6.

Kieran, S. 1993. Media seeking profit, not freedom. *Toronto Star*, December 9, p. A27.

Killer cards may get Easter ban. 1993. *Hamilton Spectator*, March 1, p. B6.

LaMarsh, J. 1977. *Report of the Royal Commission on violence in the communications industry.* Vol. 1, *Approaches, conclusions and recommendations;* vol. 2, *Violence and the media: A bibliography;* vol. 3, *Violence in television, films, and news;* vol. 4, *Violence in print and music;* vol. 5, *Learning from the media;* vol. 6, *Vulnerability to media effects;* vol. 7, *The media industries: From here to where?* Toronto: Queen's Printer for Ontario.

Lungren, D. E. 1993. Lungren to video game industry: Pull violent games from market. News release, November 16.

Mackie, R. 1993. Boyd urges consumers to boycott promoters of violent video games. *Globe and Mail*, July 14, p. A3.

Matas, R. 1999. Legal to possess child porn, B.C. court rules. *Globe and Mail*, July 1, p. A3.

On electronic child abuse: Problems and solutions. Toronto, Ont. Video recording.

Provenzo, E. F. 1993. Violence, videogames, and interactive TV. Paper presented at Conference on Electronic Child Abuse: Problems and solutions. Toronto: IPCA. Video recording.

Quill, G. 1999. Driving up the cost of violence. *Toronto Star*, June 6, p. D16.

Risdon, J. 1992. Murder: The board game. *The News* (Burnaby, B.C.), August 16, pp. 1, 3.

Saunders, D. 1999. Hollywood protest benefits Canada. *Globe and Mail*, August 20, p. C1.

Slotek, J. 1999. Money vs. morals: Guess which wins. *Toronto Sun*, February 28, p. 13.

Standing Committee on Communications and Culture. 1993. *Television violence: Fraying our social fabric.* Ottawa, Ont.: Ministry of Supply and Services.

Standing Committee on Justice and Legal Affairs. 1994. *Report on crime cards and board games.* Ottawa, Ont.: Ministry of Supply and Services.

Thall, N. 1993. Letter to the editor on the Teale trial. *Globe and Mail*, December 8, p. A18.

Top court refuses Langer appeal. 1995. *Toronto Star*, October 14, p. A4.

Toran-Harbin, N. 1993. The tides of justice. *Law Society of Upper Canada Gazette*, June, pp. 111–112.

Tyler, T. 1993a. Cable firms could be charged. *Toronto Star*, July 15, p. A10.

———. 1993b. Courts looks "foolish," professor says. *Toronto Star*, December 1, p. A4.

Warren, B. 1998. *Annual Report, 1997–1998.* Ontario Film Review Board, p. 2.

Whitney, S., and R. Abeles, eds. 1980. *Television and social behavior: Beyond violence and children.* Hillsdale, N.J.: Erlbaum.

Wilkes, J. 1993. Porn suspect faces 35 charges. *Toronto Star*, p. A11.

5

Drugs in Television, Movies, and Music Videos

George Gerbner

How well and how long most Americans live no longer hinge on medicine or fate. Preventable illness and premature death are now end products of a complex manufacturing and media marketing process.

The cultural environment, with television drama as its mainstream, has become the new frontier of health promotion and disease prevention. This is a report from that frontier.

Scenes with alcohol, tobacco, and/or illicit drugs are present in seven out of ten prime-time network dramatic programs. Scenes of drinking alcoholic beverages are seen an average of every twenty minutes, smoking every fifty-five minutes, and illicit drugs every seventy-eight minutes (fig. 5.1).

More major characters in prime-time television drink alcoholic beverages than anything else (fig. 5.2).

Since 1989–1991, the portrayal of drinking alcoholic beverages in prime time has increased significantly for major male characters. Since 1992–1994, the portrayal of drinking alcoholic beverages has increased significantly for major female characters (fig. 5.3).

Female smokers now outnumber male smokers among major characters in prime-time television (fig. 5.4).

In a sample of the 40 highest-grossing movie titles for the years 1994 through 1995, 39 (97.5 percent) contain portrayals of alcohol, smoking and/or illicit drugs (figure 5.5).

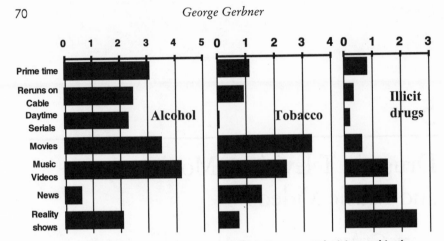

Figure 5.1.   Scenes of Alcohol, Tobacco, and Illicit Drugs on Television and in the Movies (number per hour)

Those who view the most popular music video channel see alcohol use an average of every fourteen minutes, tobacco use every twenty-five minutes, and illicit drugs every forty minutes (fig. 5.6).

The use of addictive substances is shown as generally risk-free. More than nine out of ten drinkers, more than eight out of ten smokers, and six out of ten illicit drug users experience positive health effects or no health effects (see fig. 5.7).

In television drama, illicit drug users are mostly male (1.0 percent of all

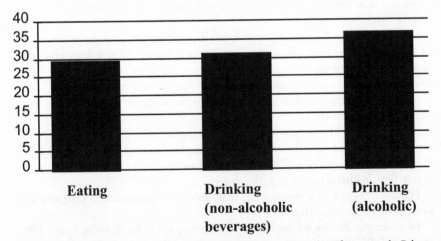

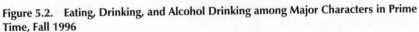

Figure 5.2.   Eating, Drinking, and Alcohol Drinking among Major Characters in Prime Time, Fall 1996

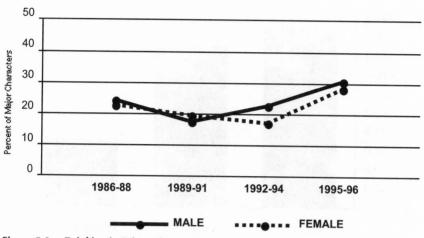

Figure 5.3.   Drinking in Prime Time, 1986–96

male characters), young and are either Hispanic and/or people of color. Nearly six out of ten are involved in violence (compared to one-fourth of nonusers), of which they are most likely to be both perpetrators and victims.

Persons of color and Hispanics are typically underrepresented in the prime-time population; however, their proportion among the illicit drug users in prime time is twice that of the proportion of all persons of color and Hispanics in the real population.

In general, addictive substances are linked to bad character rather than to negative health consequences or the danger of addiction. Only 6.1 percent

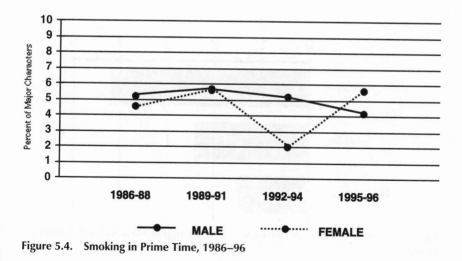

Figure 5.4.   Smoking in Prime Time, 1986–96

72   *George Gerbner*

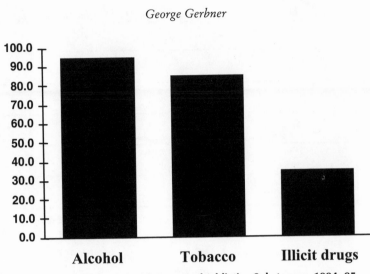

Figure 5.5.   **Percent of Movies with Scenes of Addictive Substances, 1994–95**

of drinkers and 8.9 percent of smokers, but 40.0 percent of illicit drug users, suffer negative health consequences. Only 2.5 percent of all drinking characters are shown to be problem drinkers, and only 3.3 percent of smokers are shown to be addicted. Only the use of illicit drugs is shown to be perilous. Even among these users, just 39.3 percent are identified as addicted and only five out of eleven of these addicts are shown as suffering ill health effects.

Victimization of drug users is about three times higher than the victimization rate among non-users. The proportion of fatal victimization among the users of illicit drugs (nearly 1 in 5) is the highest for any group of characters

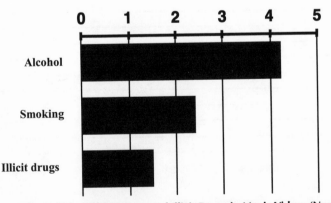

Figure 5.6.   **Scenes of Alcohol, Tobacco, and Illicit Drugs in Music Videos (Number per Hour)**

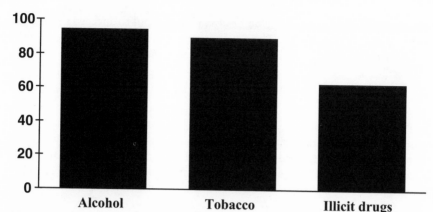

Figure 5.7. Percent of Addictive Substance Users Who Suffer No Negative Health Effects, Prime Time, All Characters

that have been analyzed over the years. Illicit drug users fail because they are characterized as criminal or evil rather than as a consequence of drug use.

MOVIES

Addictive substances appear much more frequently in movies and music videos than on prime-time television. Only one of the forty movies surveyed does not have scenes involving alcohol, tobacco, and/or illegal drugs. Two titles do not include any portrayal of alcohol, and six titles do not have any smoking. Illicit drug scenes are present in over one-third of the movies, more than twice their presence on prime-time television.

Addictive substances are portrayed over six times per hour (about one and a half times more frequently than in prime time). Movies show smoking almost as often as drinking. The moviegoer sees or hears about drinking an average of every seventeen minutes, smoking every eighteen minutes (three times more often than on prime-time television), and illicit drugs every hundred minutes.

More than half of all major movie characters use alcohol—at more than twice the rate of prime-time characters. Almost a third use tobacco, about six times the rate of prime-time characters. One out of every three movies contains an illicit drug scene. Most of them present dealers rather than users. Their main concern is with crime, action, and adventure rather than the health consequences of drug use. As in prime time, major female characters who drink are disproportionately more likely to be victimized.

Smoking shows a marked gender difference in casting and fate. Male smokers are more likely to be heroes than villains and to succeed than to fail compared to non-smokers. The major female characters who smoke, on the other hand, are more likely to be villains than heroes, and to fail than to succeed.

MUSIC VIDEOS

Music videos present addictive substances even more frequently than movies. About half of all music videos on MTV and BET channels contain some addictive substance. This proportion is constant throughout different time slots and during the entire week on both channels, exposing viewers of all ages.

A viewer of MTV sees alcohol use every fourteen minutes, compared with every seventeen minutes in the movies and every twenty minutes on prime-time television. Illicit drugs are present every forty minutes, approximately twice as often as in the movies and on prime-time television.

Music videos associate addictive substances with fun and sex. Videos that show smoking are also likely to be associated with crime. Videos with illicit drugs associate them mostly with crime.

The highest percentage of drinkers on MTV are males under eighteen. Illicit drugs are used at a proportionately higher rate by older females. BET has no underage substance users, and very few female users. In fact, BET videos rarely show main performers and other narrative characters as drinking, smoking, or using illicit drugs.

THE ADDICTS

Addiction on prime time does not merely consist of repeated or regular use of an addictive substance. It is a special category, distanced from regular use and restricted to special types of users. Only one in four frequent users are identified as addicted, and one in four addicts experience negative health consequences. But addicts are more likely than others to fail and to fall victim to violence. They are portrayed as "losers."

Addicts are likely to be male, and are likely to be Hispanic or people of color. (Less than one-fifth of "regular users" who are not depicted as addicts are in this group, while a third of the users who are shown as addicts are minority males. The female addicts, however, are all white young adults.

CONCLUSION

A child who grows up watching only three hours of prime-time television a night on one channel will have watched 32,000 characters who demonstrate tobacco use as a part of their lives. Over 2,500 tobacco smokers will have been playing central roles in the stories being told. Yet the story of negative health affects and addiction is not one of them. The child will have to view 2,200 smokers on television before seeing one who experiences negative health effects.

Each year, the four major television networks are broadcasting stories that include about 25,000 alcohol drinkers, about 6,000 tobacco smokers, and at least 1,500 illicit drug users.

The music video channels serve up an even more intoxicating batch of programming to audiences with younger overall demographics than the major networks. It must be noted, however, that 76 percent of illicit drug scenes in music videos were antidrug messages. It is thus alarming that such public health messages played no part in any of the music videos featuring tobacco, and only a few ambivalent mentions of alcohol intoxication were recorded. The risk of experiencing negative health effects is presented as minimal, even for excessive or addicted users.

In prime time, one in every five illicit drug users die, not because of their drug habit but simply because they are expendable people, often cast as murderers, criminals, or villains. Since viewers generally do not view themselves as failed or murderous villains, they will not assume that they are susceptible to the same risks. Couching the effect in terms of morality rather than the consequences of substance use and abuse compounds the danger of simply not providing accurate health information.

NOTE

This chapter was prepared with the assistance of Nejat Ozyegin and Brian Linson.

6

The Mass Media and the Health of Adolescents in the United States

Jane D. Brown and Elizabeth M. Witherspoon

In the United States, adults always have worried about the harmful effects of the mass media on children and adolescents. In the 1920s, parents were concerned about how Hollywood movies viewed in theaters allowed young people to be together unchaperoned in the darkness watching bigger-than-life scenes of kissing and romance. Our concerns have simply broadened since then as each new medium—radio, comic books, television, music videos, video games, and now the Internet—has been introduced. How do our children make sense of all these images, these ideas about how the world works? Do the media teach our youth that violence is an appropriate way to resolve conflict, that sexual intercourse comes before love, that only thin girls can be popular, that smoking, drinking, and using other drugs is cool?

The answer is not a simple one, primarily because U.S. youth are such diverse audiences, and because they have an increasing opportunity to choose which media and aspects of those media they will attend to and perhaps learn from. But, in general, the media depict a world in which unhealthy behaviors such as physical aggression, unprotected sex, smoking, and drinking are glamorous and risk-free. It would be hard for teens today to not be seduced by this media view. Unfortunately, the social scientific evidence investigating the effects of the media on adolescents' health is more robust for some health issues and some media than others.

We begin by looking at the media diet of U.S. teens to see what an array of media are available and how frequently they are used, and then we turn to what is known about the media's effects on four health issues that have been studied most comprehensively: (1) violence and aggression; (2) sex; (3) obesity, nutrition, and eating disorders; and (4) alcohol and tobacco use.

U.S. TEENS' MEDIA DIETS

How U.S. Teens Use the Mass Media

U.S. teens today are growing up in a world saturated with the mass media. Although adolescents watch less television than any other age-group, they still watch on average more than twenty hours per week, or two to three hours per day (Nielsen Media Research 1998). More portable and teen-focused media such as music and magazines are most appealing to teens, who listen to music even more frequently than they watch television—on average more than twenty-two hours per week, whether radio, CDs, or tapes.

Advertising permeates almost all media that teens attend to and probably will become even more apparent as marketers discover how lucrative the "teen market" is. American teens currently spend about $57 billion a year, an average of $68 per week per teen, and they have significant influence on other things—from food to cars—their families buy. As the teen population swells over the next decade, marketers will focus even more closely on how to persuade them to buy their products and be loyal to their brands. Marketers already are inventing new ways to get advertising in front of kids, including mediums such as school buses, paper book covers, and even cafeteria tray liners (Acuff, Reiher, and Acuff 1997; McNeal 1992; Zollo 1995). As the Web entangles schools, children will increasingly be exposed to advertising on the "educational" sites they use in their classrooms (Richards, Wartella, Morton, and Thompson 1998).

Relatively recent developments in media technology, such as satellite transmission, the remote control, the VCR, and the Internet, have expanded enormously the number of media materials available and have given teens in the United States much more control over when and where they will use them. In the next five years, other technological innovations such as digital compression will bring an estimated three hundred program choices into most U.S. homes; by 2010 most homes will have a thousand channels or "content windows" (Stevens and Grover 1998). Other media, such as radio, magazines, and movies, already are highly specialized and offer an array of content that appeals to a variety of tastes and interests. Today's teens have the opportunity to select their own media diets from a smorgasbord of possibilities.

Table 6.1.   U.S. Teens' Frequency of Use and Attractive Attributes of Mass Media

Medium	Average Use	Attractive Attributes
Music	22 hours/week	Highly specialized; portable; arousing
Advertising	In all media	Signals trends, what's cool
Magazines	Middle-class girls: daily	Shows trends, sets standards; is portable
Movies	1/mo. in theaters; frequently on VCR, on cable at home, and at friends' homes	Favorite media stars; relevant; arousing
Television	20+ hours/week	Favorite shows; familiar; relaxing; funny
Internet	Upper-class boys most frequently; 60% homes with kids have PCs	Information; chat groups; porn (?)

U.S. TEENS' MEDIA DIETS

Figure 6.1 diagrams the array of media "food groups" available to U.S. teens, using the same pyramidal structure that the U.S. Department of Agriculture created to illustrate ideal eating habits. The bottom tier, or the "grains and breads" level, in terms of U.S. teens' media use, is what Willis (1990) calls "the common culture"—the images, styles, and ideas that most youth will attend to in the media. This includes the top television shows in prime time, the top songs that play most frequently on the radio stations and simultaneously rotate on music video channels, the blockbuster movies (e.g., *Titanic*),

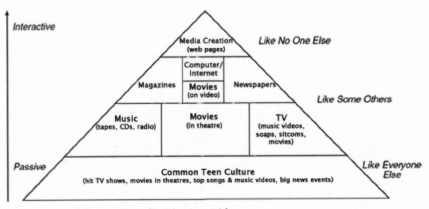

Figure 6.1.   Adolescents' Media Diet Pyramid

and magazines such as *Seventeen* and *Sports Illustrated*. These media products become the common language, the common topics of conversation. If you are an American teenager and you haven't seen the latest episode of *Dawson's Creek* or the movie *Titanic*, you may not have the cultural capital necessary to belong to the peer group of your choice.

The selection at the next two levels in the media pyramid, we speculate, is governed more by the teen's developing sense of self. The development of a firm sense of identity is a central task of adolescence. Gallatin (1975) suggested that the teen is learning in what ways he or she is like all other people, like some others, and like no others. At the common culture level, a teen is (or yearns to be) like all other people. At the next level, the teen is like only some others, for example, "skateboarders," who read *Thrasher* magazine, rent skateboarding videos, and listen to a particular kind of rap music, or "popular girls," who read *Elle* and *Cosmopolitan* magazines and watch *The Young and the Restless* soap opera. Finally, at the tip of the pyramid, teens have the opportunity to create their own media—diaries, poems, songs, videos, and, recently, Web sites—in which they are like no others.

The media nearer the top of the pyramid are increasingly interactive, requiring greater effort by the viewer or listener or reader, and they may have greater impact because the consumer is so personally involved. This is where youth who are developing "fringe" identities, such as "metalhead" or "riot grrrl" will spend most of their time because they are less likely to find others like them in the more mainstream media. The majority of media used by teens probably fall into the middle two levels—somewhat interactive, necessitating some choice, and increasingly specialized to appeal to teens' developing sense of self. This is important to keep in mind because it means that effects will not be the same for all teens, since they are not attending to the same media content for the same reasons.

HOW THE MEDIA AFFECT ADOLESCENTS' HEALTH

What do we currently know about how this extensive use of the media by adolescents affects their health? The four health issues we review here have been investigated in sufficient detail that some conclusions may be drawn. Unfortunately, much of the work focuses primarily on television, even though it is not the most important medium for most teens, and the work rarely takes into account the dramatic variation in teens' media diets. Nevertheless, we can see that the media do have an impact on adolescents' health.

Violence and Aggression

Injury and death by violence constitute the greatest public health threats to U.S. adolescents. Although crime rates among youth seem to be declining since they peaked in the mid-1990s, homicide is still the second leading cause of death for American youth (Snyder, Sickmund, and Poe-Yamagata 1996). The highly publicized murders committed by young teen boys in nonurban schools in the late 1990s has increased the public's concern that gun violence is not simply a disturbing but unavoidable problem of the inner cities.

Can the media be blamed for violent youth? Yes, at least to some extent. As with any of the health issues we examine, the media are not the sole cause, and many other factors, such as gender, developmental patterns, personality characteristics, family stability and socioeconomic status, characteristics of the community, and so on, are probably more important. In the case of aggression and violence, however, we can conclude confidently that television is one of the contributing factors. The effect of televised portrayals of violence on children has been the most extensively studied health issue in mass communication research. More than 1,000 studies using various scientific methods with a range of populations over three decades converge on the conclusion that viewing violence on television increases the probability that viewers will be fearful, will become desensitized to real-world violence, and will be violent themselves (Friedrich-Cofer and Huston 1986). Analyses suggest that 5–15 percent of violent behavior in the United States can be attributed to television viewing (Comstock and Strasburger 1990).

Despite the certainty with which most researchers would say there are direct and negative effects, and numerous public and legislative efforts to reduce the amount of violence portrayed in the media in the United States, television and movies remain saturated with violence. The most recent and comprehensive content analyses of U.S. television non-news programming (2,750 programs on 23 channels randomly selected over seven months for three years [1994–1997]) found violent material in a stable 58 to 61% of the programs. Despite the television industry's stated commitment to reduce the frequency and glamorization of televised violence, only 3% of these programs could be characterized as having an overall non-violent theme, and only 13% of violent shows portrayed the long-term negative consequences of violence such as physical and psychological suffering (Smith et al. 1998).

Fear

An often overlooked outcome of viewing on average more than 1,000 murders, rapes, and aggravated assaults per year on television is fear for personal safety in the real world. Children frequently develop long-term fears of specific kinds of people and places from seeing just one movie or television scene that frightened them (Cantor 1998). Boys are probably more likely than girls to suppress this fear, which may in turn cause anxiety and increased aggression (Sonesson 1998). Gerbner and his colleagues speculate that the fear generated at least in part by the ubiquity of violent acts on television may contribute to Americans' reluctance to relinquish their handguns, as well as their support for building more prisons and harsher penalties for criminals (Gerbner et al. 1994).

Desensitization

Interestingly, televised violence is rarely explicit or graphic. It is uncommon to see a close-up view of a gun firing, a bullet entering a victim's body, or blood, thus increasing the possibility of desensitization to violence. The simultaneous use of humor in almost half (42 percent) of the violent scenes, as well as the lack of portrayals of pain or physical injury to victims of violence, may also contribute to viewers' beliefs that violence isn't a serious act and consequently reduce their willingness to assist or intercede in real-life violence (Smith et al. 1998).

Violent Behavior

Younger children probably are more directly affected by portrayals of violence on television than adolescents, but adolescents are more likely to have access to deadly weapons and to experience interpersonal situations in which they may act on the lessons about violence they learned as children. Centerwall (1992) showed that the rate of homicide increased in the United States, Canada, and South Africa ten to fifteen years after the introduction of television and that rates of serious violence rose in children first and then among adolescents and young adults. Huesmann and Eron's (1986) cross-cultural longitudinal studies showed that children who watched more violence on television were more likely than those who watched less to be aggressive as teenagers and as young adults, even after controlling for IQ, social status, parental aggression, mobility, church attendance, and the child's baseline aggression level.

The evidence is compelling and disturbing. The media, especially television and movies that increasingly are shown on television, continue to teach our children and teens that violence is an appropriate and relatively risk-free way of resolving conflict in a scary and dangerous world.

SEX AND SEXUALITY

Although teens are waiting longer to have sexual intercourse and are using condoms more frequently than they have in the past, the rate of teen pregnancy and the incidence of sexually transmitted diseases, including chlamydia and HIV, are still higher among U.S. youth than in most other postindustrial countries in the world (Centers for Disease Control and Prevention 1998).

Some say that in the 1970s, when the U.S. television industry was last compelled to listen to public outcry about the negative effects of violence on television, it simply substituted sex for violence as the "bait" for the audience. It must have been an effective strategy, since sex is more common and explicit in media available to adolescents now than ever before. Even in the "family hour" on television (the first hour of prime time) three-fourths of programs contain sexual messages (portrayals of and talk about sex). On average, there are about eight sexual incidents per hour—more than four times as many as in 1976 (Kunkel, Cope, and Colvin 1996).

What is talked about on TV programs is done in the movies. More than two-thirds of Hollywood movies are R-rated, and teens have increasing access to these films through cable TV and rental videos. In an analysis of movies most viewed by adolescents, Greenberg et al. (1993) found an average of 17.5 sexual portrayals per movie.

Heterosexual sexual intercourse between unmarried partners is the most frequent sexual activity either talked about or portrayed in television and movies. Contraceptives, and the consequences of pregnancy or sexually transmitted diseases, are almost never discussed or depicted (Huston, Wartella, and Donnerstein 1998). One study of sex on prime-time television found a ratio of one mention of sexual responsibility, STDs or pregnancy to every twenty-seven sexual incidents, and most of these were in a joking or humorous context, for example, "better be careful, who knows who she's slept with!" (Lowry and Shidler 1993). Soap operas, a popular genre for adolescent girls, have a somewhat better record. One out of every ten sexual incidents include planning for sexual activity, discussion about "safer sex," or the negative consequences of sexual activity (Heintz-Knowles 1996), although there is little portrayal of pregnancy or the realities of raising an infant (Greenberg and Busselle 1994).

American popular music always has been and remains preoccupied with love and sex. Although music videos differ by musical genre, for example, "gangster rap" is more misogynistic than country music, which tends to focus on romantic love and breakups, music videos are, as one critic put it, a young adolescent male's sexual fantasy (Jhally 1995). The almost always scantily clad women are rarely portrayed as anything other than sexual objects to be lusted after or aggressed against (Seidman 1992).

The magazines most popular with adolescent girls are full of advertising and editorial copy about how to achieve the "look" that will attract the right kind of male (Peirce 1990). *YM*, for example, recruits readers in the following way: "If you like finding out about yourself and guys and fashion and relationships and beauty and . . . subscribe now" (*YM* 1998, p. 17). About two-and-a-half pages per issue of teen girl magazines are devoted to explicitly sexual issues, mostly in advice columns answering readers' questions about contraceptives and STDs, and articles focused on how to decide when to have sex (Walsh-Childers 1998).

MEDIA AS SEX EDUCATORS

The frequency and consistency of sexual portrayals across the media adolescents attend to and the relative reticence of other sources of information to deal with the issue of sex suggest that the media could be important "sex educators" (Roberts 1982). Teens say they would prefer to get sexual information from their parents, but more than half of adolescents report learning about pregnancy and birth control from TV and movies, and more than half of teen girls say they learned about sex from magazines (Princeton Survey Research Associates 1996).

But what are they learning? Given the dearth of information about sexual consequences, it should come as no surprise that in the United States, only a quarter of the population reports learning about STDs from the media. Fewer than half of teens can name an STD other than HIV, and only 3 percent know of chlamydia. In contrast, in Western Europe, more than three-fourths of the population say they learn about STDs from TV, books, or magazines (American Social Health Association 1996).

Relatively few studies of the potential effects of the media on adolescent sexuality have gone beyond documenting that the portrayals exist, to a large extent because of the difficulty of gaining access to teens to talk about sex. The few experimental studies that are most adequately designed to assess causality have shown that teens can learn the following:

- basic sex information (e.g., menstruation and reproduction from educational videos [Greenberg, Perry and Covert 1983])
- the meaning of words such as "homosexuality" and "prostitution" (from regular television programs [Greenberg, Linsangan, and Soderman 1993])
- that premarital sex is acceptable (from viewing music videos and prime-time television [Bryant and Rockwell 1994; Greeson and Williams 1986])

Correlational studies have also found relationships between viewing music videos and permissive attitudes about premarital sex (Strouse, Buerkel-Roth-fuss, and Long 1995). Those who view soap operas frequently are more likely to believe that single mothers have relatively easy lives and that male friends will be important in her children's lives than those who watch less often (Larson 1996). Marriage is not as pleasantly perceived. Signorielli

(1991) found that those who view television frequently were more likely to be ambivalent about the possibility that marriage is a happy way of life. Interpretation and effects of sexual media content will depend on the users' age, gender, and race as well as the teens' reasons for using the media and other factors such as parental involvement (Huston et al. 1998). For example, older teens have a better understanding of and feel more comfortable with televised sexual innuendos than younger teens do (Brown, White, and Nikopoulou 1993; Kaiser Family Foundation and Children Now 1996). Girls may use the media to learn about interpersonal relationships more than boys do (Thompson, Walsh-Childers, and Brown 1993).

We still have much to learn about the sexual effects of the media on teens. Are teens who see more portrayals of sexuality more likely to engage in risky sexual behavior earlier than those who see fewer portrayals? How do teens evaluate what they hear from other sources with what they see in the media? Are the media more compelling than other sex educators because they include the possibility of sexual passion and desire?

NUTRITION, OBESITY, AND
EATING DISORDERS

Getting comfortable in a changing body is a daily concern of most teenagers. "Looking good" becomes a preoccupation, and for some girls, especially, getting thin enough becomes an obsession. Ironically, simultaneously, more American teens are obese than ever before, primarily because they eat junk food instead of fruits and vegetables and don't get enough exercise. (Gortmaker, Dietz, and Sobol 1987; Pope et al. 1984).

The media play a role here in two ways. First, the very act of attending to the media, because it requires no physical effort, contributes to weight gain. A significant body of work with children and adults has found that the more time a person spends watching television, the more likely he or she is to be obese. Although a recent study did not find the same relationship for adolescents (Robinson, Hammer, and Killen 1993), it is reasonable to expect that media do have an impact on both the amount of time available for more physical activities and food consumption among adolescents. The more time children spend watching television, the more snack food—which is typically high in fat, sugar, and calories—they consume (Dietz 1993).

Second, the media portray food and people in a way that leads paradoxically to obesity and an obsession with thinness. Food, typically sweet snacks, are consumed or referred to three to five times per half hour on prime-time programming (Story and Faulkner 1990). Food products and fast-food restaurants are heavily advertised on television and increasingly are aimed at the teen audience (Zollo 1995). This couch potato (chip) effect may be strongest for older male teens as they return to heavier television use and less physical activity (Ozer et al. 1998).

But here's the paradox: given all this unhealthy food consumption in the media, how are most of the people in the media, especially white women, so thin and apparently healthy? Content analyses show that more than two-thirds of women characters on television are thin, but only 18 percent of the men (Silverstein et al. 1986). The shape of women's bodies, and to a lesser extent, men's, has long been subject to cultural construction. In the first half of the twentieth century, for example, American fashion magazines sold women corsets designed to achieve the perfect look, which changed periodically from rounded to angular. Now, however, "it is the body itself that acts as its own corset" as women are told they must control their bodies without benefit of bones or plastic in their underwear (Benson 1997, p. 141).

The media-depicted ideal of female beauty has become thinner and thinner over the past thirty years, and the difference between the idealized body and the average young woman has increased: models used to weigh about 8 percent less than the "average" woman in the United States, now they weigh about 23 percent less (Seid 1989). Between 1979 and 1988, two-thirds of the *Playboy* centerfold women weighed at least 15 percent less than expected based on height—and being at least 15 percent below one's expected body weight is symptomatic of anorexia nervosa (American Psychiatric Association 1994; Wiseman et al. 1990).

Teen girls are most at risk for developing eating disorders as they struggle with a body that's getting bigger in a culture that simultaneously sells them junk food and tells them they should be thin. For some girls, bulimia must appear a rational response to these contradictory messages—splurge and then purge. Chronic dieting and, most recently, strenuous exercise, not so much for maintaining health as for assuring the right body, are the other possibilities the media present. Between 1970 and 1990 in *Seventeen*, although an emphasis on fitness increased, the body shape of models became more and more "linear," and both nutrition and fitness-related articles emphasized physical appearance and weight loss as the primary reasons for paying attention to the body (Guillen and Barr 1994). The proportion of articles related to diet and exercise in the most popular women's magazines (e.g., *Harper's Bazaar, Good Housekeeping*) also has steadily increased. They include about ten times more ads and articles that endorse weight loss than men's magazines (Wiseman et al. 1990).

Effects

Unfortunately, we have relatively little scientific evidence that these media images affect the nutritional habits and physical activity of youth. But initial studies suggest that teens are paying attention to these media messages and are applying them as their own bodies develop. Demographic differences in teens' attitudes about weight correspond to media portrayals—in the United States, Anglo and Hispanic girls are more likely than black girls or boys of all races to be concerned about their weight. Close to half (44 percent) of all female adolescents think they are overweight, and 60 percent are actively trying to lose weight, although technically most are within normal weight ranges (Ozer et al. 1998). Although estimates vary widely, it is suspected that 0.5–3 percent of the general population and 4–22 percent of college-age females engage in anorexic or bulimic behavior in an effort to be thin, and these proportions have increased as media women have grown thinner over the past thirty years (Harrison 1997). In a recent national survey of 1,200 children aged ten to seventeen, 16 percent of girls and 12 percent of boys said they have dieted or exercised to look like a television character (Reflections of Girls in the Media 1997).

Although boys may be increasingly affected by the portrayals of muscular men in the media (Katz 1995), most research has focused on the effects of media portrayals on girls' eating and dieting habits. Some experimental work shows that exposure to thin media models can have immediate effects on young women's perceptions of and satisfaction with their own bodies (Sumner et al. 1993). For example, after exposure to images of thin models, bulimic patients reported lower self-esteem and increased dissatisfaction with personal body weight (Irving 1990). Meyers and Biocca (1992), in an experiment with college women without eating disorders, unexpectedly found that after exposure to thin media models, the young women actually were less likely to overestimate the size of their own bodies and were less likely to be depressed than young women who had not seen the television ads. They proposed that body-image disturbance is a two-stage phenomenon in which viewers first absorb a representation of the ideal body that is frequently found in the media, but after an initial feeling of identification realize that their body does not measure up, and become dissatisfied, perhaps depressed, perhaps motivated to achieve the ideal through dieting.

Other studies of the etiology of severe eating disorders show these are complicated illnesses unlikely to be caused solely by observation of thin media models. But it is reasonable to believe that many teens are affected by the unrealistic images of women's and, increasingly, men's bodies in the media.

ALCOHOL AND TOBACCO

It would be hard for adolescents not to see depictions of alcohol consumption in their daily use of the media in the United States. Alcohol appears in more than 70 percent of prime-time television shows, and it is drunk more frequently than any other beverage on television (Brown and McDonald 1995). More than one-third of all major characters drink alcohol, but fewer than 2 percent are characterized as having a drinking problem (Signorielli 1987). Also, beer and wine are among the most heavily advertised products on television and radio. Liquor advertising is a major source of revenue for magazines and some newspapers (Novelli 1990), and the television industry recently rescinded its long-standing voluntary restriction against advertising liquor, despite protests by health advocates.

Advertising associates alcohol with a variety of benefits that appeal to adolescents: social camaraderie, masculinity, sexual attraction, romance, escape, adventure (Atkin 1993), and few consequences (e.g., hangovers, accidents, violence, embarrassment). Alcohol advertising often depicts slices of life that focus on the drinkers and the drinking occasions rather than on the qualities of the product itself (Atkin 1987), which may be particularly appealing to teens who are using the media for ideas about how to be in the world.

Effects

The cumulative evidence from limited experimental studies and more extensive survey work with adolescents suggests that alcohol advertising on television does influence teen attitudes about drinking and does have a moderate direct effect on initiation of drinking and indirect effects on problem drinking and drunken driving (Atkin 1993). In one key survey, adolescents' exposure to alcohol ads on television was found to be more strongly correlated with both beer and liquor drinking than were parental influence, age, sex, church attendance, social status, or viewing alcohol in entertainment programming (Atkin, Hocking, and Block 1984).

The few studies that have investigated the impact of the frequent portrayal of alcohol in entertainment television are inconsistent but suggest that effects will differ depending on the characteristics of the viewer and the media they attend to (Brown and McDonald 1995). One study (Rychtarik et al. 1983), for example, found that boys who viewed a videotape of television programs that contained drinking scenes in which no negative consequences occurred were more likely than boys who saw a tape in which the drinking scenes had been edited out to believe that the good effects of alcohol are more important than the bad. No significant results were apparent for girls, perhaps because they already knew that drinking is more problematic for females than males in this culture. Boys may also see more beer advertising than girls because the sports programming they are more likely to watch is imbedded with two to five times more beer advertising than the situation comedies and dramas girls are more likely to choose (Grube 1995).

Cigarette Smoking

Although adult smoking has gradually declined in recent decades in the United States, youth smoking, after declining for years, has again begun to climb (Ozer et al. 1998). Some suggest the increase is due at least in part to the sophisticated marketing techniques developed by an increasingly defensive tobacco industry that must attract 2 million new smokers each year to preserve its market status (Centers for Disease Control and Prevention 1995).

Cigarette advertising has been banned on television and radio in the United States since 1971. Consequently, tobacco companies turned to the print media and other forms of promotion, including sponsorship of sporting events such as the Virginia Slims women's tennis tournament and the Winston Cup NASCAR races, and "special placement" of tobacco products in movies. They spend more than $6 billion—about $16 million per day (Preventing tobacco use among young people 1994). Despite the industry's arguments that they don't encourage young people to smoke (almost all new smokers are adolescents), much of this advertising and promotion activity is designed to appeal to young people. Youth-oriented popular magazines have received an increasing number of cigarette ads since 1965 (Basil et al. 1991).

Children and adolescents pay attention to cigarette advertising and readily recognize tobacco symbols and slogans (Aitken, Leathar, and Squair 1986). Some studies have shown that ad recognition is correlated with frequency of smoking, although others have found that recognition is negatively related to liking cigarettes at least among young children (Goldstein et al. 1987; Mizerski 1995). R.J. Reynolds finally withdrew its highly successful Joe Camel campaign after public outcry that preschoolers were almost as familiar with Joe Camel as they were with Mickey Mouse, and more teens than adults could correctly identify the brand when they were shown a picture of Joe Camel (Davidson 1996; Fischer et al. 1991).

Just as was found with alcohol advertising, lifestyle appeals in advertising for cigarettes may be especially attractive to adolescents, who are in the process of developing personal identities. A U.S. government survey of adolescent smokers who bought their own cigarettes found that almost all (86 percent) preferred Marlboro, Camel, or Newport cigarettes—the most heavily marketed brands (Federal Trade Commission Report to Congress 1995).

The ability to promote cigarettes via the mass media is changing in the United States, however, as courts and politicians continue to fight the tobacco industry. In late 1998, a number of states were settling with the tobacco industry for large sums of money and agreements that eliminated some forms of promotion (Fleeman 1998). But simultaneously, the tobacco and alcohol companies have stepped up spending in alternative media such as direct mail, contests, and the Internet. Some of the most recent cigarette ad campaigns, although claiming to target the "adult smoker," may be especially appealing to the rebellious or unhappy teen, who is most likely to be seduced by ad appeals. The newest Camel campaign, running in such youth-targeted magazines as *XXL—Hip Hop on a Higher Level,* features mock warnings, "Viewer Discretion Advised," and links cigarette smoking with risky sexual behavior and violence. The tobacco and alcohol industries will not give up easily what they claim is the right to advertise legal products, and youth will continue to be an important target audience for these potentially lethal products.

CONCLUSION

From an adolescent's point of view the mass media are a window on a larger world beyond family and school. Although from a researcher's point of view it is an often distorted picture of violence, misogyny, and excess consumption, to a youth it is an often appealing portrait of action, fame, and fortune. Adolescents beginning to grapple with questions of identity and the other crucial developmental tasks of adolescence (e.g., establishing cross-gender relationships, independence from parents, and occupational roles) may see the media as a "tool kit" of possible ways of being (Steele and Brown 1995).

Given the ubiquity of unhealthy behavior presented in teen media and the accumulating evidence that these portrayals and images do have an effect on those who read, view, and listen to them, we might well wonder why adolescents are as healthy as they are. Why are all teens not drunken, chain-smoking, anorexic, fat, or pregnant gun toters? Of course, the answer is that the media are not the sole cause of the health status of our youth. Adolescents come to the media with individual characteristics, from families and communities that already have pushed them in certain directions and have provided models of healthy and unhealthy behavior. Those perceptions and experiences will modify and/or enhance the effect the media have on their health in the future. But we have seen, too, that the media do have an impact, sometimes subtle, sometimes more powerful, and the potential is greater for negative rather than positive effects. What should we do to minimize the media's potential negative effects on adolescent health?

Research

We must continue to monitor and learn more about the role the media do play. We must turn attention to the array of media our teens attend to other than television. Music, magazines, and movies, and now the Internet, are vital to the everyday lives of teens, and they have been inadequately included in studies of media effects. We should adopt the idea of "media diets" and devise ways to learn more about how adolescents use media in developing a sense of themselves.

Measures of adolescents' use of media should be included in other studies of the precursors of health beliefs and behavior, as well. It is surprising how seldom measures of media consumption have been included in studies of adolescent health. Some of this is the fault of media researchers who have not developed a stable and reliable set of media measures.

Advertising

We need to pay special attention to advertising's effects not only on product consumption but also on associated behavior. For example, a current ad campaign for Mountain Dew soft drink promotes risky behavior by associating the product with "wild sports" like bungee cord jumping and wind boarding. Three product categories are especially important for teen health: cigarettes, alcoholic beverages, and food.

Media Policy

In some areas, such as aggression and violence, it is clear that changing media content could have a desirable effect. We should continue to press the media industries to reduce the frequency of violent portrayals and to change remaining portrayals so it is clear that there are other ways of resolving conflict and that violence has both short- and long-term consequences.

Regulation is a tricky business, especially of media content. It will not be easy to arrive at consensus on what we mean by dangerous images of violence or sexuality, and we have to be careful not to restrict valuable information in the process. The industry acting as a responsible steward in the public interest is the more preferable approach, but we have had little evidence in the past that the media industry can be counted on for much else than watching the bottom line. With the Internet there basically is no one responsible steward.

Media Literacy

The idea that we might be able to raise generations of critical media consumers who, by knowing how the media work, will be less seduced by their images, is a tantalizing idea. It just might work. But it will require significant resources to ensure that all who need it, get it. And in the United States, we will need to train teachers, develop curricula, convince school systems that this is another important topic they must add to already overloaded school curricula. The most important piece may be educating parents to take the media seriously, to pay attention to what their children are seeing, and to help convince the media that they should begin to act more like socially responsible members of the community.

NOTE

A previous draft of this chapter was commissioned by and presented to the Health Futures of Youth II: Pathways to Adolescent Health Conference, sponsored by the Office of Adolescent Health in the Health Resources and Sciences Administration's Maternal and Child Health Bureau (MCHB), U.S. Department of Health and Human Services, September 14–16 1998, Annapolis, Maryland.

REFERENCES

Acuff, D. S., R. H. Reiher, and D. Acuff. 1997. *What kids buy and why: The psychology of marketing to kids.* New York: Free Press.
Aitken, P. P., D. S. Leathar, and S. I. Squair. 1986. Children's awareness of cigarette brand sponsorship of sports and games in the UK. *Health Education Research* 1: 203–211.
American Psychiatric Association 1994. *Diagnostic and statistical manual of mental disorders.* 4th ed. Washington, D.C.
American Social Health Association. 1996. *Gallup study: Teenagers know more than adults about STDs.* Research Triangle Park, N.C.: ASHA.
Atkin, C., J. Hocking, and M. Block. 1984. Teenage drinking: Does advertising make a difference? *Journal of Communication* 342: 157–167.
Atkin, C. K. 1987. Alcoholic-beverage advertising: Its content and impact. *Adolescent substance abuse supplement* 1: 267.
———. 1993. Effects of media alcohol messages on adolescent audiences. In V. C. Strasburger and G. A. Comstock, eds., *Adolescent medicine: State of the art reviews,* pp. 527–541. Philadelphia: Hanley & Belfus.
Basil, M., C. Schooler, D. G. Altman, M. Slater, C. L. Albright, and N. Maccoby. 1991. How cigarettes are advertised in magazines: Special messages for special markets. *Health Communication* 3: 75–91.
Benson, S. 1997. The body, health, and eating disorders. In K. Woodward, ed., *Identity and difference,* pp. 122–167. London: Sage.
Brown, J. D., and T. McDonald. 1995. Portrayals and effects of alcohol in television entertainment programming. In *The effects of the mass media on the use and abuse of alcohol,* pp. 133–150. Research Monograph 28. Washington, D.C.: National Institute on Alcohol Abuse and Alcoholism.
Brown, J. D., A. B. White, and L. Nikopoulou. 1993. Disinterest, intrigue, resistance: Early adolescent girls' use of sexual media content. In B. S. Greenberg, J. D. Brown, and N. L. Buerkel-Rothfuss, eds., *Media, Sex, and the Adolescent,* pp. 177–195. Cresskill, N.J.: Hampton.

Bryant, J., and S. C. Rockwell. 1994. Effects of massive exposure to sexually oriented prime-time television programming on adolescents' moral judgment. In D. Zillmann, J. Bryant, and A. C. Huston, eds., *Media, children, and the family: Social scientific, psychodynamic, and clinical perspectives*, pp. 183–195. Hillsdale, N.J.: Erlbaum.

Cantor, J. 1998. *Mommy, I'm scared*. New York: Harcourt Brace.

Center for Media Education. 1997. ABSOLUTe Web: Tobacco and alcohol industries launch into cyberspace. *InfoActive Kids*, Winter, p. 1.

Centers for Disease Control and Prevention. 1995. Symptoms of substance dependence associated with use of cigarettes, alcohol, and illicit drugs—United States, 1991–1992. *Morbidity and Mortality Weekly Report* 44: 830–831, 837–839.

———. 1998. Trends in sexual risk behaviors among high school students: United States, 1991–1997. *Morbidity and Mortality Weekly Report* 47.

Centerwall, B. S. 1992. The scale of the problem and where to go from here. *Journal of the American Medical Association* 267: 3059–3063.

Comstock, G., and V. C. Strasburger. 1990. Deceptive appearances: Television violence and aggressive behavior—An introduction. *Journal of Adolescent Health Care* 11: 31–44.

Davidson, D. K. 1996. *Selling sin: The marketing of socially unacceptable products*. Westport, Conn.: Quorum Books.

Dietz, W. H. 1993. Television, obesity, and eating disorders. In V. C. Strasburger and G. A. Comstock, eds., *Adolescents and the media: State of the art reviews*, pp. 543–549. Philadelphia: Hanley & Belfus.

Federal Trade Commission Report to Congress. 1995. Pursuant to the comprehensive Smokeless Tobacco Health Education Act of 1986, cited in *Media Sharp: Analyzing Tobacco and Alcohol Messages*. Atlanta: Office on Smoking and Health, Centers for Disease Control and Prevention.

Fischer, P. M., M. P. Schwartz, J. W. Richards Jr., and A. O. Goldstein. 1991. Brand logo recognition by children aged 3 to 6 years: Mickey Mouse and Old Joe the Camel. *Journal of the American Medical Association* 26622: 31454.

Fleeman, M. 1998. Smoking on screen smolders as issue in Hollywood. *News and Observer* (Raleigh, N.C.), July 14, p. 8E.

Friedrich-Cofer, L., and A. C. Huston. 1986. Television violence and aggression: The debate continues. *Pyschological Bulletin* 1003: 364–371.

Gallatin, J. E. 1975. *Adolescence and individuality*. New York: Harper & Row.

Gerbner, G., L. Gross, M. Morgan, and N. Signorielli. 1994. Growing up with television: The cultivation perspective. In J. Bryant and D. Zillmann, eds., *Media Effects*, pp. 17–41. Hillsdale, N.J.: Erlbaum.

Goldstein, A. O., P. M. Fischer, J. W. Richards, and D. Creten. 1987. *Journal of Pediatrics* 1103: 488–491.

Gortmaker, S. L., W. H. Dietz, and A. M. Sobol. 1987. Increasing pediatric obesity in the United States. *American Journal of the Disabled Child* 141: 535–540.

Greenberg, B. S., and R. W. Busselle. 1994. *Soap operas and sexual activity*. Menlo Park, Calif.: Kaiser Family Foundation.

Greenberg, B. S., R. Linsangan, and A. Soderman. 1993. Adolescents' reactions to television sex. In B. S. Greenberg, J. D. Brown, and N. L. Buerkel-Rothfuss, eds., *Media, sex, and the adolescent,* pp. 196–224. Cresskill, N.J.: Hampton.

Greenberg, B. S., K. L. Perry, and A. M. Covert. 1983. The body human: Sex education, politics, and television. *Family Relations* 32: 419–425.

Greenberg, B. S., M. Siemicki, S. Dorfman, C. Heeter, C. Stanley, A. Soderman, and R. Linsangan. 1993. Sex content in R-rated films viewed by adolescents. In B. S. Greenberg, J. D. Brown, and N. L. Buerkel-Rothfuss, eds., *Media, sex and the adolescent,* pp. 45–58. Cresskill, N.J.: Hampton.

Greeson, L. E., and R. A. Williams. 1986. Social implications of music videos for youth: An analysis of the content and effects of MTV. *Youth and Society* 18: 177–189.

Grube, J. W. 1995. Television alcohol portrayals, alcohol advertising, and alcohol expectancies among children and adolescents. In S. E. Martin, ed., *The effects of the mass media on the use and abuse of alcohol,* pp. 105–121. Bethesda, Md.: National Institute on Alcohol Abuse and Alcoholism.

Guillen, E. O., and S. I. Barr. 1994. Nutrition, dieting, and fitness messages in a magazine for adolescent women, 1970–1990. *Journal of Adolescent Health* 15: 464–472.

Harrison, K. 1997. Does interpersonal attraction to thin media personalities promote eating disorders? *Journal of Broadcasting and Electronic Media* 41: 478–500.

Hazan, A., and S. A. Glantz. 1995. Current trends in tobacco use on prime-time fictional television. *American Journal of Public Health* 85: 116–117.

Heintz-Knowles, K. E. 1996. *Sexual activity on daytime soap operas: A content analysis of five weeks of television programming.* Menlo Park, Calif.: Kaiser Family Foundation.

Huesmann, L. R., and L. D. Eron. 1986. *Television and the aggressive child: A cross-national comparison.* Hillsdale, N.J.: Erlbaum.

Huston, A. C., E. Wartella, and E. Donnerstein. 1998. *Measuring the effects of sexual content in the media: A report to the Kaiser Family Foundation.* Menlo Park, Calif.: Kaiser Family Foundation.

Irving, L. M. 1990. Mirror images: Effects of the standard of beauty on the self- and body-esteem of women exhibiting varying levels of bulimic symptoms. *Journal of Social and Clinical Psychology* 9: 230–242.

Jhally, S. 1995. *Dreamworlds: Desire/sex/power in rock video.* Northampton, Mass.: Media Education Foundation. Videocassette.

Kaiser Family Foundation and Children Now. 1996. *The family hour focus groups: Children's responses to sexual content on TV and their parents' reactions.* Menlo Park, Calif.

Katz, J. 1995. Advertising and the construction of violent white masculinity. In G. Dines and J. M. Humez, eds., *Gender, race, and class in media,* pp. 133–141. Thousand Oaks, Calif.: Sage.

Kunkel, D., K. M. Cope, and C. Colvin. 1996. *Sexual messages on family hour television: Content and context.* Menlo Park, Calif.: Children Now/Kaiser Family Foundation.

Larson, M. S. 1996. Sex roles and soap operas: What adolescents learn about single motherhood. *Sex Roles* 351, no. 2: 97–110.

Lowry, D. T., and J. A. Shidler. 1993. Prime time TV portrayals of sex, "safe sex," and AIDS: A longitudinal analysis. *Journalism Quarterly* 70: 628–637.

McNeal, James U. 1992. *Kids as customers: A handbook of marketing to children.* New York: Jossey-Bass.

Meyers, P. N., and F. Biocca. 1992. The elastic body image: The effect of television advertising and programming on body image distortions in young women. *Journal of Communication* 423: 108–133.

Mizerski, R. 1995. The relationship between cartoon trade character recognition and attitude toward product category in young children. *Journal of Marketing* 594: 5813.

Nielsen Media Research. 1998. *1998 Report on Television.* New York: Nielsen Media Research, Inc.

Novelli, W. 1990. Controversies in advertising of health-related products. In C. Atkin and L. Wallack, eds., *Mass communication and public health,* pp. 78–87. Newbury Park, Calif.: Sage.

Ozer, E. M., C. D. Brindis, S. G. Millstein, D. K. Knopf, and C. E. Irwin. 1998. *America's adolescents: Are they healthy?* San Francisco: University of California School of Medicine.

Peirce, K. 1990. A feminist theoretical perspective on the socialization of teenage girls through *Seventeen Magazine. Sex Roles* 239, no. 10: 491–500.

Pope, H., J. Hudson, D. Todd-Yurgelun, and M. Hudson. 1984. Prevalence of anorexia nervosa and bulimia in three student populations. *International Journal of Eating Disorders* 3: 45–51.

Princeton Survey Research Associates. 1996. *The Kaiser Family Foundation survey on teens and sex: What they say teens today need to know and who they listen to.* Menlo Park, Calif.: Kaiser Family Foundation.

Reflections of Girls in the Media. 1997. *Report of the fourth annual children and the media conference.* Oakland, Calif.: Children Now.

Rich, M., E. R. Woods, E. Goodman, S. J. Emans, and R. H. DuRant. 1998. Aggressors or victims: Gender and race in music video violence. *Pediatrics* 1014: 669–674.

Richards, J. I., E. A. Wartella, C. Morton, and L. Thompson. 1998. The growing commercialization of schools: Issues and practices. *Annals of the American Academy of Political and Social Science* 557: 148–163.

Roberts, E. J. 1982. Television and sexual learning in childhood. In D. Pearl, ed., *Television and behavior: Ten years of scientific progress and implications for the 80s,* pp. 209–223. Washington, D.C.: Government Printing Office.

Robinson, T. N., L. D. Hammer, and J. D. Killen. 1993. Does television viewing increase obesity and decrease physical activity? Cross-sectional and longitudinal analyses among adolescent females. *Pediatrics* 91: 273–280.

Rychtarik, R. G., J. A. Fairbank, C. M. Allen, D. W. Foy, and R. S. Drabman. 1983. Alcohol use in television programming: Effects on children's behaviors. *Addictive Behavior* 8: 19–22.

Seid, R. P. 1989. *Never too thin: Why women are at war with their bodies.* New York: Prentice-Hall.

Seidman, S. A. 1992. An investigation of sex-role stereotyping in music videos. *Journal of Broadcasting and Electronic Media* 36: 209–216.

Signorielli, N. 1987. Drinking, sex, and violence on television: The cultural indicators perspective. *Journal of Drug Education* 173: 245–260.

———. 1991. Adolescents and ambivalence toward marriage: A cultivation analysis. *Youth and Society* 23: 121–149.

Silverstein, B., L. Perdue, B. Peterson, and E. Kelly. 1986. The role of the mass media in promoting a thin standard of attractiveness for women. *Sex Roles* 149: 519–532.

Smith, S. L., B. J. Wilson, D. Kunkel, D. Linz, W. J. Potter, C. M. Colvin, and E. Donnerstein. 1998. Violence in television programming overall: University of California, Santa Barbara study. In Center for Communication and Social Policy, ed., *National Television Violence Study*, 3: 5–220. Thousand Oaks, Calif.: Sage.

Snyder, H. N., M. Sickmund, and E. Poe-Yamagata. 1996. *Juvenile offenders and victims: 1996 update on violence.* Pittsburgh: National Center for Juvenile Justice.

Sonesson, I. 1998. Television and children's fear: A Swedish perspective. *News on children and violence on the screen* 21: 11–12.

Steele, J. R., and J. D. Brown. 1995. Adolescent room culture: Studying media in the context of everyday life. *Journal of Youth and Adolescence* 245: 551–576.

Stevens, E. L., and R. Grover. 1998. The entertainment glut. *Business Week*, February 16, pp. 88–95.

Story, M., and P. Faulkner. 1990. The prime time diet: A content analysis of eating and food messages in television content and commercials. *American Journal of Public Health* 80: 738–740.

Strouse, J. S., N. Buerkel-Rothfuss, and E. C. Long. 1995. Gender and family as moderators of the relationship between music video exposure and adolescent sexual permissiveness. *Adolescence* 30: 505–521.

Sumner, A., G. Waller, S. Killick, and M. Elstein. 1993. Body image distortion in pregnancy: A pilot study of the effects of media images. *Journal of Reproductive and Infant Psychology* 114: 203–208.

Thompson, M., K. Walsh-Childers, and J. D. Brown. 1993. The influence of family communication patterns and sexual experience on processing of a movie video. In B. S. Greenberg, J. D. Brown, and N. L. Buerkel-Rothfuss, eds., *Media, sex, and the adolescent*, pp. 248–263. Cresskill, New Jersey: Hampton.

Walsh-Childers, K. 1998. *A content analysis: Sexual health coverage in women's, men's, teen, and other specialty magazines.* Menlo Park, Calif.: Kaiser Family Foundation.

Willis, P. 1990. *Common culture.* Boulder: Westview.

Wiseman, C. V., J. J. Gray, J. E. Mosimann, and A. H. Aherns. 1990. Cultural expectations of thinness in women: An update. *International Journal of Eating Disorders* 111: 85–89.

YM. 1998. LOVE special edition. *YM* magazine.

Zollo, P. 1995. *Wise up to teens: Insights into marketing and advertising to teenagers.* Ithaca, N.Y.: New Strategist Publications.

7

Covering his Not-So-Private Parts: The Multinational and Multicultural Struggle to Regulate the Broadcasts of Shock-Jock Howard Stern

Neil Nemeth

Few people who listen to the radio, watch television, or attend movies in the United States and Canada have missed the presence of Howard Stern, the American shock-jock who has challenged and expanded the boundaries of radio since the mid-1980s. In 1995, Stern's employer paid $1.7 million to settle fines levied by the U.S. Federal Communications Commission for indecent content during the previous five years. The sum, the largest by far ever levied against an American broadcaster, represented a fraction of the revenue generated by *The Howard Stern Show*. In 1997 and 1998, Stern brought his controversial discussions of sex, gender, racism, and politics to Canada, where stations in Toronto and Montreal aired his syndicated radio program. Stern's broadcasts stimulated protests seldom seen about the content of the modern mass media (Canadian Broadcast Standards Council complaint):

> If Stern is allowed to continue broadcasting on Canadian airwaves, the hatred that he promotes and encourages will grow and fester, and will one day spew all over me and the people whom I care about. It will spew over women in the

form of harassment and violence. It will spew all over the French, because permission will be given for mud to be thrown in their faces. His filth will be hurled in a thousand different directions and will affect more than us many people, as the media have the power to reach all of us.

Yet one American listener found a defense for Stern's broadcasts (Federal Communications Commission e-mail):

I am confused about the FCC censoring radio broadcasters like Howard Stern. In my opinion, the American people have a right to hear the comments and opinions of Howard Stern. The large fines which he has received seem quite ridiculous. Also, I believe the government could use their *(sic)* time in a more sensitive manner. I am not a 'Howard Stern weirdo' but I believe that even though his opinions often differ from my own, we have a right to hear them.

Such a divergence of opinion represents a difference in culture and in values. Stern and his employers have engaged in a decade-long battle with the U.S. Federal Communications Commission over the decency of his radio program. Twice within a six-month period, the Canadian Broadcast Standards Council issued critical judgments against the two stations that aired Stern's program. The Montreal station dropped Stern's radio and network television shows, though the decision appears to have been motivated more by a desire to smooth the way for the expansion of the owner's broadcast business interests than by public discontent with the content of Stern's show. Despite the controversy, Stern's program remained among the most popular in radio (Adelson 1998). Stern earned as much as $15 million per year from his radio program, books, television programs, and a full-length movie (Colford 1996). These facts raise questions about the effectiveness of government regulation and the alternatives available to those who object to Stern's approach to broadcasting. This chapter will recap and evaluate the effort to regulate Stern's broadcasts in the United States and Canada with an eye toward identifying differences in cultural values and alternatives for people who wish to lodge complaints.

HOWARD STERN AND THE EVOLUTION OF HIS STYLE

Born January 12, 1954, Howard Allan Stern spent his early years in Queens, New York, but his family moved to the community of Roosevelt in Nassau County, Long Island, in the mid-1960s. Stern's father, Ben, worked as a radio engineer with an interest in puppetry that stimulated his son's interest in being a performer. A shy and gawky youth who stood six feet, five inches tall, Stern created a broadcast and performance studio in the basement of the family's home. The performances in the family's basement gave Stern a creative way of stepping out of his geeky persona (Colford 1996).

Stern gained his first radio experience while a student at Boston University. Even during this period, Stern realized he needed to be different to make his mark in radio: "I've got to do something different and outrageous in the business." Just as important personally, Stern met Alison Berns during his junior year. They married in 1978 and would become the parents of three daughters (Colford 1996); the couple separated in 1999 (Losito 1999).

Stern took a traditional path for a broadcaster through a series of jobs between 1976 and 1981 in Westchester County, New York; Hartford, Connecticut; and Detroit, Michigan. At DC-101 in Washington, D.C., Stern hired newscaster Robin Quivers, who would become a foil for Stern's evolving style (Colford 1996).

Stern and Quivers separated briefly when he took a job at WNBC-AM in New York in 1982, but the pair survived Stern's firing at WNBC-AM in 1985 and resurfaced at WXRK-FM in New York just two months later. Dubbed "K-Rock" in the topsy-turvy world of radio, WXRK-FM remained the base of the Stern broadcast empire, even after his entry into television, books, and movies (Colford 1996).

As the years passed and Stern became a celebrity, a significant divergence developed in Stern's on-air persona and his reported private life. The on-air Stern specialized in discussing his sex life and asserting his disgust for homosexuals and lesbians. He frequently criticized high-profile "hypocrites" such as actor Chevy Chase, talk show hosts Kathie Lee Gifford and Regis Philbin, conservative talk show host Rush Limbaugh, singer Yoko Ono, talk show host Johnny Carson, actor Michael Landon, and actress Roseanne Barr (Stern 1994). But the private Stern seemed almost "normal."

> The real Howard was a nice Jewish boy from Long Island, a devoted family man who solicitously asked friends about their own families, a health nut who scorned drink and drugs—and followed the more elusive Ayurvedic prescriptions for a healthy life, which include a sound home environment and workaday routines. . . . Then again, it was simplistic to say that the often-crude persona he presented for more than four hours each weekday morning was entirely an act. Because it was not an act. It was the other Howard, the one that Transcendental Meditation helped him tap into. As his friends and associates observed, Howard had an unusual ability to reach this other side of himself on the radio—the sex-driven, go-scratch-yourself Howard. The radio personality was not the warm and quiet Howard familiar to those who knew him off the air. (Colford 1996, pp. 252–253)

Stern cultivated a large and loyal following of listeners in the highly lucrative twenty-five to thirty-four age demographic. In addition, men made up about 70 percent of the listeners to Stern's program, and his listeners aged twenty-five to fifty-four earned more than the average of $75,000 and owned homes worth an average of about $300,000 (Colford 1996). These demographics made Stern popular with advertisers, despite the shock-jock's confrontations with the FCC: "Howard's fans will listen through every commercial wondering whether he is going to interrupt with an outrageous comment" (Ramirez 1995). Stern expanded his reach from three stations in the New York, Philadelphia, and Washington, D.C., areas in the late 1980s to a national network of about fifty stations ten years later (www.marksfriggin-.com). Clearly, Stern had changed the face of commercial radio:

> Howard Stern . . . has become one of the most influential personalities in the history of broadcasting largely because he abandoned the fixtures of the radio trade. Over the past ten years, he purged most of the rock music from his show, as well as the traffic report, time checks, and weather forecasts. He set off, unanchored in his own raging stream of consciousness. Although he has continued to call himself a disc jockey, he now presides over a talk show that echoes only the ambient rhythms of his own psyche. He weaves his offbeat and often vulgar ruminations about sex, politics, and pop culture into long, ever-curious riffs. He tells all. When he is not drawing from his own imagination, he presents tales of the dysfunctional family consisting of those who work with him inside and outside his New York studio. Part of Howard's genius is to expose his insecurities, plus those of his cohorts, and to have people identify with them. The relatively few guests invited to visit his show are mere foils. (Colford 1996, pp. xiii–xii)

HOWARD STERN AND THE FCC

The rise of Howard Stern coincided with a period of turbulence in the regulation of broadcasting in the United States. Created by congressional legislation in 1934, the U.S. Federal Communications Commission (FCC) acted as a trustee of the commercial broadcasting system and required broadcasters to operate in the public interest *(NBC v. U.S. 1943)*. While professing noninterference in the content of commercial broadcasting, the commission implemented the Fairness Doctrine in 1949 to require broadcasters to devote "reasonable time" to public issues and to air contrasting viewpoints on these issues *(In re Editorializing by Broadcast Licensees* 1949). The doctrine was always controversial because broadcasters believed it infringed on their First Amendment rights, but the U.S. Supreme Court supported its logic and some of its provisions: "[I]t is the right of the viewers and listeners, not the right of broadcasters, which is paramount" *(Red Lion Broadcasting v. FCC* 1969). In a later decision, the court used similar logic in deciding to protect unsuspecting adults and especially children from indecent but not obscene broadcasts *(FCC v. Pacifica Foundation* 1978), though later decisions provided constitutional protection for these broadcasts from 10 p.m. to 6 a.m.

(Action for Children's Television 1991, 1995). It should be noted that listeners bear the responsibility for reporting suspected indecency violations and providing documentation for their claims (www.fcc.gov). Technological advances and a gradual relaxation of regulations generally led to the commission's decision to abandon the Fairness Doctrine in 1987, a decision that was upheld in the federal courts. (102 FCC 2d 145; 2 FCC Rcd 5272; *Syracuse Peace Council v. FCC*, 867 F.2d 654 [1989]; cert. denied, 493 U.S. 1019 [1991])

Initially, Stern benefited from the commission's change in philosophy as it declined to intervene when listeners complained about his broadcasts in the early 1980s. As early as 1981, the FCC cited Stern during his days in Washington, D.C., after two listeners complained about his quizzing women callers how they achieved orgasm and a skit depicting a horse having sex with a woman. In both cases, the FCC declined to pursue the complaints, citing the agency's lack of authority to regulate the content of radio programs. The commission exhibited a similar hands-off policy about complaints concerning graphic details about bloody toilet tissue found in a restroom and Stern's description of his bathroom habits (Colford 1996). In the early 1980s, the FCC's policy was clear: Broadcast indecency was confined to uttering the seven dirty words cited in the Pacifica decision: shit, piss, fuck, cunt, cocksucker, motherfucker, and tits (*FCC v. Pacifica Foundation* 1978).

This approach changed with the advent of a more conservative commission during the Reagan administration in the 1980s. While proclaiming marketplace values, the commission followed the Reagan administration's lead in investigating the effects of obscenity and pornography with a tougher stand against coarse language on the broadcast airwaves. Stern's broadcasts that described testicles, the sexual activities of homosexuals, penis size, bestiality, and sodomy prompted a FCC inquiry in 1987. In finding Stern's broadcasts indecent, the commission attempted to articulate a clearer standard (2 FCC Rcd 2705):

> Instead, the broadcast must be examined in context to determine whether its meaning can reasonably be considered to contain patently offensive references to sexual or excretory activities and organs. Words that in one context may be innuendo or double entendre may be rendered explicit in other contexts when they are intermingled with explicit references that make the meaning of the entire discussion clear or capable only of one meaning. The latter may constitute actionable indecency.

The commission declined to hold Stern's employer, Infinity Broadcasting, financially liable, citing possible confusion over the standard of indecency. Unfortunately for Stern, the confusion would persist throughout his battle with the FCC during the next decade.

In 1990, Stern's employers faced a $6,000 FCC fine for material describing a man playing a piano with his penis at his show's Christmas party and the sexual activities of homosexuals in 1988 (5 FCC Rcd 7291). The total was based on a $2,000 fine levied on each of the three stations that broadcast Stern's show at the time: his flagship station, WXRK-FM in New York City, WYSP-FM in Philadelphia, and WJFK-FM in Manassas, Virginia. Stern believed the FCC had decided to single him out for punishment: "The FCC Chairman, Alfred Sikes, a Republican do-gooder, suddenly decided that the FCC should go after disc jockeys. Sikes took it upon himself to clean up the 'indecency' from the radio airwaves. They attempted to do that by staging a vendetta against one man—me" (Stern 1994).

Stern's employers appealed the fine, as well as all subsequent fines. In late 1992, the commission assessed a $600,000 fine against Stern's employers for airing comments about his masturbating to a picture of Aunt Jemima and a graphic parody about comedian Pee Wee Herman, who pleaded no contest in 1991 to a charge of indecent exposure in an adult movie theater in Florida (8 FCC Rcd 2688). In 1993, Stern's employers faced an additional $500,000 in FCC fines for his "describing" the alleged bathroom and sexual habits of talk show host Kathie Lee Gifford, his own bathroom habits, masturbation, the sexual apparatus of actor Richard Gere, the characteristics of women's vaginas, and a sarcastic interview with actor Woody Allen. Allen's interview discussed his affair with the daughter of his former lover, Mia Farrow (8 FCC Rcd 6790).

The commission cited Stern for using language or material that "in context, depicts or describes in terms patently offensive as measured by contemporary community standards for the broadcast medium, sexual or excretory activities or organs." (8 FCC Rcd 6790) The commission also expressed concern about the presence of children in the audience during airtime of 6 a.m. to approximately 10 a.m.—outside the so-called safe harbor for the airing of indecent broadcasts. Stern remained unrepentant.

Why is there so much shame in this country? Why are we so afraid to say what we like and to talk about sex? What happens to a man when he hears the words breasts and vagina? Will it turn him into an ax murderer? . . . There are thousands of broadcasters talking about sex every day. In fact, there are thousands of people having sex, but out of all those people, when I talk about sex, people go nuts. No one in the history of broadcasting has ever been threatened with fines close to a million dollars because he found Aunt Jemima sexy. No one, until me, that is. (Stern 1994, pp. 580–581)

The commission fined Stern's employers $400,000 in 1994 for his graphic and detailed comments about his sex life with his wife, women's underwear, vibrators, and an incestuous relationship (9 FCC Rcd 1746). Later the same year, the FCC levied an additional $200,000 in fines against Stern's employers for his discussion of masturbation and oral sex (9 FCC Rcd 6442).

Stern remained defiant in his opposition to the efforts to regulate his program.

> But I'm not gonna lie down like the rest of the sheep in the broadcast industry. The FCC—I don't know who these guys are, I don't know who elected them, I don't know what their particular political affiliations are, I don't know what their morality is, I don't know if they're having sex in the back of a bus with a little boy, I don't know anything about these people. I just want to preface my remarks with that. But I will be going to the Supreme Court to fight this. (Stern 1994, p. 568)

Stern prayed on the air that FCC Chairman Al Sikes and his colleagues would contract cancer. Former New York City Mayor Ed Koch and Senator Alfonse D'Amato (R–N.Y.) publicly defended Stern's free speech rights, but few other public figures took the same stance (Stern 1994). Yet one academic observer noted that the commission dismissed three complaints against Stern's program between September 1993 and February 1995, a period when the commission pursued several other indecency violations (Rivera-Sanchez 1997).

The expansion plans of Stern's employer, Infinity Broadcasting, intervened. The company's desire to buy three radio stations in Los Angeles and the Washington, D.C., area at a cost of $170 million ran into delays at the FCC, and Stern's problems were blamed (Andrews 1994). Ultimately, the FCC approved the purchases in early 1994 (Andrews 1994), but similar interests led to Infinity's decision to settle the pending fines against Stern by making a "voluntary contribution" of $1,715,000 to the U.S. Treasury in September 1995 (10 FCC Rcd 12245; Ramirez 1995). By then, the commission had relaxed the limitations on the number of radio stations that could be owned by a single company, and Infinity had plans to expand its holdings (Ramirez 1995). Stern told his listeners he would have continued to fight the fines had he been personally liable, but "I wasn't in on this decision, nor did I know about it, how's that?" when cornered for a reaction. "And I was plenty upset" (Colford 1996).

Later the same month, Infinity purchased seven major market stations owned by Alliance Broadcasting for $275 million (Colford 1996). A year later, Westinghouse Electric purchased Infinity for $3.7 billion (Fabrikant 1996; Landler 1996). By this time, Stern generated an estimated $22 million for Infinity and about $8 million for himself from his radio work (Colford 1996). In the four years after Infinity's "voluntary contribution" to the U.S. Treasury, four stations airing Stern's program would pay an additional $20,000 in fines for airing his comments about masturbation, urination, sexual intercourse, women's genitalia, bestiality, and incest (11 FCC Rcd 13214; 12 FCC Rcd 4147; 12 FCC Rcd 8274; 13 FCC Rcd 13869). An additional $16,000 fine for Stern's comments about his wife's sexual and urination habits and his descriptions of female genitalia was under appeal (13 FCC Rcd 17254). Clearly, the FCC fines represented pocket change in the 1990s world of broadcast high finance and corporate mergers. The vague indecency standard prompted one academic observer to remark that "without more guidance from the FCC, context makes the assessment of what is 'patently offensive' very difficult at best and practically impossible at worst" (Rivera-Sanchez 1997).

Others, including Stern himself, came to the conclusion that the shock-jock was being singled out for punishment by the FCC, though one academic study concluded that the fines assessed against Stern's employers were actually less per incident than what the agency might have levied (Rivera-Sanchez and Ballard 1998). On a wider scale, though, Howard Kurtz, media reporter for the Washington Post and host of CNN's *Reliable Sources,* argued that Stern's coarse style enlivened the mostly bland fare offered on commercial radio.

His message to those who were offended by his show was simple: Turn it off. . . . Whatever one thinks of Howard Stern, it was truly disturbing to see the full weight of the federal government brought to bear against one person for off-color humor that would barely raise an eyebrow on daytime television. It had the look and feel of a vendetta, an attempt at official intimidation. . . . Sure, he can be gross and tasteless on occasion. . . . Still, Stern's joking monologues about race and crime and politics often have the kind of passion that is all too often missing from the mainstream media. His hold on his audience is so strong that congressmen and governors come courting in the hope of winning a few favorable words. Howard Stern strips away the polite veneer of social discourse and presents himself, neuroses and all, to his audience. He pushed the boundaries of talk radio in a way that made room for a new generation of egomanics. (Kurtz 1997, pp. 276–278)

THE CANADIAN EXPERIENCE

In the 1990s, Stern expanded his media empire into television, books, and movies. After early failures in both local and network television, Stern launched a video version of his radio program on the E! Entertainment Television cable network on November 27, 1992. The cable television show was outside the FCC's jurisdiction, so it came as little surprise that Stern focused on the sexual activities of his guests. Such celebrities as comedian Gary Shandling, celebrity entrepreneur Donald Trump, singer James Brown, and singer Boy George traded barbs with Stern, who prodded his guests into revealing intimate details of their lives (Colford 1996). Stern got his wish for a network television show when CBS agreed to air the *Howard Stern Radio Show* to compete with NBC's long-running hit show *Saturday Night Live* in August 1998 (Mifflin 1998; Schlosser 1998). The *Howard Stern Radio Show* generated predictable controversy in some markets (Mifflin 1998a; Mifflin 1998b) but increased the network's viewership in its assigned time slot, even if it didn't beat *Saturday Night Live* in the ratings (Mifflin 1999).

Stern branched into the publishing world with the release of his touted autobiography, *Private Parts,* in the fall of 1993. More a continuation of his radio program than a tell-all tome, *Private Parts* became the fastest-selling book in the history of his publisher, Simon and Schuster. Stern pocketed a $1 million advance and attracted an estimated 10,000 admirers to a New York City book-signing engagement (Colford 1996). After a false start, Stern sold the rights to *Private Parts* to Rysher Entertainment, which released a movie version in the spring of 1997 (Maslin 1997). The movie debuted as the top grossing film during the week of its release (James 1997; Gates 1997; Nathan 1997). A second Stern book, *Miss America,* sold well when it was released in 1995 (Colford 1996). Stern began calling himself the "King of All Media," and his celebrity spawned an unauthorized biography with the same title (Sharkey 1997).

Stern's popularity attracted the interest of two Canadian stations, CHOM-FM in Montreal and CILQ-FM in Toronto, which began airing Stern's radio show on September 2, 1997 (Shock jock 1997). Almost immediately, Stern's broadcasts increased ratings at the two stations by 62 percent and 47 percent respectively (Ratings leap 1997), though ratings slipped as the show neared the first anniversary of its Canadian debut (Boone 1998a). Just as immediately, Stern offended thousands of Canadian listeners with comments of questionable taste, an attack on France and the French language, racist comments, sexist comments, and material deemed unsuitable for children during daytime hours. The comments about the French and the French language were particularly problematic in Montreal, where upwards of 65 percent of CHOM-FM's audience is French speaking (CHOM-FM 1997).

Equally problematic for Stern were provisions of the Canadian Broadcast Act, which provide that broadcasting should "serve to safeguard, enrich and strengthen the cultural, political, social and economic fabric of Canada." The act requires broadcasters to serve the needs and interests of Canadians with respect to "the linguistic duality and multicultural and multiracial nature of Canadian society and the special place of aboriginal peoples within that society." Finally, the act requires that broadcasters "make maximum use, and in no case less than predominant use, of Canadian creative and other resources in the presentation of programming" (www.cbsc.ca).

Stern's initial broadcast in Canada contained the following references to the French and French language:

There is something about the French language that turns you into a pussy-assed jackoff. . . . Anybody who speaks French is a scumbag. It turns you into a coward, just like in World War II the French would not stick up for us. The French were the first ones to cave into the Nazis, and certainly, certainly were overproductive for the Nazis, when they became their puppets. . . . Hey, I'm singing, Frig the French! Screw the French! You're going to have to listen to Americans now! Screw your culture and we're invading you all. For as long as it lasts! Sorry. (CHOM-FM 1997)

Off the air, Stern declined to apologize for the statements. "I can't imagine anybody would take what I say seriously. I'm a disc jockey—I'm a dope" (Stations ignore 1997; Stern won't apologize 1997).

Many of the complaints were first lodged to the Canadian Radio-television Telecommunications Commission, the Canadian equivalent of the U.S. Federal Communications Commission. The commission forwarded the complaints to the Canadian Broadcast Standards Council, a voluntary regulatory agency formed by the country's broadcasters in 1987. The council, organized in a series of seven regional councils throughout the country, established a Code of Ethics. The code contains eighteen provisions governing broadcasters' obligations, including provisions to protect human rights and eliminate "abusive or discriminatory material" and prevent sex-role stereotyping (www.cbsc.ca).

The Quebec and Ontario councils found the stations in violation of the code generally and the sex-role portrayal provisions specifically on October 17, 1997. The council's opinion recognized a significant difference in the free speech rights of Americans and Canadians. While protecting "freedom of the press and other media of communication," the Canadian Charter of Rights and Freedoms places "reasonable limits prescribed by law as can be demonstrably justified in a free and democratic society." The council interpreted the charter and Canadian values as placing stricter limits on the degree of free speech tolerance:

> The CBSC has frequently observed that freedom of expression is the basic rule which it applied in the rendering of its decisions but it believes that this principle is not absolute. It is and must be subject to those values which, in a free and democratic society, entitle all members of society, on the one hand, to speak freely while, on the other hand, remaining free from the abrogation of those values in which they and other Canadians believe. Free speech without responsibility is not a liberty; it is a license.(CILQ-FM 1998)

The stations were required to broadcast acknowledgments of the council's findings within thirty days of the decision, but they declined to remove Stern's program from the air. Instead, the Toronto station agreed to hire a producer to monitor Stern's broadcasts for objectionable content and discuss the use of digital editing technology with Stern's producers. The council found the stations' responses inadequate and began another investigation of the content of Stern's show (CILQ-FM 1998).

The council issued a second decision against CILQ-FM in Toronto on February 20, 1998, regarding Stern's broadcasts in December 1997 and January 1998. The council recognized the station's decision to employ a producer to monitor Stern's program and the acquisition of editing equipment after the airing of the programs that prompted the complaints. The complaints alleged violation of the council's sex-role portrayal portion of the Code of Ethics. Specifically, the complainants objected to Stern's repeated emphasis on women's genitals and their sexual proclivities. Stern had discussed the supposed lack of sexual appeal of cooking expert Julia Child and his desire to have sex with the mother of one of the show's guests. In a later show, Stern auditioned candidates for breast implant surgery. Other citations were made for comments that advocated violence against women, racist and abusive comments and sex acts involving children (CILQ-FM 1998).

In deciding the case, the council recognized the station's efforts to edit Stern's broadcasts to conform with Canadian standards, though it criticized the tardiness with which the necessary equipment had been acquired. The council took notice of the editing procedures put in place by the station after the incidents that prompted the complaints: seventy-seven individual edits between February 23 and March 20, 1998, that ranged from a few seconds to as long as a twenty-minute segment. It issued a judgment against the station but was willing to give the editing procedures a chance to work before pursuing additional action, including possible ouster of the station from the council and reference of future violations to the Canadian Radio-television Telecommunications Commission (CILQ-FM 1998).

In 1999, the council cited Stern for violating its ethics codes protecting human rights in making disparaging comments about the Polish people (CILQ-FM 1999a), though it supported the broadcaster's handling of Stern's alleged violation of the human rights code in discussing handicapped people (CILQ-FM 1999b).

In the meantime, one member of the commission used the approval of a request by Bravo, parent company of CHUM Limited and owner of the Montreal stations, for programming exemptions to state his views on the impact of Stern's broadcasts (CRTC holds 1998): "It represents a serious challenge to community and broadcasting standards in this country . . . (and) I am concerned that the Howard Stern Show may be the most serious threat to Canadian radio as we know it, especially to talk radio."

CHUM Limited had business reasons to take these pronouncements seriously. The license of the Montreal station was up for renewal in 1999 (Boone 1998b), and CHUM wanted to expand its cable television and news channel services throughout Canada (CHUM promises 1999). Eventually, both actions received the commission's approval (www.citytv.com).

The debut of Stern's network television show in August 1998 prompted the withdrawal of the radio program from CHOM-FM in Montreal and the television program from stations in Toronto and Montreal (Fidelman 1998; CHUM City yanks 1998). At least one observer suggested the television show merely provided CHUM with a convenient way to regain the commission's good favor by dumping Stern, since few people found the show's graphic discussion of sex-related subjects surprising (Boone 1998b). More than 140 listeners called to complain about the decision to remove Stern's radio program from the airwaves in Montreal (Boone 1998; Fine 1998). A handful of loyal Stern fans organized a protest to commemorate the first anniversary of Stern's disappearance from Montreal's airwaves (Boone 1999). Stern's radio program remained on Toronto's CILQ-FM because "we're getting half-a-million listeners a week, making it the top morning show in English Canada" (Sanders 1998). The shock-jock's listeners in Toronto "attained a post-secondary education, (were) employed as owners, managers and professionals, and (had) high household incomes of $60,000 and $80,000" (www.q107.com).

MediaWatch, a Canadian citizens group that had lodged many of the complaints against Stern's show, praised CHUM's decision to drop Stern's programs in Montreal: "Howard Stern has been dumped and it's about time. . . . CHUM has made a wise decision, albeit months after thousands of vigorous complaints, to live up to the codes and guidelines that the private broadcasters have set for themselves" (MediaWatch, August 26, 1998).

One commentator at the *Toronto Globe and Mail* criticized the decision to remove Stern's programs in Montreal:

> CHUM decided that it didn't want to tangle with Canada's broadcast codes at a time when it needed to stay on the good side of the nervous Nellies at the Canadian Radio-television and Telecommunications Commission, the federal arbiters of good taste in broadcasting. The suffocating effect of the CRTC is nothing new, nor is spinelessness masked as a sound business decision . . . Stern only exists because so much radio and TV is so unbearably bland, and a surprisingly large part of his shtick consists of tell-it-like-it-is denunciations of media figures (Val Kilmer "is such a prick"; Rose O'Donnell "is a fake"). Even at his worst, his appalling approach to risk-taking makes viewers pay attention, which is something Saturday Night Live, his rival for the late-night, zoned-out audience, gave up doing a long time ago. (Allemang 1998)

THE ROLE OF VOLUNTARY
REGULATION

The saga of Howard Stern's challenge to government regulators in two countries offers an instructive look at how media operate in an era where marketplace values dominate commercial broadcasting. The era is over when commercial broadcasters can be counted upon to eliminate programming that is sexually explicit, insensitive to racial minorities, and offensive to gays and lesbians. It is clear that too much money can be made from shock-radio and that the penalties for broadcasting indecent material are relatively minor.

Nowhere was this more the case than in Stern's five-year fight with the U.S. Federal Communications Commission. Compared with the multimillion dollar profits from airing Stern's show each year, Infinity Broadcasting's decision to make a "voluntary contribution" of $1.7 million to the U.S. Treasury to settle the pending fines makes financial sense, even if a sizable number of Americans view Stern's programs as a misuse of the public airwaves. It is instructive, though, that the decision to end the standoff and Stern's principled free-speech defense of his program was made for a capitalistic reason: the desire of Stern's employers to clear the way for the acquisition of profitable radio stations.

Even under the best of circumstances and a favorable climate, the ability of government to regulate broadcasts such as Stern's has grown increasingly suspect. Nearly a decade passed between Stern's first major clash with federal regulators and the resolution of the multiple citations against his program. The lengthy appeals process ensures that formal government regulation will remain time-consuming at best and ineffective at worst.

The Canadian experience may offer some hope to people who believe programs such as Stern's represent a misuse of the public airwaves. It is important to note, as the Canadian Broadcast Standards Council did, that the two countries have different values: "In general, the Stern show has the reputation of pushing the envelope; it is, however, to be remembered that the nature of the Canadian and American envelopes differ. . . . The Canadian approach to broadcast speech is far more cautious and reflective of the need to respect other Canadian values" (CHOM-FM 1997).

While noting these differences, CHUM's decision to drop Stern's television and radio shows seems motivated by the same general factors that influenced Infinity Broadcasting to settle the pending complaints with the FCC: eliminating the potential for government regulators to block the company's expansion plans. In an era of marketplace values in the mass media, the future of government regulation may be more indirect than the approach taken by the FCC in the late 1980s and early 1990s. Instead of relying on overt governmental regulation, the media operators may simply prune indecent content to a level at the upper reaches of social acceptability rather than threaten their profit margins. With Howard Stern, Infinity Broadcasting had it both ways in the United States: multimillion dollar profits made possible by a controversial broadcaster for the relatively small cost of a "voluntary contribution" to cover a series of fines. In a smaller country determined to protect its culture and set a higher standard, CHUM chose to sacrifice some profitability at its Montreal stations for the promise of greater profits by expanding its business interests.

The role of the Canadian Broadcast Standards Council demonstrates the advantages and disadvantages of voluntary mechanisms of media regulation: speed and the lack of decision-making authority. The council's two decisions came within a six-month period, whereas the FCC's battle with Stern lasted more than five years. The council's existence absolved the Canadian Radio-television Commission of immediate responsibility for handling the complaints and issues at hand; the FCC served as complaint processor and policy maker. The difference suggests that the council may fulfill a public relations function for the regulatory body; the council's willingness to receive and process complaints and render decisions may make it seem that action is being taken. Certainly, the citizens group MediaWatch expressed that frustration after the March 1998 decision by the Canadian Broadcast Standards Council:

> MediaWatch is calling upon the CRTC to intervene in this matter in the public's interest. Despite self-regulation by the broadcast industry in Canada, the CRTC is not removed of its legal responsibility to administer the Broadcast Act and Radio Regulations. . . . The CBSC has noted Q107's strong commitment to the self-regulatory process and their intention to comply with all applicable codes and regulations as the sole reason for not removing the member from the Council. In doing so, the CBSC seems to be turning a blind eye to the daily barrage of sexism that predominated the Stern program. (Howard Stern program, March 26, 1998)

Notwithstanding the frustration and apparent inaction, a voluntary regulatory body provides the general public and public interests groups with a convenient collection point for complaints. If there is power in numbers, the ability of the public to be counted and heard collectively offers leverage that might otherwise be absent in a broadcast environment dominated by marketplace values.

The Canadian council recognized the challenge at hand and the need to defend its country's values in its initial decision about Stern's program:

> The globalization of the late twentieth century village does not mean the abdication of the maintenance of order within Canadian borders. The existence of other standards in other parts of the global village cannot weaken the need to apply home-grown standards within the Canadian bailiwick. The bar should not be lowered in Canada just because it is set at a lesser height elsewhere in the village. There is no need for the chain of vigilance here to be as weak as its weakest links elsewhere. If, however, an alert to the re-definition of principles is called for by what is created in other parts of the village, Canadian broadcasters have consistently shown their willingness and skill to rise to such challenges.

Shock radio should be no more demanding than any other challenge which has hitherto been presented to them. (CHOM-FM 1997)

Logic suggests that the values inherent in the council's statement may not always prevail in the marketplace. Certainly, the dominant values governing Stern's program seem capitalistic: Stern's employers sacrificed the most offensive parts of the shock-jock's repertoire (fines for indecent content in the U.S. experience, the Montreal market in the Canadian experience) in the name of commerce. That public pressure assembled by a voluntary regulatory mechanism may not prove an effective substitute for direct government regulation should come as no surprise. But with advances in technology and the increased reluctance of government officials to intervene, voluntary regulatory mechanisms may represent the best—and only—defense by people who take offense at mass media content that they believe threatens national and cultural sensibilities.

REFERENCES

Action for Children's Television et al. v. Federal Communications Commission, 932 F. Supp 2d 1504 (U.S. Court of Appeals, D.C. Cir. 1991).

Action for Children's Television et al. v. Federal Communications Commission, 58 F. Supp 3d 654 (U.S. Court of Appeals, D.C. Cir 1995).

Adelson, A. 1998. A dash past Rush? *New York Times*, April 13, p. D7.

Allemang, J. 1994. Employer of Howard Stern wins F.C.C. vote. *New York Times*, February 1, pp. D1, 6.

———. 1998. In defence of the offensive Howard Stern . . . sort of. *Toronto Globe and Mail*, September 10. From the newspaper's Web site: www.theglobeandmail.com.

Andrews, E. L. 1994. F.C.C. officials see hurdles in curbing Stern's employer. *New York Times*, January 7, pp. D1–2.

Boone, M. 1998a. Stern's ratings tumble. *Montreal Gazette*, June 4. From the newspaper's Web site: www.montrealgazette.com.

———. 1998b. Take a bow, Stern: CHUM wisely scrubs talk-show host like a barnacle from the poop. *Montreal Gazette*, September 1. From the newspaper's Web site: www.montrealgazette.com.

———. 1998c. Friday will be a sad anniversary for Howard Stern fans. *Montreal Gazette*, August 22. From the newspaper's Web site: www.montrealgazette.com.

Canadian Broadcast Standards Council complaint on the council's Web site: www.c-bsc.ca.

CHOM-FM re Howard Stern Show and CILQ-FM re Howard Stern Show. 1997. Canadian Broadcast Standards Council Decision 97/98–0001 + and 97/98–0015 +. October 18.

CHUM City yanks Howard Stern off airwaves. 1998. *Toronto Globe and Mail*, August 28. From the newspaper's Web site: www.theglobeandmail.com.

CHUM promises two new channels. 1999. March 15. www.cfra.com.

CILQ-FM re the Howard Stern Show. 1998. Canadian Broadcast Standards Council Decision 97/98–0487, 488, 504 and 535, February 20.

CILQ-FM re the Howard Stern Show. 1999a. Canadian Broadcast Standards Council Decision. 97/98–1186, February 3.

CILQ-FM re the Howard Stern Show. 1999b. Canadian Broadcast Standards Council Decision. 97/98–1223, February 3.

Colford, P. D. 1996. *Howard Stern: King of all media.* New York: St. Martin's.

CRTC holds Stern broadcasters responsible. 1998. Web site maintained by Canada's Media Awareness Network, July 9: www.screen.com.

Fabrikant, G. 1996. Two radio giants to merge, forming biggest network. *New York Times,* June 21, pp. A1, D5.

FCC v. Pacifica Foundation, 438 U.S. 748 (1978).

Federal Communications Commission e-mail at the commission's Web site: www.fcc.gov.

Fidelman, C. 1998. CHOM pulls plug on Stern. *Montreal Gazette,* August 27. From the newspaper's Web site: www.montrealgazette.com.

Fine, P. 1998. Cheers and jeers greet shock jock's demise. *Toronto Globe and Mail,* August 28. From the newspaper's Web site: www.theglobeandmail.com.

Gates, A. 1997. Peering inside the heads of laughing fans. *New York Times,* March 10, p. C1.

Howard Stern program ruled in contravention of industry codes a second time! MediaWatch urges CRTC to intervene in the public's interest. 1998. MediaWatch Web site, March 26: www.mediawatch.com.

In re Editorializing by Broadcast Licensees, 13 F.C.C. 1246 (1949).

James, C. 1997. Now a nice guy and Oprah antidote: Howard Stern ogles the mainstream. *New York Times,* March 10, pp. C1, 14.

Kurtz, H. 1997. *Hot air: All talk, all the time.* New York: Basic.

Landler, M. 1996. To infinity and beyond: Is a radio deal too big? *New York Times,* June 21, 1996, pp. D1, 5.

Losito, D. 1999. Stern Shocker: Howard, wife separate; couple parts after 21-year marriage. *Radio Digest,* October 24: www.RadioDigest.com.

Maslin, J. 1997. When a scourge turns on the charm. *New York Times,* March 7, p. C3.

MediaWatch welcomes Stern's departure from CHUM airwaves. 1998. From the organization's Web site, August 26: www.mediawatch.com.

Mifflin, L. 1998. CBS backs shock-talk radio host's new TV job. *New York Times,* April 2, p. A12.

———. 1998. Tepid debut for Stern show. *New York Times,* September 2, p. E4.

———. 1998. Two more television stations dump Howard Stern's show. *New York Times,* September 7, p. C5.

———. 1999. Howard Stern has a TV hit but not a knockout. *New York Times,* February 15, p. C11.

Nathan, J. 1997. For a specialist in being abused, it's a good life. *New York Times,* March 9, sec. 2, p. 25.

NBC v. U.S., 319 U.S. 190 (1943).

Ramirez, A. 1995a. Radio giant is set for a growth spurt. *New York Times,* September 18, p. D7.

————. 1995b. $1.7 million to end Howard Stern indecency case. *New York Times*, September 2, sec. 1, pp. 32, 45.

Ratings leap for stations carrying Howard Stern. 1997. *Toronto Globe and Mail*, October 29. From the newspaper's Web site: www.theglobeandmail.com.

Red Lion Broadcasting v. FCC, 395 U.S. 367 (1969).

Rivera-Sanchez, M. 1997. How far is too far? The line between "offensive" and "indecent" speech. *Federal Communications Law Journal* 49: 327–366.

Rivera-Sanchez, M., and M. Ballard. 1998. A decade of indecency enforcement: A study of how the Federal Communications Commission assesses indecency fines, 1987–1997. *Journalism and Mass Communication Quarterly* 75, no. 1: 143–153.

Sanders, D. 1998. CHUM axes Stern's radio, television talk shows. *Toronto Globe and Mail*, August 27. From the newspaper's Web site: www.theglobeandmail.com.

Schlosser, J. 1998. Stern scores in late night. *Broadcasting*, August 24, p. 41.

Sharkey, J. 1997. Looking for fame in all the wrong places. *New York Times*, April 6, New Jersey edition, sec. 13, p. 1.

Shock jock comes to Canada. 1997. Associated Press. From the Web site maintained by Canada's Media Awareness Network, August 28: www.screen.com.

Stations ignore Stern warning. 1997. *Ottawa Citizen*, December 11. From the Web site maintained by Canada's Media Awareness Network: www.screen.com.

Stern, H. 1994. *Private parts*. New York: Pocket Books.

Stern won't apologize for insulting francophones. 1997. *Toronto Globe and Mail*, September 11. From the newspaper's Web site: www.theglobeandmail.com.

Syracuse Peace Council v. FCC, 867 F.2d 654 (D.C. Circuit 1989).

Syracuse Peace Council v. FCC, 493 U.S. 1019 S. Ct. (1991), cert. denied.

www.cbsc.ca.

www.citytv.com.

www.fcc.gov.

www.marksfriggin.com.

www.q107.com.

102 FCC 2d (1985). August 23.

2 FCC Rcd 2705 (1987). April 29.

2 FCC Rcd 5272 (1987). August 4.

5 FCC Rcd 7291 (1990). December 7.

8 FCC Rcd 2688 (1992). December 18.

8 FCC Rcd 6790 (1993). August 12.

9 FCC Rcd 1746 (1994). February 1.

9 FCC Rcd 6442 (1994). May 20.

12 FCC Rcd 8274 (1994). June 4.

10 FCC Rcd 12245 (1995). September 5.

11 FCC Rcd 13214 (1996). October 15.

12 FCC Rcd 4147 (1997). April 2.

13 FCC Rcd 13869 (1998). June 4.

13 FCC Rcd 17254 (1998). June 29.

8

Cultural Bane or Sociological Boon? Impact of Satellite Television on Urban Youth in India

Kuldip R. Rampal

Christmas Eve 1999, Chandigarh, India: France's Fashion Television, one of the fastest expanding international channels in India, is taking a break from its transmission of the latest in haute couture from the fashion houses of Paris. It is time for the latest in lingerie. Millions of Indian viewers on this Christmas Eve, still wondering what kissing would be like in Indian movies or television programming because the country's laws bar such scenes in domestic productions, are in for something elegantly provocative and sensuous. Fashion TV has just started showing the latest in lingerie. To the tune of Prodigy's "Smack My Bitch Up," models wearing eye masks purr up to the catwalk, concealing more of their faces than the parts of the body that lingerie is supposed to hide. It does not take the viewer long to sense that it is more of a display of full breasts behind the often sheer bras and bottoms left alone by Rio briefs than anything resembling Victorian era undergarments for women.

Just as the protected Indian viewer is taking all of that in, another line of high-fashion lingerie enters to the song of "Going Up, Up, Up . . . Going Down, Down, Down." The highly suggestive bras and briefs are now supplemented with suspender belts, stockings, and heels. The models have stepped down the catwalk and walk around the audience tables coyly. As if that was not enough to shake up conservative Indian sensibilities, Fashion TV gives a peek into Le Lido, one of the most famous Parisian cabarets in the world, showing bare-breasted women aplenty.

Welcome to the world of international satellite television in India. Fashion TV, which reached 30 million viewers in 125 countries in December 1999, is one of about two dozen international channels, many of them from the United States, available on cable and through roof-top satellite dishes across India (The Indian pulse, 1999, p. 4). The Internet, hugely popular in urban India through Internet cafes, is projected to have 70 million subscribers in the country by 2005.

At the dawn of the twenty-first century, Marshall McLuhan's projected global village (McLuhan 1967) is increasingly a reality made possible by the communication revolution—satellite and cable television, multinational media conglomerates such as those of Rupert Murdoch and TIME-Warner communications, and, increasingly, the Internet. This writer, having traveled to some twenty-five countries, has seen firsthand the pervasiveness of American culture being imported through a variety of media, especially movies and television programming. The *Washington Post* reported that international sales of American entertainment and software products totaled $60.2 billion in 1996, more than any other U.S. industry (American Pop, 1998, p. A1).

American television is practically everywhere, and young people are tuning it in at a viewing scale often unparalleled in the ratings levels of indigenous programming. When the Singapore Broadcasting Corporation, for example, canceled MTV for contractual reasons in 1994, young Singaporeans spoke out in frustration and rejected an alternative local music video program as "unexciting." MTV has not only been a vehicle for the globalization of American music, but it has also attracted a young audience throughout the world, even in highly conservative countries such as Saudi Arabia and Iran.

The implications of offering freewheeling Western commercial television programming and movies have long been a subject of concern and research in Western countries. How do people with substantially different social and cultural values cope with such entertainment fare? Writing in *Mass Communication and American Empire* in 1969, Herbert Schiller cautioned that the implications of the cultural influences brought about by American programming were far-reaching, especially for the developing peoples of the world. "Everywhere local culture is facing submersion from the mass-produced outpourings of commercial broadcasting in the United States," he said, adding, "to foster consumerism in the poor world [through American entertainment programming] sets the stage for frustration on a massive scale" (Schiller 1969, p. 111).

More recently, Jerry Mander, cofounder of the International Forum on Globalization, voiced a similar warning. Writing in the *Nation*, Mander (1996) said that the global media corporations of Rupert Murdoch, Ted Turner, and a few others "transmit their Western images and commercial values directly into the brains of 75 percent of the world's population. The globalization of media imagery is surely the most effective means ever for cloning cultures to make them compatible with the Western corporate vision." Revisiting the theme of the dominance of American cultural products around the world, Schiller wrote in 1998 that "the machinery of mind management is so entrenched and pervasive that nothing less than seismic movements can be expected to loosen or weaken its pernicious authority" (Schiller 1998, p. 195).

This chapter examines the sociological implications of satellite television programming, both Western and Indian, for the urban youth in India in the areas of sex, violence, and drugs. Does satellite television have adverse influences in these areas? If yes, are such influences linked to the issue of "cultural imperialism" only or to a larger set of socioeconomic variables in which "cultural imperialism" is only a part of the explanation? We will also look for indications of positive effects of satellite television. Research for this chapter is based on an examination of literature and quantitative data on the subject, as well as focus group interviews in India by this writer during the summers of 1998 and 1999.

SATELLITE TELEVISION IN INDIA

Western television's popularity in India, especially in urban areas, is traced to 1991 when CNN became prominent in the country, as elsewhere in the world, for its live coverage of the Gulf War. The availability of international television in India for the first time in its history that year was aided, in no small measure, by the introduction of economic liberalization by the government the same year. A democratic government with a pronounced economic liberalization policy would have found it difficult, had it tried, to legally keep international television out of the country.

For decades, Indians had been restricted to the fare served by state television known as Doordarshan (DD), a diet of tedious discussions by government bureaucrats, old Hindi movies with generous amounts of singing and dancing, and news programs usually promoting the government line instead of providing objective and balanced coverage. During the Gulf War, urban India was swept up in the Cable News Network craze. Satellite dish manufacturers worked overtime to provide equipment to hotels and apartment buildings and many people spent hours riveted to the first war seen live in India. But after the war, the repetitiveness of CNN and its concentration on

American news caused many Indian viewers to drift away from the American network.

In the fall of 1991, as hundreds of unregulated cable TV operations flourished in urban areas, new channels began appearing on Indian televisions courtesy of Hong Kong-based STAR-TV, including MTV, an all-day sports channel for the cricket-hungry South Asian fans, two entertainment channels carrying a heavy dose of American programming, and BBC World, a global television news channel launched by the British Broadcasting Corporation as its answer to CNN.

Practically overnight, millions of Indian television viewers, long used to DD's staid educational programming and dramas based on Indian mythology, found themselves tuning in to the likes of *Baywatch, Dallas,* and *Dynasty.* In a land where kissing has never been allowed in Indian movies or television programming, TV viewers could now experience the "sex and violence" culture long decried even in the West. Further globalization of television has brought dozens of additional channels to Indian viewers, especially since democratic India's free press laws (Freedom House 1999) allow people to set up their own satellite dishes or have access to international programming via cable television. A survey of urban youth by India's influential newsweekly *Outlook* found that more than 85 percent of the respondents spend "over two hours daily" watching television. "Sidney Sheldon is their [the Indian youth] top author, Dickens a lowly tenth" (Outlook millennium poll, 1999).

Commenting on the new phenomenon of the popularity of Western television in India, Edward Gargan of the *New York Times* wrote: "For India, a nation long padlocked to the government's version of reality, the candy-store variety of programming has brought a poorly contained giddiness" (Gargan 1991).

In early 1999, there were 20 million cable households in India, including at least 2 million multiple-TV households, and the reach of television was expanding fast. The more than forty channels that this writer observed in the northern Indian city of Chandigarh in summer 1999 included SONY Entertainment, STAR-World, STAR-Plus, STAR-Movies, STAR-News, MTV, [V] Music, Music Asia, ZEE-Cinema, ZEE-Drama, Fashion-TV from France, BBC World, CNN, Cartoon Network, National Geographic Channel, and TB-6 from Russia, in addition to the three news and variety channels of DD and many other Indian and international entertainment, sports, and news channels. The next wave in the Indian television industry was expected to arrive in the country by early 2000 in the form of direct-to-home (DTH) television planned by Rupert Murdoch's News Corporation and Indian broadcasters.

Consumption of Western English-language programming is facilitated in India by the fact that English, which is one of the official languages of the country, is widely spoken in urban areas. Indeed, according to David Dalby, eminent scholar and linguist from Great Britain, "by the year 2010 India will have the largest number of speakers of English, the world's language of communication" (Vaidya 1998).

Although Indians of all ages have been fascinated with Western television, a variety of articles and ratings surveys indicate that the youth of India are particularly enamored with Western television and the cultural values that it projects. Ratings indicate that MTV is the most popular channel among teenagers in India followed by other music channels and channels carrying dramas and movies, both Indian and Western. Programming that typically carries advisories for parents in the United States to keep inappropriate programming beyond the reach of their children is routinely available from Western channels in India without issuing such advisories as a matter of rule. The cable television industry was brought under government regulation in 1995 to manage its further expansion, but no moves were made to call for a programming code until early 1999 when the information and broadcasting minister in the federal cabinet spoke of the need for such a code (Cable operators, 1999).

In a study of Indian satellite television (Crabtree and Malhotra 1996, p.6), the authors say that "early indications suggest that the presence of Western programming via satellite has had some influence on the social discourse of middle class Indian youth." We now examine the nature of influence, if any, in the areas of sex, violence, and drugs before turning to the issue of any sociological benefits from international television.

SATELLITE TELEVISION AS A
FACTOR IN SEXUAL BEHAVIOR

Vasanthi Nail, a seventeen-year-old girl from the city of Bangalore, India's silicon valley, told the country's premier news weekly, *India Today*, in October 1997 that she listened to the Spice Girls track "I Wanna, I Wanna" over and over again because "there is some kind of subliminal message telling me to go ahead and do my own thing" (Urban Teenyboppers, 1997). Music channel's *Beach It Out with the Spice Girls in Bali* was so popular with Indian teenyboppers that the British pop group was dropping by for an India tour later that month.

The article also noted that the Spice wannabes were not stopping midway. "They have not only donned the attitude, but also their body-hugging gear. Today, it is commonplace to see groups of leggy teenage girls showing a sexy navel peeping over their hipsters." The magazine reported that this "new breed of girls are tougher because of constant Western media exposure and are also 100 percent resistant to authority." College girls often skip lectures and head for "watering holes" that run special afternoon hours for students. The magazine quoted the manager of a trendy Bombay pub as saying, "Girls now associate alcohol and skimpy clothes with hip culture."

This hip generation finds that information on sex is also widely available courtesy of media globalization. Talk shows on adultery, seductive soaps such as *The Bold and the Beautiful*, and titillating pictures on the Internet are commonly accessible in urban India today. The number of Internet subscribers in India had shot up from 120,000 in February 1999 to 500,000 by the end of the year (Half a million, 2000, p. 1). The generous share of sleaze on France's Fashion-TV, mentioned earlier, has reached a point that the authorities are beginning to get concerned about it. At a New Delhi seminar in early April 2000 called Communicating Fashion—A New Dimension, Arun Jaitley, India's information and broadcasting minister, said, "We in the Ministry are cautious and concerned that in the name of fashion channel what we are being shown is see-through dresses with disconcerting frequency" (Govt concerned, 2000).

Even Indian TV serials like *Swabhimaan* and *Kabhie, Kabhie,* which are clearly copying the commercial success formula from their Western counterparts, are spiked with illicit sexual relationships and sexual metaphors. Indian film actress Deepti Naval said that "vulgarity in Hindi songs today shows that filmmakers take the audience to be buffoons and even a little retarded. I call today's age as the 'pelvic age', where hero and heroine simply gyrate to the music" (Deepti criticizes, 1999).

Asha Das, an official in the Women and Child Development section of the Ministry of Human Resource Development, said, "I've seen TV even in the West. But ours is much more suggestive with far more innuendoes" (Sex, 1998). A fifteen-month study conducted on one hundred adolescents in India found they took most of their pointers on sex from television and movies. A twelve-year-old boy, who said he thought about girls all the time, added, "It's all there on TV—that's where I learned how to hook girls" (Sex, 1998).

Newspapers, magazines, and novels have also been found to be major influences in the early sexual awareness of adolescents. In a New Delhi school, students asked to read the newspaper as part of their curriculum suddenly discovered the graphic reporting of the Bill Clinton–Monica Lewinsky case. According to a national newsweekly (Sex, 1998), "They lapped it up—especially the jokes. One joke went like this: Why doesn't Monica open her mouth? Because—ha, ha—she harbors the evidence there." A school principal commented, "Sex has become as banal as shaking hands—it is much more in your face than ever before" (Sex, 1998).

As a result, said Dr. Achal Bhagat, a psychiatrist, "More than any generation in this century, children today experiment with sex, drugs and alcohol at a much earlier age" (Sex, 1998). A study conducted on adolescent girls in

1981 by Dr. Alka Dhal, a gynecologist, found that 90 percent of the girls surveyed had practically no knowledge about sex (Sex, 1998). In contrast, as mentioned above, television and movies are the primary sources of knowledge about sex for today's youth. Teenage pregnancies in recent years have reached an all-time high in India. For example, Health Ministry figures for the state of Maharashtra, of which Bombay is the capital, show that in 1997 girls younger than fifteen accounted for 21.7 percent of all abortions—more than 41,000—carried out in the state. There is also a sharp increase in the number of young people turning to prostitution, both as a business and as "customers" (Sex, 1998).

A 1998 study, "Child Prostitution in India," by Centre of Concern for Child Labour, found that the number of children under fourteen in commercial prostitution is increasing at the rate of 8 to 10 percent annually. Nearly 20 percent of the customers of these young prostitutes were found to be students, particularly in the urban areas. Sexually transmitted diseases were becoming a significant problem (Thirty percent, 1998).

In a 1998 survey of 3,000 young people aged fifteen to thirty-four in small and big towns by MTV-India, 29 percent of the respondents said yes to the question, Is premarital sex a way of life in the 1990s? (Ninety percent, 1998). This response may not be high by Western standards, but for the traditionally conservative Indian population this finding is very revealing about the sexual values of a significant percentage of today's youth. Others saw this finding as evidence that Western influences have not overwhelmed Indian youth, with most displaying strong traditional moorings with regard to issues like sex and marriage.

G. C. Gupta, a psychologist and professor, citing a number of studies, surveys, and trends said that the phenomenon of teenage sexuality has come to stay in the Indian society (Sexual trends, 1998). He said trends indicate that it will prosper in the twenty-first century as a consequence of "free mixing between members of the opposite sex, exposure to increasingly uninhibited mass media, more permissive family/home environment, and the desire to indulge in it just for the kick of it" (Sexual trends, 1998). Cyber romance will also be a major stimulant for the information technology-savvy young population of India, said Gupta.

SATELLITE TELEVISION AS A FACTOR IN VIOLENCE

The National Crime Records Bureau (NCRB) in India reported that in 1997 young people aged sixteen to twenty-five were responsible for 56 percent of all crimes committed in the country. In New Delhi, the country's capital, 93 percent of all serious crimes in 1998 were committed by young men trying their hand at crime for the first time. A total of 767 robberies were reported in the capital in 1998 compared with 602 in 1997, a jump of 27 percent. Of people committing robberies in the capital, most were below age thirty, a third from a middle-class background, and almost 40 percent were school educated (Rising crime, 1999).

This *Times* article also reported that the crime graph in the entire country has shot up. The following crime data were recorded in 1998: 38,000 murders, 15,000 rapes, 23,000 robberies, 900 cases of extortion, and 35,000 cars stolen. Kidnapping and abduction cases also scored high. A study on crime patterns done at India's prestigious Tata Institute of Social Sciences found in 1998 that the crime rate among youth had gone up by as much as 40 percent in the past decade. This study also found that although the youth crime wave flows across all races, classes, and lifestyles in India, there was a "noticeable increase in the number of heinous crimes committed by young people from middle-class and upper middle-class families" (Young menace, 1999).

Achal Bhagat, a New Delhi psychiatrist who runs a counseling center for troubled youth, offered the following explanation for increasing youth crime rate:

> In a world where cutthroat competition begins from kindergarten and the concept of having 'made it' is defined by satellite TV images of the rich and famous, most children today prowl tirelessly for a better deal that will free them from the restraints that their parents faced. Ambitions soar and images of making it big (cars, exotic holidays) constantly play on the mind. But when failure strikes, most can't handle it. A squeeze in the job market and the general lack of opportunities frustrate them. And soon the tremendous pressure to succeed builds up anger. (Young menace, 1999)

This view was shared by Pramod Kumar, director of the Institute of Development and Communication in the northern Indian city of Chandigarh, who said that young people "suddenly find crime and brute force has a premium" (Young menace, 1999). Several studies by non-governmental institutions in India indicate that the "sensation-seeking" younger generation facing an unemployment rate of approximately 23 percent increasingly feels insecure and socially frustrated. Crime suddenly becomes an option for a number of young people, even those coming from middle and upper middle class backgrounds, to quickly attain the lavish lifestyle they are seeking. For example, a newspaper report (Rising crime, 1999) said that a young man in New Delhi had stolen approximately $3,500 from his own house and "to impress his friends got himself a secondhand car."

At a seminar in July 1999 in Chandigarh, several school teachers attributed youth violence to satellite television in particular, although they cited the high unemployment rate and travails of social relationships faced by young people among the contributing factors. The "invasion" of young minds by violence-heavy programming on various cable channels was said to be a catalyst in the rising incidence of crime among the youth. In what is clearly consistent with Albert Bandura's modeling theory (DeFleur and Ball-Rokeach 1989, p. 212), one high school principal at the seminar said, "What they [the youth] see on television is what we get from them. They imitate their real-life heroes [role models] on the screen to become real-life heroes themselves" (School bullies, 1999).

Rajni Kothari, an eminent Indian social scientist, wrote in July 1998 that the fast pace of social and cultural changes in the country was contributing to a rising amount of tension. "We are likely to witness criminalization of tensions. Most of the problems emanate from social changes," he said (We are likely to witness, 1998, p. 4). That was also the view of some experts speaking at the World Conference on Injury Prevention and Control sponsored by the World Health Organization in New Delhi in early March 2000. Dr. Emmanuel Rozental, a surgeon at New York General Hospital, noted at the conference that economic globalization has led to increasing inequality, with concentration of wealth and power in the hands of a few and massive exclusion and deprivation among growing majorities. "Social exclusion within contexts characterized by inequity and poverty is fertile ground for all kinds of violence," Dr. Rozental said, adding that when deprivation and opulence coexist, violence is perceived as functional to the satisfaction of needs that appear otherwise inaccessible (Globalization has led, 2000).

SATELLITE TELEVISION AS A
FACTOR IN DRUG USE

A study published by the Ministry of Welfare and Development in India in 1998 found that there were 3 million drug addicts in the country in 1997, including 15,000 females. Although available research indicates that critics are not blaming satellite television directly for promoting drug use, liberal and permissive social values that run through their programming themes combined with their promotion of a sensation-seeking culture are said to be instrumental in the increasing drug abuse in the country. Drug use is also attributed to stress, peer pressure, increased availability of drugs, and often just "to experiment" with drugs. Dr. Aruna Broota, a clinical psychologist, noted that the sale of illegal drugs was on the rise in the country. Increasingly, young women were getting involved in such a trade "to make a quick buck or earn extra for that new dress or jazzy bloc heels" (Women increasingly falling prey, 1998, p. 5).

Although use of illegal drugs in India is nowhere close to that in the West, the problem is getting serious enough for national publications like *India*

Today, which came out with a cover story on the issue in its April 5 1999 edition. Entitled "Drugs: New Kicks on the Block," the investigative story said that the use of cocaine and ecstasy was on the rise, especially among wealthy entrepreneurs and young professionals, "a generation that is rich, successful and wants to party hard" (Drugs, 1999).

In what the magazine noted was a typical example of many young urban professionals trying drugs just for the fun of it, it quoted Vicky Kapuria, thirty-two, who runs a computer business and "does drugs every weekend" before going to parties: "More than half the crowd in these parties do cocaine and ecstasy. I know because only a user can spot fellow users" (Drugs, 1999).

The magazine quoted Dr. Harish Shetty, consulting psychiatrist at the National Addiction Research Center, as saying that cocaine use "is very high in this segment of kids from rich families." Another psychiatrist, Dr. Sanjay Chugh, who managed a drug rehabilitation center in a south Delhi hospital, said, "two years ago, I didn't know a single cocaine addict. Now I treat 25 to 30 cases, all of whom belong to the upper crust." Yusuf Merchant, president of the Drug Abuse Information Rehabilitation and Research Center in Bombay, said that 15 percent of his patients were addicted to cocaine, adding that "the [actual] number is higher since most of these drug addicts don't believe there is a problem." Maneka Gandhi, the country's social welfare minister, whose ministry looks after drug rehabilitation, confirmed the wide use of drugs among wealthier people: "Among a certain class this winter, there wasn't a party in Delhi that didn't have cocaine" (Drugs, 1999).

Explaining reasons for drug use, Delhi psychiatrist Dr. Achal Bhagat said: "The single-most important reasons seems to be the desperate desire to party hard—stretch those definitions of fun. Today their whole lives seem to revolve around a partying culture. They live for instant gratification" (Drugs, 1999). Such definitions of fun are increasingly being attributed to the permissive social atmosphere promoted by both international satellite television as well as privately owned Indian channels and other media. Rising frustration among the youth with high social expectations but the inability to achieve them because of the unemployment problem is also cited as a key reason for drug abuse. *India Today*'s investigative story mentioned above said that drug use is also linked with copious literature available on the Internet that explains how to do "drugs safely."

SATELLITE TELEVISION AND SOCIOLOGICAL BENEFITS

An extensive review of literature on the sociological implications of new media technologies, especially satellite television, in India indicates that there is also a positive aspect to what satellite television has to offer. For example, the huge popularity of the Hindi-language programming carried by STAR-TV for its Indian viewers has been promoting understanding of this language among non-Hindi speakers in the country. As a brief perspective, it should be noted that although fifteen different languages with hundreds of dialects are spoken in various regions and states of India, the Indian constitution provides for Hindi as the national language of the country. But Hindi is spoken by only about 40 percent of the Indian population, forcing the government to maintain English, the language inherited from British colonial rule, as an associate national language of India along with Hindi.

The Education Ministry's efforts since the 1960s to promote Hindi through its Learn Hindi campaign have often faced stiff resistance in parts of multilingual India, especially in the south, where understandably people prefer to learn and use their own language. For example, the southern state of Tamil Nadu refused to carry the Hindi news service from the national television network, DD, in the early 1990s and has been insisting that Tamil be made an associate national language. A common sentiment expressed in the south is that English has served the country well for over a hundred years, so where is the need to have Hindi as the national language. Moves to teach Hindi across India have been seen as an attempt by the Indo-Aryan people of the north to impose their culture on the Dravidian south, which the south has resisted, at times with demonstrations and riots.

Amid this continuing row came Hong Kong-based STAR-TV and then Indian satellite channels such as ZEE-TV, which began to broadcast Hindi movies around the clock. Although India's movie industry, the largest in the world (American pop, 1998), produces movies in a variety of languages, Hindi movies have attracted the best of talent and financial resources. The Bombay-based Hindi movie industry, commonly referred to as Bollywood, produces hundreds of movies every year, with a huge popularity in India and a substantial viewership in the Middle East, Africa, the Central Asian republics, and Southeast Asia.

The popularity of Hindi movies and other Hindi-language entertainment programming carried by STAR and ZEE is providing an incidental benefit. It is promoting understanding of Hindi across the country, a development that the Indian government, no doubt, welcomes. Since entertainment programming brought by satellite television does not appear to have any hidden agenda, it is apparently contributing toward addressing a sociological problem that the government has not been able to solve through its Learn Hindi policy. Rupert Murdoch, whose News Corporation owns STAR-TV, told the Indian prime minister in 1994 that Indian critics needed to tone down their rhetoric of "cultural invasion" by satellite television in view of the obvious sociological benefits that were accruing from it.

Interviews conducted by this writer with a focus group comprising ten college-aged male and female students in the northern Indian city of Chandi-garh in July 1998 about the effects of satellite television revealed another pos-itive aspect of this entertainment and information source. Although the re-spondents were often concerned that sexual content in television programming was "harmful" for children and teenagers, there was a consen-sus that satellite television had made them aware of the larger world and the possibilities and opportunities that it presented. It is this positive aspect of media globalization that the critics of "cultural imperialism" appear to have overlooked.

As this writer explored the positive aspect of satellite television with the focus group, he was reminded of the "empathy" variable that the American sociologist Daniel Lerner had spoken of as playing a central role in the soci-etal modernization process (Lerner 1958). Lerner had discovered in his re-search that media exposure cultivated one's sense of "empathy," which he defined as the capacity to see oneself in desired situations, say a preferred job or a lifestyle, that the empathic individual could then work to achieve.

The focus group members emphasized that they and their peers were con-centrating on finding ways to develop the economic ability to achieve the lifestyles that they were learning about from satellite television. A good job and a family with kids, a decent home, a car, good friends, holidays at exotic destinations, and often a pet figured prominently on their list of goals. In-deed, evidence indicates that more and more Indian students are looking toward education abroad after high school and college, either to settle abroad after education where jobs are seen to be abundant or to improve their com-petitiveness for jobs in India. Thousands of young professionals are also seeking employment visas or educational opportunities abroad to be able to further their careers.

For example, the New Delhi office of the British Council noted in late 1999 that the number of self-funded Indian students going to the United Kingdom for higher education is expected to increase to 6,000 by the year 2000, from the 1997–1998 figure of 2,193. An India-based Australian educa-tion official said that the number of Indian students going to his country for further studies is expected to jump to at least 10,000 by the year 2000 from 3,800 in 1997–1998. MBA remains at the top of the list of preferred study disciplines for Indian students in the United Kingdom and Australia, with the other popular disciplines being information technology, food processing, fashion technology, media studies, hotels, and tourism, among many others. The United States, which has historically been the favorite destination of In-dian students wanting to study abroad, still continues to attract the largest number of students from India. France and New Zealand are also becoming the countries of choice for Indian students seeking education abroad (Big demand, 1998).

A further indication that Indians view globalization generally positively, in spite of the sociological problems linked to it by many people, came from the results of an opinion poll conducted by the *Outlook* newsweekly in early March 2000 in six major cities across India. Fifty five percent of those polled said American culture posed no threat to Indian culture, whereas 33 percent said that it did. Fifty eight percent supported the entry of multinationals into India, while only 29 percent were opposed to it (U.S. should help India, 2000).

CONCLUSION

No definite conclusions were sought or can be drawn from the foregoing analysis of the available data as to the effects of satellite television in India. The available evidence appears to suggest, however, that critics of "cultural imperialism," such as Herbert Schiller, are only partially right in arguing that Western pop culture and commercially driven entertainment programming can be harmful for the youth of developing countries. Critics also need to look into the possible positive effects of exposure to Western popular culture.

It is true that many sociologists, social psychologists, teachers, government functionaries, and laypeople in India hold the permissive and promiscuous culture portrayed by satellite television as a significant contributing factor to problems in the areas of sex, violence, and drugs. One forceful reminder of that view came from an Associated Press story in late 1994. The story said that "hundreds of people sick of violence and sex on television shows have hurled their television sets out of the window" in two large apartment buildings in Bombay (Bombay residents, 1994). This action came amid rising criticism that Western soaps and game shows, and Indian song-dance sequences that are increasingly using the Western sex-and-violence formula for commercial success, are overtly violent or risqué.

The state government in Maharashtra, with Bombay as its capital, announced in June 1998 that it had asked the culture minister to police sexually suggestive lyrics in movies and music video programs. Even the federal government announced that it will have to devise a multipronged approach to meet the challenge of "cultural invasion thrown up by transnational electronic media which have invaded Indian homes" (Counter cultural influence, 1999). Fortunately for free flow of information advocates, the government was not speaking of restricting such a flow. Instead, it advocated creating an awareness on the part of producers, programmers, parents, and citizens to fight the challenge by becoming responsible producers and discriminating consumers of media (Counter cultural influence, 1999).

But social scientists also point to other contributing factors to problems involving sex, violence, and drugs that are commonly associated with media

influences. It is virtually impossible to conclusively study the effects of satellite television separate from other influential variables such as the parental
role in child rearing, unemployment, the widening income gap between the
rich and the poor linked to economic globalization, peer pressure, and stress.
At the same time, the positive effects of satellite television cannot be ruled
out. There are indications from the new awareness and motivations acquired
by young people in India that such television, indeed the information revolution at large, is instrumental in contributing to, and possibly hastening, the
modernization process of people in democratic societies. And who could
have imagined before satellite television that a Hong Kong based television
service would help in addressing India's national language problem some-
day? In retrospect, one can see why a "neutral" foreign channel would have
a better chance to accomplish that inadvertently than the state-run television
network based in the north of India. There is little doubt, therefore, that
there is more to international satellite television than just "cultural imperialism."

One other conclusion can be drawn from the experience of private commercial television in India. Having tasted the offerings of such channels—
both foreign and domestic—Indian viewers are spending far more time
watching the state-run Doordarshan (DD) television than private channels.
According to audience measurement data released in early April 2000, the
average viewer, even in a cable and satellite television home, spent fifty-four
minutes a day watching DD, compared with only seven minutes watching
the private Zee and SONY television channels. The data concluded that DD
is by far the most watched channel in the country. This finding suggests a
clear rejection of the view held by critics like Leonard Sussman of the New
York–based Freedom House that state involvement in broadcasting in democratic nations is something inherently undemocratic, warranting the listing
of such a country as "partly free." As the data indicates, audiences in India
are increasingly rejecting the sex-and-violence formula of the "free" privately run channels and rightfully so.

That is not to say that private commercial television should be banned or
heavily regulated. To the contrary, private television is natural to democratic
countries that, like India, cherish media freedoms and therefore allow the
operation and reception of such domestic and international channels. But
the public media critics and media policy makers know from experience that
private commercial television programming is designed to cater to the lowest
common denominator in public entertainment values, resulting in the exploitation of sex, violence, and drug themes for higher ratings. A public
broadcaster, such as DD, with its serious cultural, entertainment, and educational programming can provide the necessary balance, something that Indian viewers are clearly appreciating. Of course, a BBC-type public broadcaster, which maintains news-editorial autonomy, is to be preferred over a

state-run broadcasting system. It is welcome news that DD's organization is moving in that direction. However, there is clearly a strong justification for the continuing presence of a vibrant public broadcasting system in democratic states to offset what critics believe are the adverse influences of private commercial broadcasting.

REFERENCES

American pop penetrates worldwide. 1998. *Washington Post,* October 25.

Big demand for Indian students abroad. 1998. *Indian Express,* November 18. www.expressindia.com.

Bombay residents smash TV sets. 1994. Associated Press, December 26. www.ap.org.

Cable operators to be regulated. 1999. *Times of India,* March 29. www.timesofindia.com.

Counter cultural influence. 1999. *The Hindu,* March 14. www.hinduonline.com.

Crabtree, R. D., and S. Malhotra. 1996. On the ground and in the air: The commercialization of television in India. *International Communication Bulletin* 3 (fall): 3–4.

Deepti criticizes pelvic age. 1999. *The Tribune,* September 8. www.tribuneindia.com.

DeFleur, Melvin L., and Sandra Ball-Rokeach. 1989. *Theories of Mass Communication.* New York: Longman.

Drugs: New Kids on the Block. 1999. *India Today,* April 5. www.india-today.com.

Freedom House. 1999. *Freedom in the World: The Annual Survey of Political Rights and Civil Liberties, 1998–1999.* New York: Freedom House.

Gargan, Edward. 1991. TV comes in on a dish, and India gobbles it up. *New York Times,* October 29. www.nytimes.com.

Globalization has led to violence in the world. 2000. *Hindustan Times,* March 7. www.hindustantimes.com/nonfram/080300/detCIT07.htm.

Govt concerned over content of Fashion TV. 2000. *Hindustan Times,* April 9, 2000. www.hindustantimes.com/nonfram/090400/detNAT06.htm.

Half a million log on to India.com. 2000. *Economic Times,* January 3.

The Indian pulse. 1999. *Economic Times,* July 14–20. www.economictimes.com.

Lerner, Daniel. 1958. *The Passing of Traditional Society: Modernizing the Middle East.* New York: Free Press.

Mander, Jerry. 1996. The dark side of globalization: What the media are missing. *Nation.* www.escape.ca/~viking/global.html.

McLuhan, Marshall. 1967. *The medium is the message: An inventory of effects.* New York: Random House.

Ninety percent of "MTV generation" say no to pubs, discos. 1998. *Times of India,* November 13. www.timesofindia.com.

On the ground and in the air: The commercialization of television in India. *International Communication Bulletin* 31: 3–4.

The Outlook millennium poll. *Outlook,* November 8. www.outlookindia.com/19991115/poll.htm.

Rising crime is our crying shame. 1999. *Times of India,* March 16. www.times ofindia.com.

Schiller, Herbert. 1969. *Mass Communication and American Empire.* Boston: Beacon.

———. 1998. Living in the number 1 society. *Gazette* 60 (April): 2.

School bullies take to violence: Teachers attribute it to TV. 1999. *The Tribune,* July 26.

Sex: An early awakening. 1998. *India Today,* September 21. www.india-today.com.

Sexual trends in the twenty-first century. 1998. *India Today Plus.* www.india-today.com/iplus/1998_3/sex.html.

Thirty percent of sex workers are children: Study. 1998. *Times of India,* November 10. www.timesofindia.com.

Urban teenyboppers: Spice attack. 1997. *India Today,* October 13. www.india-today.com.

U.S. should help India fight terrorism. 2000. *Outlook,* March 20. www.outlook india.com/20000320/coverstory6.htm.

Vaidya, Abhay. 1998. India will soon be the centre of gravity of English. *Times of India,* November 9 1998.

We are likely to witness criminalisation of tensions. 1998. *The Tribune,* July 31.

Women increasingly falling prey to drug use. 1998. *Times of India,* August 12. www.timesofindia.com.

Young Menace. 1999. *India Today,* January 18. www.india-today.com.

9

Pornography, Perceptions of Sex, and Sexual Callousness: A Cross-Cultural Comparison

Zhou He

As new communication technologies reach an increasingly large audience and make controls over mass communication channels extremely difficult to maintain, the long-standing controversy about pornography has come to the forefront in countries around the world. Underscoring the controversy is widespread concern about pornography's pervasiveness, its relationship to free speech, and, especially, its potential impact on people in respect to sexually aggressive behavior, subordination of women, perception of sexual activities, sensitivity to women, and moral standards.

Using a sample of 409 college students from the United States, China, and Hong Kong, this study attempts to examine the impact of pornography across cultures. Specifically, it tries to explore the following general questions: What is the relationship between exposure to pornography and people's perception of sexual activities, their sensitivity toward women, and their moral values regarding sexual activities across cultures?

BACKGROUND

The United States, China, and Hong Kong were chosen as the sites for this study because they provide a testing ground for a comparative examination.

131

Pornography is rampant in these countries, which are all worried about its impact and have taken some measures to cope with this problem. Yet they are distinctly different cultures and are in different stages of experience with pornography. With these similarities and differences, they serve as good cases for a comparative examination of whether the impact of pornography is universal and whether the impact is related to the stages of contact with pornography. In this study, an assumption is made that cultures in the world encounter pornography in three stages, depending on historical, societal, and cultural tolerance of pornography. The first stage is the "initial contact," in which a country is just recently exposed to pornography that mostly comes from outside. The second stage is "discreet experiment," in which a country has experienced pornography for some time and is still unsure about the appropriate degree of tolerance. The third stage is "established tolerance," in which pornography is accepted as part of the adult culture and is legally and morally tolerated.

The United States

If we put the three cultures' experience with pornography on the three-stage continuum, the United States is obviously in the third stage. Pornographic material is legally available to anybody over eighteen in bookstores, newsstands, video stores, X-rated movie theaters, adult cable channels, pay TV, and even international computer networks such as the Internet and World Wide Web. Pornography is a lucrative business that grosses a colossal $8 billion a year.

The pervasiveness of pornography is due partly to the long tradition of free expression in the United States, partly to the public's increasing tolerance of sexually explicit materials, and partly to the vague definitions offered by the judicial system, which regulates the distribution of such materials. In the 1957 *Roth v. United States* case, for example, Supreme Court Justice William Brennan wrote for the majority opinion that the test of obscenity should be whether to "the average person, applying contemporary community standards, the dominant theme of the material, taken as a whole, appeals to prurient interest" (*Roth v. United States* 1957). In the 1973 *Miller v. California* case, Supreme Court Justice Warren E. Burger defined pornography as that which "taken as a whole, appeals to the prurient interest in sex, which portrays sexual conduct in a patently offensive way in violation of acceptable state laws, and which, taken as a whole, lacks serious literary, artistic, political or scientific value" (*Miller v. California* 1973).

The broadness and vagueness in these definitions make it extremely difficult for the law enforcement system to restrict "obscene" material, even though the Supreme Court has repeatedly ruled that such material is not protected by the First Amendment to the U.S. Constitution. Today, only two types of sexually explicit material are undoubtedly illegal in the United States: (1) that which involves extreme violence and (2) that which involves children.

Hong Kong

Hong Kong, a British colony for almost a century and recently a special region of China that is subject to a different set of laws and moral standards, is in the "discreet experiment" stage. In motion visuals (videos, movies, or laser discs), explicit sex acts can be shown only when the pubic areas are blurred out or covered and only to people who are over eighteen. In still pictures, female, but not male, reproductive organs can be exposed, and explicit sexual acts are not allowed. In verbal portrayals, anything pertaining to sex goes. All this material, however, has to be submitted to the authorities for censorship.

In Hong Kong, sexually explicit material of various kinds had been circulated in a semiopen fashion or underground for a long time under the British government's hands-off policy. Only when pressured by forces from various sectors did the British government enact the Control of Obscene and Indecent Articles Ordinance to exert some control over the traffic in 1987. However, the ordinance offered only a vague definition of what constituted obscenity and indecency, which simply classified articles into three categories: Class I: the article is neither obscene nor indecent; Class II: the article is indecent; and Class III: the article is obscene (Television and Entertainment Licensing Authority).

There was no detailed explanation of the categories. Under this law, indecent articles could be distributed to people over eighteen, but obscene articles were illegal. In 1989, the Hong Kong government established the movie rating system, which was different from the Control of Obscene and Indecent Articles Ordinance. The rating system classifies movies into three categories, with the third category being equivalent to Class II in the ordinance.

Because of the vagueness in these laws and regulations, sexually explicit material is bountiful in Hong Kong and readily available to anybody over eighteen. According to one estimate by a Hong Kong media expert, about 50 to 70 percent of the some three hundred movies produced and shown in Hong Kong each year in the mid 1990s were third-category movies, most of which are pornographic.

Unlike pornography in the United States, pornography in Hong Kong openly involves violence and minors. For example, *Hong Kong 97*, the equivalent of *Penthouse*, frequently publishes special editions of ten underage bunnies. In addition, Hong Kong's pornographic publications blatantly promote prostitution, which is illegal in Hong Kong, by giving tips, providing match-making hotline services, and carrying prostitution ads.

China

China is apparently in the initial-contact stage in its experience with pornography—despite the centuries-old tradition of pornography in the country that was marked by sexually explicit writings in the form of *Fangzhong shu* (Techniques in the bedroom) in the Han dynasty (202 B.C.–A.D. 220), the sex boom in the Tang dynasty (618–906), exquisite color block prints of sex acts in the Ming dynasty (1368–1644), and the classic *Ching p'ing mei* (Golden lotus) (China's equivalent of *Lady Chatterley's Lover*) in 1610 (Gulik 1961; Gulik 1951).

When the Communists took power in 1949, pornography was eliminated along with prostitution. As a result, two generations of Chinese were not exposed to pornography. From 1949 to 1979, there was virtually no sexually explicit material in China. There was not even a spelled-out definition of pornography. Any material that verbally or visually depicted the act of sex or exposed the female body down to the breast or up to the thigh was considered pornographic and was illegal. One of the very few pieces of pornographic material known to be circulated underground among some "delinquent adolescents" was a hand-copied fiction titled *Shaonu zhixin* (The heart of a teenage girl).

Pornography reemerged in China only when the country began its economic reforms and opened its door to the outside world in 1979. People's curiosity, desire to taste the "forbidden fruit," and revolt against the decades-long suppression of sex-related displays combined to create a tremendous market for sexually explicit material. Pornography made a sudden comeback through various underground and semiopen channels. In big cities such as Wuhan, Beijing, and Shenzhen, there were semiopen markets for sexually explicit products. In places where commercialization was carried to the extreme, such as Wenzhou in eastern China, pornographic videotapes were used as kickbacks and commissions in business transactions. Even in such remote places as Guizhou Province in southwestern China, pornographic material could be easily obtained through under-the-counter deals. Most of the pornographic materials were duplicates of originals smuggled from overseas, especially Hong Kong.

In 1986 and 1987, the newly established State Press and Publication Bureau launched two targeted raids on pornographic and erotic material. In 1988, the bureau drafted the Temporary Rules on the Identification of Pornographic and Obscene Material to cope with increasingly rampant pornography. In the rules, the bureau defined obscene material as "that which, taken as whole, portrays and promotes obscene acts, which appeals to the prurient interest in sex, leads to the corruption of the average person, and lacks artistic or scientific value" (State Press and Publication Bureau [SPPB] 1988, 151–152). It defined pornography as "that which, taken as a whole, is not obscene but contains some obscene content, which is harmful to the health and spirit of an average person, especially an adolescent, and lacks artistic or scientific value" (SPPB 1988, pp. 151–152). According to the rules, any material that fell under those two categories was illegal, and distributors of such material were subject to severe punishments, including imprisonment or the death penalty under some circumstances. Starting in 1989, the Chinese Communist Party began to wage national antipornography campaigns under the leadership of a politburo member in charge of ideology and propaganda work. Although the 1989 campaign was commonly seen as being driven more by politics following the Tiananmen movement than by a genuine concern over the pervasiveness of pornography, subsequent campaigns seemed to be motivated by the central leadership's wish to eradicate pornography. Each of these campaigns rounded up large quantities of pornographic material, as shown by the following figures of confiscated illegal, pornographic, and obscene materials reported by the national conferences on the work of "antipornography campaigns": nearly 32 million copies of illegal publications and 1 million pornographic videotapes and audiotapes in 1989–1990; more than 20 million copies of illegal publications, 510,000 pornographic videotapes, and more than 170,000 pornographic audiotapes in 1991; and more than 10 million copies of illegal publications and 120,000 pornographic videotapes in 1992 (Li 1993).

However, instead of being eradicated, pornography bounced back each time with reinforced momentum, new production techniques, and increasingly sophisticated distribution channels. Several factors combined to account for pornography's tenacity: a great demand for sexually explicit material, relaxed law enforcement at the local levels, reluctant cooperation of the public who loathed mass campaigns, corruption of government officials and police, and increasingly sophisticated and well-organized underground production and distribution networks.

PREVIOUS RESEARCH

Because of the widespread concern, the effects of pornography have been scrutinized from various perspectives over the past few decades. From the moralistic perspective, pornography is seen as being harmful to cultural values and morals. From the feminist perspective, pornography is regarded as the subordination and degradation of women and reinforcement of male dominance (e.g., Dworkin and MacKinnon 1985). From a therapeutic perspective, pornography is often seen as playing a cathartic role and serving as a "lubrication" and aphrodisiac that improve lovemaking and sexual relationship between a couple (e.g., Carins and Winshner 1962).

Despite all this scrutiny, however, empirical evidence of pornography's impact on individuals is still inconclusive and contradictory. In China, the impact appears to be more assumed than proven. A rather exhaustive search through the *Index of Newspaper and Journal Articles* (the most comprehensive in China) and leading sociological and social-issue journals found only a handful of research articles on the impact of pornography. And those articles dealt with the impact of pornography in an indirect or heuristic fashion. In a fairly comprehensive article on the harmful effects of pornography, for example, Tong (1993) listed four harmful effects of pornography: (1) eroding morals and accelerating societal chaos; (2) damaging social gender roles and gender equality, and leading to discrimination against women; (3) leading to aggression and violent crimes against women; and (4) contributing to the insecurity of women when the content is full of violence and subordination. However, the discussion was purely argumentative and often based on translated works from the West. In a study using sophisticated quantitative methods to examine the psychological characteristics of prostitutes, Wang and Xu (1993) presented a secondary finding on the impact of pornography. They reported that half of the 452 prostitutes under study claimed that they were most impressed by such hand-copied pornographic books as *Shaonu zhixin* (The heart of a teenage girl), 83 percent said that pornographic videotapes and pictorials were the strongest sexual stimulus for them, and most of them learned, actively or involuntarily, sex techniques from pornography. In another study of adolescents in a reform school, Zhang (1989) found that 30 percent of the sex crime–related people were influenced by pornographic publications. Most of the studies of pornography in China have focused on the classification and distribution of pornography (Tong 1993). The few studies of pornography's impact have mostly been conducted among convicted criminals such as prostitutes or adolescents in reform schools. Although there have been some internal investigations of pornography's impact, again mostly among convicts, these studies are not available to the public. This lack of systematic and empirical research on the impact of pornography is due to several factors: a firm belief that pornography does cause harm; the lack of social science tradition; the novelty of pornography in contemporary China; and the illegal status of pornography, which makes it difficult to research pornography's impact among individuals other than convicted offenders.

In Hong Kong, there is virtually no focused study of the impact of pornography on people. A comprehensive search through English-language journal articles and Web sites found only one academic article dealing with pornography in Hong Kong. In the article, Liu, Chung, and Wong (n.d.) offered a brief discussion of Internet pornography and suggested some regulatory measures based on the U.S. experience. The impact of pornography was implicitly assumed and taken for granted.

In the West, there is a large body of literature on the impact of pornography. However, the evidence collected so far is also inclusive and sometimes contradictory. For example, a large-scale investigation by the Commission on Obscenity and Pornography in the United States in 1970 concluded that there was no convincing evidence to show that pornography caused harm (Commission on Obscenity and Pornography 1970). However, in 1986, the U.S. Attorney General's Commission on Pornography, commonly known as the Meese Commission, reversed the findings of the 1970 investigation and concluded that pornography did cause harm and that even when sexually explicit material did not portray violence, it might be harmful to society and the family (Attorney General's Commission on Pornography 1986). In Denmark, where pornography has been legal since 1969, several studies have found that pornography did not lead to aggression against women, nor did it increase incidents of rape (Kutchinsky 1991; Kutchinsky 1985). Donnerstein (1991) suggests that there is no evidence of any harmful effects from nonviolent, soft-core pornography. In a meta-analysis of thirty works, Allen, Alessio, and Brezgel (1995) found that exposure to pictorial nudity reduces subsequent aggressive behavior, that consumption of material depicting nonviolent sexual activity increases aggressive behavior, and that use of violent sexually explicit material generates more aggression.

Most studies seem to agree that violent pornography can have an impact on aggression against women, especially when inhibitors such as fear of legal punishment are reduced (e.g., Donnerstein 1983; Donnerstein 1984). However, as Donnerstein (1991) points out in a review of research on pornography, aggressive images are the issue, not sexual images. Even here, evidence has been challenged and the observed effects questioned. In two experiments that carefully created conditions in which violent pornography should produce intended effects, for example, Fisher and Grenier (1994) found that exposure to violent pornography did not produce significant effects on men's fantasies, attitudes, and behaviors toward women. They attributed the lack of effects and the inconsistent findings of previous research on the effects of violent pornography to unreliable research procedures and conceptual limitations.

One line of research that has drawn a lot of attention is the examination of pornography's adverse impact on people's perception of reality and their sensitivity to women, not their aggressive behavior, which has been criticized as inconsistently measured. Representative of this line is Zillmann and Bryant's research. In an experiment of 160 college students, Zillmann and Bryant (1982) found that massive exposure to soft-core pornography could: (1) produce visions of people doing more of anything pertaining to sex; (2) make people regard pornography as less offensive and objectionable; (3) reduce people's willingness to ban pornography; (4) contribute to the loss of compassion for and sensitivity to women as rape victims. Some of these findings were later replicated (Zillmann 1986; Zillmann and Bryant 1988).

Despite criticisms of Zillmann's research, his line of conceptualization apparently accords with the main findings of media effects over the past few decades: media effects are more evident at the cognitive and perceptual levels than at the behavioral level.

Building on Zillmann and Bryant's line of thinking, this study attempts to examine pornography's effects on individuals' perception of sexuality, sensitivity to women, support of the feminist movement, and dispositions toward sex across cultures. The basic assumption is this: If pornography can affect people in those aspects, as Zillmann and his associates found, then the impact should cut across cultures if people are exposed to basically the same material. This assumption is based on the author's research on the pornography market in China and Hong Kong since 1994. It has been found that in those two places, people are indeed exposed to much of the same material Americans were exposed to. In Hong Kong, a major proportion of the pornographic material, especially the motion visuals, is imported from the United States and Japan (whose exported pornographic material is also popular in the United States). In China, the overwhelming majority of the material is smuggled in from Hong Kong, which contains the same mix as the Hong Kong diet.

The study hypothesized that the more exposed the subjects in those cultures are to pornography, the more likely they will be:

H1 To approve premarital sex
H2 To approve extramarital affairs
H3 To approve legalized prostitution
H4 To be lenient in their recommended sentences for rapists
H5 To have higher estimates of people engaged in anal, oral, group, and sadomasochistic sex
H6 To show less support for the feminist movement

METHOD

For ethical and legal reasons, an experiment could not be carried out in China and Hong Kong. Therefore, a survey of 170 students at Shenzhen University in China and 111 students at the Chinese University of Hong Kong was conducted in November 1994. A similar survey of 120 students was carried out in February 1995 at San Jose State University, California.

To make sure that the sample did not have any study-based predisposition on pornography, only those students who were in lower-division classes or in the beginning of upper-division classes in which sophisticated research literature on pornography's effects had not been taught were chosen for the sample. A seventeen-item questionnaire was distributed in the classes. To ensure that the students provided honest and reliable responses, they were told that their responses would be kept confidential. They were also instructed to keep their eyes on their own questionnaires. The survey was disguised as one on cultural values, not one on the effects of pornography. The most sensitive question—the one about their exposure to pornography—was placed at the very end of the questionnaire so that the students could answer it last and turn the questionnaire over to conceal their responses. The survey questions were designed to measure students' exposure to pornography, their recommended sentence for a rapist after reading a rape case in which the rapist is convicted but a sentence is pending, their perception of sexual acts practiced by people in their respective societies, and their attitudes toward the feminist movement, premarital sex, extramarital affairs, and legalized prostitution (for details, see notes to table 9.1). In the surveys, pornography was defined as "material that explicitly portrays sexual conduct, appeals to the prurient interest in sex and, taken as a whole, lacks artistic or scientific value."

Because of the illegal status of pornography in China, several additional measures were taken to ensure reliable responses. First, the survey was administered by and with the help of liberal-minded professors liked and trusted by the students at Shenzhen University. Second, some questions were carefully worded to suit the Chinese situation. For example, the question on the subjects' estimates of the percentage of people engaged in various sexual practices was worded this way: "The People's University recently conducted a national survey of sex practices. Can you provide a guess on the percentage of adults doing . . . ?" Third, the subjects were told that the survey results would be kept completely confidential and that they would be taken out of the country the next day.

For the purpose of accumulation and cross-cultural comparison, many of Zillmann's measures of perception and sensitivity were used.

Because the purpose of this study was not to generalize the findings to the population but rather to find some basic regularities across cultures, no effort was made to draw a random sample. Although a survey of this nature had its inherent limitations, it nevertheless had some merits. First, it did not rely on the one-short exposure that is often administered in most experiments; instead, it was based on the subjects' long-term and real-life exposure to pornography. Second, it avoided the extreme difficulty in picking and dividing hard-to-find subjects who did not have any prior exposure to pornography. Third, it was based on the mix of pornographic material—both violent and nonviolent—that people actually expose themselves to rather than the artificially separated diets of violent and nonviolent pornography used in experiments.

FINDINGS

General Description

The data show that college students in the United States, China, and Hong Kong differed significantly in several ways but were similar in others. Table 9.1 summarizes the major differences and similarities.

On exposure to pornography, the U.S. students had the highest score and differed significantly from both the Chinese and Hong Kong students. Surprisingly, Hong Kong students, with their ready and legal access to pornography, did not differ significantly from their Chinese counterparts. In fact, the combined exposure by both females and males was slightly lower than that of the Chinese students. On the feminist movement, the U.S. students were the most supportive and differed significantly from the Chinese students but not the Hong Kong students. What came as a surprise was that the Chinese students, who lived in a culture that had an almost radical movement for gender equality, were the least supportive of the feminist movement among the three groups, even though their support was just a little more than lukewarm. The most noticeable difference was found in the students' attitude toward premarital sex. On a 5-point scale, the U.S. students scored an average of 4.1 points, which differentiated them significantly from both the Chinese and Hong Kong students, who scored 2.9 and 2.8, respectively. However, on extramarital affairs, the U.S. students were least favorable, and, surprisingly, the Chinese students were the most favorable. All the students were very similar in their attitude toward legalized prostitution, with the average scores in the middle of a 5-point scale (meaning neither supportive nor opposed), despite the fact that prostitution was banned in China and Hong Kong and was legalized only in certain counties in Nevada in the United States. Another noticeable difference was the sentence recommended for a rapist. The U.S. students recommended the longest average sentence, whereas the Hong Kong students meted out the shortest sentence.

In their estimation of people engaged in common and uncommon sexual activities, the U.S. students gave the highest estimation and differed significantly from their Chinese and Hong Kong counterparts in all categories except for anal sex. This shouldn't come as a surprise, given the generally liberal attitudes toward sex in the United States. What was surprising was that Chinese students, who just recently started to break themselves off from the almost "puritan" Communist culture, had almost exactly the same estimates as their counterparts in the open society of Hong Kong. In fact, the Chinese students' estimate of people engaged in sadomasochistic sex was significantly higher than that by the Hong Kong students.

Given these differences and similarities, did pornography have a significant impact on the subjects' perceptions in each category from their respective starting points?

Table 9.1. A Comparison of College Students in the United States, Hong Kong, and China on Exposure to Pornography, Attitudes toward Rapist, Feminist Movement, Women, and Legalized Prostitution, and Perception of Sexual Activities (n 346)

		U.S.	Chinese	Hong Kong
Exposure to pornography[a]	Female	2.2[a]	1.5[b]	1.5[bc]
	Male	2.6[a]	2.0[b]	2.3[bc]
	Combined	2.3[a]	1.8[b]	1.7[bc]
Jail sentence for rapist[b]	Female	37.6[a]	25.2[b]	21.0[bc]
	Male	38.3[a]	26.7[b]	18.0[bc]
	Combined	38.4[a]	25.9[b]	20.1[c]
Attitude toward legal prostitution[c]	Female	2.3	1.9	2.3
	Male	2.8	2.7	2.7
	Combined	2.5	2.2	2.4
Support of feminist movement[d]	Female	4.0	3.9	3.9
	Male	3.3	3.0	3.2
	Combined	3.8[a]	3.5[b]	3.7[ab]
Women as clothes[e]	Female	1.1[a]	1.3[b]	1.1[ac]
	Male	1.6	1.6	1.8
	Combined	1.2	1.4	1.3
Attitude toward premarital affairs[f]	Female	4.0[a]	2.6[b]	2.8[bc]
	Male	4.1[a]	3.4[b]	3.0[bc]
	Combined	4.1[a]	2.9[b]	2.8[bc]
Attitude toward extramarital affairs[g]	Female	1.5[a]	2.3[b]	1.8[ac]
	Male	1.6[a]	2.3[b]	1.9[ac]
	Combined	1.6[a]	2.3[b]	1.8[ac]
Estimate of oral sex[h]	Female	68.5[a]	42.6[b]	35.7[bc]
	Male	61.8[a]	33.0[b]	41.3[bc]
	Combined	66.0[a]	37.4[b]	37.6[bc]
Estimate of anal sex[i]	Female	27.9	23.8	22.6
	Male	22.1[a]	15.5[b]	14.5[ab]
	Combined	25.7	19.8	19.9
Estimate of group sex[j]	Female	16.5[a]	8.3[b]	6.2[bc]
	Male	13.8[a]	6.9[b]	5.6[bc]
	Combined	15.5[a]	7.7[b]	6.0[bc]
Estimate of sadomasochism[k]	Female	16.0[a]	14.2[ba]	8.8[c]
	Male	13.7	13.3	7.6
	Combined	15.3[a]	13.4[ab]	8.4[c]

Note: Means with different superscripts in the rows differ from each other at the .05 level by the Student-Newman-Keuls test.

[a] A 3-point scale was used to measure the exposure to pornography, in which 1 represents no exposure, 2 represents occasional exposure (once every six months to once a year) and 3 represents frequent/massive exposure (once every two months to more than once a month).

[b] Respondents were asked to recommend a sentence for a convicted rapist. A few respondents recommended life imprisonment, which was coded as 70 years, or the death penalty, which was coded as 100 years.

[c to g] A 5-point scale was used to measure opinions on the legalization of prostitution, attitudes toward the feminist movement, the statement that "Women are clothes that can be dumped once worn out," and attitudes toward premarital sex and extramarital affairs. In this scale, 1 represents absolute objection and 5 represents absolute support.

[h to k] A percentage scale of 0–100 was used to measured respondents' estimate of people practicing oral, anal, group, and sadomasochist sex.

Premarital Sex

As the correlation analysis shows in table 9.2, pornography seemed to have a noticeable association with subjects' perceptions when the sample was examined as a whole (r = .40, p < .001). However, when the influence of country differences was controlled for, the correlation coefficient dropped to .31 (p < .001). Even though this was not a very high coefficient and did not explain much of the variance in each variable (r^2 = .09), it seemed to suggest a positive and statistically significant relationship to a certain degree.

This relationship appeared to be supported by the one-way ANOVA analysis of all the subjects by their exposure, which shows that the more exposure the subjects had to pornography, the more likely they were to approve premarital sex (see table 9.3). However, when the subjects were broken down by country, the differentiation pattern was not so neat. Within the U.S. subsample, pornography did not show any impact at all. Within the Hong Kong subsample, both the intermediate-exposure group and the heavy-exposure group differed significantly from the no-exposure group, but there was no difference between the two exposed groups. The only neat pattern was found in the Chinese subsample. Apparently, the aggregate statistics were affected by the Chinese subsample, which had the largest number (n = 177).

Based on the statistical evidence, what can be said with some confidence about H1 is that it found only mixed evidence.

Extramarital Affairs

The correlation in table 9.2 shows that pornography was almost not correlated with the subjects' attitude toward extramarital affairs (r = −.01, p <

Table 9.2. Pierson Correlation between Exposure to Pornography and Sensitivity, Attitude, and Perception Variables among All Student Subjects in the United States, Hong Kong, and China (n 346)

	Exposure to Pornography	
		Controlling for Country
Jail sentence for rapist	.09*	.04
Support for feminist movement	−.18***	−.23***
Attitude toward legalized prostitution	.23***	.19***
Attitude toward premarital sex	.40***	.31***
Attitude toward extramarital sex	−.01	.12*
Estimate of oral sex	.18**	.09
Estimate of anal sex	.06	.04
Estimate of group sex	.18***	.12*
Estimate of sadomasochism	.16**	.15**

*p < .05   **p < .01   ***p < .001

Table 9.3.   Attitude toward Premarital Sex among U.S., Hong Kong, and Chinese College Students, as a Function of Exposure to Pornography

		No Exposure	Intermediate Exposure	Heavy Exposure
U.S.	Female	3.9	4.0	4.1
	Male	3.0	4.1	4.1
	Combined	3.8	4.0	4.1
Hong Kong	Female	2.7	2.9	3.2
	Male	2.4	3.0	3.4
	Combined	2.6[a]	2.9[b]	3.3[bc]
Chinese	Female	2.2[a]	2.9[b]	3.5[bc]
	Male	2.9[a]	3.4[ac]	3.8[c]
	Combined	2.4[a]	3.1[b]	3.8[c]
All subjects	Female	2.6[a]	3.3[b]	3.9[c]
	Male	2.8[a]	3.5[b]	3.9[c]
	Combined	2.6[a]	3.4[b]	3.9[c]

Note: Means with different superscripts in the rows differ from each other at the .05 level by the Student-Newman-Keuls test.

.05). when the subjects were examined as a single sample group. When the influence of country differences was controlled for, the correlation coefficient went up to .12 (p < .05). This was also a very weak correlation. ANOVA analyses confirmed this relationship. At the level of the entire sample, pornography did not show any impact on the three different exposure groups. Within the Chinese subsample, there was a statistically significant difference. However, such a difference existed only between the heavy-exposure group and the intermediate-exposure group, not between these two groups and the no-exposure group. Therefore, H2 was clearly rejected.

Legalized Prostitution

Pornography appeared to have a mixed relationship with this variable across the cultures. It showed a moderate correlation (.23, p < .001) when the subjects were examined as a single group (see table 9.2). However, when the influence of country differences was controlled for, the correlation coefficient dropped to .19 (p < .001). Given the size of the sample (n = 346), this was obviously a fairly weak correlation.

When the three groups with different types of exposure to pornography were examined using ANOVA, exposure to pornography appeared to have a clear-cut relationship with the subjects' attitude toward legalized prostitution when all the subjects were examined as a single group. The more exposure to pornography the subjects had, the more likely they leaned toward

Table 9.4. Attitude toward Extramarital Affairs among U.S., Hong Kong, and Chinese College Students, as a Function of Exposure to Pornography

		No Exposure	Intermediate Exposure	Heavy Exposure
U.S.	Female	1.5[a]	1.3[ab]	1.8[ac]
	Male	1.0	1.5	1.6
	Combined	1.5	1.4	1.7
Hong Kong	Female	1.8	1.7	1.8
	Male	1.8	1.8	2.0
	Combined	1.8	1.7	2.0
Chinese	Female	2.3	2.3	3.0
	Male	2.4	2.1	2.7
	Combined	2.3[a]	2.2[ab]	2.8[ac]
All subjects	Female	2.0	1.8	2.0
	Male	2.2	1.9	2.1
	Combined	2.0	1.8	2.0

Note: Means with different superscripts in the rows differ from each other at the .05 level by the Student-Newman-Keuls test.

approving legalized prostitution. But a closer look at the different groups by country reveals that this relationship was not universal. Within the U.S. subsample, pornography did not make any difference on subjects' attitude toward legalized prostitution. Within the Hong Kong subsample, the difference was between the intermediate-exposure group and the no-exposure group, but not between the heavy-exposure group and the no-exposure group. As in the case of H1, the only neat pattern was found within the Chinese subsample, in which more exposure was associated with a more favorable attitude. Apparently, this pattern in the Chinese group compounded the overall pattern of all the three groups when they were examined as a single collective. What can be said, therefore, is that H3 found only weak and mixed evidence.

Sentence for Rapist

H4 found virtually no support from the data. As table 9.2 shows, the correlation coefficient was only .09 ($p < .05$), and it was even lower (.04, $p > .05$) when the influence of country differences was controlled for. The ANOVA analysis shows that exposure to pornography did not make a difference on the subjects both as a single sample group and as sub-groups (see table 9.6).

Perception of Sex Acts

In this area, exposure to pornography appeared to show a weak but positive correlation with the estimate of people engaged in oral sex ($r = .18$, $p <$

Table 9.5. Attitude toward Legalized Prostitution among U.S., Hong Kong, and Chinese College Students, as a Function of Exposure to Pornography

		No Exposure	Intermediate Exposure	Heavy Exposure
U.S.	Female	2.6	2.2	2.4
	Male	1.0	2.9	2.8
	Combined	2.5	2.4	2.6
Hong Kong	Female	2.1	2.7	2.0
	Male	1.4[a]	2.9[b]	2.9[abc]
	Combined	2.1[a]	2.8[b]	2.7[abc]
Chinese	Female	1.6	2.1	2.7
	Male	2.3[a]	2.4[ab]	3.6[c]
	Combined	1.8[a]	2.4[b]	3.3[c]
All subjects	Female	2.0	2.3	2.4
	Male	2.0[a]	2.6	3.1[c]
	Combined	2.0[a]	2.4[b]	2.8[c]

Note: Means with different superscripts in the rows differ from each other at the .05 level by the Student-Newman-Keuls test.

.001), group sex (r = .18, p < .001), and sadomasochism (r = .16, p < .01) when the subjects were examined as a whole. However, when the influence of country differences was controlled for, all the correlation coefficients dropped, with the estimate of oral sex plunging most dramatically to .09, the estimate of group sex dropping to .12 (p < .05), and the estimate of sadomasochism sliding to .15 (p < .01). This means that subjects in one or two countries differed tremendously from the rest. It also means that with all the estimates of sex practices, exposure to pornography had a weak relationship when country differences were controlled for and when all the subjects were examined as a single group (see table 9.2).

The ANOVA analysis shows some interesting results. When all the subjects were examined as a whole, the heavy-exposure group differed significantly from both the intermediate- and no-exposure groups on the estimate of oral sex, group sex, and sadomasochism, with the intermediate-group showing no statistically significant difference from the no-exposure group. When examined as separate groups by country, however, the difference disappeared on two variables—the estimate of anal sex and that of group sex—within every country group. On the estimate of sadomasochism, only the Chinese subsample demonstrated a statistically significant difference between the heavy-exposure subjects and others. On the estimate of oral sex, there was no difference among the different exposure groups within the U.S. subsample. Within the Chinese subsample, there was a statistically significant difference between the no-exposure group and the intermediate-expo-

Table 9.6. Number of Years of Imprisonment Recommended for a Rapist by U.S., Hong Kong, and Chinese College Students, as a Function of Exposure to Pornography

		No Exposure	Intermediate Exposure	Heavy Exposure
U.S.	Female	50.5[ab]	29.0[b]	47.7[ac]
	Male	70*	42.9	35.4
	Combined	52.27	32.6	41.2
Hong Kong	Female	19.6	22.7	17.2
	Male	14.4	18.2	19.0
	Combined	19.1	21.0	18.5
Chinese	Female	26.4	24.26	20.8
	Male	27.4	28.1	24.1
	Combined	26.8	26.0	23.3
All subjects	Female	25.7[a]	25.8[ab]	37.6[c]
	Male	26.3	29.2	27.9
	Combined	25.9	27.1	31.7

Note: Means with different superscripts in the rows differ from each other at the .05 level by the Student-Newman-Keuls test.
*Only one American male student did not report any exposure to pornography. Therefore, the Student-Newman-Keuls test did not show any significant difference.

sure group. However, it was the no-exposure group that had a higher estimate than the intermediate-exposure group. Only in the Hong Kong subsample was there a significant difference between the no-exposure group and both the intermediate- and heavy-exposure groups in the hypothesized direction. Based on these data, H5 apparently found very weak evidence (see table 9.7).

Support for the Feminist Movement

Exposure to pornography appeared to show a noticeable correlation with the subjects' support for the feminist movement. When all the subjects were examined as a collective, the correlation coefficient stood at $-.18$ ($p < .001$). When the influence of country difference was controlled for, the correlation coefficient rose to $-.23$ ($p < .001$), indicating that exposure to pornography was associated with decreasing support for the feminist movement, independent of country differences (see table 9.8). However, in the ANOVA analysis, this pattern was not so clear-cut. Although the aggregate data show that the intermediate-exposure and heavy-exposure differed from the no-exposure group at a statistically significant level, the breakdown data show mixed pat-

Table 9.7.   Estimates of the Percentage of Adults Practicing Common and Uncommon Sexual Acts by U.S., Hong Kong, and Chinese College Students, as a Function of Exposure to Pornography

		No Exposure	Intermediate Exposure	Heavy Exposure
Oral sex	U.S.	63.3%	63.6%	68.8%
	Hong Kong ·	28.4[a]	43.1[b]	49.8[bc]
	Chinese	46.9[a]	29.9[b]	35.9[ab]
	All subjects	40.4[a]	45.2[ab]	56.5[c]
Anal sex	U.S.	27.6	25.4	25.8
	Hong Kong	19.2	21.0	19.7
	Chinese	20.9	17.2	25.5
	All subjects	20.9	21.1	24.4
Group sex	U.S.	14.0	14.0	17.4
	Hong Kong	5.0	6.1	8.0
	Chinese	8.5	6.4	9.6
	All subjects	7.5[a]	9.1[ab]	13.4[c]
Sadomasochism	U.S.	15.0	14.9	15.9
	Hong Kong	8.1	8.4	11.9
	Chinese	12.0[a]	11.2[ab]	23.0[c]
	All subjects	10.6[a]	11.9[ab]	16.8[c]

Note: Means with different superscripts in the rows differ from each other at the .05 level by the Student-Newman-Keuls test.

terns from one group to another. Within the U.S. subsample, a statistically significant difference existed only between the intermediate-exposure group and the heavy-exposure group, with the latter showing less support for the feminist movement. Within the Hong Kong subsample, there was no difference between the three groups. The only neat pattern was found within the Chinese subsample, in which the heavy-exposure group showed the least support, the intermediate-group showed less support for the feminist movement, and the no-exposure group showed strongest support. Therefore, H6 found only very weak and mixed evidence.

CONCLUSION AND DISCUSSION

The findings of this study appear to suggest that pornography did not have a significant relationship with the subjects' perceptions and dispositions pertaining to sexuality, the feminist movement, and sexual aggression. With such classic variables as callousness to rape victims, perception of sexual reality, and support for the women's struggle for equality, exposure to pornography either showed no statistically significant relationship or only mixed

Table 9.8. Support for the Feminist Movement among U.S., Hong Kong, and Chinese College Students, as a Function of Exposure to Pornography

		No Exposure	Intermediate Exposure	Heavy Exposure
U.S.	Female	4.0	4.0	3.9
	Male	4.0	3.7	3.1
	Combined	4.0[a]	3.9[ab]	3.5[ac]
Hong Kong	Female	4.0	3.9	3.8
	Male	3.4[a]	3.4[ab]	2.4[c]
	Combined	3.7	3.7	3.6
Chinese	Female	4.1[a]	3.6[b]	4.0[ab]
	Male	3.4[a]	3.1[ab]	2.4[bc]
	Combined	3.9[a]	3.3[b]	2.8[c]
All subjects	Female	4.0	3.8	3.9
	Male	3.2	3.3	3.0
	Combined	3.3[a]	3.6[b]	3.8[bc]

Note: Means with different superscripts in the rows differ from each other at the .05 level by the Student-Newman-Keuls test.

relationships across the three cultures. In "sex liberalization" (as measured by approval of premarital sex, extramarital affairs, and legalized prostitution), pornography's role was ambiguous.

The most regular pattern of pornography's role was found among the Chinese students. On most variables in this study, exposure to pornography among the Chinese students showed a classic pattern, with more exposure being more closely associated with higher estimates of sexual acts and less support for the feminist movement. Although this finding appears to support previous research, it actually points to two lines of inquiry that seem to have been overlooked by previous research: (1) the novelty effect of pornography and (2) the cultural mentality of a society.

Of the three cultures examined, the Chinese culture is in the initial-contact stage in its experience with pornography. For the Chinese students, as well as most people in contemporary China, pornography is a novelty, which has reemerged only recently. As a result, they are not well prepared and tuned up in their encounters with the fantasized world of pornography. The impact of the first shock, the unpreparedness and the inexperience, may combine to make them more vulnerable to the impact of pornography. The same may have been true with most subjects in the classic experiments in the United States, in which people with no prior exposure were chosen and assigned to treatment and control groups. Had these subjects been exposed to pornographic materials over a long period of time, the results might have been different. Indeed, the fact that some effects were found in the Hong

Kong subsample and no effect was found on the U.S. students on most of the variables appears to support this line of thinking.

Furthermore, the Chinese culture today is undergoing tremendous changes, with the old culture almost completely disrupted or destroyed by the Communist movement (especially by such mass movements as the Cultural Revolution from 1966 to 1976) and the new commercial culture that is struggling to be established. There is a lot of chaos and a lot of confusion. This obviously contributes to the vulnerability of the Chinese students to the influence of pornography. Further evidence of the importance of cultural mentality can also be found in the U.S. students' recommendation of imprisonment terms and their responses to the feminist movement. With the widespread concern over and hatred for rampant violent crimes in the United States, and with long years of education in political correctness, it is just natural for the U.S. students to condemn rape and support the feminist movement—regardless of their exposure to pornography.

Even if pornography could influence people's perception of sexual acts in some cultures and make them estimate more people doing anything pertaining to sex, as Zillmann and Bryant (1982) found, would such an influence make people's perception of reality more accurate or more distorted? This is a question that previous researchers have left unanswered.

To check on this, the Chinese students' estimates of anal and oral sex acts were compared with data on such acts reported in a twenty-seven-city random sample survey in China in 1989 (Pan 1993). It was found that the intermediate-exposure group's estimates were the closest to the survey findings (see table 9.1.). A comparison was also made between the U.S. students' estimates in the same categories with percentages reported in the first national scientific survey in the United States in 1994 (Michael et al.). It was found that the heavily exposed group's estimates were closest to the survey figures (see table 9.9). These comparisons seem to suggest that pornography may serve an educational function when it comes to the perception of sexual practices, although we cannot say that pornography might have played an educational role in "correcting" the subjects' perception of sexual practices in the real world. This is because there was no statistically significant difference between the within-country exposure groups on the estimates of these sexual practices except for the estimate of oral sex practices by the Chinese subsample. The results of the comparison may warrant more research and prompt us to think about whether pornography does serve an educational role, especially in places where information about sex is scanty.

The data of the current study apparently leads to two conclusions. First, there is no strong evidence to suggest that pornography affects people's perceptions of sex acts, attitude toward women, and dispositions toward "sex liberalization," as measured by subjects' self-reported answers. Second, the impact of pornography, however unclear it may be, is not universal. The cul-

Table 9.9.   A Comparison of Chinese and U.S. Students' Perception of Sexual Acts and Real-Life Acts Reported in National Surveys

			Estimates by Subjects of This Study		
Country		National Survey	No Exposure	Intermediate Exposure	Heavy Exposure
China	Oral sex	31%	46.9%[a]	29.9%[b]	35.9%[ab]
	Anal sex	7	20.9	17.2	25.5
U.S.	Oral sex	72.5	63.3	63.6	68.8
	Anal sex	23	27.6	25.4	25.8

Note: The percentages of reported acts in China are drawn from a 27-city random survey in 1989 by Shui-min Pan, reported in "Sex in Recent China," *Sociological Research,* March 20, 1993. The percentages of reported acts in the United States are drawn from the first national scientific survey in the United States in 1994, reported in Michael, Gagnon, Laumann, and Kolata, *Sex in America* (Boston: Little, Brown).

tures that are in the initial-contact stage in their experience with pornography seem to be more vulnerable to the impact of pornography, whereas the cultures in later stages seem to develop a "callousness" toward pornography, or an inoculative ability to buffer pornography's impact.

NOTE

This chapter was written in cooperation with the Department of English, City University of Hong Kong.

REFERENCES

Allen, M., D. Alessio, and K. Brezgel. 1995. A meta-analysis summarizing the effects of pornography II: Aggression after exposure. *Human Communication Research* 22: 258–283.

Attorney General's Commission on Pornography. 1986. Final report of the *Attorney General's Commission on Pornography.* Washington, D.C.: U.S. Department of Justice.

Carins, B., N. Paul, and J. Winshner. 1962. Sex censorship: The assumptions of anti-obscenity laws and the empirical evidence. *Minnesota Law Review* 46: 1009–1041.

Commission on Obscenity and Pornography. 1970. *The report of the Commission on Obscenity and Pornography.* New York: Bantam.

Donnerstein, E. 1983. Erotica and human aggression. In Russel G. Green and Edward Donnerstein, eds., *Aggression: Theoretical and empirical reviews.* New York: Academic Press.

———. 1984. Pornography: Its effect on violence against women. In Neil Malamuth and Edward Donnerstein, eds., *Pornography and sexual aggression.* Orlando: Academic Press.

———. 1991. Mass media, sexual violence, and male viewers: Current theory and research. In Michael Kimmel, ed., *Men confront pornography.* New York: Meridian.

Donnerstein, E., M. Donnerstein, and R. Evans. 1975. Erotic stimuli and aggression: Facilitation or inhibition? *Journal of Personality and Social Psychology* 32, no. 2: 237–244.

Dworkin, A., and C. MacKinnon. 1985. *Pornography and civil rights: A new day for women's equality.* Minneapolis: Organizing Against Pornography.

Fisher, W. A., and G. Grenier. 1994. Violent pornography, antiwoman thoughts, and antiwoman acts: In search of reliable effects. *Journal of Sex Research* 31, no. 1: 23–38.

Gulik, R. 1951. *Erotic colour prints of the Ming period.* Privately printed.

———. 1961. *Sexual life in ancient China.* Leiden: Brill.

Howard, J., M. Liptzin, and C. Reifler. 1973. Is pornography a problem? *Journal of Social Issues* 29, no. 3: 133–145.

Kutchinsky, B. 1985. Pornography and its effects in Denmark and the United States: A rejoinder and beyond. *Comparative Social Research* 8: 301–330.

———. 1991. Legalized pornography in Denmark. In Michael Kimmel, ed., *Men confront pornography.* New York: Meridian.

Li, Y. 1993. Dalu huangchao gungun lai [The rolling waves of pornography in mainland China]. *The Nineties,* June, pp. 44–49.

Liu, I., J. Chung, and V. Wong. n.d. http://humanum.arts.cuhk.edu.hk/~cmc/eng-spark/gp02/gp02.html.

Michael, R., J. Gagnon, E. Laumann, and G. Kolata. 1994. *Sex in America: A definitive survey.* Boston: Little, Brown.

Miller v. California 413 U.S. 5 (1973).

Pan, S. 1993. Dangqian zhongguo de xingcunzai [Sexuality in today's China]. *Shehuixue yanjiu* [Sociological research] 442: 104–110.

Roth v. United States; Alberts v. California 354 U.S. 476 (1957).

Shi, F. 1993. *Zhongguo xingwenhua shi* [A history of Chinese sex culture]. Haerbin: Heilongjiang Remin Chubanshe [Heilongjinag People's Publishing House].

State Press and Publication Bureau. 1988. Guanyu rending yinhui ji seqing chubanwu de zanxing guiding [Temporary rules on the identification of pornographic and obscene material]. In *Chu liuhai shiyong fagui shouce* [A practical handbook on laws and regulations concerning the elimination of six evils]. 1990. Beijing: Police Officers Education Publishing House.

Television and Entertainment Licensing Authority. n.d. The Control of Obscene and Indecent Articles Ordinance. Hong Kong: Government Printer.

Tong, X. 1993. Woguo yinhui wupin de shehui weihai [The social harms of pornography in our country]. *Sociological Research* 453: 52–61.

Wang, J., and S. Xu. 1993. Xinsheng maiyin nuxing goucheng, shengxintizheng yu xingwei zhi yuanqi [The makeup, physical and psychological features, and behavioral causes of the newly emerging prostitutes]. *Sociological Research* 442: 111–123.

Zhang, X. 1989. Fanlan de "huangchao" [The "deluge" of pornography]. *Banyue tan* [Biweekly chat], p. 4.

Zillmann, D. 1986. Effects of prolonged consumption of pornography. In E. P. Mulvey and J. L. Haugaard, eds., *Report of the surgeon general's workshop on pornog-*

raphy and public health. Washington, D.C.: U.S. Department of health and Human Services, Office of the Surgeon General.

Zillmann, D., and J. Bryant. 1982. Pornography, sexual callousness, and the trivialization of rape. *Journal of Communication* 324: 10–21.

———. 1988. Effects of prolonged consumption of pornography on family values. *Journal of Family Issues* 94: 518–544.

10

A Lethal Combination: Sex and Violence in the World of Korean Television

Jong G. Kang

Over the past three decades, the television industry has come under continued attack because of the heavy diet of sex, violence, and mayhem it feeds to enormous audiences. Critics fear it is a diet that produces a variety of ill effects (Weaver and Wakshlag 1986). Nevertheless, the television industry continues to use sex and violence in its programming because it is an easy and relatively inexpensive way to get audiences. In the world of television, sexual message is most often depicted as a competition, a way to define masculinity and an exciting amusement for people of all ages (Silver 1995). Fights, shootouts, brutality, car chases, and sadistic violence are common gimmicks designed to capture and hold viewers' attention (Berger 1989). In fact, the television industry has claimed that television is violent because it is a mirror of society (Silver 1995).

Television programs that combine sex and violence targeted at children and teenagers are matters of great concern. Research on sex and violence has established that a steady diet of television influences viewers' conceptions of social reality in such a way that heavy viewers' beliefs about the real world are distorted by the images of television. The cultivation perspective suggests that heavy viewers of sexual and violent content believe the real world mirrors the world they see on television. Studies have shown that heavy viewing of violent programming leads to an increased likelihood of developing aggressive attitudes and behaviors. Furthermore, heavy viewing of sexual content may lead to increased sexual experience (Brown and Steele 1995).

For a number of years, communication researchers have been profiling the amount of sex and violence on U.S. television. Results from their studies have indicated that there are overwhelming amounts of sex and violence on television. Most communication researchers acknowledge that systematic analysis of television's content (known as "message system analysis") is extremely important. It identifies and assesses the most recurrent and stable patterns of television content, such as the consistent images, portrayals, and values that cut across most types of programs (Morgan 1990). Unfortunately, little attention has been paid to message system analysis in cross-cultural settings.

Message system analysis is a flexible tool for making systematic, reliable, and cumulative observations about television content. The assumption underlying this approach is that certain themes in television content are systematically related to each other and are repeated over and over again. Message system analysis allows researchers to identify almost any aspect of the television world, so they can then test its contribution to viewers' conceptions of the real world. Accordingly, it is very difficult to conduct meaningful television research in the absence of reliable, comprehensive message system data. In this regard, Tamborini and Choi (1990, p. 159) assert that communication researchers "must first do content analyses to determine the coherent set of images and messages produced by television for a given culture in order to do research on cultivation in cross-cultural settings."

INTERNATIONAL IMPLICATIONS OF
MESSAGE SYSTEM ANALYSIS

All societies produce explanations of reality for themselves and for their posterity (Gerbner et al. 1980a). In every culture, this socially constructed reality produces a coherent, homogeneous picture of what exists, what is important, what relates to what, and what is right. Television is today's central agency of the established order, and as such it serves primarily to maintain, stabilize, and reinforce—not subvert—conventional values, beliefs, and behaviors (Gerbner et al. 1980a). The goal of entertaining the largest audience at the minimum expense demands that these messages follow conventional social morality.

Since the 1960s, a considerable amount of research has been conducted on the power structure of the world of U.S. television drama, especially on the expression of sexual message and physical force as a scenario of social relationships. The findings reveal that the symbolic world of U.S. dramatic television is not like the real world. Almost since the inception of the medium,

U.S. television has painted a lousy, mean, hostile, and violent picture of the world (Gerbner 1972). However, we know very little about other countries' symbolic messages produced by television for their audiences. Although the 1980s saw a flurry of attempts to replicate message system analysis in Sweden, England, Germany, the Netherlands, Canada, and Australia, most of them focused heavily on empirical associations between television viewing and conceptions of social reality. Systematic message system analysis on available television programming in a given culture is missing in most cross-cultural research. Although message system analysis is a widely accepted methodology for establishing the composition and structure of the symbolic world, communication researchers have rarely attempted to challenge this methodology. This study attempts to examine the message system analysis data in the case of sex and violence in the world of Korean television.

TELEVISION IN KOREA

Since the Korean Broadcasting System (KBS) put its first television program on the air in December 1961, KBS transmission hours have increased from 42 hours per week in 1961 to 113 hours per week in 1999. Following KBS-TV, Munwha Broadcasting Company (MBC) aired its first program in August 1969. Since then, MBC has increased programming from 46 hours per week in 1969 to 112 hours per week in 1999. In 1990, the Seoul Broadcasting System (SBS) began broadcasts as a provincial broadcasting station covering Seoul and its surrounding areas. Currently, the four networks (KBS-1TV, KBS-2TV, MBC-TV, and SBS-TV) offer seven hours of daytime broadcasting beginning at 6 A.M. and then resume broadcasting from 4 P.M. to 1 A.M. There is no broadcasting from 1 P.M. to 4 P.M. on weekdays. However, the four networks operate an additional three hours (1 P.M. to 4 P.M.) on Saturday and Sunday. A typical programming schedule for Korean television networks begins at 6 A.M. with brief news reports. Morning programming offers mainly news, information, drama, and cultural/educational programs. For example, the four networks provide morning news, morning talk shows, home-journal shows, discussions, soap operas, and children's programs from 6 A.M. to 1 P.M.

Similar to the U.S. practice of beginning evening broadcasts with syndicated programs and cartoons followed by local news and national news before prime time, Korean networks begin their afternoons with a news brief at 4 P.M., followed by a one-hour time slot reserved for network children's programming. Generally, children's programs include cartoons, puppet shows, dramas, and educational programs. Another news brief at 7 P.M. introduces prime time. The four networks fill the next three hours with programs ostensibly suitable for family viewing, including dramas, game shows, soap operas, variety shows, news magazines, situation comedies, action adventures, occasional sports, and specials. Traditionally, networks also broadcast one hour of nine o'clock news during prime time. This news broadcast attracts many viewers and produces extremely high ratings. Over the course of the evening, each network also provides brief news reports and sports news. Late evening hours (from 10 P.M. to 1 A.M.) are usually devoted to imported programs, dramas, movies, and talk shows. The four networks sign off their broadcasting at 1 a.m. after the day's wrap-up news brief.

Weekend programming is similar to weekday programming except that it is designed to attract specific types of viewers who are demographically desirable to advertisers. Each network places weekend morning viewers in one of four categories: children, teenagers, young adults, and adults. Each network presents programs for each specialized audience. For example, MBC-TV and KBS-2TV target older children and teenagers by providing quiz shows and teen dramas, while KBS-1TV offers reruns of soap operas and talent contests for adult viewers. Weekend afternoon programming (12 P.M. to 4 P.M.) is usually filled with sports broadcasts, movies, and reruns. On weekend nights, the schedule is slightly modified to include more variety shows, situation comedies, and weekend soap operas, followed by imported movies, mostly from the United States.

Initially, Korean television networks were heavily dependent on foreign imports, mostly American, for their programming. Overall, imported programs averaged approximately one-third of total programming hours in 1969. In recent years, however, the Korean television networks have decreased imported programming hours from 16 percent in 1983 to 10 percent in 1997. In the 113 hours of weekly programming scheduled as of September 1999, MBC-TV presented 7.6 hours of U.S. programming, compared with 8.6 hours at SBS-TV, 9.2 hours at KBS-2TV, and 4 hours at KBS-1TV. This programming included shows such as *ER, Renegade, Mr. Holland's Opus, Nemesis, Police Story, Odyssey, Ghost Story, Zero Target, Viper, Burning Zone, Orlando,* and *Double Spy.*

Korean television celebrated its thirty-ninth birthday in 2000. A great deal has changed in the past four decades. There were only three hundred television sets in Korea in 1956, but that number climbed to an estimated 6.27 million by 1980. Today, television has become the favored medium in Korea, and television viewing has become the favorite form of entertainment for the mass audience. As of May 2000, Koreans owned close to 14 million television sets, a penetration rate of nearly 100 percent.

DEFINING SEX AND VIOLENCE ON
KOREAN TELEVISION

Using the postulates and methodology of the message system analysis, this study began with the selection of a two-month sample of four Korean networks' programming broadcast nationally between May and September of 1998.[1] A total of 143 programs, or a collective total of 219.8 hours of programming, from the four Korean television networks (KBS-1TV, KBS-2TV, SBS-TV, MBC-TV) were coded. Message system analysis focuses on sex and violence in the television program. An incident was considered sexual if it contained a depiction of sexual behavior, seductive display of the body, or an explicit or implied reference to intimate sexual behavior, sexual organs, or sex-related activities (Sapolsky and Tabarlet 1991). Content categories included were (1) "explicit sexual behavior," (2) "aggressive sexual behavior," (3) "suggestive sexual behavior," and (4) "verbal suggestiveness."

The four types of sexual behavior were categorized based on the content of a scene including explicit, aggressive, suggestive, or verbal depiction of sexual behavior. An incident was considered "explicit sexual behavior" if it contained physical depictions of sexual intercourse and an explicit exposure of the body (sexual organs) when both characters were involved in sexual intercourse. "Aggressive sexual behavior" was defined as explicit sexual actions or sexually suggestive exposure of the body, erotic touching that involves interpersonal touching with clear sexual overtones, and physically suggestive breast shots and derriere shots. "Suggestive sexual behavior" includes touching, kissing, hugging, and partial nudity. "Verbal suggestiveness" was defined as the expression of sexual desire or affection and references to sex, including jokes about sexual behavior.

For violence, this study employed Gerbner's definition. According to Gerbner et al. (1980a), violence is the overt expression of physical force (with or without a weapon, against oneself or other) compelling action against one's will on pain of being hurt or killed, or actually hurting or killing. Based on this definition, clear-cut violence in the sample was coded independently by the trained coders. For example, no idle threats, verbal abuse, or gestures without credible violent consequences were included. For the analysis of violence in the program samples, this study examines the frequency and rate of violent episodes, and the number of roles in which characters were the perpetrators of violence (violents), its victims, or both.[2]

PREVALENCE OF SEX AND VIOLENCE IN THE WORLD OF KOREAN TELEVISION

Together, 87 out of 141 programs sampled contained some form of sexual behavior. The 87 episodes included 244 incidents of sexual or sexually related situations—an average of 2.9 acts per program. The most frequent sexual activity was "suggestive sexual behavior." A total of 70 episodes contained 176 incidents of "suggestive sexual behavior," indicating an average of 2.5 suggestive sexual acts. Overall, Korean television networks offered viewers 1.3 instances of suggestive sex per program.

A total of forty-two "aggressive sexual behaviors" were found in fourteen programs. Most aggressive sexual behavior depicted in Korean television was intimate sexual behavior including passionate embraces, sexual touching, and physical suggestiveness of sexual acts. Verbal sexual behaviors were rarely shown in the world of Korean television. There were nineteen incidents of "verbal suggestiveness" in fourteen programs. Most verbal content consisted of dialogue related to expression of sexual desire or affection and references to sex, including jokes about sexual behavior.

Least prevalent in the world of Korean television was the appearance of "explicit sexual behavior." There was only one incident of "explicit sexual behavior" that explicitly contained physical depictions of sexual intercourse. It seems that Korean television networks tend to reflect governmental regulations and societal acceptance of not having explicit sexual behaviors in entertainment programming. In Korea, control of the broadcasting system affects networks' programming. As the Korean government regulates the content of television programming very closely, television networks tend to produce less controversial programming to stay out of trouble with the Korean government (Kim et al. 1994).

Violence on Korean television was nearly as rampant as that on U.S. television. A total of 124 out of 141 programs sampled contained some violence. The percentage of programs containing any violence accounted for 87.9 percent. And 482 out of all 1,119 characters were involved in some type of violence. Among them, victims slightly outnumbered violents by a ratio of -1.04, meaning that there were 1.04 victims for every violent. Overall, men were significantly more likely than women to become involved in some violence. Nearly one out of every three men, as compared to one out of every seven women, was involved in some violence. Men were significantly more likely than women to be victims. Adults were more likely than children and elderly to be involved.

In the world of Korean television, "good" characters were significantly more likely to become involved in violence than "bad" characters. Among "good" characters, victims outnumbered violents by a ratio of -1.07, meaning that there were 1.07 victims for every violent. By contrast, among "bad" characters, violents outnumbered victims by a ratio of $+1.74$, meaning that there were 1.74 violents for every victim. In addition, the finding indicated that there is a significant number of killings in the Korean television world. Thirty programs depicted killings. In 32 programs, 111 characters were involved in the killings.

To provide further information on sex and violence in the world of Korean television, message system analysis examined the presentation of sex and violence in the following four program-type categories: drama, cartoon, movie, and reality programming. A detailed breakdown of sex and violence across different program genres is presented in tables 10.1 and 10.2. The findings revealed that 83.9 percent of all movies contained sexual content, followed by drama (72.6 percent), reality programs (25 percent), and cartoons (20.7 percent).[3] More than one-third of characters in the movies were involved in some sexual activity (37.1 percent), averaging 3.95 acts per episode, or 2.8 acts per hour. As one might expect, cartoons had the least sexual content, with 1.08 acts per episode or 1.15 acts per hour. More than three out of four dramas depicted sexual behavior, and 19.2 percent of all characters in the dramatic programs were involved in some sexual activity. One out of every four reality shows featured sexual content, but only 4.7 percent of characters were involved in sexual material.

Reality shows contained the most violence (100 percent), followed by cartoons (96.6 percent), movies (93.5 percent), and drama (78.1 percent). As shown in table 10.2, all movie shows sampled in this study contained some violence, averaging 11.8 acts per episode, or 8.74 acts per hour. One out of two characters in reality shows was involved in some violence (50 percent). In addition, male characters were slightly more likely to be victims rather than victimizers in violent conflicts. Among males, bad characters were more likely to commit crime than their counterparts and were more likely to be involved in violence.

In twenty-eight out of twenty-nine programs, more than one out of two cartoon characters got heavily involved in violence (54.9 percent) with 11.7 acts per program, or 11.87 acts per hour. Overall, male characters were more likely to be involved in some violence than female characters: adult men, male children, and robots (or unidentified machines) were more likely to be involved in some violence than adult women and female children, but they show high positive violent-victim ratio when involved. "Good" cartoon characters were victims of the most violence relative to their ability to inflict it on others. Nearly two-thirds of characters in the movies were involved in some violent acts (62 percent). Movies imported from the United States significantly contributed to the prevalence of violent acts in Korean television.

Table 10.1. Prevalence of Sex on Korean Television

Type (Number of Total Episodes)	Program Involved (%)	Number of Total Characters	Characters Involved (%)	Sexual Content Per Program	Sexual Content Per Hour
Movie (31)	26 (83.9)	205	76 (37.1)	3.95	2.8
Drama (73)	53 (72.6)	619	119 (19.2)	1.9	.93
Reality (8)	2 (25)	64	4 (4.7)	1.17	1.15
Cartoon (29)	6 (20.7)	251	10 (4)	1.08	1.15

Table 10.2.   Prevalence of Violence on Korean Television

Type (Number of Total Episodes)	Program Involved (%)	Number of Total Characters	Characters Involved (%)	Violent Content Per Program	Violent Content Per Hour
Movie (31)	29 (93.5)	205	127 (62)	11.8	8.74
Drama (73)	57 (78.1)	619	185 (29.9)	4.75	2.8
Reality (8)	8 (100)	64	32 (50)	8.5	7.2
Cartoon (29)	28 (96.6)	—	—	11.7	11.87

Examination of the message system analysis showed that four Korean television networks broadcast thirty-one movies in a two-month period, of which twenty-three movies were imported from the United States.

In the world of Korean dramatic television, nearly one out of three characters (29.9 percent) were involved in some type of violence.[4] Male victims outnumbered violents, while female violents outnumbered victims. Children and adolescents of both sexes, however, were seldom involved in violence. But as they age, their chances of involvement in violence increase. Interestingly, "good" characters were more likely than bad characters to be both violents and victims. In general, the characters most involved in violence in the world of Korean television were classified as adults and "bad" characters. It seemed that male and "bad" characters of both sexes were mostly likely to be both violents and victims. However, children and elderly were the "safest" people in the world of Korean television.

IMPACT OF SEX AND VIOLENCE ON KOREAN TELEVISION

The message system analysis revealed a significant amount of sexual depiction. Overall, more than two-thirds of programs included sexual content. Among the four types of television genres, the findings indicated that movies contained the highest amount of sexual and violent contents. Suggestive sexual content in the movies was predominantly used to refer to the common types of sexual behaviors—touching, kissing, hugging, and partial nudity.

The majority of programs except cartoons contained sexual material. Despite the widespread presence of sexual content in Korean television, sexual content involving children and teenagers was not found. The Korean television networks have been encouraged by the government to air what they perceive as "quality" programs. Accordingly, all four television networks have striven to meet the moral and ethical guidelines stipulated by the government. The Korean culture, in addition, is one in which the traditions dominant in Asian culture are mixing more and more with new Western thinking. The results create a situation in which Korean society is somewhat uncomfortable with the portrayal of something as private as sex, while at the same time demanding its depiction in entertainment. Korean viewers do not accept the level of sex present in the programming of some Western nations. The Korean government responds to these societal and cultural values by imposing regulations on the entertainment industry to limit the sexual content contained on television (Kim et al. 1994). In this respect, Korean television networks try hard to ensure that sexual content meets government standards while still satisfying viewer demand. For this reason, Korean television appears more restrictive than U.S. or European television in depicting sexual content (Kang et al. 1993). Thus explicit sexual content is seldom broadcast.

In general, Korean television appeared to portray sex without any reference to subsequent consequences. The vast majority of sexual content was not accompanied by any messages about sexual risks or responsibilities. Unfortunately, in their efforts to attract young viewers, Korean television networks emphasized entertainment values that are loaded with manifest sexual content and made little effort to teach young viewers the dangers of unprotected sex leading to pregnancy and other complications.

The message system analysis also revealed a significant amount of violence: more than half of all programs on Korean television contained some kind of violence and nearly one out of two characters were involved in it. The findings indicated a trend of high violent depiction in movies. More than one-third of characters in the movies were involved in some violent acts. Movies produced in the United States were a significant factor in increasing the number of violent acts in Korean television. Because U.S. movies shown on Korean television have a high rate of violence, the findings show violence to be much more prevalent than it would have been if the research focused solely on Korean original programs. Although the U.S. violence index was higher than the Korean violence index (Kang et al. 1993), these findings clearly illustrated that violence in the world of Korean television was nearly as rampant as that of U.S. television. Thus the possible social and cultural effects of these U.S. movies have concerned parents and educators in Korea. This concern has prompted a flurry of activities over the past year in Korea: the passage of legislation requiring the family television viewing hour; an agreement by the television industry to develop a system for rating television programs regarding their sexual and violent content; and new rules requiring television networks to produce more family-oriented programming.

According to the trade press, international growth in new technologies such as cable and satellite has created a "significant increase in the demand for American television product, and sales are thriving" (Coates 1985, p. 12). U.S. entertainment programs dominate the ratings and the program schedules in many countries. This domination has generated a great deal of concern about the impact of these programs on the importing societies. As U.S.

television programs flood the market in other countries, it becomes increasingly important to understand their influence on audiences in these countries (Gunter 1979). With this influx of American programming into other countries, many countries, like Korea, expressed concern about the possible effects of sex and violence depicted in U.S. programs. While evidence of the sexual and violent content depicted in the imported programs continues to grow, little is known about the degree to which viewer behaviors are shaped by that programming. Future studies should therefore focus on the degree with which viewer beliefs and values are transformed to conform to the world of U.S. television.

In sum, the pervasiveness of sex and violence in this study was based on the cultural aspects depicted in the world of Korean television. But we should understand that Koreans still live in a society blending Western and traditional cultures. Currently, Korea is experiencing unprecedented moral trauma: rising divorce rate, epidemic teenage promiscuity, and the demise of family values. In this process, we should understand that symbolic messages and images produced by television in a given culture might reflect the country's social values, media system, and cultural diversity. Accordingly, any investigation that overlooked the structural differences in a given economic, social, cultural, and political background would be incomplete and meaningless. This problem may possibly be solved through more cross-cultural comparison involving other countries and cultures. It is hoped that the message system analysis conducted in this study can serve as a foundation leading to the examination of foreign television's content.

NOTES

1. The data was obtained from the latest measurements of Cultural Indicator Project of Korean television programs reported by Ho Sun Sung. See *Report on the 1998 Korean Cultural Indicator* (Seoul, Korea: Korean Broadcasting Commission 1998).

2. The MSA data were collected by the Korean Broadcasting Commission and analyzed by Ho Sun Sung, and I greatly appreciate his making them available for these analyses. I would like to thank Hye Sun Jeon who were involved in the data collection efforts drawn on in this chapter.

3. The sample includes selected programming on all four networks aired during a two-month period (May and September) in 1998. After five intensive training periods, each program was coded independently by six trained observers.

4. For the analysis of violence in the program samples, this study examined the frequency and rate of violent episodes, and the number of roles in which characters were the perpetrators of violence (violents), its victims, or both. According to Gerbner et al., these data are called "prevalence," "rate," "role," "involvement," and "risk ratio," respectively:

Prevalence is the percent of programs containing any violence in a particular program sample. Prevalence is calculated both as percent of programs (percentP) and as percent of program hours containing violence.

Rate expresses the frequency of these acts in units of programming and in units of time.

Role is defined as the portrayal of characters as violents (committing violence) or victims (subjected to violence), or both and yields several measures. They are percent of violents out of all characters in a sample; percent of victims out of all characters in a sample; all those involved as violents or as victims or both (percentV); percent of killers (those committing fatal violence); percent of killed (victims of lethal violence); and all those involved in killing, either as killers or as killed (percentK).

Involvement occurs in a scene of overt physical force, and an "involved" character may commit or suffer violence or both. For example, a victimized character is clearly hurt, killed, or compelled to act under a credible threat of pain or death. A violent perpetrates these actions, and both characters' choices are written into the script as part of characterization and plot element.

Risk ratio signifies a character's chances for positive or negative outcome once involved in violence. It indicates the burden of risk with which each dramatic and social type enters the arena. The violence-victim ratio denotes chances for being a violent or a victim. The killer-killed ratio marks the risk of killing or being killed. Involvement in violence and in killing may range from 0 to 100 percent of a particular group. Risk ratios are obtained by dividing the more numerous of these two roles by the less numerous with each group. A plus sign indicates more violents and killers, a minus sign more victims and killed. A ratio of 1.00 means that they are even, a ratio of 0.00 means that there are none. When there are only violents or only killers shown, the ratio will read + 0.00. Conversely, when there are only victims or only killed, the ratio will read 0.00.

REFERENCES

Andison, F. S. 1977. TV violence and viewer aggression: A cumulation of study results, 1956–1976. *Public Opinion Quarterly* 41: 314–331.

Berger, G. 1989. *Violence and the media.* New York: Franklin Watts.

Brown, J. D., and J. R. Steele. 1995. *Sex and the mass media.* Menlo Park, Calif.: Kaiser Family Foundation Press.

Clark, C. S. 1993. TV violence. *Congressional Quarterly* 312: 265–288.

Coates, C. 1985. World sales good despite strong dollars. *Electronic Media,* February 16, p. 26.

Corder-Bolz, C. 1981. Television and adolescents' sexual behavior. *Sex Education Coalition News* 3: 40.

Eron, L. D. 1982. Parent-child interaction, television, violence, and aggression of child. *American Psychologist* 1372: 197–211.

Gerbner, G. 1972. Violence and television drama: Trend and symbolic functions. In G. A. Comstock and E. A. Rubinstein, eds., *Television and Social Behavior,* vol. 1, *Content and Control.* Washington D.C.: Government Printing Office.

————. 1977. The real threat of television violence. In J. Fireman, ed., *TV book: The ultimate television book.* New York: Workman.

Gerbner, G., L. Gross, M. Jackson-Beeck, S. Jeffries-Fox, and N. Signorielli. 1978. Cultural indicators: Violence profile no. 9. *Journal of Communication* 28: 176–207.

Gerbner, G., L. Gross, M. Morgan, and N. Signorielli. 1980a. The mainstreaming of America: Violence profile no. 11. *Journal of Communication* 30: 10–29.

————. 1980b. Television violence, victimization, and power. *American Behavioral Scientist* 235: 705–716.

Gerbner, G., and G. Larry. 1976. Living with television: The violence profile. *Journal of Communication* 26: 173–199.

Gunter, J. F. 1979. *The United States and the debate on the world information order.* Washington D.C.: Academy for Educational Development.

Hur, K. K. 1982. International mass communication research: A critical review of theory and methods. In M. Burgoon, ed., *Communication Yearbook* 6. Beverly Hills, Calif.: Sage.

Josephson, W. L. 1987. Television violence and children's aggression: Testing the primary, social script, and disinhibition predictions. *Journal of Personality and Social Psychology* 535: 882–890.

Kang, J. G., W. Y. Kim, K. Kim, and S. Kapoor. 1993. The case of violence in prime-time television drama in the U.S., the Netherlands, and Korea: Message system analysis. *World Communication* 22: 30–36.

Kim, K., W. Y. Kim, and J. G. Kang. 1994. *Broadcasting in Korea.* Seoul: Nanam Publishing House.

Morgan, M. 1990. International cultivation analysis. In N. Signorielli and M. Morgan, eds., *Cultivation analysis: New directions in media effects research.* Newbury Park, Calif.: Sage.

Morgan, M., and N. Signorielli. 1990. Cultivation analysis: Conceptualization and methodology. In N. Signorielli and M. Morgan, eds., *Cultivation analysis: New directions in media effects research.* Newbury Park, Calif.: Sage.

Peterson, J. L., K. A. Moore, and F. F. Furstenberg Jr. 1991. Television viewing and early initiation of sexual intercourse: Is there a link? *Journal of Homosexuality* 21: 93–118.

Peterson, R. A., and J. R. Kahn. 1984. Media preferences of sexually active teens. Paper presented at the meeting of the American Psychological Association, Toronto, Canada.

Pingree, S., and R. P. Hawkins. 1981. U.S. Programs on Australian television: The cultivation effect. *Journal of Communication* 31: 97–105.

Ridley-Johnson, R., T. Surdy, and E. O'Laughlin. 1991. Parent survey on television violence viewing: Fear, aggression, and sex differences. *Journal of Applied Developmental Psychology* 12: 63–71.

Sapolsky, B., and J. Tabarlet. 1991. Sex in primetime television: 1979 versus 1989. *Journal of Broadcasting and Electronic Media* 35: 505–516.

Silver, M. 1995. Sex and violence on TV. *U.S. News,* September. www.usnews.com/usnews/ISSUE/SEX&VIOL.HTM.

Tamborini, R., and J. Choi. 1990. The role of cultural diversity in cultivation analysis.

In N. Signorielli and M. Morgan, eds., *Cultivation analysis: New directions in media effects research.* Newbury Park, Calif.: Sage.

Weaver, J., and J. Wakshlag. 1986. Perceived vulnerability to crime, criminal victimization experience, and television viewing. *Journal of Broadcasting and Electric Media* 30: 141–158.

11

Women, Media, and Violence in the New South Africa: Disciplining the Mind (the Body Is Irrelevant)

Arnold S. de Beer and Karen Ross

Violence is commonly acknowledged to be one of the most pressing problems troubling the new South Africa. Pervasive and endemic violence exists at every level of society. It is blamed for many of society's ills: the unwillingness of overseas businesses to invest, the "brain drain" of (mostly white) expertise, poverty, and increasing unemployment. But as Bowie (1997, p. 24) argues, more important is its "crippling effect, both physical and psychological, on the humanness of both the victims and the perpetrators of violence." Ten years into the new constitutional order, "the specter of crime continues to stalk the corridors of power and the psyches of ordinary citizens" (Van der Spuy in Mbeki 1999, p. 265).

The news media in South Africa is one of the primary definers of the many public debates on violence. One of the main issues on the news agenda is the way the media portrays violence against women. This is the topic of this chapter.

A BRIEF HISTORY OF NEWS MEDIA AND GENDER PORTRAYAL

The media is not only the portrayer of the periodic incidences of violence, but plays a crucial cultural function in its gendered framing of public aware-

167

ness and the discourses they present. But how does the media "do" this exactly? How is the media involved in the perpetuation of ideas and ideologies that protect the status quo, in which men largely remain in positions of authority and decision making in news organizations in South Africa. At the same time, the status quo undermines the potency of women to be greater than the sum of their body parts.

Much research, particularly studies using feminist perspectives, has concentrated on analyzing the way in which women are portrayed in popular media (see, e.g., McNeil 1975; Tuchman et al. 1978; Butler and Paisley 1980; Gallagher 1988; Davis 1990; Cumberbatch et al. 1994; Gunter 1995; Macdonald 1995; Raycheva 1995; Cowie 1998; European Commission 1999), or on how women consume media products (Wober 1981; Hobson 1990; Douglas 1994; Arthurs 1994; Millwood Hargrave 1994; Ross 1995a; Baehr and Gray 1996) or analyzed the experiences and position of women professionals working in media industries (Women's Broadcasting Committee 1993; Dougary 1994; Gallagher 1995; Carter et al. 1998; Van Zoonen 1998; Hartley 1998). It is outside the scope of this chapter to look at the second and third themes mentioned above, but we will discuss the ways in which women are persistently sexualized in and by news media (both broadcast and print) in reporting on violence. We will also argue that even women who occupy positions of authority (e.g., elected parliamentarians) within the socioeconomic contexts of their nation-state are, nonetheless, commodified by a media imperative that too often reduces them to a base sexuality (see Ross 1995b; Ross and Sreberny-Mohammadi 1997; Ross and Sreberny, forthcoming).

A growing body of women-centered theory looks critically at the way in which political and media institutions function to exclude or limit women from their operational orbits (see, e.g., Fraser 1989; Benhabib 1992; Van Zoonen 1994). However, less work has been done internationally and in South Africa on the ways in which women are reported as subjects and objects in media reports on violence within the context of women as victims of sex crimes and domestic violence.

Whether one subscribes to the theory of the power of the media to influence opinions and attitudes or not, the fact remains that media reports are influential (Katz 1987, p. 28; Ramaprasad 1983, pp. 122–123; Shaw 1979, pp. 96–97). They play a role in shaping public understanding of crimes against women and affect attitudes toward victimized survivors and perpetrators of violence. Eventually, these reports have an impact on the way abused women are perceived and the nature of assistance offered to them by the public, the police, and the criminal justice system.

In the long run, media reports influence politicians who legislate on these issues, as well as the parents and educators raising the next generation. Within the South African context, organizations such as the umbrella Soul City (1999) have started a number of campaigns to raise public awareness about violence against women. The media is considered important by these organizations because it can reflect women's experiences, raise public awareness, and encourage a critical, informed understanding of the situation. On the other hand, poor coverage can endorse existing perceptions that perpetuate violence against women and lead to the further victimization of survivors.

South African media have reported on the following types of violence experienced most by the country's women:

- sexual harassment
- rape
- domestic violence
- forced prostitution, or trafficking, of women
- female genital mutilation/circumcision (less common)
- being burned as witches (women who are thought to be "bad" witches who brought on "evil spells" in the community)
- rape-murders
- sexual serial killings
- intimate femicide by a husband or boyfriend

The issue we raise in this chapter is part of the debate raging in South Africa: does the media trivialize violence toward women, or does it increase people's awareness of the problem? Media researchers cannot afford to ignore the media whether it trivializes or raises awareness about critical social issues. Through research and publishing, "shoddy, biased reporting must be challenged, and informed, insightful coverage encouraged" (Vetten 1999, p. 1).

It is therefore of considerable interest, given the (virtually) unquestioned authority and veracity accorded to the news media, to explore precisely how women are routinely portrayed. The push toward globalization, with its attendant conglomeratization and reduction in diversity, forces an urgent exploration of how women are framed in a constantly shrinking news source pool, with fewer journalists doing more tasks.

Though a number of journalists in South Africa already actively contribute to the challenge of ending violence against women (Soul City 1999, p. 4), their efforts are often typically constrained by traditional news processes. Such constraints include deadlines, uninformed editors and copy editors, limited access to sources of information, as well as laws surrounding what may and may not be reported in relation to violence against women. Given the often sexist nature of newspaper content, the pressure to sell newspapers and magazines, or to attract advertising revenue leads not only to the sensationalization of stories but also to the skewing effect of the social phenomenon of violence against women.

We argue that the kinds of stories, perspectives, and interests we see and read in news media on violence against women are inextricably bound up with the kind of relations that take place in newsrooms themselves as sites of cultural production (see Carter, Branston, and Allen 1998). What is true of the media, especially in the West in general, is also applicable to South Africa: "We know from our own observations [that] the news the country is given is largely what is considered newsworthy by men—produced, directed, edited, and shot overwhelmingly by men" (Women's Broadcasting Committee 1993, p. 6).

Studies of women and their portrayal around the world show a consistent picture of denigration, sexualization, and trivialization when the media report stories featuring women. For example, research undertaken by the Dutch public sector broadcaster, NOS (1994), found a number of subtle ways in which news media are biased against women: in interviews, women are far more likely to be referred to by their first name rather than title; women are more likely to be addressed in familiar terms; when women's names are captioned on screen, they are less likely to have their occupation referred to; there is often a tendency for interviewers to be overly familiar with women interviewees, making jokes or paying compliments. Men are often brought on after women to reinforce or validate the points they made; women are more likely to be questioned about their emotions or private circumstances than men, who are usually asked about work or practical activities (e.g., see the personal information expected by the media from Ivy Matsepe-Casaburi when she was appointed first black and woman chairperson of the SABC board, in de Beer 1993).

These findings are mirrored by similar studies in other places, which look at the portrayal of women in single nation-states. In a "poacher-turned-gatekeeper" study, the British group Women in Journalism did an analysis of their own and their colleagues' practice in relation to gender and news reporting, using compare/contrast strategies to analyze three case studies (Christmas 1996). One of the concluding remarks was that "it seems clear that sometimes news desks go onto auto-pilot, trotting out clichés and stereotypes when, in fact, the woman in the story before them is unique" (Christmas 1996, p. 11).

BRTN, the public broadcaster in Belgium, did a study of women and television in which a panel of forty people gave their impressions on whether programs were dominated by men or women, and the kinds of images portrayed about each (Michielsens 1991). The secretary of state for emancipation in Belgium, Miet Smet, argued, "I am convinced that if a larger percentage of women are employed in creative and management functions, the image of women in the programs will be presented in a different and more correct way" (cited in Michielsens 1991, p. 4).

Neves (1994), in a study of gender and portrayal on Portuguese television, demonstrated significant differences in image between men and women and found that programs covering subjects of particular interest to women were often shown at awkward times: only men were seen to read news during the week—the women were brought in for the less serious weekend slots. Of all political interviewees in news and current affairs, 97 percent were men and 80 percent of all "expert" interviewees were male.

Many of the studies described above are now several years old and generally focus on only one national context. However, more recent comparative work (both European and international) demonstrates that the patterns of gendered representation that have been seen over the past twenty years have scarcely changed. Women still feature less frequently than men do in simple volume terms. When they do feature, they are often contained and constrained in a narrow range of story types that emphasize their sex and sexuality. It is also important to note that women are especially, more often than not, treated as victims rather than survivors of sexual abuse and violence. This happens via the commodification of their bodies as ornaments in print news media and, increasingly in the 1990s, as seductive sirens who lead important men to their political death.

The Global Media Monitoring Project (MediaWatch 1995), which grew out of the Women Empowering Communication Conference in Thailand in 1994, had women from seventy-one countries monitoring the output of the national daily news media for one day in January 1995. Among other findings were the following: only 9 percent of politicians interviewed were women; 18 percent of "professionals" were women; but 97 percent of homemakers were women. Importantly, nearly one-third of news reports involving women portrayed them as victims compared with 10 percent of male interviewees.

What does the discussion above say about women's role and function in modern societies? In a recent study, the European Commission (1999) looked at images of women in the media across the European Union. The rather gloomy conclusion of the report repeats the low volume of women's appearances in the media across all genres, and argues that women are overrepresented as victims, usually of violence, often sexual in nature (Bens 1992; Cumberbatch, Maguire, and Woods 1994; Bueno Abad 1996). Women are also often subject to overly sensational reporting (NOS 1994 1995; Michielsens and Ten Boom 1995). The portrayal of women in advertising has scarcely shifted in its stereotypical casting, and "the most that can be said is that change in media gender images is hesitant and contingent" (European Commission 1999, 13).

The EU report found that "old" forms of gender stereotype have recently been introduced as a consequence of political and economic upheaval, so that in the case of Germany, reunification has resulted in a new emphasis on women as mothers and housewives. In former Eastern European countries, demands for "Western" goods and services, including "easy sex," have encouraged the reemergence of women as sex objects in popular media discourse in those already ravaged and now ravished countries (Reading 1996; Marinescu 1995; Roventa-Frumusani 1995).

Several studies that have used qualitative approaches to women and news have, apart from the examples quoted above, looked at the media's treatment of women and violence, and in particular, the media's reporting of sex crimes (Kitzinger 1992; Lees 1995; Cuklanz 1996).

Peck (1987) argues that press reporting of rape and sexual assault is just another way in which men deliver thrills to each other under the guise of responsible, professional, and ethical reporting practices. Women who are the target of male violence are routinely portrayed by the media as "victims" rather than "survivors," placing them as eternally passive and dependent, and their lives entirely circumscribed by the whim of men. Pictures of assailants are captioned with phrases like "sex monster," "crazed animal," or "fiend," labels that distance these men from the ordinary variety, implying that normal men do not do these things, only maniacs (see the discussion below of the SABC rape advertisement with Charlize Theron as spokesperson).

In Britain, the law was changed in 1993 in order for a young man under the age of fourteen to be convicted of rape. The media carried reports that suggested that "the public" was concerned at "moves which could put more young children behind bars" (*Guardian*, November 12, 1994). But at the dawn of the new millennium, do we really believe that a fourteen-year-old adolescent is still an innocent child, given everything we know about childhood and sexuality? (The opposite of this question was raised in South Africa in 1999 when a father got a rather lenient prison sentence for raping his daughter, discussed below).

Soothill and Walby (1991) undertook one of the most thorough studies of sex crime reporting in the late 1980s in which every item on sex crimes identified in sixteen national and regional newspapers in Britain for one year was analyzed. The authors were highly critical of the way in which the press chose to report sex crimes, suggesting that the problems of newspaper reporting could be summarized under four headings:

- seeking the sensational (sex beasts and girls who deserve what they get)
- producing a cascade effect (everyone is tainted, including families)
- embracing a narrow definition of crime (stranger rape as normal)
- providing information and explanation (but not any illuminating analysis other than the sensational aspects)

The framing of sexual assaults as "unusual occurrences" carried out by "unnatural men" encourages the view that such crimes are both rare and the result of individual pathology requiring a law-and-order response rather than a general social problem requiring a social reform solution. In the late 1990s, the evidence of this kind of framing is still disturbingly similar.

Women who have experienced sexual assault are often described as "girls" irrespective of their age. The "moral status of the victim is often portrayed as ambivalent in murder trials [and] there is a range of behaviors and relationships which provide a variety of ways of blaming the victim" (Soothill and Walby 1991, p. 46). Judgments at a number of recent rape trials, including those described under the new category of "date rape," have provoked considerable criticism when judges have suggested that women who wear makeup or short skirts are asking for everything they get and that if they dress "provocatively," they shouldn't be surprised if men get the "wrong idea" and act on their erroneous assumptions. Such blatant sexism ignores the evidence that the majority of convicted rapists are friends or acquaintances of the women they attack. But the media message is clear: men can't help their biological urges and women must dress "modestly" if they are to avoid sexual assault. It is thus women who have to bear the burden, in every sense of the word, of men's inadequacies; women who must modify and change their behaviors; women who are the guilty ones.

If news media provide the way in which we get information about our world, news values seem to be inherently masculine, perpetuating sexist stereotyping through the presentation, style, tone, and language of stories that are about women. Nowhere is the articulation of power so clear as when the media show women as victims of male violence and aggression. Within the South African context this has become a major issue.

To accept the media's often held response that it merely reflects on real life is to accept that conflict is a natural and normal component of relations between women and men, rather than a symptom of the way in which men and women are socialized into viewing each other (Peck 1987). While the very nature of news genres demands conflict, excitement, and disaster, news stories tend to simplify contexts and provide only the most superficial of analyses. Television news in particular is especially prone to the snappy sound bite and sensational photo opportunity (de Beer and Steyn 1996).

What this (very) brief overview of research studies on women and news demonstrates is that the relationship between gender and news media is extremely problematic:

- Women who feature as subjects in news stories about sex, violence, and drugs are often stereotyped.
- Women rarely feature in news media because of the strong or powerful actions they have taken or the heroic deeds they have carried out.
- The way in which women are often framed as news subjects seems to suggest that women are at their most interesting when they are in the

most pain, when they experience the most suffering, when they are victims.

How, then, does the media in a newly democratized country (at least as far as its modern liberal-democratic constitution is concerned) deal with gender issues and violence against women?

What, if any, differences are discernible in a South African mediascape that comprises a good proportion of practitioners who are still relatively new to the game and who could, in principle, provide very different narratives because of their very different experiences when compared with news media professionals operating within the context of well-established democracies?

In 1997, the South African Gender Commission organized a symposium on issues relating to gender and media. The numerous papers presented and discussed during the conference painted a depressing, if unfortunately predictable, picture of gender-stereotyped representations. The images of women, which dominate in other parts of the world, were alive and well and thriving in the new South Africa: woman as clotheshorse, as mother, as victim.

Media practitioners attending the conference acknowledged a degree of "culpability" of the "charges" leveled against their profession and agreed that the media, as cultural producer and potential change agent, had some responsibility to construct more diverse and accurate portrayals of women (Le Roux 1997, p. 3).

As discussed with regard to other national media, women as victims of sex crimes and domestic violence are one of the most common themes of the media's reporting of women-focused news narratives. What brings an added twist in the South African context is the fact that many high-profile cases also concern high-profile men, often politicians, and they are often able to put out "their" side of the story while the women involved are rendered mute and invisible.

Lisa Vetten (1998, p. 8), at the Center for the Study of Violence and Reconciliation, argued that "as a general point, of course men accused of rape are entitled to present their version of events, as are the women concerned. But when women are not given this opportunity, then coverage of rape rapidly degenerates into a media trial by innuendo and speculation."

But the way in which rape cases are dealt with by the media is by no means uniform. Vetten (1998) goes on to argue that the often contradictory ways in which news stories concerning women rape victims are constructed could as easily encourage as discourage more women to come forward to file charges. Using the example of Nombonis Gasa, who was raped in 1997 on Robben Island, she suggests that the assault was widely and schizophrenically reported on, with Ms. Gasa being portrayed at various times as a liar, a survivor/heroine, an indulged government favorite, or MP Raymond Suttner's wife. One Afrikaans newspaper, along with some members of the SAPS [South African Police Service] denounced Ms. Gasa as a liar who concocted a false rape allegation; simultaneously, *Femina* (a woman's) magazine, honored her as a woman of courage. (Vetten 1998, p. 5)

The schizophrenia with which the media sometimes choose to report on sex crimes continues to provoke a tense debate over the precise role that the media plays in, on the one hand, trivializing sexual violence against women and routinely discrediting women's testimony, and on the other, helping to highlight what has become an almost endemic problem and thus encouraging more women to report such crimes to the police. Of course, as Vetten (1998; 1999) and others have said, the media probably does both simultaneously. Groups such as Women's MediaWatch ensure that some of the more outrageous excesses of the media in relation to gender and portrayal are closely scrutinized and publicized. This is done through newsletters and, more widely, through print and broadcast media.

But still the beat(ing) goes on, as we will argue and show in the next sections.

WOMEN, MEDIA, AND VIOLENCE IN
SOUTH AFRICA

In this section, we briefly discuss the issue of media, women, and violence within a political, juridical, and sociocultural media context in South Africa. Though we keep the discourse approach as a vehicle for our discussion, we acknowledge the interacting role social factors, operating in different social subsystems, could play in a problematic issue such as violence against women (e.g., see de Beer and Steyn 1996; de Beer 1998).

Political Context

South Africa's transformation to a democracy was made possible, as associate editor Matshikiza of the *Mail and Guardian* argues, by the extraordinary levels of sympathy generated by media reports of apartheid and the sustained efforts of many South Africans and others to overcome it, but

now we have the increasingly unpalable (*sic*) revelation of an evil in our midst that threatens both to undermine the gains of the last decade and to turn the legacy of international sympathy into a sense of derision and contempt. We (presently) live in a society that continues to be divided in many aspects, yet, appears to be united in a culture of lawlessness and criminality. (Matshikiza 1999, 62)

Apartheid was regarded as a crime against humanity, and its many forms were legally enshrined. Likewise discrimination against women was codified in legislation. Now South Africa shares with a very few countries in the world a constitution that outlaws gender discrimination (Piliso-Seroke 1999).

However, the South African constitution's Bill of Rights is inadequate to curb violence against women. What is still missing is a clear legal definition of all aspects of the right to equality; human dignity; life; freedom and security; slavery, servitude, and forced labor; privacy; freedom of association; freedom of movement and residence; access to courts; and the right to have access to health care, food, water, and social security.

Apart from deficiencies in the constitution, women also face many different hidden discriminatory laws. For instance, the definition of rape is too narrow. Also, while legal aid usually goes to males who have to appear in civil and criminal cases, the same support is not available for women who have to file for child support (Bezuidenhout 1999).

In order to correct some of the main constitutional and other legal restrictions, the Commission on Gender Equality (CGE) called on the government in 1999 to take gender considerations into account in its review of its proportional representation system—which has been a key factor in increasing the participation of women in politics, and consequently their role in lawmaking.

The GCE maintained that a "government for men by men cannot be a democracy for the people by the people." The commission urged all political parties to introduce voluntary 50 percent quotas for women candidates in the next election, to be held in 2004. (After the 1999 elections, women represented 27 percent of the members in parliament. Women have obtained almost 30 percent representation in provincial parliaments and cabinets, and 60 percent representation as deputy ministers [GCE media release 1999]).

The relative success of women in politics did not translate into social life, where the specter of violence against women remained "one of the single most important social issues" facing women in South Africa (Gray and Sathiparsad 1997).

As South African president Thabo Mbeki stated on Women's Day 1999, South Africans would never be able to say their country has achieved full freedom from the suppression of the past if women remain on a day-to-day basis the target of violent crime and if they have to live in continued fear (Gibson 1999).

This position was confirmed by independent election commissioner Thoko Mpumlwana. On a women's day, she said that South Africans must not believe that women's struggle to stop violence against them is unnecessary because South Africa is now a free country. "We have a good constitution, but reform is now necessary in order for women to take their rightful place" (GCE media release 1999).

Some of these reforms have to take place within the juridical context.

Juridical Context (Courts, Penal System, and Police)

Trust in the South African judicial system has taken a downward dive over the last ten years. Crime has become "a national disaster," but, argues Matshikiza (1999), "the endemic prevalence of crime has many sociological origins stemming from the country's apartheid past." In the 1980s, the "ongoing war against state authority and young people in the townships was sowing the seeds of a warped society, where war trauma would become an almost universal experience, and distinctions between right and wrong would become hopelessly blurred." The challenge ahead was how to deal with the legacy of the past and the reality of the present.

Efforts to deal with the reality of crime at the turn of the millennium were producing no results, mainly because the court and the police systems have come to a dangerously low level of ineffectiveness. More and more individuals and groups were either crying out to take the law in their own hands or to actually execute their revolt in the form of kangaroo courts and mob murders. Just before the 1999-elections, Pan-Africanist leader Stanley Mogoba called for the amputation of ears, legs, and other "revolting" limbs while the vigilante group, Pagad (People Against Gangsterism and Drugs), held Cape Town in fear through its militant tactics.

As the *Citizen* warned when the idea of castrating rapists became popular, "the prospect of inflicting pain upon rapists and rendering them impotent (would stir) the bloodlust of an angry society." Inkata Freedom Party MP and spokesperson Sue Vos maintained that "the thought of . . . chemical castration will concentrate a lot of male minds, probably more so than the death penalty. . . . Is it time we found out? Men are the problem, so why are we not prepared to consider the one thing that truly terrifies them?" (*Citizen,* October 29, 1999, p. 12).

The risk that victims of violence who are not supported and treated may themselves become perpetrators of violence was a hard reality. This was evident in the revenge fantasies and revengeful acts that were reflected in the public's demand for more violent policing of criminals and especially in the rise of self-administered justice and the wide support for the death penalty.

Women victims of rape or assault in South Africa face a criminal justice system that is too often unable or unwilling to assist them in their efforts to seek redress (MacDougall 1997). The police and the courts are often disinterested in the treatment of women, while medical staff members lack the training to collect and interpret the medical evidence crucial to an investigation and the eventual prosecution of rape or sexual assault.

Problems the public experienced with the police force were considered to be an important reason for the high rates of violence and crime (Cain 1997, pp. 2–3). These problems include the following:

- Police were rather poorly trained, demoralized, demotivated, and poorly paid.
- Very little recruiting for the police was done since 1994 and new yearly budgets did not allow for new recruits.
- The police force was not big enough to handle the workload.
- The public did not trust the police because of corruption present in the force over the past few years (*Beeld*, November 2, 1999, p. 1; see an editorial on police crime in *Beeld*, August 12, 1999, p. 14, and an editorial on the total incapability of the police to deal with the crime situation, *Beeld*, August 23, 1999, p. 10).

Apart from the failings of the police system, the court and penal systems offered no particular reason for hope. The courts in South Africa were at a point where they could not handle the cases before them (Cain 1997, pp. 3–4).

As far as the penal system was concerned, prisoners were almost escaping on a daily basis, while fewer and fewer criminal cases were reported to the police and hardly any ended up in court. A very small percentage of convictions were dealt with. Two examples would suffice: of all murders reported in 1998, 46 percent were referred to the state prosecutors. A quarter of those referred went on trial and of those less than 15 percent ended in convictions. Consequently one out of every 6.6 reported murders led to a conviction. The same pattern was found with regard to rape cases: the percentages were 44.9 percent and 17.7 percent. Eventually one out of eleven rapes that went to court led to conviction. In a media release on December 14, 1999, in Johannesburg UNICEF stated that one out of four young women and children in South Africa's first experience with sexual intercourse would be through acts of violence (SABC TV News at 8).

The inadequacy of the court system to protect women who have been raped was emphasized when a nineteen-year-old Pretoria student dropped charges against fourteen men who gang-raped her, even though the police said they had a solid case on the basis of forensic evidence. The victim said she did not want to face the ordeal of the trial and fear of retribution (*Citizen*, October 29, 1999, p. 4).

Women's groups suggested that one of the remedies for the situation was to dramatically make the minimum bail conditions tougher for people accused of crimes against women and children. By 1999, any person charged with rape in which the victim was raped more than once or by more than one person or when the accused knew he had HIV/AIDS at the time of the rape, had to satisfy the court that "exceptional circumstances" existed to be released on bail. The same onus rested on an accused when the person raped was seriously assaulted or under the age of sixteen; or when indecent assault on a minor or the infliction of grievous bodily harm was involved. People charged with rape under any other circumstance than those listed above, or any form of indecent assault on a minor, now also had to satisfy the court that the "interest of justice" would permit release on bail. Activists immediately demanded that it should be only in extremely exceptional circumstances that such accused were released on bail. (For the discussion, see Schönteich 1999; Pieters 1999; three 1999 *Beeld* editorials cited earlier; Abarder 1999; Thompson 1999).

Sociocultural Context: The Breakdown of Public Morality

Mass media provides for the expression of moral sensitivities through material that the audience uses to relate to personal views of morality, such as respect for authority and women. Though mass media depictions of crime and violence do seem to intensify personal concerns about safety, they also blunt the sense of morality (see Breytenbach 1998).

A number of concerned spokespeople in South Africa have blamed the rise of crime, and especially violence against women, on the decline in public morality. Many would probably agree that the violence stemming from the political struggle preceding the 1994 democratic elections had been transformed into criminal violence with socioeconomic foundations. As Radhika Coomaraswamy, the United Nation's rapporteur for violence against women, has contended (ANC 1997), "More than 40 years of apartheid had brutalized society in South Africa" (also see Mangold and Goldberg 1999).

Conservative spokespeople lay the blame for the spiraling specter of violence on the breakdown of specifically religious life and values in South Africa. Though the irony is more often than not missed—that apartheid was fostered in South Africa in the name of Christianity—conservative and right-wing groups believe that the trend of violence is directly related to the total breakdown of religious and moral authority.

According to Cain (1997, p. 4), South Africans used to be honest, hard-working, law-abiding people who respected the life and property of others in South Africa; this is no longer true. He also attributes this decline in morality mainly to a decline in belief in Christian values.

In reality, the exercise of apartheid was "profoundly dehumanizing . . . justified as a defense of Christian and democratic values, it required the systematic demolition of self-insight and of the sense of reality of other people" (Swift 1997). As Marais (1999) argues, what South Africa requires in post-apartheid society is a sense of peace that would require strategies aimed at restoring and improving stability and normative order.

Some women activists in South Africa, however, argue that religion might in effect have a negative subtle, though direct influence on violence against women. The Christian religion (see Booyens 1999), as practiced by most of the 70 percent of South Africans who call themselves Christians, is with little doubt patriarchal. Though the Bible never explicitly defines God's gender, "God the Father" is almost universally accepted as male. Booyens (1999, 28) argues that, on the basis of God's "maleness," some men in South Africa claim the power to pronounce: "God is a man—I am a man; therefore, by implication, I am just as almighty and all-knowing, and I have the power to order and demand at will." In a society still dominated by men who prefer sex above any other kind of activity, the consequence of such an attitude seems obvious (*Beeld*, September 24, 1998, p. 24).

However, one of the clearer signs that South Africa was no longer re-garded as a "Christian society" by government is found in the new constitu-tion. In the pre-1994 constitution, the preamble began: *In humble submis-sion to Almighty God.* In the new constitution these words were omitted. Carl Niehaus, a senior member of the ANC, explained the changes as fol-lows: A secular constitution would "base morality on enhancing public good" rather than on intimations of "God, revelation, heaven or hell." Con-sequently, South Africa would in time become a "secular state," in which norms other than Christian ones might prevail (South African Institute of Race Relations 1995/96 Survey, 474).

Deleting religious references in the constitution could be seen as part of the tendency toward more inclusive democracy. This is in direct conflict with the exclusiveness of the old South Africa. Nation building and the cre-ation of an inclusive South African community are now important principles fostered by the ANC government. This is also illustrated in the preamble of the new constitution:

> We, the people of South Africa . . . Believe that South Africa belongs to all that live in it, united in our diversity. We, therefore, through our freely elected repre-sentatives, adopt this Constitution as the supreme law of the Republic so as to heal the divisions of the past and establish a society based on democratic values, social justice and fundamental human rights. (1996, p. 1)

Built into the constitution is also the principle of equality:

> The Republic of South Africa is one, sovereign, democratic state founded on the following values: Human dignity, the achievement of equality, and the advance-ment of human rights and freedoms. (1996, p. 5)

The media placed a secular stamp on society by reducing religious broadcasting on television to about 1 percent of total airtime a week (Anon 1999). Even so, the Christian influence in South Africa is still reflected in the remaining religious airtime on SABC TV:

Christianity	70 percent
African traditional religions	10 percent
Hinduism	7.5 percent
Islam	7.5 percent
Judaism	5 percent

Whether the Christian influence of "love thy neighbor as you love yourself" is still applicable in the new South Africa becomes a moot point when one considers that most violence against women is perpetrated within family and friend circles.

The changes in the constitution and in society came around at a time when sex became a growing global industry, especially through the process of globalization and the impact of the Internet. A country that had previously banned literary works such as *Lady Chatterly's Lover* and magazines such as *Playboy* was hit by an avalanche of hard-core pornography ("Publication Board approves Hustler," *Citizen*, October 29, 1999, p. 8; Els 1995; *Weekly Mail and Guardian*, October 23, 1998).

Even spokespersons with high struggle and freedom credentials were voicing concern about the new wave of promiscuity and breakdown of moral barriers (Abrahams 1999). Ethicists seem to agree that no state or society can peacefully exist without public consensus on what is good or bad, right or wrong. Laws in themselves are not enough. Unbridled lawlessness and other forms of anarchy are warning signs that moral decline is taking place. Since the classical period, it was acknowledged that even with the best constitution, a "good" civilization still needed general respect for life, respect for others and the property of others, and eventually self-respect (Esterhuyse 1999).

Whereas one of the famous struggle slogans in the 1970s and 1980s was "No normal sport in an abnormal society," *Beeld* (July 22, 1999, p. 8) argued in an editorial that it was abnormal for a society to accept crime at the level it was experienced. What was clearly needed, *Beeld* said, was a realignment of moral values throughout society.

In order to escape its present malaise of crime and violence in South Africa, it seems that nothing less than a moral renaissance will be needed. (Esterhuyse 1999; also see the conclusion of this chapter for President Thabo Mbeki's vision for South Africa).

CASES IN POINT: RAPE AND
DOMESTIC VIOLENCE

Though it is not possible in scientific terms to claim a causal relationship between overt sexual and other forms of violence in the media with changes in society's attitudes and moral values, one cannot shy away from the reality that sex has become a major issue on the news and public agenda. At a conference on the question whether the news media could change individual behavior that results in domestic violence in Latin American and surrounding countries, there was a strong feeling that there exists a particular relationship between these elements. There was a general feeling that television, radio, and the press are often the crucial elements in any large-scale effort to deal with this devastating problem (Constance 1998, pp. 80–81). The same could also hold true for South Africa, as the following discussion will show.

Rape

In October 1999 South African President Thabo Mbeki (*Citizen*, October 28, 1999, p. 1) released a statement disclaiming the high figures given for rape cases in South Africa. Most activist and other concerned organizations paint another picture.

Every seventeen seconds a women is raped in South Africa. This information is part of a report that suggests reported rape to have increased significantly over the past decade. This can be ascribed to the increase of both the incidence of rape and the willingness of the women to report it.

According to the Crime Intelligence Management Centre of the South African Police Service, a total of 52,160 cases of rape or attempted rape were reported to the police in 1999, with 49,280 assaults reported in 1998 (*Beeld,* April 13, 1999, p. 11). There were 125.5 rape cases or rape attempts per 100,000 of the South African population in 1997. The figure was 115.8 in 1998. Although cases of rape and maltreatment of children have decreased by 12 percent in 1998 over the preceding year, the number of such occurrences remains alarmingly high—2,368 incidents in 1997 and 2,083 in 1998. There were 537 incidents of sexual relationships with minors in 1997 and 474 incidents in 1998 (Bothma 1999, p. 11). Moreover, police are of the opinion that only 2.8 percent of all rape incidents were reported in 1994.

Other facts according to the South African Central Statistic's 1999 report suggest the following:

- Between 1994 and 1996, the number of reported rapes per 100,000 of the population increased from 105 to 119. This increased to almost 2 million women being raped in 1997. This figure dropped for the first time in 1998 when 49,280 rapes were reported to the police.

- About 28–30 percent of adolescents report their first sexual experience was forced, and 16 percent of young men interviewed by CIET Africa in 1998 who knew somebody who was raped, believed that the survivor "enjoyed it" and "had asked for it." The consequence of this kind of "reasoning" shows up in South African courts, as will be shown later on.

Domestic Violence

From South Africa's brutalized history, its family life now has to find ways to heal not only broken relationships but also a traumatized society as a whole. In a society still divided by race, color, gender, education, and economic status, family life has to be restored. According to Marcus (1997):

> The worst legacy the new South Africa has inherited is the way in which its people were abused. (The challenge) is not about casting blame or making excuses, but about recognizing that the society of today grew out of brutalization and anguish of yesterday. The challenge is to start, however painstakingly, to heal the nation. (Marcus 1997)

As in the case of rape, there is an opinion among researchers that the news media can help change the individual behavior of the perpetrators of domestic violence by reporting more carefully on the reality of this kind of abuse. The media can raise public awareness to build the consensus needed to give greater protection to abused women and children. In short, there is consensus that no large-scale effort to eradicate this devastating social problem could be tackled without intervention by the media.

According to the Commission on Gender Equality (CGE), violence against women has reached epidemic proportions. It is estimated that one in four women in South Africa are victims of domestic violence. Statistics show that 54 percent of the people in the magistrate's courts who plead guilty to killing are guilty of killing their own wives. Reports on domestic violence in South African families are a familiar feature in newspapers (De Bruin 1999; Kühne 1999).

Brynard (1999) reports that husbands or friends are responsible for between 70 percent and 80 percent of all violence against women, and according to the Department of Justice, one out of every four of South African women has experienced violence at home (assault and rape). In 45 percent of the cases, the violence was witnessed by another person. The incidence of rape of children has doubled between 1994 and 1997, from 7,500 cases reported per year to almost 15,000.

In 1997, a total of 2,368 and in 1998 a total of 2,083 cases of brutality (excluding sexual crimes, assault, and murder) were reported against children.

This was 5.7 and 4.9 out of every 100,000 children in the population. Though there was a lower number of assaults on children reported in 1998, indications were that this kind of crime was on the increase due to the extensive coverage of child pornography on the Internet and the use of children as sex workers (Coetzee 1999).

Deputy justice minister Manto Thsabalala Msimang concedes: "We do not appear to have an integrated and holistic national program on the elimination of violence against women and children. It is an anathema to the vision of a non-sexist society based on equality, freedom and respect for human dignity, a vision enshrined in our constitution."

Flaws in the criminal justice system, according to Hamber and Lewis (1998), intensify the desire for retribution, and insensitive and judgmental behavior by police discourages victims from reporting crime. In the South African situation, this is particularly true for child victims and victims of domestic violence and rape. This has an adverse and detrimental effect on media coverage of violence against women.

In a society where domestic violence has become endemic, under-reporting in the media has become a major problem, since only the most gruesome crimes eventually reach the newspapers and become part of the public agenda. The result is a belief that most crime is of a violent nature, committed by unknown assailants. Consequently, common crimes in South African homes, like wife battery and child abuse, are concealed through a blurring of images.

THE NATURE OF SEX-RELATED INFORMATION IN THE SOUTH AFRICAN MEDIA

Due to South Africa's strict censorship laws during the apartheid regime, little or no explicit sex or sex-related violence were encountered in the media.

In line with its tradition, SABC radio and television offer no explicit sexual material, although the odd film and TV series such as *Silk Stalkings* may include rather explicit sex scenes. On the other hand, independent radio stations and the South Africa–based international MNet have pushed the sexual boundaries further. Radio 702 has presenters known to crack jokes and make remarks that are sexually suggestive, if not offensive. The station's policy is that listeners can tune in to another station if they do not like what they hear.

As a number of researchers argue, reporting on VAW should not be seen in isolation of reporting on sex and related matters in the media.

Newspapers and Magazines

When South African newspapers and magazines report on sex-related matters, more often than not sexual crime is the subject. The following brief, impressionistic overview summarizes the reporting by some main newspapers and family magazines of this issue.

Mail and Guardian

Apart from the *Sunday Independent,* the *Mail and Guardian* is the closest thing South Africa has to a quality newspaper. Over the last few years, it has made an attempt to highlight the plight of women and sexual abuses against them. At the time of writing, the issues of the newspaper (September–October 1999) showed a remarkable sensitivity to this question:

- A sympathetic report on the dangers highway women sex workers have to face, following the death of two women in Pretoria (September 11, 1999).
- An exposé of child pornography on the Internet (September 11, 1999).
- Interviews with students doing sex work on campus in order to raise money (September 18, 1999).
- In one of the many reports on the American president Bill Clinton's sexual encounters with Monica Lewinsky, the report tries to define the concept "having sex with."
- In a wide-ranging report about the sexual revolution, the conclusion is reached that "total sexual freedom is not possible without respecting other peoples' feelings" (September 23, 1999).
- Quoting the views of the Sex Worker Education and Advocacy Task Force (Sweat), an understanding that "prostitutes provide an essential service" is put forward (September 23, 1999).

Beeld

As the biggest and foremost Afrikaans daily in South Africa (De Beer and Steyn 1996), the newspaper has an open approach to sexual and related matters (Van Vlastuin and Froneman 1999; and De Beer 1998). In September 1999, *Beeld* reported on the views of Pope John Paul II regarding numerous sexual practices: child pornography, the need to revise traditional views on gays and their role in the church, the question of gays being "spouses" in terms of the law, the HIV crisis in South Africa, the possibility that AZT would bring hope to women who had been raped, life imprisonment for serial rapists, and the sex worker trade in Africa.

The same kind of reporting was also found in dailies such as *Cape Times* and the *Star,* as well as Sunday papers such as *Rapport* and *Sunday Times.*

Sarie, De Kat, and Men's Health

Within the scope of this discussion, some attention will be paid to three interesting South African magazines, namely, *Sarie* (a traditional, rather conservative Afrikaans family magazine aimed at women readers); *De Kat* (a kind of avante garde Afrikaans thirty-something magazine); and *Men's Health* (one of the new genre of magazines that appeared in the postapartheid era).

Sarie, a weekly Afrikaans magazine aimed at a female audience, is becoming more and more open-minded regarding articles on sex and sexuality. Most of these articles have the common purpose of informing and educating, mostly with the purpose to enrich and strengthen relationships and marriages.

A few articles will be identified. In *Sarie* (February 21, 1999) the article "Hup vir jou huwelik" (New life for your marriage) is typical *Sarie* in addressing the topic of sex. The article "Begin 'n rewolusie tussen die lakens" (Start a revolution in bed) contains the same kind of information.

In the September 22, 1999, edition, the article "Rondslaap is uit, maagde is in" (Loose sex is out, it is fashionable to be a virgin) follows on others advising readers against HIV/AIDS and the problematic nature of a promiscuous lifestyle.

De Kat, a South African glamour Afrikaans magazine, was taking the lead in the media sex revolution in more than one way. Although at times shocking to conservative readers, it nevertheless dealt with the facts and issues its audience wanted to read about—readers hardly ever comment negatively on its editorial policy regarding sexual matters.

De Kat was the first South African magazine to report on the controversial sex pill for men, Viagra, while a number of its recent editions carried pictures of seminaked models and celebrities—a far cry from its conservative Afrikaans beginnings.

Men's Health

The South African edition of the international *Men's Health* magazine doesn't hesitate to publish articles on sex, and frequently these articles are written in explicit detail. The June 1999 edition of *Men's Health* had "Great Sex Anywhere" (an article about different "interesting places" for sex) and the pros and cons of each (Quarry 1999, pp. 42–48). The same edition features an article on Viagra, which the author of the article tests (White 1999, pp. 89–90). Another article gives tips on how to handle it when you realize the girl you've been after is a lesbian (Tuugan 1999, p. 116).

"Seven ways to remind her how sexy she is" was published in the edition of August 1999 (Huyward 1999, pp. 136–141). In the article "Sex Clinic: Let Her Give You a Physical" nine "tests" are suggested for couples to examine one another's health—all of them with a sexual undertone (Beavan 1999, pp. 48–49).

The July 1999 edition features the article "Thirty-One Sex Mysteries Explained" on the cover (Guveld 1999, pp. 38–44). The title of the article "Six Moves That Hit the Spot" (Veilleux 1999, pp. 158–159) doesn't need any further explanation.

The September 1999 edition contains the same kind of articles. The article "Give Her the Body You've Always Wanted" is described on the contents page with the following sentence: "Put your cunning sex workout into action—you get to have your wicked way, she gets to firm up her bits in the process" (Heaner 1999, pp. 42–48). Another article with sex as the topic in this edition is "Couples: Is She Lying about Sex? Women Give Their Honest Opinions" (Maxted and Trapp 1999, pp. 188–189).

The Internet

Most of the established South African newspapers and magazines, as well as a number of alternative publications and NGOs, publish their Web sites on the Internet. Many of the South African news pages on the Internet (e.g., Independent Online [IOL]), contain information on sex-related topics that is not published in print or hard copy format.

There is a heavy emphasis on articles dealing with rape. Because of changes in South African legislation on the punishment of rapists, news on rape cases gets extensive publication, for instance, Independent Online featured an article (September 5, 1999) about three teenage women who were raped after a beauty competition in three unrelated cases. The next day, it reported on the verdict in a case in the high court in Bloemfontein: the rapist of two young women was sentenced to jail for ten years and six years, "to run concurrently." Public outrage over this verdict led to the parliament wanting to summon the judge to explain his verdict. The judge's verdict was further undermined by his comment that his verdict should be seen against the background that one of the "girls had been naughty, for she had sex two days before the rape."

THE MEDIA: HOW VIOLENCE AGAINST
WOMEN (VAW) IS PORTRAYED

The South African media overflows with reports and information on sex and sexuality. In magazines and broadcast media, this reporting seems to have become quite "normal." On public television and radio, some programs contain sexual information, but not during peak times. In "family" magazines, such articles are mostly informative and entertaining, seldom explicit or in extremely bad taste. In newspapers and magazines, however, extended space is given to the reporting of the negative side of sex (i.e., sexual violence and abuse).

In general, since 1994, and especially over the last five years, the South African media in general have made definite progress in dealing with gender-related issues and, more specifically, violence against women. This was especially clear in a number of news events during 1999, including the following.

The Ntini Rape Court Case

South Africa's first international black cricketer, Makhaya Ntini, aged twenty-two, won his appeal against a rape conviction and a six-year jail term that had nearly ruined his sporting career (*Citizen*, October 30, 1999, p. 1). Though Ntini was "exhilarated," antirape groups and prominent South African women organizations were "aghast and saddened." They did not welcome the appeal decision, saying it was devastating news. This followed earlier outrage when it turned out in media reports that Ntini was still eligible for the South African cricket team while awaiting his appeal case (*Citizen* 1999, p. 1; *Beeld* 1999, p. 4).

"Real Men Do Not Rape Women" Advertisement

There was overwhelming support in the media, as well as in letters to the editor, for the South African–born international actress Charlize Theron's TV antirape advertisement, when the Advertising Standards Authority (ASA) banned this ad. The South African Commission on Gender Equality and a wide range of gender activist organizations protested against the banning of the advertisement. The *Sunday Independent* (1999–10–10, 08) stated in a major editorial that the ASA "should hang its head in shame" for its "priggish self-righteous ban." The antiban campaign also received wide support from other media. In the television 109-word advertisement script, Theron said the following:

Hi, I'm Charlize Theron. People often ask me what the men are like in South Africa. Well . . . consider that more women are raped in South Africa than any other country in the world; that one out of three women will be raped in their lifetime in South Africa. And perhaps, worst of all that the rest of the men in South Africa seem to think that rape isn't their problem. It is not easy to say what the men in South Africa are like, because there seem to be so few of them out there.

The ASA eventually removed the ban after finding that the commercial did not discriminate against men (*Citizen*, October 23, 1999, p. 1).

The Foxcroft Verdict

At a time when the issue of rape tended to overshadow almost all other forms of reporting and editorial comment in South Africa, Judge John Foxcroft caused an outcry and a wave of anger, not only from women activist groups but eventually from the public at large through letters to the editor, when he sentenced a fifty-four-year-old man to seven years in the Cape high court for raping his fourteen-year-old daughter. Foxcroft became infamous almost overnight for his ruling that "while raping one's daughter was *morally reprehensible*, the act was *confined* to his daughter, and that, therefore, the man did not pose a threat to society" (italics added). While the new South African law mandated the minimum sentence of life imprisonment, Foxcroft argued that the girl "had a good chance of recovery."

What made this verdict exceptional was that it followed two earlier cases in which a judge in Bloemfontein argued that since a fifteen-year-old had sex previously, though not with the perpetrator, she was "naughty," and he sentenced the man who had raped her and another minor at gunpoint to ten years. And in a second case an eighteen-year sentence, rather than life imprisonment, was upheld on the grounds that the rapist had had "an unhappy childhood" (Stucky 1999).

The Campaign by Journalist Charlene Smith

Perhaps for the first time in South Africa's history, a woman journalist who had been raped took the issue to public forums and made violence against women a burning topic on the national news and public agenda. Without letting down, Smith campaigned for the right of women who had been raped to speak out and to put an end to the travesty (Smith 1999).

I Will Not Lie Down and Die

In a spate of articles and reports on rape, the following reports appeared on one page of the *Citizen* (October 29, 1999, p. 4): "Chemical castration not an option: Zuma; Gang-rape victim drops charges; Guilty of raping and killing gran, 113." Women who were raped were still mainly called victims. In the same month the *Mail and Guardian* published an almost full-page picture of "rape survivor" Amy Brown with the caption: "I was raped in front of my kids. I am HIV positive. I will not lie down and die" (*Mail and Guardian*, October 15, 1999, pp. 1–2), as well as an article by Charlene Smith (mentioned above), who interviewed a gang-rape survivor who refused to let her attackers get her down (also see Stucky 1999).

THE MEDIA: WHAT TO DO?

The way VAW is being dealt with in the South African media is a high priority for women's groups and other NGOs working on finding answers to this
issue. For these groups, it is especially important that media workers at all
levels will be sensitized to the problem and know how to deal with it, not
only in a regular' way, but also in innovative ways that would facilitate understanding and action. At a workshop on violence against women and the
media, organized by the Commission on Gender Equality, examples were
discussed and then reporting guidelines were formulated (Commission on
Gender Equality 1998, p. 31).

Newspaper Headlines

As an example of the way violence against women is negatively portrayed,
a number of newspaper headlines were discussed, for example, "Policeman
among 3 killed as lovers' tiff ends in tragedy." The husband came across his
wife and a policeman at a picnic. He shot both of them dead and then turned
the gun on himself. The policeman made it into the headline but not the wife
(headline from the *Star,* August 25, 1999).

Another newspaper headline read, "Wife killed after argument over pie."
The woman had objected to her husband that a pie was not a suitable meal
for a six-month-old baby. He grabbed the baby from her arms and shot his
wife in the head. The wife was portrayed as almost being responsible for her
own death over such a stupid thing as a "fight over a pie" (headline source
not cited).

Guidelines

A number of guidelines were proposed for media workers and their media
when dealing with VAW:

- Violence against women should be accorded the importance it deserves
  in terms of how stories are written and placed in the media.
- Perpetrators of violence should be named wherever possible.
- Stories should be based on a variety of sources and, whenever possible,
  should include the views of the victims themselves in a way that does
  not lead to further suffering.
- Information about support services should be made available—
  especially by the public broadcaster.
- Training should be given to journalists and producers to sensitize them
  to the importance of reporting in a more sympathetic way toward
  women who have suffered from violence.

- Regular reports should be made available regarding the social and economic costs a country faces when dealing with violence against women.
- Reporting in a way that subtly shifts the blame from the perpetrator to the woman using arguments such as the woman being responsible for the crime committed against her, or the justification of the crime due to drunkenness or provocation, should be avoided.
- Names and photographs of perpetrators should appear regularly and wherever possible.
- Sexist language should be avoided.
- If possible, contact details of organizations for victims of violence should be provided on programs and reports.
- Reports should acknowledge the criminality of violence and mention details of sentencing.
- The dignity of the victim is paramount. Sensitivity should be used before reporting details such as the sexual nature of the act or levels of undress of the victim. Care should be taken not to sensationalize the report or degrade the victim. This should be applied to headlines, titles, and visual images.
- Myths about violence against women occurring in particular racial, ethnic, or social groups should be dispelled by broadcasters if the information is of no relevance to the report or program.
- Reports on violence against women should reiterate community disapproval of crimes of this nature.

Information Programs

It was also suggested that information programs should be instated to help media workers come to grips with VAW:

- A balance should be struck between the reporting of violence against women and the portrayal of women as victims, and the programs about women who have survived and overcome violence.
- The media should report on initiatives and strategies that successfully combat violence against women.
- Programs of an analytical nature should determine whether victims of violence wish to be interviewed, and if organizations working on issues around violence against women should be interviewed to provide exploration of the details of these types of crimes.
- The complex factors underlying the psychological and social factors on violence against women should be explored.
- Programs about violence against women should indicate the different forms violence against women take (i.e., sexual, emotional, and physical).

- Finally, the long-term impact and consequences of violence against women should not be overlooked.

THE GLOBAL SITUATION

South Africa is experiencing the effects of globalization at an increasing level. As Gill Marcus (1997) states, "South Africa cannot achieve its objectives without embracing the challenges of globalization . . . I have no doubt the women of South Africa will rise to the challenge, work to stop the abuse of women, strive to protect, cherish and nourish the girl-child. Formal apartheid is ended, and the new fight is about being equal citizens of a state where all have the right to live and dream, not in the fear of hunger and illness, but in hope of a future (within the context also of globalization) that brings peace and stability, prosperity and fulfillment."

In this context, as Marcus (1997) shows, violence against women and children is a global issue. As UNICEF indicated, progress is not just about economic and quality of life indicators, it is also to be judged by the degree of protection women have against discrimination and violence. Violence against women and children undermines a nation's health and stability (Marcus 1997).

South African media portrays a large number of sexually related issues occurring especially in Western countries, for example, child pornography on the Net, the "fundamental, constitutional right of women to have an orgasm" (*Mail and Guardian*, March 19, 1999).

CONCLUSION

"South Africa will only be truly free, once women are safe" (*Beeld*, August 2, 1999). This sentiment, expressed by President Thabo Mbeki on the South African 1999 Women's Day, encapsulated much of what has been published in print and broadcast media about violence against women. For Mbeki and his government, violence against women was not confined to empty rhetoric. As the *Saturday Star* (October 16, 1999, p. 10) showed, the government was also "acting on its pledge to end violence against women." At the time of this writing, a directive was being issued for the judicial system to hasten the trial of sexual crimes, and effective prosecutions by a well-trained team was also promised. This was an important step because in the myriad crimes that clog the judicial system, violence against women and children did not, until August 1999, enjoy the priority it deserved, when the government declared it a month in which awareness of the empowerment of women would be highlighted (*Beeld*, August 5, 1999, p. 13).

For the *Saturday Star* and most law-abiding citizens, the way forward was clear. It was necessary to help restore the people's faith in the justice system. Deeds were needed, not just the announcement of another plan without any action to back it up ("They're waking up at last," *Saturday Star,* October 16, 1999, p. 10):

It is not just because cynical, crime-battered South Africans are tired of 'grand plans.' Effective action is critical because every day that South African women and children live in fear makes a mockery of our constitution and Bill of Rights.

Too many women and children are suffering and dying for us to simply wish the problem away.

To this end, there is perhaps no better way to clear the way for the future than Mbeki's (1999) inaugural speech when he accepted the presidency of South Africa:

I have seen our country turn asunder as these, all of whom are my people, engaged one another in a titanic battle, the one to redress a wrong that had been caused by one to another and the other to defend the indefensible.

I have seen what happens when one person has superiority of force over another, when the stronger appropriate to them the prerogative even to annul the injunction that God created all men and women in His image.

I know what it signifies when race and color are used to determine who are human and who, subhuman.

I have seen the destruction of all sense of self-esteem, the consequent striving to be what one is not, simply to acquire some of the benefits, which those who had imposed themselves as masters had ensured that they enjoyed. I have experienced a situation in which race and color are used to enrich some and impoverish the rest. I have seen the corruption of minds and souls as a result of the pursuit of an ignoble effort to perpetrate a veritable crime against humanity. I have seen concrete expression of the denial of the dignity of a human being emanating from the conscious, systematic oppressive and repressive activities of other human beings.

There are the victims parade with no mask to hide the brutish reality—the beggars, the prostitutes, the street children, those who seek solace in substance abuse, those who steal to assuage hunger, those who have to lose their sanity because to be sane is to invite pain.

Perhaps the worst among these, who are my people, are those who have learnt to kill for a wage. To these, the extent of death is directly proportional to their personal welfare. And so, like pawns in the service of demented souls, they kill in furtherance of the political violence in KwaZulu/Natal. They murder the innocent in the taxi wars. They kill slowly or quickly in order to make profits from the illegal trade in narcotics. They are available for hire when husband wants to murder wife and wife, husband.

Among us are the products of our immoral and amoral past, killers who have no sense of the worth of human life, rapists who have absolute disdain for the women of our country, animals who would seek to benefit from the vulnerability of the children, the disabled, the old, the rapacious who brook no obstacle in their quest for self-enrichment.

All this I know and I know to be true because I am an African! Because of that, I am also able to state this fundamental truth that I am born of a people who are heroes and heroines. I am born of a people who would not tolerate oppression. I am of a nation that would not allow that fear of death, torture, imprisonment, exile, or persecution should result in the perpetuation of injustice.

The great masses, which are our mother and father, will not permit that the behavior of a few results in the description of our country and people as barbaric patient because history is on their side, these masses do not despair because today the weather is bad. Nor do they turn triumphal when, tomorrow, the sun shines.

Whatever the circumstances they have lived through and because of that experience, they are determined to define for themselves who they are and who they should be.

The Constitution, whose adoption we celebrate, constitutes an unequivocal statement that we refuse to accept that our Africanness shall be defined by our race, our color, our gender or our historical origins.

It is a firm assertion made by us that South Africa belongs to all who live in it, black and white. It gives concrete expression to the sentiment we share as Africans, and will defend to the death that the people shall govern.

It recognizes the fact that the dignity of the individual is both an objective which society must pursue, and a goal, which cannot be separated from the material well being of that individual. It seeks to create a situation in which all our people will be free from fear, including the fear of the oppression of one national group by another, the fear of disempowerment of one social echelon by another, the fear of the use of state power to deny anybody his or her fundamental human rights, and the fear of tyranny. (Mbeki 1999)

NOTE

The first author is indebted to Karen Ross for being the primary writer of the sections up to the South African situation. This chapter started out as an honor's project with final-year women journalism students in the School of Communication and Information Sciences, Potchefstroom University, South Africa. Lizelle Erasmus, Hanlie Raath, Estie Steyn, Corneli van Aarde, Jeandré van Tonder, and Susan van Vuuren are thanked for their input.

REFERENCES

Abarder, G. 1999. Leading Pagad critic shot dead. *Star* 19: 1.

Abrahams, L. 1999. PC attitudes cultivate an ethos of disrespect. *Sunday Independent*, p. 1011.

ANC. 1997. Briefing, Cape Town.

Arthurs, J. 1994. Women and television. In S. Hood, ed., *Behind the screens,* pp. 82–101. London: Lawrence & Wishart.

Baehr, H., and A. Gray, eds. 1996. *Turning it on: A reader in women and media.* London: Arnold.

Beavan, C. 1999. Let her give you a physical. *Men's Health.* August, pp. 48–49.

Benhabib, S. 1992. *Situating the self: Gender, community, and postmodernism in contemporary ethics.* Cambridge: Polity.

Bezuidenhout, N. 1999. Vroue ly steeds onder 'versteekte diskriminasie' (Women still suffer from hidden discrimination). *Beeld,* March, p. 8.

Booyens, H. 1999. Jy mag maar, dis net 'n vrou (You may, because it's only a woman). *Insig,* November, pp. 28–29.

Bothma, P. 1999. 24,875 Mense in 1998 vermoor (24,875 people murdered in 1998). *Beeld* 11 (April): 13.

Bowie, M. D. 1997. Media violence. *SAMJ* editorial, January, p. 871.

Breytenbach, D. 1998. Influence of the mass media and politicians on public perceptions of crime. Paper read at the annual conference of the South African Development Association, Rand Afrikaans University, Johannesburg.

Brynard, K. 1999. How free are we? *Insig,* August, p. 20.

Bueno Abad, J. R. 1996. *Estudio longitudinal de la presencia de la mujer en los medios de communicacio de prensa escrita* (Longitudinal study of the presence of women in the written press). Valencia: Nau Libres.

Butler, M., and W. Paisley. 1980. *Women and the mass media.* New York: Human Sciences Press.

Cain, E. P. 1997. *Crime in South Africa: Its causes and solutions.* Potchefstroom: Institute for Reformational Studies.

Carter, C. 1998. When the "extraordinary" becomes "ordinary": Everyday news of sexual violence. In C. Carter, G. Branston, and S. Allan, eds., *News, gender and power,* pp. 219–232. London: Routledge.

Carter, C., G. Branston, and S. Allan, eds. 1998. *News, gender, and power.* London: Routledge.

Christmas, L. 1996. *Women in the news: Does sex change the way a newspaper thinks?* London: Women in Journalism.

Coetzee, S. 1999. Kinderpornografie op internet kring uit (Child pornography on the Internet increases). *Beeld,* August, p. 1011.

Commission on Gender Equality. 1997. Submission to the independent Broadcasting Authority on the code of conduct for broadcasters by the commission on gender equality, Johannesburg.

———. 1998. What's lust got to do with it? *Rhodes Journalism Review,* July, p. 31.

Constance, P. 1998. Private violence in the public eye. *Unisa Lat. Am Rep,* January–June, p. 141.

Cowie, E. 1998. Images of women and filmic identification. In N. Dakovic, D. Derman, and K. Ross, eds., *Gender and media,* pp. 35–60. Ankara: Mediation.

Cuklanz, L. M. 1996. *Rape on trial: How the mass media construct legal reform and social change.* Philadelphia: University of Pennsylvania Press.

Cumberbatch, G., A. Maguire, and S. Woods. 1994. The portrayal of women on British television: A content analysis. In *Broadcasting Standards Council perspectives of women in television*, pp. 24–59. Research Working Paper 9. London: BSC.

Davis, D. M. 1990. Portrayals of women in prime-time network television: Some demographic characteristics. *Sex Roles*, 23, no. 5–6: 325–332.

de Beer, A. S. 1993. Baas van 'n bontspan (Boss of a mixed team). *De Kat*, February, pp. 50–53.

de Beer, A. S., ed. 1998. *Mass media toward the millennium*. Cape Town: Van Schaik.

de Beer, A. S., and E. F. Steyn. 1996. Towards defining news in the South African context: The media as generator or mediator of conflict. *South African Journal of Sociology* 273: 90–97.

De Bens, E. 1992. Televisie als cultuurmediator (Television as a cultural mediator). *Commuicatie* 221: 1–21.

De Bruin, G. 1999. Gesin se heerlike vakansie aan kus eindig in nag van verskrikking (Family's wonderful holiday at seaside ends in horror). *Rapport*, June 13, p. 12.

De Bruin, P. 1999. Regstorm woed voort om gay "gades" (Juridical storm about gay "spouses" intensifies). *Beeld*, May 5, p. 19.

Dougary, G. 1994. *The executive tart and other myths*. London: Virago.

Douglas, S. 1994. *Where the girls are: Growing up female with the mass media*. New York: Random House.

Dugmore, H. 1998. Elke dier sy taboe (Every animal's taboo). *De Kat*, May, pp. 72–76.

Els, J. 1995. Harde pornografie tref SA (Hard pornography hits SA). *Insig*, April, p. 12.

Esterhuyse, W. 1999. Suid-Afrika benodig 'n morele renaissance (South Africa needs a moral renaissance). *Finansies and Tegniek*, August, p. 28.

European Commission. 1999. *Images of women in the media*. Brussels: EC.

Fraser, N. 1989. *Unruly practices: Power, discourse, and gender in contemporary social theory*. Minneapolis: University of Minnesota Press.

Gallagher, M. 1988. *Women and television in Europe*. Brussels: Commission of the European Communities.

———. 1995. *An unfinished story: Gender patterns in media employment*. Paris: UNESCO. Includes reports on mass communication, p. 110.

GCE media release. 1999. Johannesburg, October 20.

Gibson, E. 1999. Land eers werklik vry as vroue veilig is (Country really free when women are free). *Beeld*, August, p. 10.

Gray, M. M. A., and R. Sathiparsad. 1997. Violence against women in South Africa: An analysis of media coverage. *Social Work* 343: 267–280.

Gunter, B. 1995. *Television and gender representation*. London: John Libbey.

Hamber, B., and S. Lewis. 1998. Crime's worst horror is all in the mind. *Sunday Times*, April, p. 1.

Hartley, J. 1998. Juvenation: News, girls, and power. In C. Carter et al., eds., *News, gender, and power*, 47–70. New York: Routledge.

Heaner, M. K. 1999. Give her the body you've always wanted. *Men's Health*, September, pp. 42–48.

Hobson, D. 1990. Housewives and the mass media. In Stuart Hall et al., eds., *Culture, media, language*, pp. 105–114. London: Hutchinson.

Huyward, K. 1999. Seven ways to remind her how sexy she is. *Men's Health*, August, 136–141.

Kitzinger, J. 1992. Sexual violence and compulsory heterosexuality. *Feminism and Psychology* 23: 399–418.

Kühne, I. 1999. Tienerselfmoord in SA "kan nie meer geïgnoreer word" (Teenage suicide in SA not to be ignored any further). *Beeld*, April, p. 15.

Lees, S. 1995. Media reporting of rape: The 1993 British "date rape" controversy. In D. Kidd-Hewitt and R. Osborne, eds., *Crime and media: The post-modern spectacle*, pp. 107–130. London: Pluto.

Le Roux, G. 1997. Editorial: Gender Commission symposium on gender and media. *Women's MediaWatch Newsletter* 4: 3.

Lötter, F. 1999. SA voor in vroue-regte (South Africa ahead regarding women's rights). *Beeld*, March, p. 12.

Macdonald, M. 1995. *Representing women: Myths of femininity in popular media.* London: Edward Arnold.

Mangold, T. 1999. Armed with that toxic charm. *Sunday Independent*, August 26, p. 13.

Marais, S. 1999. *Violence in South Africa*. National Trauma Research Program.

Marcus, G. 1997. On women in South Africa. Speech delivered at a Women's Day luncheon, August 8, p. 10.

Marinescu, V. 1995. Does Angela walk alone? Women and media in the Romanian case. Paper presented at the International Association of Media and Communication Research annual conference, Slovenia, June.

Matshikiza, J. 1999. An evil in our midst. *Siyaya: Crime and Policing*, Winter, pp. 62–64.

Maxted, A., and J. K. Trapp. 1999. Is she lying about sex? *Men's Health*, September, pp. 188–189.

Mbeki, T. 1999. I am an African. In M. Gitanjali, ed., *Between unity and diversity: Essays on nation-building in post-apartheid South Africa*, pp. 11–15. Idasa: David Philip.

McNeil, J. 1975. Feminism, femininity, and the television show: A content analysis. *Journal of Broadcasting* 19: 259–269.

McQuail, D. 1987. *Mass communication theory: An introduction.* London: Sage.

MediaWatch. 1995. *Global media monitoring project: Women's participation in the news.* Ontario: National Watch on Images of Women MediaWatch.

Michielsens, M. 1991. Women in view: How does BRTN portray women? Brussels: BRTN.

Michielsens, M., and A. Ten Boom. 1995. Portrayal of victims. Paper presented to the EU/EBU conference, Reflecting Diversity: The Challenge for Women and Men in European Broadcasting, London, June.

Millwood Hargrave, A. 1994. Attitudes towards the portrayal of women in broadcasting. In *Broadcasting Standards Council: Perspectives of women in television*, pp. 6–23. Research Working Paper 9. London: BSC.

Neves, H. 1994. Address to the Prix Niki conference, Lisbon, March.

NOS Gender Portrayal Department. 1994a. *Interviewtechnieken in talkshows* (Interview techniques re male and female guests in Dutch talk shows). Hilversum: NOS.

————. 1994b. *Report to Bectu conference: Whose point of view?* London, June.

————. 1995. *Interviewtechnieken in acualiteitenprogramma's* (Interview techniques on male and female guests in Dutch current affairs features). Hilversum: NOS.

Peck, J. 1987. Violence against women. In K. Davies, J. Dickey, and T. Stratford, eds., *Out of focus: Writings on women and the media.* London: Women's Press.

Pieters, M. 1999. Afkap van ledemate het te veel nadele (Cutting off limbs has too many drawbacks). *Beeld*, February, p. 1.

Piliso-Seroke, J. 1999. Untitled speech by the chairperson of the Commission on Gender Equality during the African Human Rights Day celebration in Pretoria, October 21.

Quarry, P. 1999. Great sex anywhere. *Men's Health*, June, pp. 42–46.

Raycheva, L. 1995. Women in Bulgarian mass media in the period of change, 1989–1994. Paper presented to the International Association of Media and Communication Research annual conference, Slovenia, June.

Ross, K. 1995a. *Women and the news agenda: Media—Ted reality and Jane public.* Discussion papers in Mass Communication no. MC95/1. Leicester: Centre for Mass Communication Research, University of Leicester.

————. 1995b. Gender and party politics: How the press reported the Labour leadership campaign, 1994. *Media, Culture, and Society* 174: 499–509.

Ross, K., and A. Sreberny. In press. Bodies politics: Women, politics, and news media. In A. Sreberny and L. Van Zoonen, eds., *Women's politics and communication.* Cresskill, N.J.: Hampton.

Ross, K., and A. Sreberny-Mohammadi. 1997. Playing house: Gender, politics, and the news media in Britain. *Media, Culture, and Society* 191: 101–109.

Roventa-Frumusani, D. 1995. Images of women in the postcommunist society and media: Romania's case. Paper presented at the International Association of Media and Communication Research annual conference, Slovenia, June.

Schönteich, M. 1999. Our ineffective criminal justice system needs fixing, and denying bail won't help. *Sunday Independent*, October 9.

Sexist shame of rape advert ban. 1999. Editorial. *Sunday Independent*, October 10, p. 8.

Smith, C. 1999a. Asmal: School rapes a national crisis. *Mail and Guardian*, October 15, p. 7.

————. 1999b. I was raped, I have HIV, but I will. . . . *Mail and Guardian*, October 15, p. 2.

————. 1999c. Rape victims are people too: This is our story. *Marie Claire*, June, p. 56.

————. 1999d. SA rape gets more violent. *Mail and Guardian*, June 11, p. 6.

Soothill, K., and S. Walby. 1991. *Sex crime in the news.* London: Routledge.

Soul City. 1999. *Guidelines for reporting on violence against women: South African Institute of Race Relations 1995–1996 survey.* Johannesburg: STE Publishing.

Soul City Institute for Health and Development Communication. 1999. *Why should we take violence against women seriously?* SA: STE Publishing.

————. 1999. *Rape in South Africa.* SA: STE Publishing.

Stucky, C. 1999. Judges accused of bias in favor of leniency over sentences for rape. *Sunday Independent*, October, p. 5.

Swift, A. 1997. The battle to prove that "real men do not abuse women." *News Scan International.*

Thompson, D. 1999. Boendoehof-slanery geprys (Bundu court hitting praised). *Beeld*, April 29, p. 1.

Tuchman, G., A. Daniels, and J. Benét, eds. 1978. *Hearth and home: Images of women in the mass media.* New York: Oxford University Press.

Tuugan, I. 1999. Yes, I'm a lesbian: Now leave me alone. *Men's Health*, June, p. 116.

Van Vlastuin, E., and J. D. Froneman. 1999. Afrikaans papers reporting on gambling, drugs, and being gay. *Ecquid Novi* 20, no. 2: 63–85.

Van Wyk, A. 1999. Vrouehaat, magteloosheid en verveeldheid (Hating women, feeling powerless and being bored). *De Kat*, September, pp. 61–63.

Van Zoonen, L. 1994. *Feminist media studies.* London: Sage.

———. 1998. One of the girls? The changing gender of journalism. In C. Carter, G. Branston, and S. Allan, eds., *News, gender, and power,* pp. 33–46. London: Routledge.

Vetten, L. 1998a. Reporting on rape in South Africa. *Women's MediaWatch, 1998.*

———. 1998b. Reporting on rape in South Africa. *Women's MediaWatch Newsletter* 3: 5–8.

———. 1999. *Reporting on rape in South Africa.* Centre for the Study of Violence and Reconciliation, Women's MediaWatch.

White, W. 1999. One pill makes you larger. *Men's Health*, June, pp. 89–90.

Wober, J. M. 1981. Television and women: Viewing patterns and perceptions of ideal, actual, and portrayed women's roles. London: Independent Broadcasting Authority.

Women's Broadcasting Committee. 1993. *Her point of view.* Andover: BC/Bectu.

12

Media, Violence, Drugs, and Sex in Turkey

Alev Yemenici

This chapter, which is based on a survey, will discuss Turkish students' views regarding the role of national and international media in promoting violence and aggressive behavior in general and against women in particular. The portrayals of women as sex objects and drug use will also be discussed.

Media studies in Turkey and abroad have long emphasized that heavy portrayals of violence in media can contribute to violent behavior among maladjusted individuals consuming such media on a prolonged basis. However, there are differing views on the degree of effects of media on children and adults. It has been believed that the studies of mass communication do not provide enough information on the kind and degree of these effects. McQuail argues that

> there can be no question of the media being a primary cause and we have no real "explanation" of patterns of thought, culture and behaviour with deep social and historical roots. Furthermore, it makes little sense to speak of "the media" as if they were one thing, rather than an enormously diverse set of messages, images and ideas, most of which do not originate with the media themselves but come from society and are sent "back" to society. It is thus not at all easy to name a case where the media can plausibly be regarded as the sole or indispensable cause of a given social effect. (1990, pp. 80–81)

According to Sobowale (1983), there are two schools of thought: "One school argues that the media actually transmit violence and encourage people to acquire aggressive behavior." According to the proponents of the other school, "the media simply do not have such potency." However, "the evidence on both sides is inconclusive" (1983, p. 221).

In Turkey, the media have been gaining strength and importance in turning the society into a world that is gradually becoming susceptible to direct or indirect expressions of violence and representations of women as figures of desire. As the media constitute a powerful means of control and influence, it is very likely that in the near future, the media will determine new social norms and the boundaries of acceptable behavior along with the perception of women from only a male perspective. In other words, the media influence on the society as "all-powerful propaganda agencies brainwashing a susceptible and defenceless public," is inevitable, leading to the fact that the media will propel " 'word bullets' that penetrate deep into its inert and passive victims. All that needed to be done was to measure the depth and size of penetration through modern scientific techniques" (Curran, Gurevitch, and Woollacott 1990, p. 58). Consequently, this study aims to ascertain the influence of media on Turkish youth, focusing mainly on their views, attitudes, and emotions regarding the media-related issues just identified.

This is a descriptive study conducted in Ankara, the capital city of Turkey. Thirty-six Turkish students (twenty-one female and fifteen male) from Middle East Technical University, Department of Foreign Language Education, participated in this study. The age of the subjects ranged between eighteen to twenty-two. The subjects were from a variety of backgrounds. They were administered a questionnaire to help discover their opinions and attitudes.

The subjects watched a variety of TV programs (news on TV, commercials, two talk shows, one reality show, movies, and music clips) and read two different newspapers and two magazines for two weeks. After each viewing or reading they were asked to write their opinions and answer a set of questions designed to help the students analyze the nature of the program viewed or material read. After a two-week period, they were asked to form an attitude regarding the programs viewed and materials read, elaborating on the impact of media on youth regarding the issues mentioned above.

This paper presents database information analyzed according to a framework adapted from Sobowale (1983). The present study investigates the role of the mass media as a distributing, facilitating, defusing, magnifying, and/or mediatory agent as perceived by Turkish university students.

GLOBALIZATION

Technological advances in the media make the world grow smaller each year. The largest and most modern media in the hands of economically well-developed nations of the world such as the United States and some European countries provide a heavy flow of news and entertainment programs from these information- and entertainment-producing countries to the Second World and Third World countries. This flood makes the developing countries receptive of global information. The incoming information may be in the form of movies, music clips, newspaper, magazines, and various TV programs. And satellites enable huge amounts of information to travel around the world at the speed of light. The speed of information transfer and technology come to dominate the mass media markets in the developing countries.

There is a high level of American and European influence on Turkish private televisions and cinema. On some Turkish private TV channels there is a direct transfer or adoption of the American model of broadcasting. American-produced serials and movies account for more than half of the programs on some private TVs. For instance, on Saturdays the exported programs on the major Turkish TV channels constitute 34 percent of total programming on the average. However, this number amounts to 100 percent on some channels, such as Maxi TV and Supersport. On Cine 5 the exported programs constitute 88 percent of the whole.

Researchers have offered the following criticisms of global information transfer:

- The flow of information is unequal, with too much information originating in the West and not enough representing the developing nations.
- There is too much bias against, and stereotyping of, the developing or "less developed" countries.
- Alien values are foisted on the Third World by too much Western (mainly American) "communication imperialism."
- Western communication places undue emphasis on "negative" news of the Third World—disasters, coups, government corruption, and the like.
- The Western definition of "news" (meaning atypical and sensational items) is unrealistic and does not focus enough attention on development news (items helping in the progress and growth of the country).
- Too much of the world's information is collected by the big news agencies, giving the news a biased (Western) slant. (Merrill, Lee, and Friedlander 1994, pp. 416–417)

Another criticism comes from Gerbner (1995). "Violence on television is an integral part of a system of global marketing. . . . The system inhibits the portrayal of diverse dramatic approaches to conflict, depresses independent television production, deprives viewers of more popular choices, victimizes some and emboldens others, heightens general intimidation and invites repressive postures by politicians that exploit the widespread insecurities it itself generates" (p. 549).

The present study further explores whether international media have an important influence on the national media, whether the criticisms of the Turkish audience display similarities with the criticisms mentioned above, and whether the national media adopt foreign models of program making and broadcasting.

BACKGROUND

Violence is one of the most pervasive problems in Turkey. Mass media are believed to play a significant role in producing, distributing, magnifying, and legitimating violence. Gerbner (1995) argues that violence reflected in drama and news demonstrates power as "it portrays victims as well as victimizers. It intimidates more than it incites. It paralyzes more than it triggers action. . . . It shows one's place in the 'pecking order' that runs society" (p. 548). Violent behavior and sexual elements in TV programs make children and youth prone to aggressive reactions and violent acts (Köknel 1996). Research has shown that violence plays an important role in the ratings struggle on Turkish private TV channels (Özal 1996; Akarcalı 1996). According to Akarcalı (1996), violence has become an integral part of commercial TV and has been extensively used in cartoons, news, and adult programs sending subliminal messages (pp. 553–554). Some studies designed to expose the correlation between TV violence and the increase in the aggressive behavior in Turkey suggest that there is some evidence indicating a rise in social violence and suicide rates. Heper (1996) emphasizes that a young girl committed suicide after she had watched *Inferno*, a horror film. Another victim was an eight-year-old student from Üsküdar who hanged himself after he had deeply been affected by the TV. Heper argues that the violent main characters on TV set bad examples for children and youth, which leads to the dissemination of violence throughout the country. Programs and movies that build around violence introduce techniques that show how crime can be committed. According to some experts, five-year-old children who watch violent programs on TV every day by the age of fifteen will have been acquainted with 18,000 ways of how to commit acts of sexual harassment, assault, fighting, and torture. According to a study done in 1994, the violence rate on Turkish TV is 62 percent and on a Sunday a child is reported to watch more than six hundred violent acts on seven different channels that display killings of more than five hundred people. Pamuk, a clinical psychologist, argues that reality shows are a threat to children and youth as they gradually lose their faith in the society they live in when they start to think that everybody they meet on the streets can kidnap children and kill their parents at any time (Heper 1996). Those who lead a life in such doubt will inevitably use force to feel safe (Heper 1996). According to Rigel (1996a) children aged five to seven in

Turkey perceive negativity in news programs intensely and regard news of death and accidents as the most important news events. Their first reaction is fear, which is followed by aggressive behavior as they grow older. According to research done in 1994 in Turkey, 68 percent of the subjects said that the mass media encouraged violence (Gezgin 1996, p. 559). Gezgin argues that when movies, serials, reality shows, and news portray violence, they attract attention. However, as the violence in the programs is hidden and subtly interwoven in the texture of the program, it creates a negative impact on the audience before they realize that this is so (p. 559). News programs are selling death and blood to the audience. Other research demonstrates that children are exposed to 150–200 movies and serials out of 400 in a week that host scenes of battering, fighting, rape, theft, assault, poisoning, and bombing (Köknel 1996). Rigel's study (1996b) reveals that 7.92 percent of the Turkish subjects liked watching violence on TV or in movies in 1994 while in 1995 this number amounted to 15.4 percent, indicating that violence provides pleasure for the audience, directing them toward new models of aggression that will lead to an environment in which the person can use these models freely with pleasure (Rigel 1996b). Gradually people will be desensitized toward overtones of violence and will be raising mentally, psychologically, and morally delinquent children. Rigel argues that the Turkish audience watches injustice in life in reality shows and may easily transform themselves into dangerous individuals. These individuals who have learned how to derive pleasure out of violence will constitute the human material for these programs any time (1996b, p. 590).

Research indicates that advertisements support a male image with overtones of violence. For instance, an ad for Dell computers shows a painting in which some cowboys are shooting at Indians who are chasing them. "The copy reads 'Being Able to Run Faster Could Come in Real Handy' " (Katz 1995, p. 137). This ad presents violence that is "depicted as defensive, a construction that was historically used to justify genocide" (p. 137).

Similarly, it has been claimed that for rating concerns, the issue of sex and news regarding drug use and alcohol consumption have been exploited by the private TV channels in Turkey. However, these findings are not enough to associate the impact of media with the increase in social crime directly (Palabıyıkoğlu 1997). According to Alemdar and Erdoğan (1994) in the United States there is pressure on youth who want to be a part of the popular culture to at least try marijuana. Since the youth in developing countries have a strong tendency to imitate the developed countries, youth may start using drugs extensively in the future (p. 68).

How are women represented in the news? A study carried out by Boom and Michielsens (1996) reveals that slightly more than 35 percent of the victims in West European TV news are women victims. In their research, this percentage amounts to 71 percent. Boom and Michielsens (1996) emphasize that women are overrepresented as victims because they are underrepresented in other areas of media coverage (p. 189). They claim that if lower status is attached to a role, then the role is represented by women. In other words, women are represented as victims of violence (rape, murder, battering), which assigns women the role of signs (Rakow and Kranich 1991) that "carry rather than create meaning" (Boom and Michielsens 1996, p. 188). As signs of violence, they represent consequences of events and actions. In some cases the perpetrators of crime are magnified, whereas the female victim is silenced. In addition, though the perpetrator might be guilty of murder in addition to "incest, adultery and statutory rape," "his actions were excused while the woman was blamed for her own murder" (p. 196). Boom and Michielsens conclude that news as a "primarily masculine narrative . . . uses the 'woman-sign' to illustrate the private consequences of men's public action. . . . The female victim is pre-eminently the product of a patriarchal ideology in which boys don't cry; they only die or get wounded. In the portrayal of female victims, certain 'rules' must be obeyed: keep it 'clean,' private and emotional. Overdo the personal violence against them, but neglect them if they dare to accuse you" (p. 197).

Women are represented in commercials as either housewives or sex objects. When women are seen from a pornographic stance, this directly influences the attitudes of society. The advertisements that sell women's bodies create a social climate in which "the marketing of women's bodies–the sexual sell and dismemberment, distorted body image ideal . . . as sex objects–is seen as acceptable" (Kilbourne 1995, p. 125). One drawback of this image is that women's self-image can be affected deeply by the "subliminal impact of advertisements" that may influence their relationship with society as women are represented as an object that can be brutalized (p. 125). Bass (1995) argues that college-age men exposed to a few slasher films "are more likely than other men to believe that the victim of an actual rape deserved what she got. They are also less likely to want the rapist to be punished" (p. 186). Bass emphasizes that a study carried out by a psychologist revealed that "young men exposed to popular films like *Getaway* and *Swept Away,* which combine sex and violence, were more accepting of violence toward women than those who had seen other types of films. A larger percentage of these men also said they might try to force women into sexual acts against their will, as long as they were assured of not being caught" (pp. 186–187). In a study, attitudes of college-age men who were exposed to nonviolent sexually explicit films and others who watched slasher films were compared. The results revealed that "if no violence surrounds the sex, sexually explicit films do not appear to make viewers more callous toward victims of violent crime" (p. 187).

The representation of women in slasher films or in movies that equate masculinity with violence and action and femininity with passivity conveys a negative image. The violent scenes reflect a climate in which "male domineering and violence against women seem erotic" (Dines and Humez 1995, p. 162). And this concept immediately reduces the role of women to sex object.

Aldoğan (1996) studied how the image of the woman was used and how women were represented in the Turkish mass media. Pictures of women on the front pages of newspapers display the beauty of the woman. Here news content is not important. If the woman is used on the third pages of newspapers, she portrays the image of the victim. They should be battered, raped, or killed or undergo an accident to appear on these pages. Their pictures are dramatically contrasted with their pictures taken from their family albums. These women are either victims of sadistic crimes or victimizers who killed their husbands. On the Turkish private TV channels, in the news programs or reality shows only the woman who is victimized has news value. It is not easy to determine whether the programs that display women as victims have a didactic purpose or whether they send subliminal messages. On the second and last pages of newspapers, women who are models, actresses, and singers are displayed. The news content of these pages is insignificant. Women mostly appear on the magazine and TV pages of newspapers surrounded with hot gossip. In other words, women are regarded as a sign of sex or victim. This is women's usual role. Other than this usual role, when women appear on the newspaper, their femininity is almost always emphasized. If the woman on the newspaper is a lawyer than her profession is specified with a linguistic determiner "female" and she becomes a "female lawyer" (p. 1320). This linguistic clue indicates that "women are under-represented in other areas of media coverage" (Boom and Michielsens 1996, p. 189).

FRAMEWORK

The framework that is used for the analysis of the impact of the media draws on Sobowale's study (1983). Sobowale analyzes the effect of the media as positive or negative. The role of the media as defusing agents and as mediating agents constitutes the positive effect of the mass media. When the media function as distributing agents, facilitating agents, and magnifying agents, this function constitutes the negative effect.

The Mass Media as Distributing Agents

The media distribute news, circulating information about achievements of governments and conflicts between countries. "It is probably reasonable to argue that without the mass media individual nations would not know a lot of what they know about the rest of the world. In that case, perhaps, there might be fewer international conflicts" (Sobowale 1983, p. 224). According to Sobowale, the mass media disseminate "dysfunctional" as well as functional "information, such as violence, both at the national and the international level" (p. 225).

The Mass Media as Facilitating Agents

The mass media have a strong influence on what people pay attention to. According to Sobowale (1983), this is what makes the world a "global village" (p. 225); the mass media put "international violence on the agenda of their international audiences" (p. 225). This media influence is important because it makes people abroad or at home aware of the existence of crime and violence, though it does not "command people to commit crime" (p. 225).

The Mass Media as Magnifying Agents

The mass media are influential in that they tell the audience what importance they should give to one particular news event. The degree of importance they assign to a news event, the headline they use, or the angle at which the TV camera is focused determine their judgment about the worth of the news event and thus help manipulate the perception of the audience. In other words, the news event in the hands of the mass media can very well be magnified and turned into sensationalism.

The Mass Media as Defusing Agents

The mass media spread information instantaneously nationally and internationally. This not only leads to the defusing and facilitating roles of the media but also brings about some fast and effective solutions to the problematic situations. For instance, the fast speed of the news regarding disputes among countries brings about international diplomatic efforts "to defuse crises before their potentially dangerous fallouts begin to spread" (Sobowale 1983, p. 227).

The Mass Media as Mediatory Agents

The mass media, distributing news events all around the world almost instantaneously, bring to the world's attention a variety of conflicts and crises, assuming the role of a mediating agent. The world, in return, aims at bringing and keeping these crises and conflicts under control. This may lead to "peaceful resolution of conflicts" (p. 229). On the one hand, the media "set nations or individuals warring against one another," while on the other, they "promote dialogue among them" (p. 229).

In this chapter we will examine the questionnaire results within the framework of the roles of the media as facilitating, distributing, magnifying, defusing, and mediatory agents as described above.

DESIGN AND PROCEDURES

This study is a descriptive study. The intention is to analyze the subjects' attitudes toward the influence of media regarding the issues of sex, violence, and drug use. The subjects were administered a questionnaire with twelve survey questions that investigated their attitudes. To analyze the results of the questionnaire, Sobowale's framework was taken as a point of departure and his definitions of the roles of the media were taken as the basis.

The questionnaire comprises twelve survey questions that were designed to explore the subjects' emotions, attitudes, and reactions, in other words, their conception of the mass media as an influential social institution in Turkey and of the national media as having been influenced by the international media or not. The programs that were analyzed are categorized as follows:

News programs: *Show Haber* and *Star Haber*
Sports magazine programs: *Televole* (on two different channels)
Talk Shows: *Hülya Avşar Show* and *Zaga Show*
Reality Show: *Arena*
Newspapers: *Hürriyet* and *Star*
Magazines: *Tempo* and *Aktüel*
Music Clips, action movies, and commercials

These particular news programs, sports magazine programs, talk shows, magazines, and newspapers were selected because they were reported to have a higher rating than the other programs, newspapers, and magazines on the market.

RESULTS AND ANALYSIS

The questionnaire results displayed in table 12.1 indicate that news programs are full of violence. Thirty-six out of thirty-six subjects (100 percent) found elements of violence in news programs. Similarly, the element of sex constitutes 81 percent of the programs specified. Only 11 percent of the subjects said the news programs make news regarding drugs. Fully 81 percent of the subjects think that sports magazine programs contain elements of sex and 28 percent think they observed elements of violence in these programs. However, none of them found drug-related issues in these programs. Ninety-four percent of the subjects stated that talk shows are based on sex-related issues and 58 percent found elements of violence in these programs. None reported issues regarding drugs. Sixty-seven percent of the subjects found sex-related news, 44 percent found violence-related news, and 11 percent read drug-related issues in the newspapers. Fifty-six percent of the subjects think that the specified magazines use sex, 6 percent think they use violence, and 17 percent think they use drug-related news as material for consumption. Seventy-five percent of the subjects found sex, 28 percent found violence, and 8 percent found drug use in music clips. Fifty percent found sex, 78 percent found violence, and 11 percent found drug-related issues in action movies. Eighty-nine percent thought that commercials are based on sex, 25 percent found elements of violence in commercials, and none observed drug-related issues. The subjects specified the fact that although there are elements of violence, sex, and drugs, the reality show, *Arena,* does not exploit these issues but highlights a social problem that needs to be cured. Eleven percent of the subjects found sex, 31 percent found violence, and 28 percent found drug-related issues in *Arena,* but all of them emphasized that issues of sex, violence, and drugs are not exploited and sensationalized in *Arena.* Four subjects stated that these issues are exaggerated from time to time.

Analysis of the Questions

The twelve survey questions and the responses elicited are summarized below.

• Do you get emotionally involved in these programs when you watch them? How do you react?

The subjects indicated that none of them was emotionally involved in these programs. However, they believe that children and laymen whose educational level is not as high will definitely be emotionally involved and negatively affected by these programs.

Table 12.1. Distribution of Sex, Violence, and Drugs in TV Programs and Newspapers

	Element of Sex	Element of Violence	Drugs
News	81% (29/36)	100% (36/36)	11% (4/36)
Sports magazines	81% (29/36)	28% (10/36)	—
Talk shows	94% (34/36)	58% (21/36)	—
Reality shows	11% (4/36)	31% (11/36)	28% (10/36)
Newspapers	67% (24/36)	44% (16/36)	11% (4/36)
Magazines	56% (20/36)	6% (2/36)	17% (6/36)
Music clips	75% (27/36)	28% (10/36)	8% (3/36)
Action movies	50% (18/36)	78% (28/36)	11% (4/36)
Commercials	89% (32/36)	25% (9/36)	—

• Do you get emotionally involved in the news and magazine articles when you read them? How do you react? (In other words, are you affected positively or negatively, or do you remain neutral?)

The subjects thought that newspapers sensationalize news events, putting emphasis on rape, suicide, crime, and disasters, and making use of violence and death to the level of exaggeration. Though they are not emotionally involved, laymen and children, they believe, will be negatively affected in the long run.

• If you find these programs/articles/pieces of news entertaining to watch/read, please explain why.

None of the subjects reported that they were entertained by the scenes of violence and sex in the programs specified. They reported that because of the constant emphasis on such scenes some of them stopped watching these programs altogether.

• Do you think people/children who watch these programs/read the articles are encouraged to commit violent acts
against self
against human beings and animals
against things

All of the subjects firmly believed that these programs, except for *Arena,* the reality show, encourage people to commit crimes of all sorts. These programs were reported to encourage aggression, desensitization, and a sense of vulnerability due to fear.

• To what extent is physical aggression encouraged?

The subjects stated that the action movies, news programs, sports magazine programs, music clips, and the specified talk shows encourage physical aggression.

• To what extent is verbal aggression encouraged?

The subjects thought that the sports magazine programs and the talk shows encouraged verbal aggression.

• Do you think these programs and articles display aggression-supporting environments?

Movies, news about violence and rape, pictures in newspapers, and music clips were reported to support aggressive environments.

- Do you think these programs and articles will have short-term/long-term negative/harmful effects on children/adults?

The subjects thought that if broadcasting of violence continued, it would have long-term negative influence on adults and children.

- Do you perceive direct or indirect violence in them? In other words, is violence directly observable?

The subjects observed direct violence in news programs, newspapers, music clips, and action movies. In the sports magazine programs, talk shows, and commercials, they thought violence is implied.

- Do you think women are exposed as sex objects? Do you think this representation of women may lead to violent acts toward women in our society?

Most of the subjects believed that women are exposed as sex objects in news programs, sports magazine programs, talk shows, newspapers, magazines, music clips, and some movies and commercials. They firmly believed that this denigrates women's place in society and is contributing to women's battering in some circles.

- Do you think these programs/news spots, and articles create sensationalism regarding drug use, thus drawing disproportionate attention on the issue?

The subjects did not think that drug use draws disproportionate attention. On the contrary, in *Arena,* the issue is discussed from many perspectives, drawing attention to the harmful effects of drugs, thus warning the society to take precautions and creating awareness on the part of the parents.

- Do you think international media have an important effect on the national media? In what sense? Please specify. Do they adopt foreign models of program making and broadcasting and/or transfer models directly?

The subjects believed that international media have an important influence on the national media. They thought the image of women as sex objects is borrowed from the international media. Furthermore, moviemakers and program producers who search for global markets sell entertainment-laced violence, promoting international aggression and sex. The subjects believed that international media export hi-tech violence methods. In addition, they stated that in movies and serials foreign values are imposed on the public. Most of the subjects believed that news of international importance should be broadcast on Turkish TV, and they thought the national media should broadcast important news more than sensational news of crime, sex, and disasters. In addition, they stated that the national media should be very careful with issues such as satanism so that both the national and the international media should not drive society into fear and panic. Sometimes pictures and news on foreign newsmagazines frighten people; therefore, the role of the national media, they believe, should be to reduce fear encoded in the issue, focusing on information rather than exaggeration and sensation. More than half of the subjects (62 percent) stated that the national media (especially news coverage and music clips) adopt foreign models of broadcasting.

CONCLUSION

The results of the analysis indicate that the subjects thought sex and violence are pervasively used in the specified TV programs, magazines, and newspapers in Turkey. The mass media circulate and instantaneously disseminate international and national news of violence, putting special emphasis on either a woman's body as a commodified image or grisly scenes of violence. Especially the specified news programs on the Turkish private TV channels constantly broadcast news of violence, displaying the victims, which may lead to desensitization in real-life situations as "people without real-world experience with violence are more likely to accept as real the fictionalized portrayal of violence on television and film and buy into the idea that there is no suffering or agony attached to that violence" (Bass 1995, p. 188). This type of audience has no chance of avoiding violence.

The subjects in this study reported that they developed a habit of not watching these programs because of the direct or indirect negative impacts they may have on them. This finding is in contrast with Rigel's (1996b) findings that there was a group of audience who derived pleasure from explicit messages of violence. The present finding indicates that university students have become mature enough to reject the message of violence inherent in many programs. They think the constant repetition of scenes of violence and magnified news events penetrate very deeply into their minds, involving the audience as victims or victimizers in each program. Furthermore, the mass media force people to be aware of different types, methods, and levels of violence through movies, videos, music clips, and serials. Though programs that involve violence are not highly rated, "violence may help sell programs cheaply to broadcasters in many countries despite the dislike of their audiences" (Gerbner 1995, p. 554). In addition, according to Gerbner (1995) violence on TV is a product of global marketing. Violence dominates an increasing share of the world's screens despite its relative lack of popularity in any country. Its consequences go far beyond inciting aggression (p. 548). Therefore, though these programs have low average popularity, they capture young viewers "that advertisers want to reach and by extending their reach to the global market hungry for a cheap product" (Gerbner 1995, p. 555).

According to the results of the analysis in the present study, the role of the media as a distributing and facilitating agent makes it possible for people with violent instincts to learn different ways to actualize their intentions. In the programs analyzed, scenes of crime and violence are repeatedly shown on private TV channels, and especially women are depicted as passive victims of threatening violence. In addition to this, the mass media magnify various news events through the headlines and pictures they use or through the dimension they give to the scenes. When the cameras fix on scenes of brutal violence over and over again, they convey negative messages, leading the audience to think that since this news is in the headlines or repeatedly on the screen, it must be newsworthy; thus disproportionate attention is given to crime and violence. According to Sobowale (1983), this has two major consequences. First, the audience may feel sympathy for the perpetrators of crimes. They may think that they committed crimes mainly because they were wronged or because of their oppressive circumstances. Second, the audience may have feelings of extreme anger and hatred toward the perpetrators. These two reactions have been reported by the participants in this study.

According to Sobowale (1983), "the ubiquity of the mass media and the immediacy of their information dissemination" bring about the prevention of violence. The subjects have reported that the Turkish media, especially the reality shows, draw attention to the issue of drug use, its harmful effects, and urgent precautions. All the subjects agreed that the mass media are very careful with this social phenomenon. The media tend to create awareness and fear as well as empathy and concern regarding the victims of drugs so that drug use has a dissuading influence on the public. In other words, in *Arena,* violence, sex, and drugs become a legitimate and even necessary cultural expression for the good of society. The mass media undertake the role of a mediatory agent when they "set in motion a complex network of mediation" as they bring "the existence of conflicts, crises and violence to the attention of the world" (Sobowale 1983, p. 226). The Turkish media function as a mediatory agent whenever there is an obvious threat to the mental, physical, or psychological health of the public; however, the degree of prominence they attribute to the news events disturbs the audience greatly and they suffer the broadcasting of violence daily.

All the programs contain elements of sex. Talk shows, commercials, music clips, news, sports magazine programs, and movies, along with newspapers and magazines, support an image of the woman as a sex object that denigrates women's social status. These programs and news sources that depict women along the lines of sexuality promise the audience bodily arousal, indicating a society obsessed with sexuality. According to Jhally (1995), "the end result is that the commodity is part of an increasingly eroticized world—that we live in a culture that is more and more defined erotically through commodities" (p. 82). The media's role as a distributing, facilitating, and mediatory agent reinforces the image of women as sex objects, continually sending subliminal messages to the public subconscious. Asena (1996) states that today in Turkey women's beauty is foregrounded in the mass media; the image of women is used for eroticism or as passive victims of crimes committed by males. In order not to hurt men's feelings, male photographs are not used in news of sex scandals but women are fully exposed. In other words, *Arena* emphasizes that the woman is used as an image of commodity that aims to please men. According to Yalçin and Yurdakök (1999), TV programs very often present sex as dangerous, abusive, and exciting. The concept of marriage is important only for women, and extramarital love affairs are encouraged as if they were socially acceptable (p. 37).

Subjects have reported cases in which women internalize the role imposed by the media only to learn their limitations as women. In other words, they are forced to accept a degraded and passive image. As the subjects are aware of this influence of the media, most of them reported that they prefer not to watch these programs because they find the content repellent and degrading. Most believe that instances and scenes of different forms of sexual violence depicted in the mass media and woman's public image as a sex object lead to more violence directed to women. It is very likely that when people are exposed to long-term violence in movies, TV programs, or newspapers, violent behavior will be a likely outcome as more impressionable people will tend to believe, without questioning, what they see and those who are ready to commit violent acts tend to imitate violent behavior especially when they witness, in some movies, that the perpetrators are rewarded.

When we look at the whole picture, the Turkish students who participated in this study wish to watch programs that do not threaten people's physical, mental, and psychological health and moral values in the long run. They do not want to be steeped in a distorted reality in which violence and erotic images are intermingled. They do not want to see women as overvictimized or overrepresented as sex objects and underrepresented as respectable members of society. They no longer wish to raise children who will grow up violent or addicted to the passive or active expression of violence.

The data in this study are not rich enough to provide elaborate generalizations regarding the effect of the mass media on sex, crime, and drug use. More case studies need to be done on the issue. However, this study has presented an attitude survey as to how university students perceive the role of the national and international mass media in Turkey. The Turkish students refused to take in distorted images of women and instances of violence that threaten the structure of the society. They believed that mass media should take on a constructive role to contribute positively to the psychological and social development of children and teenagers who are believed to be most vulnerable to the harmful effects of explicit/implicit messages of violence and sex abuse.

REFERENCES

Akarcalı, S. 1996. Televizyon ve şiddet (Television and media). *Yeni Türkiye* 11: 553–557.

Aldoğan, Y. 1996. Medyanın kadına bakış açısı (Representation of women in media). *Yeni Türkiye, 12,* 1318–1321.

Alemdar, K., and İ. Erdoğan. 1994. *Popüler kültür ve iletişim* (Popular culture and communication). Ankara: Ümit Yayıncılık.

Asena, D. 1996. Medya ve kadın (Media and women). *Yeni Türkiye* 12: 1323–1324.

Bass, A. 1995. Do slasher films breed real-life violence? In G. Dines and J. M. Humez, eds., *Gender, race, and class in media,* pp. 185–189. London: Sage.

Boom, A. T., and M. Michielsens. 1996. Illustrating human suffering: Women as victims on the news. *Yeni Türkiye* 12: 1323–1324.

Curran, J., M. Gurevitch, and J. Woollacott. 1990. The study of the media: Theoretical approaches. In O. Boyd-Barrett and P. Braham, eds., *Media, knowledge, and power,* pp. 57–79. London: Routledge.

Dines, G., and J. M. Humez, eds. 1995. *Gender, race, and class in media.* London: Sage.

Gerbner, G. 1995. Television violence: The power and the peril. In G. Dines and J. M. Humez, eds., *Gender, race, and class in media,* pp. 547–557. London: Sage.

Gezgin, S. 1996. Göstergesel şiddet (Symbolic violence). *Yeni Türkiye* 11: 558–560.

Heper, D. 1996. Basın meslek ilkeleri, medya ve şiddet (Principles of press, media, and violence). *Yeni Türkiye* 11: 547–549.

Jhally, S. 1995. Image-based culture: Advertising and popular culture. In G. Dines and J. M. Humez, eds., *Gender, race, and class in media,* pp. 77–87. London: Sage.

Katz, J. 1995. Advertising and the construction of violent white masculinity. In G. Dines and J. M. Humez, eds., *Gender, race, and class in media,* pp. 133–141. London: Sage.

Kilbourne, J. 1995. Beauty and the beast of advertising. In G. Dines and J. M. Humez, eds., *Gender, race, and class in media,* pp. 121–125. London: Sage.

Köknel, Ö. 1996. *Bireysel ve toplumsal şiddet* (Individual and social violence). İstanbul: Altın Kitaplar Yayınevi.

McQuail, D. 1990. Processes of media effects. In O. Boyd-Barrett and P. Braham, eds., *Media, knowledge, and power,* pp. 80–107. London: Routledge.

Merrill, J., J. Lee, and E. J. Friedlander. 1994. *Modern mass media.* New York: HarperCollins.

Özal, Ö. 1996. Medya ve şiddet (Media and violence). *Yeni Türkiye* 11: 550–552.

Palabıyıkoğlu, R. 1997. Medya ve şiddet (Media and violence). *Kriz Dergisi* 5, no. 12: 123–126.

Rakow, L. F., and K. Kranich. 1991. Woman as sign in television news. *Journal of Communication* 41, no. 1: 8–23.

Rigel, N. 1996a. Haberin gizli tüketicisi çocuk (Child as the secret consumer of news). *Yeni Türkiye* 11: 561–589.

———. 1996b. Reality show ve haber programlarının 94–95 karşılaştırmalı etki analizi (A comparative analysis of the influence of reality shows and news programs in 94–95). *Yeni Türkiye* 11: 590–635.

Sobowale, I. A. 1983. The impact of the mass media on international violence. In T. Adeniran and Y. Alexander, eds., *International violence*, pp. 221–230. London: Sage; New York: Praeger.

Yalçin, S. S., and K. Yurdakök. 1999. Televizyon ve çocuk (Child and television). *Hacettepe Tıp Dergisi* 30, no. 1: 36–41.

13

Media, Sex, Violence, and Drugs: Egypt's Experience

Hussein Y. Amin and Hanzada Fikry

The Republic of Egypt is located in the heart of the Arab world, with Arabic as its official language. Islam is the religion of the state, with a large minority of Coptic Christians. Despite a cosmopolitan atmosphere, both religions as well as a deep-rooted Arab culture have considerable impact on the Egyptian tradition and lifestyle. Media and politics go hand in hand in Egypt. Three men who ruled Egypt after the 1952 revolution, excluding Mohamed Naguib who headed the government for two years (1952–1954), shaped the development of modern mass media in Egypt but dealt with the issues of media violence, sex, and drugs differently. The first was Gamal Abdel Nasser, president of Egypt from 1954 to 1970, who developed and implemented severe rules of censorship; the second was Anwar el Sadat, president of Egypt from 1970 to 1981, who introduced opposition parties; and the third is Egypt's current president, Hosni Mubarak, who has relaxed strong government control of the media (Napoli and Amin 1997).

Nasser realized from his first days as a ruler of Egypt that political parties controlled the press. Non-Egyptians owned most publishing houses. Realizing the power of the press in mobilizing the public, Nasser made his move in 1960 by nationalizing the Egyptian press. All media organizations had to surrender their ownership to the country's only legal political organization, the National Union, later renamed the Arab Socialist Union. The ownership of the nation's four large private publishing houses—Dar al-Ahram, Dar

219

Akhbar al-Yom, Dar al-Hilal, and Dar Rose al-Yousuf—was transferred to the National Union, which already owned Dar al-Tahrir publishing house (Rugh 1989). These and other changes were designed by Nasser to permit the government to mobilize the press behind his socialist policies, as was already the case with the state broadcasting system (Nasser 1990). On October 26, 1954, the Muslim Brotherhood fired shots at Nasser while he was giving a speech in Alexandria (El Attar 1998). The attack gave Nasser a reason to launch a major attack on the Muslim Brotherhood and keep their political activities at a minimum (Stephens 1971).

Nasser's successor, Anwar el Sadat, theoretically adopted an open attitude toward the press, but in practice, his policies with regard to the press were ambivalent (Napoli and Amin 1997). Sadat restored the right to establish political parties, which also were given the right to publish newspapers. The four major opposition parties in Egypt are El Ahrar, the socialist party; El Wafd, the rightist party; El Tagamo'a El Watani, a leftist party; and El Am'al Alashtraki, the socialist labor party with Islamic influences (Amin and Napoli 1997). They each have their own newspapers. The most important and the only daily opposition newspaper is *El Wafd*. The most important of the other major opposition party papers is El Am'al's weekly *Al-Shaab* (The people) and El Tagamo's and El Watani's weekly *El Ahali* (Natives) (Napoli 1995).

Political violence struck heavily on January 18–19, 1976. Violence and demonstrations erupted in almost all major cities in Egypt following the government's sudden increase of basic food prices. Thousands of people were killed and wounded (Nasser 1990). President Sadat did not want the Egyptian press to cover the riots, but the press conducted several campaigns blaming the government for the riots (El Attar 1998). Members of a Muslim fundamentalist group assassinated President Sadat in 1981. The Egyptian media's coverage of political violence raised the public's concerns about violence in the society.

Hosni Mubarak—unlike his two predecessors—moved toward more press freedom and lifted many restrictions. The Egyptian press under Mubarak operates far more freely than it did under the two previous regimes and more freely than in the majority of Arab and African countries (Napoli and Amin 1997). By 1992, a bigger number and wider range of titles were being published than ever before by a host of private and energetic publishers (Tresilian 1992).

A wave of political violence erupted in the country, eventually reaching the president himself, when an assassination attempt was carried out as his motorcade drove from the Addis Ababa airport in Ethiopia. The president was on his way to attend a meeting of the Organization of African Unity. Immediately after the attempt on his life, Mubarak returned to Egypt. The Egyptian media not only gave full-scale coverage of the event from the point of Mubarak's return to the country, but they sent reporters to investigate the event in Addis Ababa and the Sudan (El Attar 1998).

At the dawn of the twenty-first century, Egyptian media remain generally conservative, always monitored, and usually subject to some form of censorship. Newspapers and magazines have provided a clamorous and lively forum for the nation's conservative and modernist tendencies. Many periodicals propagate ideas and movements for economic and political reforms, feminism, secular liberalism, religious conservatism, trade unionism, and so forth (Vatikiotis 1991).

The relaxation of censorship and the partial opening up of the economy after years of socialist controls have also cleared the way for a revitalization of the magazine press, especially under the pro-Western government of President Mubarak. Until 1981, the year that Sadat was assassinated, the number of publications of all types licensed to operate in Egypt was only 77. Since the 1980s, however, more than 300 publications of all types have been licensed, including many magazines for hospitals, airports, companies, the military, and various trades. But special interest consumer magazines have also begun to create a market for themselves on Egyptian newsstands. The biggest category of new special interest magazine is devoted to religion (Amin and Napoli 1994).

COVERAGE OF SEX, VIOLENCE, AND DRUGS

In the past few years, the issues of sex, violence, and drugs have begun to surface in the Egyptian media. *Rose El Yousuf,* a leading magazine in the country, started a campaign to expose the sexual behavior of some prominent figures in the country. The highly popular campaign outlined their alleged involvement in sex scandals. Although the magazine was accused of indulging in yellow journalism, the campaign was successful in bringing the issue to public debate.

Violence against women in the country is generally ignored by the media. One researcher has found that this social problem receives little exposure in the Egyptian press (El Dessouky 1997). In addition, the Egyptian reader is not getting important information and in-depth coverage and analysis of sex-related crimes. The main reason for limited coverage of this crime is the traumatic impact of sexual violence on the victim and the family and friends, and on the society in general. It is a cultural dimension that avoiding any publicity about the incident is desirable in order to maintain the reputation of the victim. However, the Ma'adi gang rape incident in 1985 and the Attabah (a district in Cairo) sexual assault in 1992 were major incidents that gave a boost to the coverage of sexual violence against females in Egypt (El Dessouky 1997).

There is a good chance today that a viewer turning on television will find images of dead bodies in the news or a dramatic series built around a murder or other violent crime. Crime news had a limited coverage in terms of content and space in print media in Egypt, but this situation has changed with the acceleration of terrorist acts since the early 1990s. *Akhbar Al Hawadas* (Crime news) is a prominent tabloid newspaper in Egypt and the Arab world that specializes in crime news. The weekly publication was established on April 9, 1992. The reporting in the newspaper is intended to support the idea that "crime doesn't pay" and also to discuss problems facing young Egyptians, such as unemployment, drug use, and lack of opportunities (Tewfik 1992).

In recent years, many Egyptian government and opposition media have become concerned over the intensive media coverage of terrorism. The Egyptian media have covered attacks on the minister of interior, Hassan el Alfi, in August 1993, on the Nile cruise ships, and on tourists (El Kotby 1995). Other acts of terrorism that had national and international media exposure and triggered debates on media and violence in Egypt were a series of bombs blasts in March 1993 and the attack on tourists in Luxor.

The Egyptian government and the media view the function, roles, and responsibilities of the media when covering terrorist events from differing viewpoints. Terrorists seek publicity in order to gain attention and inspire fear and respect in order to gain some sort of public understanding for their cause (El Kotby 1995). The Egyptian government, through its media, strives to gain the public's understanding, cooperation, restraint, and loyalty in its efforts to limit any harm from terrorists that might be inflicted on society and its efforts to punish people responsible for terrorist acts. News coverage of terrorism in Egypt has been criticized in recent decades, and that criticism is not without basis. There is probably no type of news event that presents more obstacles to coverage or has the potential for greater manipulation of the media than incidents of terrorism.

One criticism faced by the media is that much of the coverage lacks objectivity and that the media define terrorism on the basis of who committed the acts of violence rather than what acts were committed. Thus violent acts by groups opposed to political leaders would be labeled terrorism and those who perform them called terrorists, but similar acts by groups supported by political leaders or the media would not be so characterized. The media coverage, therefore, rests on a particular meaning associated with terrorism. In addition, media have also been criticized for their tendency to ignore "average" terrorist acts, the small-scale violence that occurs daily, instead concentrating coverage on spectacular or large-scale acts of violence. Most coverage of terrorism focuses on the extraordinary acts of terrorism. Media audiences, therefore, come to associate terrorism only with spectacular events perpetrated by disaffected persons (Paletz 1992).

The media also always aim to be the first with the story and make it as dramatic as possible, values that sometimes conflict with the need to be professional and accurate. Most of the time, Egyptian media do not focus as much on the coverage of terrorist attacks as they do on presenting opinions after the event. Moreover, since this topic is of great sensitivity to the government, its top aim has been to censor such coverage as much as possible. Another important goal that the government always attempts to achieve is to separate the terrorist from the media to deny the terrorist a platform. The government desires to present terrorists as criminals. The government seeks publicity and media support for its fight against terrorism to help diffuse tension in the society over this problem. Keeping the public reasonably calm is an important policy objective. At the same time, the government uses the media to boost its image so that its legitimacy won't be questioned.

Many TV series have participated in the governmental campaign against Islamic fundamentalism. The series showed these groups as terrorists who, because of their wrong interpretation of Islamic doctrines, destroy much of the good in the society. Soon enough, the terms "violence" and "terrorism" were associated with these groups throughout Egypt (Labib 1999). Foreign media began to do the same because they often base their reports on the information provided in the Egyptian media (El Kotby 1995).

CENSORSHIP, MEDIA GLOBALIZATION, AND CLASH OF CULTURES

Many Egyptians have expressed concerns about the information that is coming from the West. They view the constant flow of Western pop culture as a threat to their civilization and culture. Although such tensions have existed for more than a hundred years because of the popularity of Western media, especially print media, the sudden and addictive impact of Western popular cultural products such as video games, music CDs, computer software, films, and television programs has intensified the defensiveness of the Arab world (Gher et al. 1998).

Islamic societies in general are notably protective of their traditional religious and social values, and their conventions. The Egyptian society is generally conservative, with a tendency to shelter its culture and protect its national identity. The Arabic and Islamic dominions are inseparable on these points and are justifiably proud of their role in preserving the use of the Arabic language and Middle Eastern customs through their media, which dominate the Arab region.

Arab countries have responded to Western media infiltration, imagined or real, through severe rules of censorship. The Freedom Forum has stated that censorship is rigorously applied in most countries of the Arab world (Gher et al. 1998). In the West, freedom of expression is a basic individual right and is protected by judicial authority. In Egypt, media censorship is easily tolerated and even expected as a type of civic responsibility. Thus the clash of cultural values ensues.

For several decades since the 1920s, the Egyptian film industry remained the third largest in the world after the Indian film industry and Hollywood. Its dedicated fan club of more than one million Arabs stretches beyond Egyptian borders to the whole region. Generations of Egyptian stars became idols for men and women of all ages, formulating their concepts of purity and seduction, good and evil, and beauty and power. Typical scenes of wrestling between the villain and the lead actor, alluring and loose women who would soon die or turn into saints, and naive, misled men drinking off their failures in a bar filled the big screen, defying many social restrictions. But the films would one way or another conclude that justice, purity, and honesty must prevail (Farid 1981).

The first law defining the function of the Office of Censorship was issued in 1975. Under this law, the censors exercised their authority by ordering the removal of any scene conflicting with religion and national security, official government positions on issues of economic policy and foreign relations, and social ethics and traditional norms (El Shenawi 1994). During the 1960s, the articles of this law were made effectively irrelevant due to the nationalization of most of the production companies. In the Egyptian film industry, more daring topics and themes were discussed. Drug abuse, prostitution, and violence were the focus themes of many films in the 1970s and 1980s.

Egyptian radio and television programming policies still reinforce to a great extent cultural and national traditions and values. The system prohibits content that creates social confusion or criticizes the principles and traditions of Arab and Islamic society. Thus television adhered to the more conservative line in its production of local dramas emphasizing the family norms starting with *El Kahhira Wel Nas* (Cairo and its people) in the late 1960s to *Layali El Helmiya* (Nights of Helmeya district) in the 1990s. On the other hand, concerns over the cultural impact of films, TV dramas, or programming on Egyptian families, especially the middle classes, had its direct effect. Accordingly, the rules of censorship included prohibition of any material that threatened family ties or condemned family values.

Accordingly, sex scenes in foreign TV miniseries, mainly American series like *The Rich and the Poor* and later *Falcon Crest,* were censored. Others that dealt with taboos or portrayed divorce as a solution to family problems were shown for months to Egyptian viewers, then under pressure from conservative and religious groups were totally banned from the screen. These include *Dallas* and *The Bold and the Beautiful* in the late 1980s and early 1990s (El

Shenawi 1994). Some countries fear possible political and/or religious repercussions resulting from this influx of alien values. The anti-Western, Islamic fundamentalist reaction to the suddenly easy availability of pop culture has strengthened in the last decade.

Islamic groups, such as the Muslim Brotherhood, disapprove of their members using the media, specifically television, which is felt to have a negative, corrupting, immoral influence on Muslims. Public fear of these negative influences is documented in every Arab state. This has caused many governments to tighten control on audiovisual content through censorship. The government's fear of destabilization led to censorship of any material that violated rules of decency either by sound, picture or performance (Schleifer 1995).

Islam forbids consumption of drugs and alcohol as well as gambling, and that is why all Arab countries, including Egypt, censor any content that encourages such vice. In some modern feature films and television serials, outlaws and criminals are shown as heroes of the drama, which is not defensible within the Arab world. Some scenes in *El-A'ela* (The family) TV series, directed by Ismail Abdel Hafez, were banned in response to a direct order from Al-Azhar, Islam's premier religious institution. The deleted scenes included ridicule of a religious personality (El Shenawi 1999).

Criticism of the government's handling of radio, film, and television broadcasts has been continuous, particularly over the question of creativity. Egyptian producers and directors argue that censorship kills the spirit of creativity. It has become a problem that they face in every stage of preparing the movie. Monieb El Shafie, head of the Chamber of Cinema Production, has stated that censorship has become a monster that "rips films up under the false justification of protecting the public. Also, members of the Censorship Unit are not specialists and know nothing about art. In the end, the real victim is the quality of Egyptian cinema" (El Shenawi 1994). Tewfik Saleh, an Egyptian producer, stated that in the 1960s there was much more freedom of expression than there is now. In addition, the Censorship Unit was very different in the way it operated. He feels that today, each censor makes up his own standards and implements them without the other censors' knowledge (El Shenawi 1994). Producer Mohamed Khan said that the Censorship Unit is more of a dictator than an agency operating within the framework of clear guidelines. Its rules are vague and it treats artists with little respect. This causes a lot of strain for the artist in all stages of preparing his work. There is no way that a film of great meaning and impact can be made in such a repressive climate.

A young singer was reported to have cut his hair and changed his wardrobe so that the Censorship Unit could accept his work. Most producers and directors are frustrated with the Censorship Unit. The films that you see today are not the visions of the production teams but are those of the censors

(El Shenawi 1994). Scriptwriter Waheed Hamid stated that the censor is a conscience, not an authority. He mentioned that one of the censors at the Radio and Television Union refused an advertisement for a foreign film because the heroine tells one of her neighbors, "I am pregnant." The censor said that "pregnant" is an obscene word that implies sex and that makes the use of this word taboo. They don't permit this word but allow ads that depict Egyptian women insultingly (Farid 1981).

Coverage in the Egyptian newspapers of the censorship controversy did not eliminate or reduce censorship. The government in fact responded with more censorship by establishing a Higher Council for Censorship (Farid 1981).

As early as the 1930s, the late King Fouad of Egypt banned the film *Lasheen*, which portrayed a ruthless dictator ruling the country. An initial draft law for censorship was first issued in Egypt during World War I after a series of realistic films were released that discussed problems of Egyptian society. The law forbade raising any political or social issues or portraying poverty scenes so that Egyptian films could be good propaganda for the country. The law was obviously a reflection of the opinions of people working in the industry at that time, such as director Ahmed Badrakhan, who limited scenes shot in night clubs, gambling casinos, and horse racing tracks. On romantic themes, he said, they should by no means go beyond a story of two women fighting over one man or vice versa (El Shenawi 1994). Fifty years later, the same theme was used by female director Inas El Degheidy in her film *Dantella* (Lace), in which the whole cast was criticized in local newspapers for its daring sexual scenes between each woman and the man she wanted to win.

After the 1952 revolution, censorship law was abolished and replaced with general instructions. A few years later, special censorship regulations were issued that took a conservative line. During Nasser's rule, the film *Sha' men el-Khouf* (Some fear) was banned by the state-run censorship board because it depicted symbolically the love–hate relationship between Egypt and its dictator ruler and finally the revolt of the people. There is a strong sensitivity about any criticism or portrayal of the national leadership, officers of the state, court, military and security officers, and religious leaders. In addition, treatment of other countries with praise, satire or contempt is prohibited (Boyd 1982). In 1976, amid a wave of films on drugs and seduction, the Ministry of Information and Culture issued a decree officially returning to the 1948 censorship law with a few minor changes. In recent years, different political forces, including westernized liberals, Islamic fundamentalists, and dogmatic leaders, have competed over how far films should be allowed to go in their treatment of social issues. The conflicts reached courtrooms in many cases.

In 1984, two feature films—*Darb El Hawa* (Road of love), directed by

Hossam Eddin Mostafa, and *Khamsa Bab* (Door five) with leading actress, sex symbol, and producer Nadia El Guindi—were banned for sexual connotations and obscenity. A court order was issued later releasing the second film. In the 1990s, Islamic conservatives went to court to ban or at least partially censor the freewheeling annual musical *Fawazeer* (Riddles) shown daily on television in the Muslim holy month of Ramadan. No court order was issued to ban the program, but a more conservative dress code was ordered for the musical group (El Shenawi 1994).

In Egypt, as in the Arab world at large, obscenity, partial nudity, sexual titillation, and premarital sexual relations, as well as frequent sympathetic treatment of lesbianism and homosexuality as an acceptable alternative lifestyle, are not merely undesirable but are considered potent insults in Arabic society (Schleifer 1995).

In all Arab states, such audiovisual materials are prohibited by laws or restricted by codes of ethics. The law says that Egyptian media content should not promote indecency or sexual excitement (ERTU 95). Any materials in the Egyptian media that offend Islam or include negative statements about religions or beliefs, or even depict a religious symbol, have been traditionally taken out. In the mid-1990s, leading comedian Adel Imam took it upon himself to fight the wave of fundamentalism by presenting two films that looked at the nuances of this radical trend: *El-Irhab was Al-Kabab* (Terrorism and grilled meat), by young director Sherif Arafa, and *El Irhaby* (The terrorist). *Al Mohager* (The immigrant), by veteran film director Yousef Chahine, was taken to court by pro-Islamists demanding a ban on the film for depicting the life of the prophet Joseph. Chahine won the case, and his film was shown in more than twenty cinema houses all over Egypt. His next film, *El Maseer* (The destiny), focuses on a medieval Arab thinker who fought radical ideas through science and art (El Shenawi 1999).

Drug issues in Egyptian movies reached a peak when most of the movie billboard in a Cairo street depicted people doing drugs. These kinds of advertisements provoked the anger of parents, who saw the ads as portraying youngsters enjoying drugs. One official report stated that antidrug campaigns in Egyptian media resulted in more people doing drugs. The report claimed that youth already knew about drugs and how to consume them. The antidrug campaign was stopped for a short period of time. Several committees were formed to deal with the issue and resulted in putting together popular radio and television programs to increase awareness about drug issues among youth (Labib 1999).

As in most Arab countries, the government in Egypt owns and operates radio and television broadcasting. Egypt has a centralized broadcasting system for radio and television that was introduced after the Egyptian Revolution in 1952. The main reason for centralized broadcasting in Egypt is the government's desire to preserve national unity. Egyptian governments embrace the broadcast media as a political tool and have been keenly interested in keeping these technologies out of hostile hands (Boyd and Amin 1993). One more reason for centralized control of these institutions is the relatively low literacy rate in the Arab world. Since radio and television have the ability to overcome or bypass the problem of illiteracy, they are frequently used as an arm of the government to guide and mobilize the public (Boyd and Amin 1993). The broadcast system is subsidized by state authorities and only partially financed by advertising revenues. Egypt's broadcasting products are by far the most popular and influential in the Arab world.

Knowledge of the English language is minimal among the general Egyptian population, yet foreign material—especially American—is commonly dubbed or subtitled for Egyptian consumption. Its strong appeal to Egyptian viewers goes back to the 1960s, when they were first introduced to popular programs such as _I Love Lucy, Peyton Place_, and _The Fugitive_. Despite the language barrier, they hooked millions of Egyptians to their TV sets two or three evenings every week. The baby boom generation got its first taste of science fiction from U.S. series, such as _Lost in Space_ and _Time Tunnel_, that were shown weekly. After the 1973 war with Israel, Sadat changed allegiance from the Soviet Union to the West, especially the United States. This new political orientation was directly reflected in Egyptian television. Popular programs like _Ikhtarna Lak_ (We chose for you) broadcast full segments of U.S. entertainment programs, talk shows, and weekly series such as _The Six Million Dollar Man_ and _The Bionic Woman_. These were later adapted into Egyptian films that introduced the idea of violence for the sake of defending society against evil. During President Hosni Mubarak's rule, beginning in 1981, more foreign (mainly U.S., British, and French) programming has increasingly appeared on the Egyptian television schedule (Amin 1998).

Music Television (MTV), received in Egypt via satellite broadcasting, has been accused of including too much sex and violence, thus arousing much criticism in the country. Many researchers have argued that MTV presents too much aggression, drug use, sexual activities, and sex-role stereotyping (Abdullah 1996). Music Television came to Egypt through Cable News Egypt (CNE) in 1990. Since its introduction, it has become very popular and also the subject of heated debate. Researchers argue that, among other things, there is a dangerous dose of sex and violence presented to the target audience of MTV through their favorite music channel. MTV also has had an impact on music in Egypt, resulting in a huge wave of Egyptian rock music. The authorities have moved to censor the local music also. In 1999, young popular singer Mostafa Kamar shot abroad three video clips that included Asian women dancing with him. The songs were banned because, according to the censor, the movement and attire of the women was "obscene." The video clips are shown and seen by Arab as well as Egyptian viewers on regional satellite television (El Shenawi 1999).

Television violence and its effects on Egyptian children are coming under discussion in many academic and professional circles. Television is to a large extent the main, if not the only, medium for children's entertainment in Egypt. One school of thought in Egypt considers television a school for teaching and learning violence. In this school, youngsters are never taught that violence is in itself reprehensible. Two Egyptian researchers (Emad el Din and Bahaa 1990) stated that television programs that include violence and crime should be limited and should not be presented at a time when children are watching television. The lesson the children usually get is that violence is a great adventure and solves problems. Many Egyptian working parents complain that television content is filled with violence (Emad el Din and Bahaa 1990). Other research suggested a causal relationship between watching violent programs and adolescent attitudes toward conformity and aggression (Kamhawi 1994).

National organizations and professional associations, like the National Center for Motherhood and Childhood and the National Center for Sociological and Criminological Studies, have often condemned violent programs on television (Labib 1999). Recently the Egyptian government established committees that investigated this issue and recommended public education campaigns to inform people about the impact of television violence (Labib 1999). Censorship is not generally a sufficient option when it includes limiting access to information. Egyptian radio and television think tanks recommended that broadcast regulations have similar limitations, but self-regulation in response to public demand and opinion could be effective for reducing the potential effects of violence. One recommendation was that broadcasters ensure a balance of "prosocial" programs showing healthy cooperative behavior, counteracting the harmful, antisocial messages in violent, aggressive images. Other recommendations were to start a rating system to rate all broadcast programs in the different networks in the country (National Satellite Committee file 1996).

Egyptian television used to be prohibited from broadcasting programs that included statements that encourage violations of the law, display excessive violence, and include references to betting or gambling (Boyd 1982). The situation is different now because Direct Broadcast Satellite (DBS) is competing with the national channels. Direct Broadcast Satellite bypasses government broadcast institutions and reaches Egyptian audiences directly. Satellite broadcasting is gaining popularity, and there are currently more than a million satellite dishes across the country serving more than 7 million Egyptians. The uncensored programming available on the satellite stations has created a firestorm of debate in the country. Strongly held conventions in the Arab world are shocked by full or even partial nudity, especially of women; simulated sexual intercourse and episodic sadism and masochism; the public transmission of obscene speech; premarital sexual relations and the treatment of homosexuality as a publicly acceptable lifestyle; and role reversals in which representatives of law and order are portrayed as villains while outlaws and other criminal types are portrayed as misunderstood romantic heroes. These conventions are almost universally held to be paramount in public life, even by individuals or elites who may ignore them, relatively speaking, in their own private lives and in their own private entertainment. Some authorities in Egypt banned viewing satellite television broadcasts in coffee shops in 1994, but the government immediately lifted this ban. The Egyptian government made it clear that they were going to adopt an "open window" policy that will allow Egyptians to purchase or rent satellite dishes (Amin 1996).

In response to the foreign material on satellites, Egypt launched Nilesat with the objective of strengthening Egypt's own broadcast environment. Although Nilesat carries some foreign programs, Egyptian officials say it is better to provide the option for the viewers instead of getting it from the outside. Many services on Nilesat broadcast materials are considered liberal. ERTU currently broadcasts the Nile TV specialized package from the satellite. This package includes Nile Drama (TV movies, soap operas, and drama), Nile News, Nile Sports, Nile Culture, and Nile Children, as well as educational channels. The Showtime package includes ART/1st NET and was originally established with the intention of satisfying both Arabic speakers and international/English-speaking viewers (Amin 1998).

One major issue that reflected the difference of cultural roles in communication messages between the Egyptian media and the international media was the coverage of a story on female circumcision that CNN broadcast in 1994 (Amin and Napoli 1995). The CNN story focused on a ten-year-old female having a circumcision operation without her prior knowledge. The CNN story aroused a firestorm in the Egyptian media, which accused the network of trying to destroy the national image of Egypt and tarnish the reputation of the state (Amin and Napoli 1995). But the CNN story on circumcision made public discussion on the issue no longer a taboo, so the Egyptian media started a campaign against circumcision after this story.

VCRs have led more and more Egyptians to turn away from the country's television because of the controlled television news and entertainment. Egyptians found a way to bypass government control over the broadcast schedule. They started to gain control over the materials they want to watch, including programs with seminudity and violence, instead of the programs that are heavily cut by government censors. However, the government moved to censor the content of the videos also (Amin and Boyd 1993).

The Internet is growing slowly but steadily in Egypt, with more than fifty online service providers, such as EgyptNet, available for its citizens. Internet coffee shops were introduced to the country and a good number of Web sites are currently functional and growing. Dial-up access telephone numbers in

Cairo are available for connection from any Egyptian city. Many Egyptians have access to major providers such as America Online and CompuServe through some Egyptian Web sites (Leo et al. 1998). Growing intolerance has been strongest in Egypt, where Islam is a dominant creed and where Islamic extremists have been arguing that banning communication and/or data systems is the religious and moral salvation of the people.

Such posturing creates fear among Arab peoples and pressures Arab governments to apply strict censorship to information resources. Some Egyptians fear the danger of political/religious repercussions of this influx of alien values through the Internet. Strident and uncompromising, the Islamists' messages convey confrontation rather than ecumenicism, a message of perseverance rather than fraternity, the closing up and turning inward of a rich culture rather than an opening out of it as part of a community of learning and exploration (Gher et al. 1998). Many voices expressed antagonism and rejection to the materials that are offered by the Internet. One case of Satan worship was covered in a major magazine in Egypt blaming the Internet for bringing foreign values, including sex and violence, to Egyptian households. The case resulted in the arrest of teens who were seen as participating in the Satan worship. Later it was discovered that the youth were only dancing in black coats.

CONCLUSION

In conclusion, while Egypt is building a civil society, the Egyptian people, government authorities, nongovernmental organizations, and media have a certain role to play in creating a healthy media environment and limiting destructive influences on viewers. A media policy is needed that addresses the issues of media and violence, enhances media violence awareness and responsibility among the public, and avoids mechanisms that could encourage unacceptable behavior in susceptible individuals. Egypt must address the ever changing environment in the media worldwide and reconsider the practice of censorship as a final solution for any problem that may arise. This is perhaps best achieved by creating a balance between censorship and regulation, which have limitations in the extent to which they can control what Egyptian people consume from the media. In addition, this balance can be developed with the help of the new technology, which can assist individuals in controlling what information is received or accessed in their households.

On the other hand, the Egyptian people's awareness can be enhanced through public health and public promotion campaigns that inform people of the harmful effects of sex and violence in the media and by educational campaigns to teach children and adults the discriminatory skills necessary for healthy use of the entertainment and information media.

At the beginning of a new millennium, with the formation of the digital platform and the creation of multiple channel environments, it is important for the Egyptian media to realize their responsibilities toward their audience and to be more careful with what they provide for them. When these audiences include children, who may be easily influenced by what they see, the media must not abuse this power but rather use it in the most appropriate manner. Also, considering how sex and drugs in the media affect youngsters and others, and the tremendous amounts of violence on television, which can have a negative and aggressive effect on both children and adults, the media need to reconsider the content of what they display. While Egyptian media might show the wars, terrorism, crimes, and violence that is going on around the world, they should also, at the same time, emphasize other values such as peace, love, and harmony found in and among societies. Finally, a well-rounded and balanced approach of portraying both the good and the evil is important instead of concentrating on one and leaving out the other. This is particularly important in countries such as Egypt, where the media function under the authoritarian system and the role of the government is to direct the media on what to portray, how to portray it, and how much attention to give to those portrayals.

REFERENCES

Abdullah, R. A. 1996. The uses and gratification of music television in Egypt: Why kids want their MTV. Master's thesis, American University in Cairo, Egypt.

Amin, H. Y. 1996. Broadcasting in the Arab world and the Middle East. In A. Wells, ed., *World broadcasting*. Norwood, N.J.: Ablex.

————. 1998. American programs on Egyptian television: Prospects and concerns. In Y. R. Kamalipour, ed., *Images of the U.S. around the world: A multicultural perspective*, pp. 319–334. Albany: State University of New York Press.

Amin, H. Y., and J. J. Napoli. 1994. The specialized magazine trend in Egypt: Development and consequences. Paper presented at the Eleventh Annual Intercultural/International Communication Conference IIC, Miami, February 3–5.

————. 1995. Clash of communication cultures: CNN in Egypt. Paper presented at the Twelfth Annual Intercultural/International Communication Conference IIC, Miami, February 2–4.

————. 1997. De-Westernization of media studies: The Middle East experience. Paper presented at a Workshop on De-Westernizing Media Studies, Seoul, Korea, November 16–20.

El Attar, M. 1998. Investigative reporting in Egypt: A case study of Rosa El Yousf magazine. Master's thesis, American University in Cairo, Egypt.

Boyd, D. A. 1982. *Broadcasting in the Arab world*. Philadelphia: Temple University Press.

El Dessouky, A. Farouk. 1997. Egyptian press coverage of sexual violence against females. Master's thesis, American University in Cairo, Egypt.

El Din, E., and M. Bahaa. 1990. *Dalil el walidin ela tanmiah el tifel* (Parents' guide for child development). Cairo, Egypt: National Center of Childhood and Motherhood.

Douglas, D. A., and H. Y. Amin. 1993. The impact of home video cassette recorders on the Egyptian film and television consumption patterns. *European Journal of Communications* 18, no. 1: 2–7.

Egyptian Radio and Television Union (ERTU). 1995. Printout, Ministry of Information, Cairo, Egypt.

Farid, S. 1981. Fi Al Cinema AlArabieh in Arab Cinema. Beirut: Dar el Taleiah lil Teba'ah WA Al Nasher.

Gher A. L., H. Y. Amin, and M. el-Nawawy. 1998. Communications, culture, and the Islamic world entering the twenty-first century. Paper Presented at Muslims and the Information Superhighway Conference. Islamic Society of North America. 1999, April 10–12, Indianapolis.

Kamhawi, R. A. 1994. The relationship between exposure to television violence and committing anti-social acts by adolescent male juveniles. Master's thesis, American University in Cairo, Egypt.

El Kotby, D. Amal. 1995. Newspaper coverage of terrorism: A content analysis of Al Ahram and the New York Times. Master's thesis, American University, Cairo, Egypt.

Labib, Saad. 1999. Interview by author, December 2, Cairo, Egypt. Labib is a media expert with Egyptian Radio and Television Union (ERTU).

Napoli, J., and H. Amin. 1997. Press freedom in Egypt. In W. Jong-Ebot and F. Eribo, eds., *Communication and press freedom in Africa*. Boulder: Westview.

Napoli, J. J. 1995. Assessment of Egyptian print and electronic media. Status report submitted to the United States Agency for International Development.

Nasser, M. K. 1990. Egyptian mass media under Nasser and Sadat. *Journalism Monographs* 124 (December).

National Satellite Committee. 1996. File, the Egyptian Radio and Television Union. Cairo, Egypt.

Paletz, D. I. 1992. *Terrorism and the media*. Newbury Park, Calif.: Sage.

Rugh, W. A. 1989. *The Arab press*. Syracuse: Syracuse University Press.

Schleifer, S. A. 1995. MMDS in the Arab World. Paper presented at the Broadcast Education Association Conference, Las Vegas, Nevada, April 7–11.

El Shenawi, T. 1994. Al cenima wa qalil men alseiasah (Cinema and a little bit of politics). Cairo Film Festival, Cairo, Egypt.

———. 1999. Personal interview, Cairo, Egypt.

Stephens, R. 1971. *Nasser: A political biography*. New York: Simon & Schuster.

Tewfik, Samir. 1992. Interview by author in Cairo, Egypt, April 9. Tewfik is editor in chief of *Akhbar Al Hawadas* Crime News, *Akhbar elYoum* newspaper.

Tresilian, D. 1992. Egypt's publishing industry is very far from gathering dust. *Cairo Today* 66–70 (January): 118–120.

Vatikiotis, P. J. 1991. *The history of modern Egypt*. London: Weidenfeld & Nicolson.

14

Sex, Violence, and Terrorism in Hollywood's International Political Imagery

M. Mehdi Semati

In the post–Cold War era, Middle Eastern terrorism has become a central theme in Hollywood's international political imaginary. In order to explore the emergence and development of this theme, this chapter examines the cultural-political contexts and film critics' reaction to three high-profile 1990s action films. Two analytics are introduced to specify the subtle shifts in cultural sensibilities between Hollywood's 1980s and 1990s depictions of Middle East terrorism. One analytic (ultramasculinity) is based on the argument that the "hard bodies" (ultramasculinism) of the 1980s heroes underwent a transformation that sought to project a "kinder, gentler" image of masculinity in the 1990s. The other analytic (Orientalism) is based on four logics for depicting the Middle East. The analyses reveal that the 1990s films, in line with the cultural and political tenor of the time, deployed a "kinder, gentler" sensibility while maintaining a set of Orientalist ideologies prevalent in the 1980s films. The depiction of the Middle East in the 1990s is insidious in that these films promote the racism of the 1980s films in a kinder, gentler multicultural disguise.

FILM AND POLITICS

Before turning to a discussion of these films, I would like to state a set of theoretical assumptions and positions informing the overall approach this chapter takes toward films and the larger sociopolitical context of their emergence. Some film theorists who advocate the "apparatus theory" have argued that the "invisible" editing style of Hollywood films, its linear narrative structure, and the projection environment of film (the "apparatus") necessarily implicate the viewers and the viewing experience in particular ideological positions and relationships (see essays in Rosen 1986). Others have discussed political representation and ideological inflection of popular films without appealing to such arguments and assumptions. Prince (1992), for example, has argued that "political representation and ideology in film are a matter of content and the ways it is inflected by image, narrative design, and other attributes of style." Instead of assuming that continuity editing, for example, "necessarily embodies, a priori, an ideological framework or position," he argues, "stylistic structures of Hollywood movies may be deployed to express and portray a range of political material" (p. 6). This range of materials is structured by a set of imperatives operating in Hollywood (e.g., the economically driven need to appeal to a heterogeneous audience, the emphasis on the entertainment value of a film, Hollywood's preference for certain genres, etc.) and in American politics and society (intellectual frameworks and political traditions more generally). In this context, Prince asks, How is one to understand the political nature of Hollywood films? "The answer," he argues, "is in an indirect, mediated, and symbolic process whereby Hollywood films reference salient clusters of social and political values and, through the operations of narrative, create a dialogue through and with these values and, on occasion, transform or revise them (within the world of the narrative)" (p. 7). To the extent that the fictional world of Hollywood narrative embodies or questions established social and cultural values the society holds toward real-world historical and political issues (e.g., the question of terrorism), and to the extent that the fictional world of these films necessarily draws from such values, popular films are decidedly political. Here "political" means "the realm of collective values and fantasies that underlie and inform socioeconomic systems and behavior in the real world" (p. 7). In short, Hollywood films embody and respond to the "social" and the "political" from start to finish. Additionally, topical filmmaking, either as a commercial imperative to appeal to a large heterogeneous population or as a byproduct of the collaborative nature of filmmaking or as a "democratic" tendency toward social relevance, has always been the characteristic of American cinema responsible for its mass appeal both domestically and transnationally (see Semati and Sotirin 1999). The circulation of Hollywood films with appeal to both

domestic and transnational audiences, films producing international political imagery within an increasingly transnational market, warrants political
analysis.

THE REAGAN ERA AND HOLLYWOOD'S INTERNATIONAL POLITICAL IMAGERY

The discourse of "the Middle East" offered by Hollywood in contemporary
popular culture is thoroughly dominated by the issue of terrorism. It was
during the 1980s that "a trend toward featuring the exotic, tumultuous Middle East as the perfect setting for high-action films occurred" (Fuller 1995,
p. 192). The political climate within which these films emerged in the 1980s
was the era of Ronald Reagan (and continued into the early 1990s under
George Bush's presidency). This era has been characterized by aggressive
militarism as a response to the perceived erosion of the supremacy of American power in the international political scene. The preceding presidency of
Jimmy Carter incurred perceived and real losses that damaged and challenged America's credibility as a superpower. The "loss" of Nicaragua and
Iran, the invasion of Afghanistan by the Soviet Union, the hostage crisis in
Iran, along with Carter's preoccupation with human rights issues, all symptoms of a weakened America, had led to a call for a renewal of the projection
of American power around the globe.

One of the central themes of the Reagan presidency and its approach to
foreign and domestic policy was a "resurgent America" (see Prince 1993).
The invasion of Grenada, the American sponsorship of the Contras' war
against Nicaragua, the bombing of Libya, and a host of other CIA secret
wars and covert actions around the world are among the elements that constitute the effort to renew the projection of American power around the
globe. This aggressive militarism (culminating in Bush's massive military operation in the Persian Gulf) was part of a renewed Cold War by Reagan to
reassert American leadership after a period of perceived decline.

The call for projecting American power during the Reagan era entailed aggressive Third World intervention policies around the world. Much of U.S.
foreign policy during this period was predicated on perceived Soviet Union
aggression, which needed to be stopped at all costs. In a highly ideological
form, not unlike the good-guy bad-guy dichotomy of Hollywood films,
conflicts around the world were explained in terms of a U.S.-Soviet (communism–"free world") dichotomy. The right was after the old anticommunism
scare of the 1950s. At this point, anxieties about monolithic communism,
however, did not have as much political resonance as they did in the 1950s.
Instead, "terrorism" emerged as one of the most potent ideological signifiers

of the era. In Prince's (1992) view, "terrorism" became "a term which functioned essentially as a synonym for communism but was sufficiently new and vivid that it could carry a great deal of political freight, unlike the somewhat discredited anti-communism" of an earlier era (p. 31). The threat of terrorism, as "Russia's secret weapon," thus became a major theme in the new Cold War, as reflected in various mainstream media discourses of the period (see Prince 1993).

Hollywood welcomed this call to a renewed projection of American power by producing a cycle of films that celebrated militarism, patriotism, and superior American military technology and power. As Kellner (1995) has argued, the Hollywood films of the 1980s "nurtured this militarist mindset and thus provided cultural representations that mobilized support for such aggressive policy" (p. 75). And as Prince (1993) has argued, Hollywood's response to America's "aggressive international posture" was to produce a "cycle of invasion-and-rescue films that collectively argued for the need to project strong American military power overseas" (p. 240). Drawing from the Cold War imagery that preceded this cycle of films, films such as *Top Gun* (1986) and *Rambo* (1985) "dramatized heroic ideals of empire," and the mighty heroes of these films "functioned as personification of a national will and warrior spirit encoded by the foreign policy rhetoric of the Reagan period" (p. 240).

This "new" Cold War in the context of a weakened (and later disintegrated) Soviet Union brought with it a new evil and foreign enemy of global proportions. The replacement of the Soviet Union as the foreign and evil enemy with the "Arab" evil enemy was well anticipated by films such as *Delta Force* (1986), *Iron Eagle* (1986), and *Iron Eagle II* (1988). Films such as *Iron Eagle* and *Iron Eagle II* presented an Arab "superenemy which eventually found its incarnation in Saddam Hussein and Iraq" (Kellner 1995, p. 83; see also Prince 1993). A list of major Hollywood productions that projected the need for resurgent American military power may include *Top Gun* (1986), as well as *Rambo* (1985), *Red Dawn* (1984), *Rocky IV* (1985), *Invasion USA* (1985), *Rambo: First Blood Part 2* (1985), and *Rambo III* (1986). And it is in this context that one can explain the cycle of films that depicted the Middle East as the setting for political and military intervention. A list of these films appearing in the 1980s includes *Three Days in Beirut* (1983), *Treasure of the Lost Desert* (1983), *Glory Boys* (1984), *Not Quite Jerusalem* (1984), *Hell Squad* (1985), *Iron Eagle* (1986), *The Retaliator* (1986), *Delta Force* (1986), *Death Before Dishonor* (1987), *Counterforce* (1987), *Wanted Dead or Alive* (1987), *Steal the Sky* (1988), *Trident Force* (1988), *Warbirds* (1988), *Iron Eagle II* (1988), *Cover Up* (1990), and *Navy Seals* (1990).

ORIENTALISM AND
ULTRAMASCULINITY: AN ANALYTIC
FRAMEWORK

In this section an analytic framework is introduced in order to explore Hollywood's international political imaginary in the 1990s. Two analytics are introduced to specify the subtle shifts in cultural sensibilities between Hollywood's 1980s and 1990s depictions of Middle East terrorism. One analytic (Orientalism) is based on four logics for depicting the Middle East. The other analytic (ultramasculinity) is based on the argument that the "hard bodies" (ultramasculinism) of the 1980s heroes underwent a transformation that sought to project a "kinder, gentler" image of masculinity in the 1990s.

The portrayal of the Middle East as a setting for high-action films during the 1980s belongs to a particular tradition in Hollywood, which itself is a part of a larger ideological framework. The portrayal of the Middle East, along with other cultures of North Africa and Asia, in the Western popular imagination has been characterized as a form of "Orientalism" (Edward Said 1979). Orientalism, as a particular conception of these regions and their cultures by the West that has sustained its colonial and imperial aspirations, is a particular ideological discourse of nationality, race, and Otherness. Deeply embedded in the Orientalist tradition, Hollywood's cinematic practices historically have incorporated the Middle East as an exotic setting for various narratives, from melodramas to action-adventures (see Bernstein and Studlar 1997).

As Prince (1993) has argued, "To the extent that an Orientalist outlook existed within the culture, furnishing an interpretive framework to orient film production, it could also function to situate the meaning of real-world historical events, such as the Persian Gulf War" (p. 243). Once subjected to such a frame, historical events become culturally and politically constructed discourse. It is in this sense, he argues, that the verbal and visual rhetoric of the Gulf War and the rhetoric of the cycle of films produced in the 1980s depicting the Middle East could be understood "as sets of mutually interrelated cultural images operating in synergy" (p. 243). Both of these are drawn from the same cultural, political, and epistemological macrocosm. To capture this commonality, Prince investigates the affinities between the rhetoric of recent Hollywood films dealing with military conflict in the Middle East and the verbal and visual rhetoric of the Persian Gulf War.

There are four shared assumptions and logics that characteristically unite the anti-Arab (or more accurately anti-Middle Eastern) films of the 1980s. First, they view the Middle East as that which exists outside time and history. This view is indeed a feature of the Orientalist tradition according to which diverse cultures are reduced to an undifferentiated mass without cultural or historical specificity. Second, the confrontation of the West and the Middle East is always re-presented as an eternal struggle between the forces of civilization and savagery. Third, "Arabs" are routinely stereotyped as backward and incompetent. And finally, the audiovisual rhetoric of the East–West confrontation is a background against which the use of high-tech weaponry is celebrated, glamorized, and promoted. These four logics constitute the first analytic for considering Hollywood films depicting the Middle East in the 1990s.

Another characteristic that unifies the films of the 1980s depicting the Middle East is the ultramasculinism of the heroes of these narratives. These heroes are by and large the military types. They are the "tough guys," super-macho fighting machines: Chuck Norris, Sylvester Stallone, and Steven Seagal have made successful careers playing these characters. Janet Maslin (1987) of the *New York Times* in her review of *Death before Dishonor* argues that "the movies are looking for a few good men, to change the face of American foreign policy and out-Rambo Rambo in the process."[1] Matthew Gilbert (1990) of the *Boston Globe* in his review of *Navy Seals* refers to the characters and the setting in this film as "big boys and their toys." Caryn James (1990) of the *New York Times* in her discussion of the same film speaks of the excessive "macho heroics" and "firepower." Along with excessive machismo, these films engaged in unreserved chauvinism. Writing on the films of this period, the critics often spoke of an explicit jingoism and chauvinism that characterized this cycle of films. Vincent Canby (February 23, 1986) of the *New York Times* points to the way Iron Eagle and Delta Force "exalt blunderbuss chauvinism." Michael Blowen (1991) of the *Boston Globe* (1991) refers to *Navy Seals* as "jingoistic silliness." Geoff Brown (1991) of *The Times*, referring to *Navy Seals* and the films in that tradition, argues, "Here is the ancient, cheesy plot about a crack troop of men, patriotic and xenophobic to the core, dedicated to the fulfillment of impossible missions." Canby (February 14, 1986) refers to *Delta Force* as "fanciful chauvinist fiction."

Writing on the New Right conservative movement of the 1980s, which supported the "Reagan revolution," Lawrence Grossberg (1988) argues that the conservative movement sought not to redefine the nation but to establish a new relationship between the people and the nation. The particular arena in which this new relationship was established was "in the conjuncture of economics and popular culture rather than that of economics and the State" (p. 32). Drawing on this observation, Susan Jeffords (1994), in a book titled *Hard Bodies: Hollywood Masculinity in the Reagan Era*, argues that "during the Reagan era popular culture became the mechanism not simply for identifying but for establishing the relationship between the people and the State, through the articulation of that State as the unified national body of masculine character." Thus the reformulation of that relationship between the people and the nation, "as reconfigured in the popular discourses of militarism, patriotism, individualism, family values and religious beliefs, was accomplished largely through the rearticulation of both the individual and the nation in terms of masculine identities" in a way that actions by the nation and the individual were assumed to be "impinging on and in many ways determining the other" (pp. 13–14). In this context she argues that the 1980s films, through the depiction of the "hard bodies" of these superheroes articulated a particular image of masculinity (bodies of Sylvester Stallone, Chuck Norris, Arnold Schwarzenegger, and Steven Seagal, for example). The image, argues Jeffords (1993), is that of "the hard-fighting, weapon-wielding, independent, muscular, and heroic men of the eighties" (p. 197).

Jeffords (1993; 1994) locates a shift in the portrayal of masculinity in the aftermath of the Reagan era. Through analyses of a series of films released in the early 1990s, Jeffords (1993) argues "a changed image of U.S. masculinity is being presented, an image that suggests that the hard-bodied male action heroes of the eighties have given way to a 'kinder, gentler' U.S. manhood" (p. 197). She borrows a phrase from Janet Maslin's reflection on a male character that such characters are "ready to reassess the mad excesses of 80's materialism from an aggressively mellow 90's point of view" (p. 197). This is meant to be the end of Cold Warriors. And "while eighties men may have muscled their way into our hearts, killing anyone who got in their way, nineties men are going to seize us with kindness and declarations that they are changed, 'new men' " (p. 198). This "kinder, gentler" image of masculinity constitutes our second analytic.

Using the four shared logics of the cycle of films produced in the 1980s (discussed by Prince 1993), and the "hard bodies" (ultramasculinity) of the 1980s heroes and their subsequent transformation into "kinder, gentler" heroes (discussed by Jeffords 1993; 1994), we have a framework against which we can compare the films made in the 1990s. With this background, let us look at three high-profile films of the 1990s that depict the Middle East.

HOLLYWOOD'S INTERNATIONAL
POLITICAL IMAGERY AFTER
REAGANISM

A list of high-profile films released in the 1990s that depict terrorism may include the *Die Hard* series throughout the 1990s, *Passenger 57* (1992), *Patriot Games* (1992), *Crying Game* (1992), *Under Siege* (1992), *In the Name of the Father* (1993), *True Lies* (1994), *Under Siege 2* (1995), *Sudden Death* (1995), *Broken Arrow* (1996), *The Rock* (1996), *Face/off* (1997), *The Jackal* (1997), *Executive Decision* (1996), *Long Kiss Goodnight* (1996), *Air Force One* (1997), *The Peacemaker* (1997), *Devil's Own* (1997), *The Siege* (1998), and *Arlington Rd.* (1999). Clearly, terrorism has become a convenient lens through which Hollywood addresses political issues. Of these films, *True Lies, Executive Decision,* and *The Siege* address the Middle East substantially.

In this section, I argue that *True Lies* (1994), despite its "outrageously unflattering ethnic stereotypes" of Arabs (Maslin 1994), and despite its own intentions, by turning international terrorism into a topic for "domestic comedy" already indicates the 1990s sensibility of a "kinder, gentler" era. What is insidious about the sensibility that *True Lies* introduces is that it serves racist and sexist representations in the guise of "kinder, gentler."

True Lies

True Lies, based on a French film called *La Totale,* tells the story of a superagent by the name of Harry Tasker (Arnold Schwarzenegger) who works for an agency named Omega Sector: The Last Line of Defense. Harry has managed to hide his identity from his wife, Helen (Jamie Lee Curtis), for the last fifteen years by pretending to be a computer sales rep; a total bore as far as she is concerned. *True Lies* may be divided into three segments. The film begins with a sequence in which, in the tradition of James Bond films, Harry emerges out of a frozen lake in Switzerland wearing a black tie under his wet suit. Once in the Swiss mansion where an Arab tycoon, named Jamal Khaled, has thrown a high-class party full of international villains, he manages to download files from Khaled's computer. This sequence demonstrates Harry's superspy finesse not just by the killings he engages in, but by his skills in tango and in speaking various languages (the subtitles tell us his Arabic is perfect. Presumably, his Arabic is as perfect as his English!)

In the next sequence, Harry goes home after a long day at work. Before he goes inside the house to his wife, his wisecracking sidekick, Gib (Tom Arnold), reminds him to put his wedding ring back on. After a scene of domestic life, during which Harry's daughter Dana (Eliza Dushku) steals money from Gib, we are inside the Omega Sector. Harry's boss, played by Charlton Heston wearing an eye patch reminiscent of James Bond characters, wants to know if Harry and his team have uncovered anything substantial in their last assignment in Switzerland. We are told that the records downloaded from Khaled's computer suggest some connection between a certain four nuclear warheads and a Middle Eastern terrorist group known as Crimson Jihad.

In the second segment, Harry discovers that his wife appears to be having an affair with a used-car salesman by the name of Simon (Bill Paxton), who is pretending to be a secret government agent. Harry and his team use all of the Omega's spying capabilities to spy on his wife and Simon. They eventually abduct Simon and Helen. Speaking to Helen in electronically altered voices through a two-way mirror, Harry and Gib ask Helen a series of questions. Helen is asked if she has ever slept with Simon (the answer is no), and if she loves her husband (the answer is yes). She is asked why she is having this relationship with Simon, to which she replies, "I guess I needed something. It felt really good to be needed and trusted and feel special." In order to redeem herself, Helen is asked to pose as a prostitute for a man in a hotel room and place a bug near a phone. The man pretending to be a French spy is none other than Harry in a disguise. As soon as Helen finds out her husband is involved, terrorists burst into the room and snatch both of them.

The third segment is already on. During this segment, the terrorists manage to detonate an atomic bomb and vaporize an island off the coast of Florida. Harry and Helen team up in killing terrorists. In the meantime, Dana is kidnapped by the terrorists and in the final chase scene she is dangling from a Harrier jet piloted by none other than her dad. Harry ends up killing all the terrorists, and his identity remains secret to the press. The final sequence of the film shows Helen and Harry, as a couple, working as spies for the same government agency.

What did not escape the attention of the press was the degree to which this film was a deviation from other films in the genre, in its mixing of "action-adventure" and "romantic comedy." As Jian Ghomeshi (1994) of the *Toronto Star* put it, *True Lies* "has won raves for what is being hailed as a novel mixture of 'high adventure' and 'romantic comedy.' " Referring to *True Lies* as a "domestic epic" and attributing that label to writer-director James Cameron, Rita Kempley (1994) of the *Washington Post* calls it "a weird hybrid of action juggernaut, buddy cop caper and reactionary soft-core pornography." Michael Wilmington (1994) of the *Chicago Tribune* calls Arnold Schwarzenegger in *True Lies* "Ozzie Nelson as James Bond, a killer robot who loves his family."

The film is referred to as a comedy. As Jay Carr (1994) of the *Boston Globe* puts it, "Although its body count is high, *True Lies* is a comic thriller." Lynn Smith (1994) of the *Los Angeles Times* calls it a "self-deprecating comedy. Sort of." Amy Schwartz (1994) of the *Washington Post* claims that *"True Lies* is being widely reviewed as a campy spoof, with villains who, as *People* magazine put it, 'generate reprehensible villainy without ever seeming truly hateful.' " Wilmington (1994) claims that *"True Lies* is played as if it's a lark, a big joke."

The novelty of combining "high adventure" and "family values" caught the attention of many critics. Maslin (1994) claims that "the film's ultimate combat sequence, with Mr. Schwarzenegger flying an airplane that may just kill one of his next of kin, manages to combine shoot'em-up excitement with something resembling family values." Referring to the "subplot" involving Helen and Harry's relationship, Smith (1994) claims that the subplot "finds family values triumphing over danger, glamour and sex. Sort of." Mick La-

Salle (1994) of the *San Francisco Chronicle* argues that *True Lies* is "the story of a dysfunctional family that comes together in murder and mayhem, the story of a dissatisfied housewife who finds her calling by teaming up with her husband and killing everybody in sight." Kempley (1994) claims that "Harry must save not only the world but his marriage." Susan Wloszczyna (1994) of *USA Today* claims that "Cameron invents a new kind of family therapy that saves your marriage and the world."

True Lies in its attempt to combat international terrorism within the confines of the discourse of family becomes a sitcom, a variation of domestic comedy. This film is the 1990s answer to patriotism in the cycle of films made in the 1980s. At one point Simon propositions Helen: "If not for me—do it for your country!" Nuclear terrorism is deployed to restore the withering nuclear family. The anxieties about the nuclear family here are projected onto the discourse of nuclear terrorism. In arguing that *True Lies* turns the topic of international terrorism into a domestic comedy and a discourse of "family," I do not mean to suggest that the discourse of family is absent from the cycle of films made in the 1980s. *Iron Eagle* (1986) provides an example. In this film, a teen fantasy of rescue adventure, the total destruction of the evil Arab enemy by the teen hero is used as a rite of passage of sorts in which the hero establishes himself as a dutiful son.

It is possible to argue that Hollywood films collapse various political perspectives by elaborating a set of traditional American myths (the west and the frontier, gangster and the city, small town life, etc.). Here family is one of those myths (Ray 1985). In such an argument, the deployment of the discourse of the family is a matter of cinematic convention. But there is more to this deployment. The saliency of that discourse, or the imagery of the family, is a matter of responding to the domestic ideological and political currents in the context of its deployment. As Prince (1992) has argued, in the guise of the father figure (and through narratives expressing threats to that figure), the new Cold War films developed a discourse about the country and national politics. In this sense, *True Lies* follows the same line. What is different about *True Lies* is its "comedic" approach. More importantly, in *True Lies* the international political imaginary, the "vision of empire," to use Prince's terminology, becomes inward-looking. This is the end of the Reagan era and the beginning of Bill Clinton's presidency.

The novel contribution of *True Lies* is the introduction of a distinctively 1990s sensibility, one that takes the mix of terrorism, sex, and violence to a new political imaginary. The negative reaction to the film by the critics reveals the darker side of the 1990s sensibility embodied by *True Lies*. Kempley (1994) calls *True Lies* "a slick, sick espionage thriller featuring Arnold Schwarzenegger as the James Bond of the '90s. It's really the same old Arnman, except that he defends traditional American values like misogyny and xenophobia while dressed in a tux." Moreover, *True Lies*, "far too technologically bloated for its cartoony plot, overestimates the human tolerance for high-tech mayhem." Giles Whittell (1994) of the *Los Angeles Times* refers to the film as "Schwarzenegger's latest orgy of celluloid mayhem."

Many critics find the treatment of women and Arabs in *True Lies* particularly disturbing. Maslin (1994) refers to Gib's wisecrack ("Women, can't live with them, can't kill them") as the "film's most desperately unfortunate wisecrack." Kempley (1994) mocks the depiction of the Arab terrorists as "a pack of Islamic fruitcakes" and claims that "in a ludicrous twist, Harry, disguised as her john, realizes that the soul of a topless dancer lurks within the little woman [Helen]." Antonia Zerbisias (1994) of the *Toronto Star*, reflecting on a statement by Simon ("the Vette makes them wet"), refers to *True Lies* as "sexist hate with a punchline." Smith (1994) complains that "women are slapped and called bitches more than once. By movie's end, they have become as violent as the men." Aimee Miller (1994) of the *Los Angeles Times*, in her reflection on the bumbling Arab terrorists and their treatment of women, comments that "they chant prayers before detonating atomic missiles. They slap women around, using them as human shields. They kidnap children. They even videotape their terrorist threats for the American media (too bad they can't remember to recharge the batteries first)." Kenneth Turan (1994) of the *Los Angeles Times* claims that the film's depiction of "unshaved Arabs" and women "leave[s] a sour taste." In *True Lies*, he continues, "a strain of crudeness and mean-spirited humiliation, especially toward women, runs through the film like a nasty virus, vitiating all it touches."

In citing these critics I want to establish more than their outrage at the depiction of particular groups in the film (at whose expense the jokes are made). I also want to point out the consensus among the critics in the way *True Lies*, in mixing sex and violence in the name of fun (trying to make us laugh), establishes a new sensibility for depicting international terrorism. As we shall see, *Executive Decision* (1996) follows the same trajectory in embodying the 1990s sensibility.

Executive Decision

In this section, I argue that *Executive Decision* develops an ironic attitude toward international terrorism that reflects the same "kinder, gentler" sensibility. It also embodies the "multicultural" sensibility of the 1990s in the way it at once acknowledges and deploys insidiously the convention of the genre in depicting Middle East terrorism.

In *Executive Decision* (1996) an Arab terrorist group hijacks a 747 jet full of passengers heading for Washington, D.C. Nagi Hassan (David Suchet), the leader of the hijackers, has a number of demands to release his hostages. Among them is the release of a fellow terrorist by the name of Jaffa (Andreas

Katsulas), who is being held by American authorities. His demands are actually nothing more than a decoy to cover up the fact that he has on the plane a large quantity of recently stolen deadly nerve gas DZ-5 ("the poor man's atomic bomb," according to the film), enough to poison "the entire eastern seaboard of the United States."

The lead is played by Kurt Russell as Dr. David Grant (a title tells us he has a Ph.D.). Grant, an expert in international terrorism working for a think tank as an intelligence analyst, uncovers Hassan's diabolical plan. He is forced to join an antiterrorism commando unit headed by Colonel Austin Travis (played by Steven Seagal in military fatigues) because of his familiarity with Hassan's career as a bad guy. Grant, in his tux and wearing eyeglasses throughout the film, and the antiterrorist commandos fly a new stealth superjet equipped with a fancy antidecompression tunnel and manage to slip into the belly of the plane in midflight. They kill all the terrorists and neutralize the very sophisticated bomb and land the plane safely.

One of the most striking elements in *Executive Decision* is the casting of Steven Seagal as the head of the antiterrorist commando unit, the kind of role that made his career. As soon as he appears in the opening sequence of the film, involving a raid on a hideout of some terrorists, he begins displaying his usual ultraviolent throat-slashing drills. Perhaps in reference to the changing landscape of the hero of the action-adventure genre in the 1990s, his character is killed twenty minutes into the film.

Many critics brought up the casting of Steven Seagal. Rob Salem of the *Toronto Star* (1996) tells its readers that "if nothing else, *Executive Decision* must be commended for giving us only as much Steven Seagal as is absolutely necessary. In less enlightened times, *Executive Decision* would have starred Steven Seagal." He warns the readers that "I don't want to give too much away here—suffice it to say that Seagal's relative contribution here is pretty much a moot point after the first reel." LaSalle (1996) warns readers, "If you're planning to see *Executive Decision* because Seagal is in it, don't bother." Ray Mark Rinaldi (1996) of the *St. Louis Post-Dispatch* tells its readers that "wisely, this story emphasizes Russell and the squad's resourcefulness and pulls the plug early on Seagal's macho, throat-slashing maneuvers." Roger Ebert (1996) of the *Chicago Sun-Times* claims that "the movie succeeded in really surprising me, because, while trying to board the plane, Seagal is sucked out of the tube and into the jet stream."

In an exchange with Seagal's character (Colonel Austin Travis), Grant asks him why he is involved in this operation if he does not believe Grant's theory about Hassan's plans. He replies by saying: "Who the hell else is going to do it. You?" While Grant has no answer for this question, by the end of the film we learn that the answer the film provides is a resounding yes. The casting of Kurt Russell is important in a number of ways. In a *New York Times* report on the decision to cast Kurt Russell for the lead, Josh Young (1996) spells out a number of considerations. He claims that "the consensus among movie executives is that the forty-five-year-old actor is sexy enough to attract women, vulnerable enough to be unthreatening to men and bankable enough to appeal to studios." His image, we are told, is that of "the hunk as Everyman." Moreover, "the consensus among many students of film is that Mr. Russell's success is due in part to his ability to play a gonzo type with heart and soul." Additionally, quoting the film critic Molly Haskell, he refers to Russell as "a thinking man's action hero who appeals to both male and female audiences." She is quoted as saying, "There's nothing macho about him. There are not many actors who can be physically graceful without being bullies and who can play intellectuals and also tough guys." She characterizes Russell as "boyish and virile." In short, the casting of Kurt Russell is meant to produce a different kind of action-hero that stands in contrast to the macho heroes of 1980s films. Other casting choices, such as a carefully selected ethnic mix of the members of the commando unit, reflect the 1990s multicultural sensibility as well.

Executive Decision reflects the 1990s sensibility in a novel way by developing a self-reflexive stance toward the conventions of the genre in depicting the Middle Eastern terrorists. The film invites its audience to accept the conventions of the genre as simply that—conventions—and get on with the business of enjoying a good action flick. This is what Ebert (1996) is referring to when he claims that *Executive Decision* is a "movie for people who are sophisticated enough to know how shameless the film is, but fun-loving enough to enjoy its excesses and manic zeal."

There are two ways to establish what I am calling the film's self-reflexiveness: either through plot and character motivation or through elements that do not have much relevance to the plot. Let me give examples of the elements that are not related to the plot first. At some point in the film one of the flight attendants finds a map of the United States. Ebert (1996) refers to this map in his review where he claims that one of the flight attendants "gets the movie's single funniest moment, when she discovers, in the terrorist's jacket, a map labeled 'Washington, D.C.' " Why does he think this map is funny? Because "the map is singularly unhelpful, since all it shows is a dot identified as 'Washington,' surrounded by concentric circles of, I guess, spreading toxic gases." The second example is the way in which the film invokes James Bond in relation to its main character, Dr. Grant. Russell's character in the film is referred to as double-o-seven (and "pretty boy") by another character (from the tux, to the martini drink, to the blonde he is trying to befriend right before he is called up for the mission, etc.).

Another example is the tongue-in-cheek music that closes the film as the credits roll—a snappy song by Frank Sinatra. The lyrics tell us that it is good to travel to foreign lands and nice to "wander the camel route to Iraq." Such music and lyrics at the end of a film dealing with an airplane hijacked by a pack of Middle Eastern terrorists invite the audience to enjoy the fun of the silliness they have just watched.

This self-reflexivity may also be revealed in the plot and the "motivation" for a "character." One example is the motivation for the bomb maker. He is an Algerian by the name of Jean Paul Demou who used to work for the government of Iraq as a nuclear engineer. His family was killed during the Gulf War. His political grievance about the past, expressed in terms of personal history, is meant to give the terrorist a political motivation. Another example is the terrorist second in command. Once Hassan manages to get the authorities to release Jaffa (the leader of the group that Hassan was a member of), he refuses to terminate the mission. The movie suggests that all along Hassan has been the mastermind behind all the complications. In a speech that is a patchwork of all the clichés about Muslims (babbling about infidels, Allah, Islam, etc.), he tells Jaffa that he is going to use "the sword of Allah" to "strike deep within the heart of the infidel." At this point the film manages to surprise the critics by trying to present some of the terrorists as somewhat reasonable! The terrorist second in command on board the plane refuses to carry on the mission since Jaffa has been released. He protests to Hassan that "this has nothing to do with Islam. This is not Allah's will. You're blinded by your hatred. I will have nothing to do with it."

The critics' reaction to this aspect of the film points to the cynicism on the part of the filmmakers in deploying the very conventions (stereotypes) they themselves find convenient. Ebert (1996) in his review made this observation: "A moderate among his [Hassan's] followers steps forward, shouts 'This has nothing to do with Islam!' and is shot. His function is to get the filmmakers off the hook: Hassan is a fanatic, see, and not to be taken as typical of his co-religionists. (It would have been easy to make the terrorists members of a non-sectarian movement, and I wish they had; what purpose does it serve to slander a religion?)." Mike Clark's (1996) review for *USA Today* makes this point when he says, "In a slick ethno-political tightrope act," the script by Jim and John Thomas presents the hijackers as fanatical followers of a fairly "reasonable" terrorist [Jaffa]. Susan Stark (1996), film critic for the *Detroit News*, argues that while "characterizing the terrorists as Muslims on a suicidal mission who finally break away from their own leader in their zeal" is not exactly "pushing the envelope," it "does give the effort an aura of currency."

Such is the multicultural sensibility of the 1990s. Although the film awkwardly acknowledges stereotypes in depicting the Middle East, it assumes that such an acknowledgment, as a "kinder, gentler" gesture reflecting 1990s liberalism, will redeem its conventional approach. In the next section we will see how *The Siege* perfectly embodies the 1990s sensibility in that it advances a reactionary cause in the name of a well-meaning liberalism.

The Siege

The Siege was released in 1998, a decade after the Reagan presidency ended and in the aftermath of the Oklahoma City bombing. Given this historical framework, it was in a position to tap into the political and cultural anxieties of the post-Reagan era and the political currents during the Clinton presidency. In this context, I argue that *The Siege*, following *Executive Decision*, acknowledges the stereotypes in depicting the Middle East. The film, in line with the 1990s multicultural liberal sensibility, deploys the very stereotypes it explicitly finds deplorable.

The Siege is set in New York City. A group of terrorists executes a series of explosions terrorizing the city. Among the victims are a busload of people blown to pieces in front of the ever present news cameras, a Broadway theater, whose "list of victims is a veritable Who's Who of the city's cultural leaders," and a federal building, which houses the FBI's agents, some of whose 600 victims we have come to know throughout the film as an ethnically diverse team of good agents. An FBI agent by the name of Anthony (Hub) Hubbard (Denzel Washington) is in charge of the investigation. He is a man of impeccable moral character who strongly defends the United States constitution and the civil liberties of all American citizens. In the course of the investigation, Hub finds out that a CIA agent by the name of Elise Kraft (Annette Bening), who has intimate (literally as well) connections with the terrorists, is also investigating the case.

Once the combined efforts of the CIA and FBI prove inadequate to solve the case, the government brings the army into the action. The president declares martial law (hence the film's poster art of heavily armed soldiers marching across the Brooklyn Bridge) and places the city under the control of a very patriotic Gen. William Devereaux (Bruce Willis). Looking for terrorists, Devereaux conducts a house-to-house search in Brooklyn with its sizable population of Arabs and Arab-Americans. In the course of herding Arabs into an internment camp in a stadium, he also imprisons the thirteen-year old son of Frank Haddad (Tony Shalhoub), a Lebanese-American FBI agent who happens to be Hub's sidekick. Once Hub and Elise discover that Samir (Sami Bouajila), an Arab informant who is intimately involved with Elise, is the very (and the last) terrorist they are after, the case is closed and the martial law is lifted.

In his relentless pursuit of terrorists at all costs, Devereaux tortures and kills one of the Arab-American suspects. At the beginning of the film, he is also shown to be behind the kidnapping of an Iraqi religious leader (among whose followers is Samir) by the name of Sheik Ahmed bin Talal (who looks remarkably like the infamous Osama bin Laden) without the knowledge of the president of the United States. The accusations of murder and of conducting his personal foreign policy become the factors that bring down the hawkish General Devereaux. It is Hub who delivers the warrant for his arrest and the film ends with the release of Haddad's son.

The film's claim to originality is the use of an Arab-American character. Haddad is the film's imagined victim of a political world where "Arabs" of various political and professional persuasions are not distinguishable. Unlike many of the films in this genre, The Siege goes to the trouble of giving voice to an "Arab," albeit as a naturalized American citizen. In contrast to Hub, and even Elise, he has a family life, and we see him in his domestic environment. The injustice inflicted upon his family, however, is acknowledged by Hub, the decent FBI agent. In an exchange with Devereaux, Hub tells the general that he should release Haddad's son since his father is a federal agent. Devereaux's response is that he is also a Shiite. Strictly speaking, Haddad is only a victim and his character has no political weight in the narrative since he expresses no political view. Moreover, it is through Haddad's character that the film tests loyalty to one's country (America in this case). In short, through this character the film is acknowledging that there are some racist individuals (Devereaux and his gang) out there.

The film also includes, albeit in fleeting moments, the voice of Arab-American leaders. In a gathering where Hub is dispatching his agents to go after Arab terrorists he tells them "just got off the phone with the leaders of the Arab community. We got their complete support and cooperation. They love this country as much as we do." (Of course the film is unaware of the irony in referring to Arab-Americans as "they." How can they be as much American as "we" are if they are still "they"?). In another scene, resembling a press conference, where Hub is expressing outrage at the work of Arab terrorists, a character stands up and says he is from some Arab anti-defamation league and that "we will continue our support."

In addition to such gestures, the film is peppered with comments that are meant to protect the film from charges of racism. Elise speaks of a Beirut that she used to know as "an exotic Paris." Her first boyfriend, we are told, was a Palestinian! At some point she tells Hub that her father used to say Palestinians "seduce you with their suffering." In the midst of the outcry against the Arab community and the rounding up of Arabs in New York, we hear an off-screen voice asking, "What if they were black people? What if they were Italian?"

More importantly, following *Executive Decision* in its attempt to grant terrorists political grievance, *The Siege* tries to grant Samir and his terrorist friends some form of political grievance. At one point in the film we learn that Elise had been training Iraqi dissidents inside Iraq in an attempt to "destabilize" Saddam Hussein's regime. With the help of Samir, Elise had been recruiting individuals from among Sheik Ahmed bin Talal's followers to overthrow Saddam's government. Because of a "policy shift," according to Elise, reminiscent of George Bush's abandonment of anti-Saddam dissidents at the end of the Gulf War, the Sheik's followers are left on their own for Saddam to slaughter. In an exchange with Hub, Elise with teary eyes admits that the terrorists are here in New York City because she had helped them escape Saddam by providing visas for them. What did Elise teach terrorists to do back in the Middle East? "How to make bombs," as Hub puts it. "They are here," as Hub continues, "doing what you taught them to do." In this context, the film is making the point in a confused fashion that the terrorist killers terrorizing New York City are themselves ultimately the victims of their circumstances! In short, through its liberalism the film tries to distinguish itself from other films in the genre in that it, as one critic put it, "dares to take on the facile, hurtful anti-Arab patter of countless recent, cheesy thrillers" (Stark 1998).

One of the most striking reactions to the film by the critics in the popular press was the rejection of its so-called liberalism. Ebert (1998) answers the question, What if the film depicted other ethnic groups in this context? "By way of illustration, it is unlikely, even unimaginable, after recent history, that a fantasy like *The Siege* would be made about the internment of Japanese or Jewish Americans." The film "went off track," according to Joe Holleman (1998), film critic for the *St. Louis Post-Dispatch*, because it had "too many 'important' messages." He mocks the film's attempt at a "Hollywood civics lesson." "Let's get this straight: Dictatorship, bad. Freedom, good. Love, good. Hate, bad. Director Edward Zwick gets so politically correct that, inspired by old Coca-Cola commercials, he has a scene near the end that has at least one actor from every known race, color, creed, age and gender marching arm in arm through the streets." Carr (1998) claims that the film "mostly goes through the motions of being high-minded while dishing out the same cliffhanging genre thrills." Geoff Pevere (1998) of the *Toronto Star* is explicit on this point: "Welcome to the curious world of the liberal action movie, an oxymoronic universe where mayhem is checked by sensitivity, guilt galvanizes gunplay, and talk and action campaign democratically for equal representation." He adds that the film is so "committed to the politically worthy but dramatically stultifying need to give all sides their due," that even "Willis's martinet neo-fascist is ultimately exposed as a fundamentally decent guy." Jian Ghomeshi (1998) of the *Toronto Star* argues that "here is a Hollywood movie that appears to have its makers repeatedly apologizing for living up to the very tradition of its genre." What is insidious about the film is the way "it cloaks its offensive typecasting and hawkish ideas in the veneer of a well-meaning liberal sensibility. It advances a right-wing agenda with a skilled and experienced liberal approach." His argument is that "making a jingoistic action film that has the U.S. military triumphing over a well-known enemy composed of racist caricatures is not as easy as it once was. Not when you want credulity, not when you want to be taken seriously, and not in the racially and sexually 'correct' late-1990s."

The Siege was rejected by most critics for the way it simplistically resolves all the problems it might have posed by depicting as the source of all wrong-doings a renegade general (who is meant to represent someone resembling the Oliver North of the Reagan presidency, who conducted his "personal foreign policy"). As Ebert (1998) puts it, "The movie awkwardly tries to switch villains in the third act." Turan (1998) claims that "the rationale for going to martial law feels like a contrivance" and that the script "loses a level of plausibility." LaSalle (1998) argues that the film "derails" because of "an amazing strategic blunder in the story. Here's a movie about people blowing up. The villain should be whoever is setting those bombs. Instead, *The Siege* concentrates on the crimes of the general, who uses the imposition of martial law in New York as an excuse to deny citizens their constitutional rights."

The scapegoating of General Devereaux in *The Siege* is in line with the liberal sensitivity of the 1990s, also embodied by *True Lies* and *Executive Decision*. In the next section I will argue that *The Siege* is politically incoherent given the ideological agglomeration it insidiously engages.

THE PERSISTENCE OF VISION

In order to explore the cultural and the political tenor of the 1990s as reflected in the depiction of the Middle East, I now return to the two analytics of "kinder, gentler" men (and era) and Orientalism in light of the foregoing discussion of *True Lies, Executive Decision,* and *The Siege.*

Both *True Lies* and *Executive Decision* reflect the shift that Jeffords (1993; 1994) locates in the image of masculinity in the early 1990s. Both of these films attempt to respond and draw from the political current and the nomenclature of the post-Reagan era enunciated by George Bush's "kinder, gentler" slogan. As Maslin (1994) puts it in her review of *True Lies,* "Mr. Schwarzenegger is not in the habit of playing either jealous or romantic husbands, but *True Lies* brings out a gentler, funnier side of him, too." In the case of *True Lies,* Jeffords's (1993) argument is particularly instructive. She asks, What happens to the heroes of the 1980s? The answer, she says, is one word: family. The film, in expressing its anxieties regarding family, as we have already seen, turns into a sitcom. "Situation comedy" in the language of television criticism is a variation of the "domestic" comedy in which family (and parental authority) is the organizing principle behind its discourse (see Newcombe 1974). In another Schwarzenegger film, *Kindergarten Cop* (1990), the lead character, in line with the early 1990s male characters, prefers to be a father instead of a warrior. In *True Lies* the terrorist-fighting, world-class spy wants to have it both ways. He is at once a family man and a warrior. As Jeffords argues (1993), "Retroactively, the men of the 1980s are being given feelings, feelings that were, presumably, hidden behind their confrontational violence" (pp. 144–145).

Of course the film is not entirely comfortable letting go of the warrior spirit. This is perhaps because the conservative men who were behind the making of this film, Arnold Schwarzenegger and James Cameron, held on to the remnants of a Reagan-era heroism that is now outdated. Ultimately the film turns the entire family into warriors instead of turning the warrior into a dad. By the film's end, daddy, mommy, and the kid all have their violent moments of triumph against the bad guys. Wilmington (1994) calls *True Lies* a "cinematic oxymoron" full of contradictions: "a nice bloody, sadistic family romp, full of hilarity, death and comical lunatics trying to blow up cities, all about a dad who's a killer, a mom with a talent for striptease and whoring and a daughter who runs away with the key to the bomb." Sex (and misogyny) and violence turn out to be the real family values that bring the family together, a result of the ideological incoherence of mixing "family values" (the conservative slogan of the early 1990s) with the old Cold Warrior spirit of the 1980s (the conservative consciousness of the 1980s). As I have already pointed out, there is nothing kind or gentle about the treatment of women and Arabs in *True Lies.*

The "kinder, gentler" approach is also pursued by *Executive Decision.* As I have already argued in the previous section, the casting of Kurt Russell is an attempt to show a "gentler" kind of action hero. But more importantly, in killing Steven Seagal's character—the warrior of a bygone era who seems out of touch with the world around him—*Executive Decision* makes it clear that we are in the age of "bookish" heroes. As LaSalle (1996) tells the readers in his review of the film, "Usually it's a Seagal world, and everybody else just lives there. But here Seagal is forced to inhabit the more affable universe of Kurt Russell, and he looks out of place."

The film's self-reflexivity on the issue of portraying Arabs as terrorists is perhaps the most significant sign that the ideological monotony of this discourse is being acknowledged. Either by tongue-and-cheek devices (the map, the closing music, etc.) or by portraying some terrorists as somewhat reasonable, the film is self-conscious for deploying the very convention of the terrorist film genre it is a part of and a contributor to. One of the most striking features of this film is its efficiency in executing the very conventions of the genre. Without wasting any time it moves quickly from one plot complication to the next. As Turan (1996) puts it, "Everything about *Executive Decision* is familiar except how crisply its conventional story is executed." He adds that although this film is "unremarkable in broad outlines," it should please "those who appreciate old-fashioned craft." The film belongs to the action-adventure genre, which relies on visceral and kinetic effects driven by plot complications. In this context the larger question asks whether such a genre has intrinsic limitations for developing "characters" with feelings, emotions, and motivations. Although answering such a question is beyond the scope of this chapter, I want to point out that the attempt by the filmmakers (vis-à-vis its self-reflexivity) to give some of its "characters" something resembling "motivation" might be doomed given such structural limitations. Such a gesture on the part of the filmmakers runs up against the demands of the genre. But such a gesture is an indication that the ideological monotony of the Middle Easterner-as-terrorist is being acknowledged. More importantly, this gesture reflects the political and cultural "kinder, gentler" sensibility of the 1990s. Such a sensibility has a darker side to it, which is crystallized by *The Siege.*

As mentioned earlier, one of the most striking reactions to *The Siege* in the popular press was the rejection of its liberalism. The film's liberalism might be understood in a number of ways: it is as an element of the "multicultural" sensitivity of the 1990s; it is another "I feel your pain" moment characteristic of Clinton's era; it is another "political correctness" gesture; it is an example of a "kinder, gentler" Hollywood. That liberalism was rejected for the insidious ideological agglomeration it engages: the leftist and liberal sensitivity is put to work for the most reactionary cause. On the one hand, the film admits the racism of cultural stereotyping. On the other hand, it engages in the stereotyping it finds so offensive. At the end, a renegade general comes to take all the blame and we all feel good about ourselves for holding racist stereotypes. It is much easier to see through the reactionary films of the 1980s than such a "liberal" film.

The critics' reaction is understandable given the manner in which the film skillfully taps into cultural anxieties and fears about Islam and Middle Easterners. The film begins with stock footage of President Clinton reacting to a terrorist act. We are then presented with a series of shots intercutting between the fictional world of the film and footage from the coverage of terrorist bombings. The real-world events (and the fear they might have generated) are put in the service of the fictional world of *The Siege* (the real geopolitical world is ultimately irrelevant for such a film).

The film's crisp and well-crafted images of menacing Arabs and Muslims are particularly disturbing. Maslin (1998) argues that "the film's stark images of scheming Arab villains often speak louder than its diplomatic words." Ghomeshi (1998) argues that "in a few crucial scenes, the film marries Islam and Muslim practices with terroristic violence." He asks, "Where are the writers' liberal sensitivities when they meticulously depict a Muslim Arab completing a deeply religious act by strapping bombs across his torso and terrorizing a female hostage?" (The treatment of the only female character, the only character whose sexuality is questioned, raises the same question. As Michael O'Sullivan (1998) of the *Washington Post* puts it, "What a shame, therefore, that in its puritanical treatment of the only strong female character, the otherwise politically correct police story is blithely unaware of its own closet misogyny.''). Arguably, the image of a van full of explosives going for a building in New York is a composite image that collapses all the distinctions between international and domestic terrorism (from the World Trade Center bombing to the Oklahoma City bombing), capitalizing on the fear of threatening Muslims.

Maslin (1998) pointed out that "among the film's most ominous shots is one panning from a New York mosque to the Manhattan skyline, which looks like one big tempting target in the context of this story." In this shot the camera moves from a close-up of a Muslim chanting a call for prayer to reveal the skyline, as if to suggest the threat of Islam in the very heart of the West. Indeed, what this film shares with many of the films in this genre (including *True Lies* and *Executive Decision*) is a plot that has terrorists trying to penetrate U.S. soil. Of course the fear of terrorist bombing in the aftermath of the World Trade Center bombing and the Oklahoma City bombing may be understandable. The inescapable conclusion is that *The Siege,* as David Denby (1998) of the *New Yorker* put it, "is peddling fear," the fear of the threatening other in the midst of "us." (See Semati 1997.)

It is a commonplace these days to claim that Islam has become the "evil empire" formerly represented by the Soviet Union. The neat coordinates of the Cold War geopolitical world that kept everything in a strict communists-and-us framework are gone. *The Siege* makes a reference to this fact. Hub, tired of dealing with a CIA agent who seems to have no patience for the legal procedures necessary to obtain a search warrant, tells Elise, "I am sorry the Cold War is over and all your little masters of the universe CIA types got to work in Afghanistan, Russia, or Iran, or wherever the hell it is, but this ain't the Middle East." Hub's comments attest to the troubling confusion and the anxieties the loss of the Cold War has brought. In response to Hub's comments, we may read the "subplot" of the film (terrorists trained by CIA terrorizing an American city) as the case of the West fighting its own demons (the same way Saddam's "fourth largest army in the world" was a gift from the West in its strategy of containing Iran under a "dual containment" policy). Of course the film does not entertain such a political reading since it is too busy victimizing everyone (including the terrorists) by the only bad apple (the renegade General Devereaux).

In this context it is instructive to consider Slavoj Zizek's insightful analysis of the tendency toward victimization, a characteristic of the contemporary "liberal-democratic" West. Zizek (1994) delineates the logic of such a tendency: "The Third World other is recognized as a victim—that is to say, *in so far as he is a victim*" (p. 215). True anxiety in the encounter with the other comes about when the other refuses to play the role of the victim (hence the good terrorists and the bad terrorists). What is crucial in his analysis is that the contemporary universalization of the notion of the victim blends two aspects. On the one hand, compassion with the local victims of the Third

World "frames the liberal-democratic (mis)conception of today's Great Divide" between those who are "in" and those who are "out." On the other hand, the victimization of the citizens of the liberal-democratic societies renders the other a potential threat, "encroaching upon the space of [one's] self-identity" (pp. 215–216).

Such an understanding of the role of victimization reveals the political and cultural tenor of the "kinder, gentler" 1990s reflected in the films under discussion. If the analytic of the "kinder, gentler" 1990s reveals a darker side of the multicultural sensibility of the post-Reagan era, let us see if the second analytic (Orientalism) presents a different picture of the same era. Here the second analytic, based on Prince's (1993) argument about the four logics in the portrayal of the Middle East, is deployed in order to see if the underlying logic in such a portrayal has changed in the 1990s.

First, apart from an occasional vague reference to Saddam Hussein or Palestine, the lack of geographical and national specificity of the "Middle Easterners" in all of these films transforms the "Middle East" into something that exists outside of time and history. The lack of specificity works to translate the various national, cultural, and political currents of the Middle East into a "hazy, nebulous, threatening Other, a projection of political and cultural anxieties that are stripped of their historical basis and are assigned to regions of the world in generalized, superficial, and essentially mythological terms." Such a geopolitics works "to remove the terrain of the Middle East from history and from a knowable politics" (Prince 1993, p. 246).

Second, the portrayal of the Arabs and the Middle Easterners as brutal people capable of torture and other violent acts, in comparison with the "Westerners" who love and respect the sanctity of life, renders the Other uncivilized and savages. It matters little if a film has an "Arab" character that is friendly to us when the overwhelming number of them are portrayed as brutal. Indeed, such an attempt is the old cunning device of "some of my best friends are . . ." designed to be a defensive mechanism. As Prince (1993) points out, such a confrontation between the West and the Arabic cultures projected in these films is part of a larger historical reality in which the West has viewed Islam with fear and suspicion and as a threat to Christianity (see Said 1979). Third, if the portrayal of the cultures and religions of the Middle East in a dichotomy of the civilized versus the savages is expressed in terms of moral oppositions, another set of oppositions, true to the oldest form of Orientalist ideology, depict the other as technologically backward and incompetent. Needless to say, the victory over the enemy in all of these films necessarily entails depicting the incompetence they possess when it comes to technology. What else would one expect from "towel heads" or "sand niggers," to invoke terms used in *The Siege*?

Finally, the audiovisual rhetoric of the East–West confrontation is used as a background against which the use of high-tech weaponry is celebrated, glamorized, and promoted. This is one of the most strikingly consistent features of all of these films. As many critics point out, the celebration of high-tech weaponry and the deployment of audiovisual gimmickry have become the obligatory cliché in the genre. Such a highly romanticized image of weapons of destruction and death promotes an image of war, not unlike the image of the Gulf War, which is far from the reality of death and destruction that war creates. This is a world in which instruments of death are eroticized, weapons of destruction have sex appeal, and war itself is sexy.

The most significant conclusion we can draw from the consideration of *True Lies, Executive Decision,* and *The Siege* through the two analytics is an alarming one: a "kinder, gentler" sensibility is deployed to advance a set of Orientalist ideologies. In comparison to the 1980s, what makes the depiction of the Middle East in the 1990s particularly insidious is that these films promote the racism of the 1980s films in a kinder, gentler multicultural disguise.

CONCLUSION

This chapter set out to compare three high-profile films released in the 1990s to a cycle of films released in the 1980s in order to examine the shifts in Hollywood's representations of Middle East terrorism in the post-Reagan era. Two analytics made up the framework for the analysis. Film critics' reactions to *True Lies, Executive Decision,* and *The Siege* indicate that each was viewed in the context of current cultural-political sensibilities. Two analytics guided further analysis of the representational shifts that distinguish the 1980s films from the three 1990s films. One analytic (ultramasculinity) supported the argument that the "hard bodies" (ultramasculinism) of the 1980s heroes underwent a transformation that sought to project a "kinder, gentler" image of masculinity in the 1990s films. The other analytic (Orientalism) was based on four logics for depicting the Middle East. The analyses revealed that all three films deployed a "kinder, gentler" sensibility while advancing a set of Orientalist ideologies. These films insidiously promoted the racism of the 1980s films in the guise of a kinder, gentler multicultural sensibility. This depiction is a form of cultural violence more dangerous than the glorification of violence in the earlier action films. Although the depiction of (physical) violence may be disturbing, the cultural violence of the 1990s films has more cultural (and ultimately political) significance.

In the fictional world of the 1980s films, violence always wins over diplomacy, weapons take precedence over negotiations, and carnage and mayhem are the only ways to bring about resolution. The politically correct multiculturalism of the 1990s films does not eschew such physical violence but adds a different kind of violence, a cultural violence of representation that obliterates what cannot be assimilated. The troubling violence these films inflict on the diverse peoples and cultures of the Middle East, and on the viewers, lies not in what they depict but in what they fail to represent: the Middle East as a place where people live their lives, get married, go to work every day, enjoy food, go to school, listen to music, pay mortgages, live everyday lives . . . lives not so extraordinary.

NOTES

The author thanks Patty Sotirin and Dennis Lynch for their comments on earlier versions of this chapter.

1. Film reviews consulted for this chapter were obtained through a LEXIS-NEXIS database search using the title of the films and the word "review" as key words (page numbers for film reviews are therefore not applicable).

REFERENCES

Bernstein, M., and G. Studlar, eds. 1997. *Visions of the East: Orientalism in film*. New Jersey: Rutgers University Press.

Blowen, M. 1991. *Navy Seals* is a jingoist's dream. *Boston Globe*, February 22. LEXIS-NEXIS.

Brown, G. 1991. Belly laughs and bottom lines. *The Times*, June 27. LEXIS-NEXIS.

Canby, V. 1986a. *Delta Force*. *New York Times*, February 14. LEXIS-NEXIS.

———. 1986b. Don't mess with celluloid tigers. *New York Times*, February 23. LEXIS-NEXIS.

Carr, J. 1994. Arnie, you're no 007. *Boston Globe*, July 15. LEXIS-NEXIS.

Clark, M. 1996. *Executive Decision*: Lay 'em off. *USA Today*, March 15. LEXIS-NEXIS.

Denby, D. 1998. Looking for salvation in *The Siege*. *New Yorker* 74, no. 35: 114–115.

Ebert, R. 1994. Secret agent man. *Chicago Sun-Times*, July 15. LEXIS-NEXIS.

———. 1996. *Executive* calls the shots; *Air Scare* is goofy fun. *Chicago Sun-Times*, March 15. LEXIS-NEXIS.

———. 1998. *The Siege* gets mired in muck of prejudice. *Chicago Sun-Times*, November 6. LEXIS-NEXIS.

Fuller, L. 1995. Hollywood holding US hostage: Or why are terrorists in the movies Middle Easterners? In Y. R. Kamalipour, ed., *The U.S. media and the Middle East: Image and perception*, pp. 187–197. London: Praeger.

Ghomeshi, J. 1994. Well-meaning and dangerous. *Toronto Star*, November 15. LEXIS-NEXIS.

Gilbert, M. 1990. *Seals* drowns in its own dreariness. *Boston Globe*, July 20. LEXIS-NEXIS.

Grossberg, L. 1988. *It's a sin: Essays on postmodernism, politics, and culture*. Sydney: Power.

Holleman, J. 1998. Cop thriller with strong cast goes from bad to worse. *St. Louis Post-Dispatch*, November 6. LEXIS-NEXIS.

James, C. 1990. Teen-age mutant ninja seals, grown up and in the navy. *New York Times*, July 20. LEXIS-NEXIS.

Jeffords, S. 1993. The big switch: Hollywood masculinity in the nineties. In J. Collins, H. Radner, and E. Preacher Collins, eds., *Film theory goes to the movies*, pp. 196–208. New York: Routledge.

———. 1994. *Hard bodies: Hollywood masculinity in the Reagan era*. New Jersey: Rutgers University Press.

Kellner, D. 1995. *Media culture: Cultural studies, identity, and politics between the modern and the postmodern*. New York: Routledge.

Kempley, R. 1994. Reactionary action. *Washington Post*, July 15. LEXIS-NEXIS.

Laclau, E. 1990. *New reflections on the revolution of our time*. London: Verso.

LaSalle, M. 1994. Schwarzenegger's *Lies*: Larger than life. *San Francisco Chronicle*, July 14. LEXIS-NEXIS.

———. 1996. Russell, Seagal don't quite fly in *Decision. San Francisco Chronicle*, March 15. LEXIS-NEXIS.

———. 1998. *Siege* bombs. *San Francisco Chronicle*, November 6. LEXIS-NEXIS.

Maslin, J. 1986. *Iron Eagle*: A tale of teen-age military rescue. *New York Times*, January 18. LEXIS-NEXIS.

———. 1987. *Death Before Dishonor. New York Times*, February 20. LEXIS-NEXIS.

———. 1994. Schwarzenegger as a Walter Mitty with weapons. *New York Times*, July 15. LEXIS-NEXIS.

———. 1996. Airline terrorists meet a techie and a toughy. *New York Times*, March 15. LEXIS-NEXIS.

Miller, A. 1994. Arab American Groups Blast Schwarzenegger Film. *Washington Post*, July 22. LEXIS-NEXIS.

Newcombe, H. 1974. *TV: The most popular art*. Garden City, N.Y.: Anchor.

O'Sullivan, M. 1998. Complexity under *Siege. Washington Post*, November 6. LEXIS-NEXIS.

Pevere, G. 1998. Wussy *Siege* mentality. *Toronto Star*, November 6. LEXIS-NEXIS.

Prince, S. 1992. *Visions of empire: Political imagery in contemporary American film*. New York: Praeger.

———. 1993. Celluloid heroes and smart bombs: Hollywood at war in the Middle East. In R. E. Denton Jr., ed., *The media and the Persian Gulf War*, pp. 235–256. London: Praeger.

Ray, R. B. 1985. *A certain tendency of the Hollywood cinema, 1930–1980*. Princeton: Princeton University Press.

Rinaldi, M. 1996. This thriller is literally up in the air. *St. Louis Post-Dispatch*, March 15. LEXIS-NEXIS.

Rosen, P. 1986. *Narrative, apparatus, ideology: A film theory reader*. New York: Columbia University Press.

Ryan, M. 1988. The politics of film: Discourse, psychoanalysis, ideology. In C. Nelson and L. Grossberg, eds., *Marxism and interpretation of culture*, pp. 477–486. Urbana: University of Illinois Press.

Said, E. 1979. *Orientalism*. New York: Vintage.

Salem, R. 1996. Macho boys and toys keep action thumping. *Toronto Star*, March 15. LEXIS-NEXIS.

Schwartz, A. 1994. Satire, stereotype, Schwarzenegger. *Washington Post*, July 22. LEXIS-NEXIS.

Semati, M. M. 1997. Terrorists, Moslems, fundamentalists, and other bad objects in the midst of us. *International Journal of Communication* 4, no. 1: 3–49.

Semati, M. M., and P. J. Sotirin. 1999. Hollywood's trans-national appeal: Hegemony or democratic potential? *Journal of Popular Film and Television* 26, no. 4: 176–188.

Smith, L. 1994. The truth is, there's more to *Lies* than action. *Los Angeles Times*, July 21. LEXIS-NEXIS.

Stark, S. 1996. Unfriendly skies. *Detroit News*, March 15. LEXIS-NEXIS.

———. 1998. *The Siege* gets past stereotypes that bog down most. *Detroit News*, November 6. LEXIS-NEXIS.

Turan, K. 1994. The secret life of *True Lies*: Exciting action is undercut by film's meanness. *Los Angeles Times*, July 14. LEXIS-NEXIS.

———. 1996. Making the right *Decision*. *Los Angeles Times*, March 15. LEXIS-NEXIS.

———. 1998. Crafting a *Siege* mentality. *Los Angeles Times*, November 6. LEXIS-NEXIS.

Whittel, G. 1994. Action hero holds his breath for spills at box office. *The Times*, July 13. LEXIS-NEXIS.

Wilmington, M. 1994. *True Lies* foiled by tangled web of contradictions. *Chicago Tribune*, July 15. LEXIS-NEXIS.

Wloszczyna, S. 1994. *True Lies* produces a classier action hero. *USA Today*, July 15. LEXIS-NEXIS.

Young, J. 1996. A movie tough guy with a heart of gold. *New York Times*, March 24. LEXIS-NEXIS.

Zerbisias, A. 1994. *True Lies* denigrates women and "Arabs" Bond-type bimbos. *Toronto Star*, August 12. LEXIS-NEXIS.

Zizek, S. 1994. *The metastases of enjoyment: Six essays on woman and causality*. New York: Routledge.

15

Between Globalization and Localization: Television, Tradition, and Modernity

Marwan M. Kraidy

Obituaries for the nation-state have pointed to the tide of globalization from above and to subnational local forces from below as indicators of the end of the nation-state. Against these dire predictions, the nation-state has turned out to be a particularly resilient form of political economic and sociocultural organization. Instead of the destruction of the nation-state caught in the double bind of globalization and localization, we see that the national is the context in which the global and the local are articulated, sometimes in the form of conflict with varying degrees of intensity, at other times peacefully.

This chapter argues that national television in the nonindustrialized world is the point of articulation of globalization and localization. Television is the site in which global modernity and local tradition struggle to define national values and identity. It is the prime mirror in which the nation sees itself as an "imagined community" (Anderson 1983). As such, in the era of globalization, television is the prime space in which the foreign and the domestic are redefined. Television is the main channel by which the tentacles of Western culture, with the usual dose of commercialized sex and violence, reach into the national space of traditional societies.

Using Lebanese television as a case study, this chapter will discuss the following questions: How does television reflect the struggle over national values between tradition and modernity? Is sensationalist content (such as sex and violence) always a product of Western, mainly U.S. culture, or can such content be home bred? And if such is the case, what discourses (moral, religious, statist, corporate, popular) does such content attract within the nation? Finally, what is the real role that television plays in defining national identity?

To achieve these goals, in this chapter I will first survey "cultural imperialism" and "globalization," the principal paradigms of thought that have attempted to grasp the complex cultural interactions spawned by transnational media between industrialized countries and nonindustrialized nations. Second, I will focus on Lebanon as a case study, with a brief look at Lebanon's historical and cultural context, and a survey of the development of mass media in the country. Third, I will describe and analyze the issue of "morality on television," a controversy about television content that rocked Lebanon between November 1997 and January 1998. Finally, I will discuss the discourses imbricated in the controversy to address how the localizing pull of tradition and the globalizing push of modernity clash on national television. I conclude with implications about the role of television in shaping national identity and recommendations for further research.

CULTURAL IMPERIALISM

Cultural imperialism has been one of the dominant paradigms in international communication over the past three decades. This perspective is based on the belief that "authentic, traditional and local culture in many parts of the world is being battered out of existence by the indiscriminate dumping of large quantities of slick commercial and media products, mainly from the United States" (Tunstall 1977, p. 57). Studies within the imperialism paradigm expressed fears of the "cultural homogenization" and "cultural synchronization" (Sreberny-Mohammadi 1987, p. 120) by global, predominantly Western, popular culture. Although perceived as a monolith by its opponents, cultural imperialism includes diverse perspectives. Tomlinson (1991) distinguishes four different but overlapping types of cultural imperialism: cultural imperialism as media imperialism, cultural imperialism as nationalistic discourse, cultural imperialism as a critical perspective on global capitalism, and cultural imperialism as a mode of criticism of modernity. Perhaps because of this internal diversity, the concept of cultural imperialism has been mired with ambiguity, as conveyed by Mattelart (1979), who wrote that the concept "has too often been used with ill-defined meaning" (p. 57).

Calls for a revision of the concept of cultural imperialism (Straubhaar 1991; Sreberny-Mohammadi 1997) have criticized the paradigm as "broad and ill-defined, operating as evocative metaphor rather than precise construct" (Sreberny-Mohammadi 1997, p. 47). This revisionist perspective, in addition to new technological, economic, and political changes affecting international communication, pushed "cultural imperialism" to yield to the concept of globalization as the main theoretical framework for international media exchanges, processes, and effects (Tomlinson 1991).

GLOBALIZATION AND LOCALIZATION

The term "globalization" was first used in the late 1950s (Waters 1995). Like cultural imperialism, "globalization" is understood from a variety of perspectives. Giddens (1990) defines globalization as the "intensification of worldwide social relations which link distant localities in such a way that local happenings are shaped by events occurring many miles away and vice versa" (p. 64). Robertson (1992) defines it as "the compression of the world and the intensification of consciousness of the world as a whole" (1992, p. 8). "Globalization" refers to the interconnected complexity of contemporary worldwide processes (Robertson 1994), described by Hannerz as a global "ecumene . . . a region of persistent culture interaction and exchange" (1994, p. 137).

According to Tomlinson (1991), globalization has superseded cultural imperialism as the large conceptual umbrella covering the study of international communication and culture. For the purposes of this chapter, we will work within the general perspective identified by Tomlinson as the fourth type of cultural imperialism, focusing on a critique of imperialism as the spread of modernity. I agree with the general orientation of this theoretical perspective as an overall strategy to understand international communication. However, I question some of the tactical implications that derive from a critique of imperialism as a spread of modernity.

First, the term "imperialism" does not address the complexity and ambivalence that characterize transnational processes. Elsewhere I suggested the term "glocalization" as an alternative to both "imperialism" and "globalization" in international communication research (Kraidy 1999a). Second, an implicit assumption of imperialism understood as the spread of modernity is that when the perceived moral ills of modern (i.e., Western) society, such as promiscuous sexuality, violence, and extreme individualism, appear on television in Western societies, they are always imported. Third, and as a result of the first two lines of questioning of imperialism, I propose an examination of television as a site of struggle, in which the pressures of modernity and tradition are obliquely expressed. This stands in sharp contradistinction to imperialism's direct and somewhat deterministic perspective.

This brings me to an often neglected area in the study of international culture and communication of exchanges. Our understanding of globalization will remain incomplete unless we comprehend the flip side of the coin, localization. Following the three lines of scrutiny that I directed to the concept of imperialism, I advocate an understanding of the "local" as "tradition." A variety of perspectives on the local have emerged since Geertz's writings on "local knowledge" (1983). Under this umbrella can be included the active audience formation in cultural studies (Ang 1985; Morley 1980) and geography and urban studies ((Entrikin 1991; Galland 1996), and more recent formulations of "disjuncture" by Appadurai (1996) and of "disembedding" by Giddens (1990). In international communication, Braman (1996) offered what is probably the most sustained theoretical treatment of localization. The bottom line in all these arguments is that the local is a crucial context and a heuristic perspective from which we can understand globalization. This is why Lebanese television will be used as a case study of the articulation of the global in the local.

THE NATIONAL CONTEXT: LEBANON

One of the world's smallest nation-states, Lebanon is located in western Asia on the shores of the Mediterranean Sea. The country's location at a civilizational crossroads translated into a tumultuous history of foreign invasions, internal divisions, and a diverse culture. In a way, both history and geography determined Lebanon's position as a "betwixt-and-between" nation, a hybrid culture (Kraidy 1999a) borrowing from neighboring civilizations but preserving a distinct identity made out of an elusive mixture of heterogeneous elements. Lebanon is believed to have been a political-geographic entity before the country took its present shape and borders in the third decade of the twentieth century. The modern republic of Lebanon was born with the promulgation of the Lebanese constitution in 1926; independence from the French mandate followed in 1943. The constitution defined Lebanon as a representative democracy and established separate legislative, executive, and judicial branches. It also guaranteed voting rights for all citizens aged twenty-one, civil liberties, freedom of speech and of the press, and religious freedom, thus laying strong foundations for civil society (Kraidy 1998).

With a population of about 3.7 million, contemporary Lebanon is a dynamic mosaic of eighteen officially recognized religious groups, ranging from Shii Muslims to Armenian Catholics and including several small, "unorthodox" Christian and Muslim denominations. This diversity is reflected in language use, as Arabic and French are Lebanon's official languages, Armenian is spoken by a sizable community, and English competes with French as the lingua franca of business and the intelligentsia. Political pluralism, religious diversity, and cultural hybridity have coalesced around a fundamental identity dilemma between Lebanon's Arab soul and Western veneer, leading to internal conflicts, partly fueled by external factors, such as the 1974–1990 war.

LEBANESE TELEVISION BEFORE AND
DURING THE 1974–90 WAR

Because of Lebanon's size, geographical location, tumultuous history, and regional role, the country's mass media have developed distinctly from regional trends (Boulos 1996; Boyd 1991; Kraidy 1998, 1999b). The Lebanese press has catered to the country's diverse communities in an atmosphere of relative freedom, with prohibitions on categories such as national security or attacking heads of state. Beirut attracted dissident Arab intellectuals, artists, and journalists who freely opposed Arab rulers in the pages of Lebanon's newspapers and over its airwaves. As a result, Arab states regularly pressured Lebanon's governments to restrain the Lebanese mass media (Kraidy 1998). It is crucial to recognize these external factors affecting Lebanese media and culture because regional pressure from neighboring Arab countries is a key factor that would affect Lebanese television in the 1990s (Kraidy 1999b).

Radio and television broadcasting arrived in Lebanon relatively early compared to most Arab countries. The French launched radio broadcasting in the country in the late 1930s for anti-Nazi propaganda purposes, which was taken over by the state after World War II (UNESCO 1949). Lebanon did not have many radio stations until the arrival of numerous nonlicensed private stations, spawned by warring factions during the war (Kraidy 1998). Television was launched in 1956 as a private-public partnership. The first station, La Compagnie Libanaise de Télévision, then the only private Arab television, was followed by Télé-Orient, a second commercial company. A 1977 merger of the two stations created Télé-Liban, a semiprivate station (Boulos 1996) defined as "national" television (Kraidy 2000).

After the first decade of the war, dozens of private radio and television stations claimed the Lebanese airwaves. These stations began as subsidized political mouthpieces. Soon many shifted to an advertising-supported format whose viability was secured by taxes levied by militias who ran them and pirated foreign programming. For example, the Lebanese Broadcasting Corporation (LBC), launched by the Lebanese forces paramilitary formation, first appeared on the Lebanese television spectrum in August 1985, with pirated foreign comedy shows such as *The Benny Hill Show* and local newscasts. Since then, LBC, now LBCI (I is for International), has maintained itself at the top of audience ratings (Kraidy 1998). Private radio stations broadcast a colorful blend of Lebanese folk music, classical Arabic songs, French popular music, Latin dance music, American and British rock, and jazz and blues (Kraidy and Khalil 1995). Television offered a varied (and in the early years mostly pirated) mixture of Egyptian soap operas and feature films, international news, French drama, American police series, French and German documentaries, British comedies, and Mexican telenovelas in addition to local news, public affairs, game shows, and drama (Kraidy 1999a).

BETWEEN THE GLOBAL AND THE LOCAL: LEBANESE TELEVISION IN THE 1990S

The postwar years in Lebanon witnessed an unprecedented proliferation of unlicensed radio and television stations. The 1995 Broadcasting Law (or, as it was known in Lebanon, the "audiovisual law") gave broadcasting a sorely needed regulatory framework, but it was criticized for giving broadcast licenses to prominent politicians only. The legislation licensed four stations: the Lebanese Broadcasting Corporation International (LBCI), Future Television, the National Broadcasting Network (NBN), and Murr Television (MTV). All stations were at least partially owned by government officials or prominent politicians (Kraidy 1998).

By licensing only a few television stations and stipulating regulatory procedures that neutralized the private stations' political agendas, the 1994 audiovisual law set the ground rules for competition on a commercial basis (for a detailed treatment of the economic turn in Lebanese television, see Kraidy, 2000, forthcoming). Although Lebanon had always had a freewheeling economy and a tradition of private enterprise, these entrepreneurial tendencies were temporarily overshadowed in the media industry during the war. The commercial aspects returned in force with the implementation of the audiovisual law.

Television competition was cutthroat, as the four licensed stations fought for audience share. In fact, the competition in the television industry can be described as a race between Future Television, NBN, and MTV to catch up with LBCI, the undisputed leader in Lebanese television. Even during the war, when LBCI was the mouthpiece for the Lebanese Forces (Christian) militia (which was a political party at that time), the station was managed like a commercial corporation. The bottom line was as important, if not more important, than the party line. Its programming grid included programs specifically targeted at Lebanon's Muslim audience, notably during the Muslim holy month of Ramadan. But with other stations with talent and capital competing for the Lebanese audience, Lebanese television took a downward turn toward controversial and sensational content.

Historically, the Lebanese television industry has been reluctant to make substantial investments in local programming (Boyd 1991). This tendency goes back to the early days of television, where profits were rarely re-invested in local productions. The few local dramatic productions were long-running serials with popular success. In general, the industry preferred low-cost Egyptian soap operas, French drama, and American police series. Since the late 1980s, these were complemented by a substantial staple of Mexican and Venezuelan telenovelas (Kraidy 1999a).

In the 1990s, Lebanese television stations were forced to produce locally for two reasons. First, the 1994 audiovisual law, among other things, put regulatory pressure on television stations to have more local productions. Second, with the end of the war and Lebanon's attempts to regain its due place in the international community of nations, law enforcement returned, in effect forcing television stations to abandon their heavy reliance on pirated programming and pay premium prices for legally purchased imports. Consequently, local programming became a financially reasonable option.

In the 1990s, Lebanese television stations produced several relatively successful dramatic series, such as Télé-Liban's *The Storm Blows Twice,* a series depicting the conflicting forces of tradition and modernity in Lebanese society (see Kraidy 1999a). However, social and political talk shows, much cheaper to produce than television drama, rapidly became the staple of Lebanese prime time (Kraidy, forthcoming).

Political talk shows featured guests from Lebanon's political elite discussing current affairs with the host, usually with a studio audience and live telephone calls coming in from across the nation. These shows did much to rock the boat of the political status quo, stirring controversy and maintaining constant scrutiny on the regime in place. They were also a major reason behind state attempts, somewhat successful, to muzzle news and political programs on television (Kraidy 1999b).

TRADITION AND MODERNITY: HOW TALK SHOWS ARTICULATE MARKETS AND MORALS

It was the social talk show, however, that struck at the core of Lebanon's predicament as a betwixt-and-between nation. These were studio shows that featured a charismatic host tackling a predetermined theme. Some talk shows had a sit-down interview format between the host and one or two guests, similar to *Larry King Live.* Examples include MTV's *al-Haki Baynaatn*a (Words between us) hosted by star Lebanese broadcast journalist Maguy Farah. Others featured a discussion among a panel of "experts" with studio audience participation, moderated by a host who is mobile on stage. Such programs included MTV's *Sajjil Mowkaf* (Take a stand) and LBCI's *al-Shaater Yehki* (May the brave speak up).

The themes tackled in these talk shows were often taboo issues in Lebanon. Even though Lebanon is socially liberal in the Middle Eastern context, it is nonetheless a relatively conservative society. The seeds of controversy were planted by then President Elias Hrawi, who, during his last year in office (1998), pushed for a reform of the marriage code to allow civil marriage. In Lebanon, civil matters are the prerogative of religious courts, and civil marriage is not allowed by law. Hrawi's proposal triggered a wave of support among some politicians, students, youth, women advocacy groups, and progressive social constituencies, and an equally strong wave of opposition from other politicians and religious leaders.

The civil marriage issue had already mobilized the defenders of tradition and progress alike. Consequently, it is not really surprising that controversy erupted when social talk shows discussed taboo issues such as premarital sex, the body, incest, sexual abuse, homosexuality, cohabitation, and prostitution in a no-holds-barred fashion during prime time. The first reaction to these shows came during a keynote address to the International Catholic Union of the Press (UCIP) by the information minister, Bassem al-Sabaa. In his speech, the minister referred to a meeting he had had the previous week with television executives, which had resulted in a "gentlemen's agreement" not to air "immoral programming." The minister warned the industry that "free competition does not give the media the right to overstep the boundaries of ethical and cultural values" (Darrous 1997b). The answer to the minister's warning came indirectly, ten days after his speech. In an interview with the *Daily Star*, Elie Nakouzi, host of *Sajjil Mow'af*, explained and defended the democratic potential of talk shows, saying, "That's what we want—to give people the chance to have their say face to face. I don't want to shut people up. After all they have come to talk, and I let them. My only limit is if people become abusive. I will not allow this to happen" (Baradhi 1997).

These two statements, one by a government official and the other by a television talk show host, illustrate two opposing views about the role of the media in society. For the minister, there were unspecified "moral and cultural values" that had to be respected and reflected in the media. His concern is one of order and respect for tradition, appealing to community standards. The talk show host, on the other hand, saw the media as an agent of democracy, as an arena for public debate. His concern was with civic discourse and modern values, focused on individual rights. These two discourse about television talk shows illustrate how television is the site where morals and markets enter the public sphere.

In the meantime, then minister of information, Bassem al-Sabaa, became more specific in his criticism and asked a rhetorical question: "Why, in one month, were a number of programs broadcast on rape, homosexuality, premarital sex, and incest, as if this was the true problem in Lebanon? The goal, not to raise social issues, may have involved politics or advertising" (Dick

1997). The drop that caused the bucket of controversy to spill over came during an episode of LBCI's *al-Shaater Yehki*. Audience members shared their experiences of incest in telephone calls in which their anonymity was protected. In the same week, Télé-Liban's management canceled an episode of *Nas Min Dahab* (Golden people) about the body, under pressure from the Ministry of Information.

In interviews with the press, Télé-Liban CEO, Jean-Claude Boulos. revealed that he was under pressure from government officials not to broadcast programs dealing with taboo issues, mainly of a sexual nature (Darrous 1997a). A December 12, 1997, article in the *Daily Star* described Boulos as "defensive about the matter" and quotes him as saying that "the Lebanese are the smartest and most mature audience in the world. The audience decides what to watch or not, and I can't impose anything on them" (Darrous 1997a). This statement introduces another argument, this time a civic and progressive discourse of audience activity and personal responsibility, in support of controversial programming on television.

The issue of morality on television appeared to reach a denouement when news broke on December 12 that the "TV morals row" was just "a 'camouflage' for ratings war" (Darrous 1997a). So-called anonymous sources had revealed that Future Television had instigated the television morality debate because it was losing the ratings war and had been unable to bridge the substantial audience gap with LBCI. Although Future Television executives denied the accusations, the fact that the issue faded away soon after the allegations were made suggests an air of truth to them. This last episode of the debate on morality on television confirmed the role played by the economics of television in stirring and shaping public controversy.

A December 9, 1997, editorial in the *Daily Star* articulated tradition and modernity and the various discourses that such an articulation attracts, succinctly but eloquently:

> Protecting the moral fabric of the nation by, among other measures, ensuring the decency of what is broadcast on television and radio . . . is a function of government that carries with it responsibilities. . . . The charge is that in these hard times [television] producers are scraping the bottom of the sensationalist barrel to attract a greater viewing audience and therefore an increased share of the declining advertising pot . . . two important factors emerge . . . first . . . very few subjects should be totally off limits for discussion in what is purportedly a free society . . . second it may be undesirable but it is understandable that, in common with their peers round the world, TV stations might resort to shock tactics to improve viewing and advertising figures. (TV and morals, 1997)

CONCLUSION

The editorial quoted above encapsulates the situation of national television: caught between the external, global forces of modernity on one hand and the internal, local forces of tradition on the other. In an age of increasing commercialization of television, in which the model of public broadcasting has either been shattered or is being eroded, programming tends to gravitate toward the sensational and controversial. In Lebanon, as elsewhere, television stations have become businesses accountable to boards of shareholders concerned primarily with the bottom line. The problem in Lebanon is compounded by the heavy burden of postwar reconstruction, since the government has been eager to attract foreign investment. In order to do that in the prevailing neoliberal market ideology, public spending has to be reduced. This trend toward public disengagement and privatization is visible in the developing world from Mexico to Indonesia, with the World Bank, the International Monetary Fund, and the World Trade Organization as ultimate enforcers.

This global trend—this spread of capital as modernity's race horse—is countered by local reactions that mobilize traditional social, cultural, and moral values to face the modernizing tide and the changes it brings. Social talk shows on Lebanese television clearly illustrate how national television becomes a site of struggle that attracts a variety of opposing discourses that can be moral, religious, civic, political, or economic. In analyzing these discourses, we should not forget that by broadcasting controversial programming, national television is in fact doing a favor to society by bringing important but long buried issues to the surface of public debate. In doing so, television performs a function that goes beyond that of a mirror in which society can see itself. It is a slap in the face constantly reminding us that presumably "modern" forms such as sexual content and sensationalism are not always imported from the West. It is a constant reminder that national identity and values are contested, that tradition is always reinvented, and that modernity is always questioned. Rather than emphasizing television's presumed "effects" on audiences and national identity, future research needs to focus on unraveling the role of television as a site of articulation in which the binary oppositions between the global and the local, the textual and the social, the modern and the traditional, are questioned, undone, and reformulated.

REFERENCES

Anderson, B. 1983. *Imagined communities: Reflections on the origins and spread of nationalism*. London: Verso.

Ang, I. 1985. *Watching Dallas*. London: Methuen.

Appadurai, A. 1996. *Modernity at large: Cultural dimensions of globalization*. Minneapolis: University of Minnesota Press.

Baradhi, A. 1997. TV's Nakouzi wants to talk about it now. *Daily Star*, December 1.

Boulos, J. C. 1996. *La Télé: Quelle histoire!* [Television: What a history!]. Beirut: Fiches du Monde Arabe.

Boyd, D. A. 1991. Lebanese broadcasting: Unofficial electronic media during a prolonged civil war. *Journal of Broadcasting and Electronic Media* 353: 269–287.

Braman, S. 1996. Interpenetrated globalization. In S. Braman and A. Sreberny-Mohammadi, eds., *Globalization, communication, and transnational civil society*, pp. 21–36. Cresskill, N.J.: Hampton.

Darrous, S. 1997a. TV morals row a "camouflage for ratings war." *Daily Star*, December 10.

———. 1997b. TV stations told to stay within bounds of taste. *Daily Star*, November 25.

Dick, M. 1997. Sabaa criticizes the "worst image of society." *Daily Star*, December 9.

Entrikin, J. N. 1991. *The betweenness of place: Towards a geography of modernity.* Baltimore: Johns Hopkins University Press.

Galland, B. 1996. De l'urbanisation à la glocalisation [From urbanization to globalization]. *Terminal* 71–72 (Autumn).

Geertz, C. 1983. *Local knowledge: Further essays in interpretive anthropology.* New York: Basic.

Giddens, A. 1990. *The consequences of modernity.* Stanford: Stanford University Press.

Golding, P., and P. Harris. 1997. *Beyond cultural imperialism: Globalization, communication, and the new international order.* London: Sage.

Hannerz, U. 1987. The world in creolization. *Africa* 574: 546–559.

———. 1994. Cosmopolitans and locals in world culture. In M. Featherstone, ed., *Global culture: Nationalism, globalization, and modernity*, pp. 237–252. London: Sage.

Kraidy, M. M. 1998. Broadcasting regulation and civil society in postwar Lebanon. *Journal of Broadcasting and Electronic Media* 423: 387–400.

———. 1999a. The local, the global, and the hybrid: A native ethnography of glocalization. *Critical Studies in Mass Communication* 164: 458–478.

———. 1999b. State control of television news in 1990s Lebanon. *Journalism and Mass Communication Quarterly.*

———. 2000. Television and civic discourse in postwar Lebanon. In L. Gher and H. Amin, eds., *Civic discourse in the Middle East and digital age communication.* Norwood, N.J.: Ablex.

Kraidy, M., and J. Khalil. 1995. Hello out there: Cultural politics and programming tactics on Lebanese radio. Paper presented at the Popular Culture Association annual convention, Philadelphia, April 12–15.

Mattelart, A. 1979. *Multinational corporations and the control of culture: The ideological apparatuses of imperialism.* Newark, N.J.: Harvester.

Morley, D. 1980. *The "nationwide" audience: Structure and decoding.* London: BFI.

Robertson, R. 1992. *Globalization: Social theory and global culture.* London: Sage.

———. 1994. Mapping the global condition: Globalization as the central concept. In M. Featherstone, ed., *Global culture: Nationalism, globalization, and modernity*, pp. 15–30. London: Sage.

Sreberny-Mohammadi, A. 1987. The local and the global in international communications. In James Curran and Michael Gurevitch, eds., *Mass media and society,* pp. 136–152. London: Edward Arnold.

———. 1997. The many faces of imperialism. In P. Golding and P. Harris, eds., *Beyond cultural imperialism: Globalization, communication, and the new international order.* London: Sage.

Straubhaar, J. 1991. Beyond media imperialism: Asymmetrical dependence and cultural proximity. *Critical Studies in Mass Communication* 81: 29–38.

Tomlinson, J. 1991. *Cultural imperialism.* Baltimore: Johns Hopkins University Press.

Tunstall, J. 1977. *The media are American.* Beverly Hills: Sage.

TV and morals. 1997. *Daily Star,* December 9.

UNESCO. 1949. *Press, film, radio.* Paris: UNESCO.

Waters, M. 1995. *Globalization.* London: Routledge.

Epilogue

Kuldip R. Rampal

Two important developments took place in September 2000 that are appropriate to note as a preface to the epilogue for this book: the Millennium Summit, organized by UN Secretary-General Kofi Annan, and the findings of a fifteen-month study by the U.S. Federal Trade Commission on the marketing of restricted movies, music, and video games to children and teenagers.

The Millennium Summit, attended by leaders from more than 160 countries on September 6–8, issued a report on the nature, quality, and implications of increasing globalization and the critical issues surrounding it. Entitled *We the Peoples: The Role of the United Nations in the Twenty-First Century*, the report noted in the "Globalization and Governance" section that "for many people globalization has come to mean greater vulnerability to unfamiliar and unpredictable forces that can bring on economic instability and social dislocation, sometimes at lightning speed. . . . There is mounting anxiety that the integrity of cultures and the sovereignty of states may be at stake" (Annan 2000). The report said that the economic sphere can't be separated from the more complex fabric of social and political life. "To survive and thrive, a global economy must have a more solid foundation in shared values and institutional practices—it must advance broader, and more inclusive, social purposes," it said.

When the economic and cultural spheres are sent shooting off on their own trajectories without regard to the complex fabric of social life of peoples around the world, they carry worrisome implications, the report noted. "Globalization has also created new vulnerabilities to old threats. Criminal networks take advantage of the most advanced technologies to traffic around the world in drugs, arms, precious metals and stones—even people. Indeed, these elements of 'uncivil society' are constructing global conglomerates of illicit activities." The report went on to say that "more than ever, a robust international legal order, together with the principles and practices of multilateralism, is needed to define the ground rules of an emerging global civilization within which there will be room for the world's rich diversity to express itself fully."

The Federal Trade Commission study mentioned above was ordered by President Clinton in 1999 shortly after the massacre at Columbine High School in Littleton, Colorado. In its report released on September 11, 2000, the FTC noted that the study was done with the background that, while opinions vary, many studies have led experts and public health organizations to believe that viewing entertainment media violence can lead to increases in aggressive attitudes and behavior in children. Although scholars and observers generally have agreed that exposure to violence in entertainment media alone does not cause a child to commit a violent act, there is widespread agreement that it is, nonetheless, a cause for concern. Exposure does seem to correlate with aggressive attitudes (FTC: Text, 2000).

The report deplored what it called the "pervasive and aggressive marketing" of violent entertainment to children. It said that the vast majority of the best-selling restricted movies, music, and video games were deliberately marketed to children as young as twelve. The commission also released an internal memorandum, believed to be from a movie studio about an R-rated film, that said its promotional "goal was to find the elusive teen target audience and make sure everyone between the ages of 12–18 was exposed to the film" (FTC: Text, 2000).

The commission examined a sample of movies, recordings, and video games selected because they were best-selling products or those judged most likely to appeal to young people. It found that in the vast majority of the cases, advertising had been aimed at children. All fifty-five music recordings with labels that indicated explicit content were marketed to children younger than seventeen. So were thirty-five of the forty-four movies rated R, or 80 percent, and 83 of the 118 video games, or 70 percent.

In his testimony on the study to the Senate Commerce Committee on September 13, FTC Chairman Robert Pitofsky said that all three industries should improve the usefulness of their ratings and labels by establishing codes that prohibit marketing R-rated/M-rated/explicit-labeled products in media or venues with a substantial under-17 audience. It was also noted that for parents to make informed choices about their children's entertainment, they must understand the ratings and the labels, as well as the reasons for them. That means the industries should all include the reasons for the rating or the label in advertising and product packaging and continue their efforts to educate parents and children about the meanings of the ratings and descriptors. Industry should also take steps to better educate parents about the ratings and labels (FTC testimony, 2000).

The day the FTC released its report, President Clinton condemned the abuses cited in the report and said that he would support government restraint if the industry did not curb advertising aimed at underage teens. Key presidential candidates Al Gore and George W. Bush also took note of the study and said that if elected they would take the necessary actions to rein in the industry's marketing practices.

The two candidates faced this issue again during their third presidential debate in St. Louis, Missouri, on October 17, 2000. When a mother in the audience asked how the candidates felt about the idea that the nation's popular culture was making it more difficult to rear children, both men noted they were fathers, which allowed them to appreciate the issue. They also had tough words for Hollywood.

Bush said that "government ought to stand on the side of parents teaching their children right from wrong and the message is often undermined by pop culture. We can work with the entertainment industry on things like family hour." Gore recalled how his wife, Tipper, who was in the audience, once discovered that one of their daughters brought home a record with lyrics he described as awful and she "hit the ceiling." He noted that Mrs. Gore then began a successful campaign to have records labeled for content (Berke 2000).

Interestingly, several of the contributors to this volume have suggested the kinds of problems attendant in the freewheeling media and cultural globalization that are implied in the two reports mentioned above.

Nancy Snow best captures the problem associated with media globalization in its present form when she says that "the global media system serves mostly advertisers and shareholders," adding that "democracy falters in a global media age because the selling of goods and not the telling of stories today drives our means of communication." She is right when she says that for the world's wired generation, most of what we know, or think we know, we have never personally experienced. We live in a world erected by the stories we hear and see and tell, mostly from television. Too bad, she says, that the stories we receive are mostly driven by ratings rather than by a strong public service role of television.

In a keynote speech to the Radio-Television News Directors Association on September 15, 2000, CNN star foreign correspondent, Christiane Amanpour, appeared to echo Snow's concerns:

> The powers that be . . . the moneymen, have decided over the last several years
> to eviscerate us. It actually costs a bit of money to produce good journalism . . .
> to travel, to investigate . . . to put on compelling viewing, to give people a reason

to watch us. But God forbid they should spend money on quality . . . no, let's just cheapskate our way into the most demeaning, irrelevant, superhyped sensationalism we can find. (Amanpour 2000)

Amanpour could have added that it costs money to produce quality original entertainment programming. Instead, as American media scholar Herbert Schiller has told us for years, global media barons find it much cheaper and more convenient to buy rights to air Hollywood television reruns—many of a titillating variety containing liberal doses of violence—and put them on their international satellite and cable channels. Exposed to the provocatively dressed women in, say, *Baywatch,* or hip-gyrating ones on MTV's international channels, or practically naked ones in the lingerie shows of France's global channel Fashion TV, one can imagine why the traditionally protected viewers of most of the non-Western world may be left confused about their cultural bearings and what to make of the new world of entertainment around them. Even in the West, the permissive television offerings of today are the result of a gradual liberalization of sociocultural values over several decades. It seems implausible to transmit, without appropriate viewing advisories, highly permissive programming to traditional societies that would not have been tolerated even in the United States and other Western countries until recent years.

It seems obvious that the steps taken in the United States in recent years—such as a ratings system for television programming and the introduction of the V-chip in television sets to allow parents to keep questionable programming from reaching their children—will need to be promoted overseas as well. The FTC recommendation calling for responsible marketing of entertainment products to teenagers in the United States could also apply to the purveyors of media products worldwide. Equally important, to refer to the UN Millennium Summit report once again, media globalization needs to operate within the framework of sensitivity to the social and cultural values of target audiences, especially when their values are of a particularly conservative nature. Rose Dyson puts it well when she says in her chapter that "distortions to the democratic process itself, brought on by globalization, trade liberalization and, as George Gerbner frequently points out, increasing reliance on sex and violence as cheap industrial ingredients because they sell well in a global economy and translate easily into any language, must be challenged."

When international satellite broadcasters are insensitive to the values of receiving nations, they in fact put the continuation of media globalization at risk—even in open, democratic societies. Witness the recent example of India, the largest democracy in the world, where cable television screens in some 800,000 homes in New Delhi, the nation's capital, went dark for three days in late September 2000. The reason was a strike by cable television operators who were protesting against amendments to the Cable Television Networks (Regulation) Act of 1995 under which they could face action for content that violates government codes. The operators had said it was unfair to hold them responsible for content such as liquor advertisements or obscene programs beamed by satellite channels (Reuters 2000).

Having said that purveyors of entertainment and pop culture globally need to do so responsibly so as not to violate or offend the sociocultural values of receiving nations, it must be emphasized that it has not been conclusively established that questionable behavior in the areas of sex, violence, and drugs is linked to globalized media. As Brown and Witherspoon point out in their chapter, the media are not the sole cause of the health status of our youth. Adolescents come to the media with individual characteristics, from families and communities, that already have pushed them in certain directions and that have provided models of healthy and unhealthy behavior. Those perceptions and experiences will modify and/or enhance the effect the media have on their health in the future.

As Brown and Witherspoon add, however, the media do exert an impact, sometimes subtly, sometimes more powerfully, and the potential is greater for negative than for positive effects. What should we do to minimize the media's potential negative effects on adolescents' health? The authors rightly suggest that we must continue to monitor and learn more about the role the media do play. We must turn attention to the array of media our teens attend to other than television. Music, magazines, and movies, and now the Internet, are vital to the everyday lives of teens, and have been inadequately included in studies of media effects. We should adopt the idea of "media diets" and devise ways to learn more about how adolescents use media in developing a sense of themselves.

Finally, the possible positive effects of media globalization on the youth around the world, especially in developing countries, and on the modernization process of individual nations need to be looked into systematically by media researchers and other social scientists. As Rampal notes in his chapter, the Hong Kong-based STAR-TV's popular Hindi language programming and movies have promoted the understanding of this language across India. Sociologically, such a development would be considered a significant prelude to the unification of multilingual India, a cherished hope of Indian policymakers since the country's independence. Are there other sociological benefits that accrue from globalized media to developing nations? Do globalized media, even with their questionable programming content, stir what Daniel Lerner called the "empathy" factor in well-adjusted youth in a way that makes them more active achievers? There are certainly indications of that, as noted in Rampal's chapter, but this area needs further study. From a research standpoint, the study of media globalization and its relationship to the issues of sex, violence, and drugs in this book has raised some very significant issues for further scholarly investigation.

REFERENCES

Amanpour, Christiane. 2000. Christiane Amanpour electrifies RTNDA2000 attendees. September 15. www.rtnda.org/news/2000/asera.shtml.

Annan, Kofi. 2000. We the peoples: The role of the United Nations in the twenty-first century. September 8. www.un.org/millennium/sg/report/full.htm.

Berke, Richard L. 2000. Bush and Gore, in last debate, stage vigorous give-and-take. *New York Times,* October 18. www.nytimes.com/2000/10/18/politics/18DE-BA.html.

FTC Testimony. 2000. Federal Trade Commission testifies on marketing violent entertainment to children. September 13. www.ftc.gov/opa/2000/09/violtestimony.htm.

FTC: Text of the Report. 2000. September 11. www.ftc.gov/os/2000/09/index.htm#13.

Reuters. 2000. Indian cable TV operators call off strike. September 28. about.reuters.com/dynamic/india_en_nSP341743.html.

Suggested Readings

Abramson, P., and R. Inglehart. 1995. *Value change in global perspective*. Ann Arbor: University of Michigan Press.

Acuff, D. S., R. H. Reiher, and D. Acuff. 1997. *What kids buy and why: The psychology of marketing to kids*. New York: Free Press.

Adeniran, T., and Y. Alexander, eds. 1983. *International violence*. London: Sage; New York: Praeger.

Anderson, B. 1983. *Imagined communities: Reflections on the origins and spread of nationalism*. London: Verso.

Ang, I. 1985. *Watching Dallas*. London: Methuen.

Appadurai, A. 1996. *Modernity at large: Cultural dimensions of globalization*. Minneapolis: University of Minnesota Press.

Baehr, H., and A. Gray, eds. 1996. *Turning it on: A reader in women and media*. London: Arnold.

Berger, G. 1989. *Violence and the media*. New York: Franklin Watts.

Bernstein, M., and G. Studlar, eds. 1997. *Visions of the East: Orientalism in film*. New Jersey: Rutgers University Press.

Boyd, D. A. 1982. *Broadcasting in the Arab world*. Philadelphia: Temple University Press.

Boyd-Barrett, O., and P. Braham, eds. 1990. *Media, knowledge, and power*. London: Routledge.

Braman, S., and A. Sreberny-Mohammadi, eds. 1996. *Globalization, communication, and transnational civil society*. Cresskill, N.J.: Hampton.

Butler, M., and W. Paisley. 1980. *Women and the mass media*. New York: Human Sciences Press.

Cantor, J. 1998. *Mommy, I'm scared*. New York: Harcourt, Brace.

Colford, P. D. 1996. *Howard Stern: King of all media*. New York: St. Martin's.

Commission on Obscenity and Pornography. 1970. *The report of the Commission on Obscenity and Pornography*. New York: Bantam.

Cuklanz, L. M. 1996. *Rape on trial: How the mass media construct legal reform and social change.* Philadelphia: University of Pennsylvania Press.

Davies, K., J. Dickey, and T. Stratford, eds. 1987. *Out of focus: Writings on women and the media.* London: Women's Press.

Denton, R. E., Jr., ed. 1993. *The media and the Persian Gulf War.* London: Praeger.

Fireman, J., ed. 1977. *TV Book: The ultimate television book.* New York: Workman.

Fraser, N. 1989. *Unruly practices: Power, discourse, and gender in contemporary social theory.* Minneapolis: University of Minnesota Press.

Gallagher, M. 1988. *Women and television in Europe.* Brussels: Commission of the European Communities.

Geertz, C. 1983. *Local knowledge: Further essays in interpretive anthropology.* New York: Basic.

Gerbner, G., H. Mowlana, and H. I. Schiller, eds. 1996. *Invisible Crises.* Boulder: Westview.

Giddens, A. 1990. *The consequences of modernity.* Stanford: Stanford University Press.

Golding, P., and P. Harris. 1997. *Beyond cultural imperialism: Globalization, communication, and the new international order.* Thousand Oaks, Calif.: Sage.

Goldstein, Tom, ed. 1989. *Killing the messenger: One hundred years of media criticism.* New York: Columbia University Press.

Greenberg, B. S., J. D. Brown, and N. L. Buerkel-Rothfuss, eds. 1993. *Media, sex, and the adolescent.* Cresskill, N.J.: Hampton.

Grossberg, L. 1988. *It's a sin: Essays on postmodernism, politics, and culture.* Sydney: Power Publications.

Hall, Stuart, ed. 1990. *Culture, media, language.* London: Hutchinson.

Heintz-Knowles, K. E. 1996. *Sexual activity on daytime soap operas: A content analysis of five weeks of television programming.* Menlo Park, Calif.: Kaiser Family Foundation.

Huesmann, L. R., and L. D. Eron. 1986. *Television and the aggressive child: A cross-national comparison.* Hillsdale, N.J.: Erlbaum.

Huston, A. C., E. Wartella, and E. Donnerstein. 1998. *Measuring the effects of sexual content in the media: A report to the Kaiser Family Foundation.* Menlo Park, Calif.: Kaiser Family Foundation.

Inglehart, R. 1997. *Modernization and postmodernization.* Princeton: Princeton University Press.

Jeffords, S. 1994. *Hard bodies: Hollywood masculinity in the Reagan era.* New Jersey: Rutgers University Press.

Jones, S. 1997. *Virtual culture: Identity and communication in cybersociety.* London: Sage.

Kamalipour, Y. R., ed. 1995. *The U.S. media and the Middle East: Image and perception.* Westport, Conn.: Greenwood.

———. 1997. *The U.S. media and the Middle East: Image and perception.* Westport, Conn.: Praeger.

———. 1999. *Images of the U.S. around the world: A multicultural perspective.* Albany: State University of New York Press.

Kamalipour, Y. R., and T. Carilli, eds. 1998. *Cultural Diversity and the U.S. Media.* Albany: State University of New York Press.

Kamalipour, Y. R., and H. Mowlana, eds. 1994. *Mass media in the Middle East: A comprehensive handbook.* Westport, Conn.: Greenwood.

Katz, Elihu, and Paul F. Lazarsfeld. 1955. *Personal influence: The part played by people in the flow of mass communication.* New York: Free Press.

Kaufman, Will, and Heidi S. Macpherson. 2000. *Transatlantic studies.* New York: University Press of America.

Kellner, D. 1995. *Media culture: Cultural studies, identity, and politics between the modern and the postmodern.* New York: Routledge.

Kidd-Hewitt, D., and R. Osborne, eds. 1995. *Crime and media: The post-modern spectacle.* London: Pluto.

Lerner, D. 1958. *The passing of traditional society: Modernizing the Middle East.* New York: Free Press.

Macdonald, M. 1995. *Representing women: Myths of femininity in popular media.* London: Edward Arnold.

Mattelart, A. 1979. *Multinational corporations and the control of culture: The ideological apparatuses of imperialism.* Newark, N.J.: Harvester.

McChesney, R. W., ed. 1994. *Telecommunications, mass media, and democracy.* New York: Oxford University Press.

McLuhan, M. 1967. *The medium is the message: An inventory of effects.* New York: Random House.

McQuail, D. 1987. *Mass communication theory: An introduction.* London: Sage.

MediaWatch. 1995. *Global media monitoring project: Women's participation in the news.* Ontario: National Watch on Images of Women MediaWatch.

Merrill, J., J. Lee, and E. J. Friedlander. 1994. *Modern mass media.* New York: Harper-Collins.

Michael, K., ed. 1991. *Men confront pornography.* New York: Meridian.

Michael, R., J. Gagnon, E. Laumann, and G. Kolata. 1994. *Sex in America: A definitive survey.* Boston: Little, Brown.

Nordenstreng, K. 1984. *Mass media declaration of UNESCO.* Norwood, N.J.: Ablex.

Nordenstreng, K., and T. Varis. 1974. *Television traffic—A one-way street? A survey and analysis of the international flow of television programme material.* Paris: UNESCO.

Prince, S. 1992. *Visions of empire: Political imagery in contemporary American film.* New York: Praeger.

Ray, R. B. 1985. *A certain tendency of the Hollywood cinema, 1930–1980.* Princeton: Princeton University Press.

Rugh, W. A. 1989. *The Arab press.* Syracuse: Syracuse University Press.

Said, E. 1979. *Orientalism.* New York: Vintage.

Schiller, H. 1969. *Mass Communication and American empire.* Boston: Beacon.

Seid, R. P. 1989. *Never too thin: Why women are at war with their bodies.* New York: Prentice-Hall.

Signorielli, N., and M. Morgan, eds. 1990. *Cultivation analysis: New directions in media effects research.* Newbury Park, Calif.: Sage.

Thirestein, J., and J. R. Kamalipour, eds. 2000. *Religion, law, and freedom: A global perspective.* Westport, Conn.: Greenwood.

Tomlinson, J. 1991. *Cultural imperialism.* Baltimore: Johns Hopkins University Press.

Tunstall, J. 1977. *The media are American.* Beverly Hills: Sage.

Van Zoonen, L. 1994. *Feminist media studies.* London: Sage.

Waters, M. 1995. *Globalization.* London: Routledge.

Wells, A., ed. 1996. *World broadcasting.* Norwood, N.J.: Ablex.

Withey, S., and R. Abeles, eds. 1980. *Television and social behavior: Beyond violence and children.* Hillsdale, N.J.: Erlbaum.

Zillmann, D., J. Bryant, and A. C. Huston, eds. 1994. *Media, children, and the family: Social scientific, psychodynamic, and clinical perspectives.* Hillsdale, N.J.: Lawrence Erlbaum.

Zollo, P. 1995. *Wise up to teens: Insights into marketing and advertising to teenagers.* Ithaca, N.Y.: New Strategist Publications.

Index

About the Editors and Contributors

Yahya R. Kamalipour is professor of mass communications and head of the Department of Communication and Creative Arts, Purdue University Calumet, Hammond, Indiana. His most recent books are *Images of the U.S. around the World: A Multicultural Perspective*, *Cultural Diversity, and the U.S. Media* (with T. Carilli), and *Religion, Law, and Freedom: A Global Perspective* (with J. Thierstein). An active member of a dozen national and international organizations, he has received several significant awards, including the 1996 Distinguished Scholarship Award in International and Intercultural Communication from the National Communication Association, and the 1996 Edgar Mills Award for Outstanding Service in Communication from the Communicators of Northwest Indiana. In addition to giving numerous invited speeches and making mass media appearances and interviews, Kamalipour has written articles that have appeared in professional and mainstream publications in the United States and abroad. He holds a Ph.D. in communication (radio, TV, film) from the University of Missouri–Columbia, an M.A. in mass media from the University of Wisconsin–Superior, and a B.A. in communication (public relations) from Minnesota State University.

Kuldip R. Rampal is a professor of mass communication at Central Missouri State University in Warrensburg. His research on development communication, political communication, press regulation, media ethics, international broadcasting, and international press has appeared in a variety of books and journals. He has coauthored a reference book, *International Afro Mass Media: A Reference Guide*. He has traveled to some twenty-five countries in connection with his research work. In recognition of his publications on Confucianism and press and political liberalization in Taiwan, the government of the Republic of China awarded him the 1993 International Communication Award. In 1992, Rampal received the Byler Distinguished Faculty Award from Central Missouri State University. In 1992–1993 Rampal was a visiting professor at Singapore's National University and in 1994–1995 at Nanyang Technological University, where he also served as a part-time assistant news editor at the *Straits Times*. In recent years, he has taught in Sweden and the Netherlands. He holds a Ph.D. in journalism from the University of Missouri School of Journalism and an M.A. in journalism from Boston University.

ABOUT THE CONTRIBUTORS

Hussein Y. Amin (Ph.D., Ohio State University; M.A., Helwan University, Cairo, Egypt) is an associate professor in the Department of Journalism and Mass Communication at the American University in Cairo. In 1997, he was appointed acting director of the AUC's Adham Center for Television Journalism. Amin is chairman of the Space Committee of the Egyptian Radio and Television Union (ERTU). He is a member of several broadcasting organizations, including the Egyptian Radio and Television Union, the governing body of Egypt's broadcasting stations, and the Higher Committee for Specialized NileSat Television Networks. His research interests include transnational broadcasting, Egyptian and Arab media systems, global broadcasting, new communication technologies, and the impact of these new technologies on national development. He has published widely on these topics, with more than twenty-eight chapters and articles in professional journals and forty conference presentations in English and Arabic to his credit.

Jane D. Brown (Ph.D., mass communication, University of Wisconsin–Madison) is a James L. Knight Professor in the School of Journalism and Mass Communication at the University of North Carolina in Chapel Hill, where she has taught since 1977. Her research focuses on how adolescents use and learn from the mass media about health.

Junho H. Choi (M.A., Yonsei University, Seoul; University of Illinois, Chicago) is a doctoral student in the Department of Communication at Purdue University. He has published in *Communication Research*. His interests center around the social uses of the Internet and globalization. He is currently working on a network analysis of interorganizational alliances in cyberspace.

James A. Danowski (Ph.D., communication; Michigan State University, 1975) is a communication professor at the University of Illinois in Chicago.

He studies macrolevel processes linking communication technology and cultural values. He was founding chair of the Human Communication Technology Interest Group (now Communication and Technology Division) of the International Communication Association (ICA, 1977–1981) and was elected chair of ICA's Information Systems Division (1989–1992). Accordingly, he is a former ICA vice president and board of directors member.

Arnold S. de Beer is editor of *Ecquid Novi*, the South African research journal for journalism, and editorial board member of *Journalism Studies*. He is division head of Media and Society of the African Council for Communication Education. He has read papers at the AEJMC, ICA, and IAMCR, and he has published on news flow and the media in South Africa.

Rose Dyson (Ed.D., adult education, University of Toronto) is a consultant in media education, chairs Canadians Concerned About Violence in Entertainment (C-CAVE), and is a member of the Cultural Environment Movement. Her most recent book is *Mind Abuse: Media Violence in an Information Age.*

Hanzada Fikry has been a visiting lecturer at the American University in Cairo since 1996, teaching print and broadcast journalism. She received her B.A. and M.A. from the same university. She has worked as a print and broadcast journalist for seventeen years, serving as a correspondent for United Press International for four years and ABC News for twelve years. She has also written for *U.S. News and World Report* and *The Times* (of London) and has published articles in *Omni* magazine, *Conde Naste's Traveller, Arab News,* and *Al Sharq Al Awsat.* She was vice chairman of the Foreign Press Association from 1987 to 1990.

George Gerbner (Ph.D., University of Southern California) is Bell-Atlantic Professor of Communications at Temple University, Philadelphia. He is the founder and president of the Cultural Environment Movement, dean emeritus of the Annenburg School of Communication, and a former editor of the *Journal of Communication.* In addition to numerous speeches, media appearances, and articles, he has authored and/or edited a dozen books on mass media effects and international communication.

Zhou He (Ph.D., School of Journalism, Indiana University) is an associate professor of journalism and mass communication in the School of Journalism and Mass Communications, San Jose State University, as well as in the Department of English, City University of Hong Kong. His published academic books include *The Voice of America and China* (coauthor, 1994), *Mass Media and Tiananmen Square* (1996), and *Chinese Media: A New Perspective* (coauthor, 1998). His research work has appeared in *Journalism and Mass Communication Quarterly, Journal of Communication, Journalism Monographs*, and *Gazette*.

Jong G. Kang (Ph.D., University of Massachussetts–Amherst) is a professor in the Department of Communication at Illinois State University in Normal, Illinois. He teaches a variety of courses in broadcast production and mass communications. His articles have appeared in *Journalism Quarterly, Communication Research Report, World Communication Journal,* and *Journal of Asian Pacific Communication.* He has coauthored a book, *Broadcasting in Korea* (1993), and has written several book chapters.

Marwan M. Kraidy (Ph.D., Ohio University) is an assistant professor in the School of International Service at American University in Washington, D.C., where he teaches theory, international communication, popular culture, and new media technologies. His work has appeared in several journals and books published in the United States, Europe, and the Middle East. He received the 1998 Ralph Cooley Award for Top Paper from the International and Intercultural Communication Division of the National Communication Association.

Neil Nemeth (Ph.D., Ohio State University) is an assistant professor in the Department of Communication and Creative Arts, Purdue University Calumet, where he teaches reporting, editing, law, ethics, and mass media courses. His principal research interest is in media accountability, and he has focused most of his attention on the work of newspaper ombudsmen. He has published scholarly articles in books and journals, including *Newspaper Research Journal* and *Southwestern Mass Communication Journal.*

Thomas J. Roach (Ph.D., Northwestern University) is a tenured professor at Purdue University Calumet where he teaches graduate courses in rhetorical inquiry and undergraduate courses in public relations. His doctoral dissertation, "Dissolution of Objectivity: The Third Face of Power and the American News Media," received a national dissertation of the year award in 1994 from the National (Speech) Communication Association. Prior to his teaching career, he served as the corporate director of internal communication at Carson Pirie Scott.

Karen Ross is director of the Centre for Communication Studies at Coventry University, United Kingdom. She has published widely in the field of race, gender, and representation in popular media and is currently writing a book on women politicians and the media. Her books include *Black and White Media: Black Images in Popular Film and Television* (1996), *Gender* *and Media* (1996), *Cultural Pluralism in Global Ecumene* (2000), and *Managing Equal Opportunities in Higher Education* (2000).

M. Mehdi Semati (Ph.D., University of Missouri–Columbia) is an assistant professor of communication in the Department of Speech Communication, Eastern Illinois University. His research and teaching areas include international communication, film and television theory and criticism, cultural politics and political representation, and media production. His publications include articles in *Critical Studies in Mass Communication, Journal of Popular Film and Television,* and *Journal of International Communication.*

Nancy Snow is associate director of the Center for Communications and Community, UCLA, and the author of *Propaganda, Inc.: Selling American's Culture to the World* (1998).

Elizabeth M. Witherspoon is a doctoral student in the UNC–CH School of Journalism and Mass Communication and is an assistant professor at Elon College, Elon, North Carolina. Her primary research interest is health communication.

Alev Yemenici is an assistant professor in the Department of English Language and Literature, Middle East Technical University, Ankara, Turkey. She is interested in computer studies, cross-cultural communication, literature, and mass media.